Producing for TV and New Media

Producing for TV and New Media

A Real-World Approach for Producers

Second Edition

Cathrine Kellison

AMSTERDAM • BOSTON • HEIDELBERG • LONDON
NEW YORK • OXFORD • PARIS • SAN DIEGO
SAN FRANCISCO • SINGAPORE • SYDNEY • TOKYO

Focal Press is an imprint of Elsevier

ELSEVIER

Focal
Press

Focal Press is an imprint of Elsevier
30 Corporate Drive, Suite 400, Burlington, MA 01803, USA
Linacre House, Jordan Hill, Oxford, OX2 8DP, UK

Library of Congress Cataloging-in-Publication Data
Kellison, Cathrine.
   [Producing for TV and video]
   Producing for TV and new media: a real-world approach for producers /
by Cathrine Kellison. – 2nd ed.
        p. cm.
   Previously published as: Producing for TV and video, 2005.
   Includes index.
   ISBN 978-0-240-81087-4 (pbk. : alk. paper) 1. Television–Production and direction.
   2. Video recordings–Productions and direction. I. Title.
   PN1992.75.K38 2009
   791.4502′32–dc22

                                                                            200806271

British Library Cataloguing-in-Publication Data
A catalogue record for this book is available from the British Library.

ISBN 978-0-240-81087-4

For information on all Focal Press publications
visit our website at www.elsevierdirect.com

09 10 11 12 13 5 4 3 2 1
Printed in the United States of America

CONTENTS

Producing as a career and a lifestyle grabbed me years ago, but like many of the people you'll meet in the pages of this book, I didn't start off as a producer. Writing was my passion. I liked the process, and was able to earn a living with feature-length screenplays (eight were optioned and one made…badly), short stories, magazine articles, movie reviews, educational curricula. Then, after moving from L.A. to NYC, I was offered a job at NBC as a writer/producer. I knew what a writer did, but a producer? I said yes immediately—I'd figure out the producing part later.

That simple yes was the launch pad for this journey called producing for television—and now, for new media—that shows no sign of slowing down. I've written and/or produced hundreds of television hours in almost every genre, for NBC, CBS, ABC, PBS, for broadcast and nonbroadcast, from two-minute movie trailers to two-hour in-depth documentaries to a CBS special.

Each project has exposed me to a range of experiences—I can research new ideas, then write the scripts; I've shot in locations from the exotic to the mundane; I get to play with footage and sound and graphics in postproduction; I almost understand the parameters of finance; I've had the pleasure of interviewing celebrities, academics, and visionaries, on-camera and off; I've tested the range of my own patience and endurance; and, best of all, I've been honored to work with, and learn from, extraordinarily creative and talented people.

Producing has always felt natural to me. As the oldest of four kids, I mastered the skills of delegating, nurturing, cajoling, and outright bribery at an early age. I could convince my brother and sisters that making me a sandwich was a noble task rather than drudgery. When I was 12, I started a summer vacation newspaper, *The Shack*, and I gave each sibling a job: to report a new deer-sighting, draw treasure maps, make up riddles, sell ad space. I wrote the lead stories, designed it, and gave myself top billing…in essence, I've been producing all my life.

Producing is in my DNA. My parents were documentary filmmakers back in the day when nonscripted content was a labor of love, poorly funded, and rarely seen by large audiences. With a small dedicated crew, they directed, produced, and shot documentaries around the globe, shooting for weeks at a time. Through them, I learned about exotic places with unpronounceable names, heard stories of trekking into areas where the only common language was a smile. They loved what they did: the planning, the shoots, the weeks of editing. They found challenges and payoffs in each phase. And above all, they valued teamwork.

This family collaborative, its passion and fun, has shaped my world view of producing; it's also been essential in producing this book. My mother, Allie Clayton, provided nonstop inspiration, much of the book's graphic format design, and transcribed hours of interviews. My oldest daughter, Joan Johnsen, was also a valiant transcriber; Jonna McLaughlin, my middle daughter, and her best friend Becky Teitel, contributed their sage advice and experiences as former students of producing and now are producers themselves; and my third daughter, Simone McLaughlin, essentially constructed the glossary. My husband, Jeffrey McLaughlin, shared his considerable knowledge of postproduction, and supported me throughout the long writing process with his belief in my vision. Overseeing this family endeavor is the generous guiding spirit of my father, John Clayton, whose humor, vision, and belief in his team were the stuff of legend. His grin could light up any set.

Writing this book allowed me to explore my own producing experiences, and to combine or contrast them with those of dozens of other professionals interviewed for both editions. Each chapter was reviewed by a team of college students who were studying producing and offered their candid feedback and perspectives. Jackie Muldower contributed unswerving support, extensive research and review, and compiled references. Adam Wager offered his clarity to the text and its overall tone. Michael Krepack gave me consistent access to the latest developments in new media; Ashley Cooper Kerns, Joanna Kerns, and Nicci Marciante helped reshape, clarify, and update the legal chapter. Daisy Montfort and Noah Workman chipped in long hours on behalf of this book, and Alexandra Palmieri, Alex Holson, and Jaclyn Paris contributed to the Student Recommended Resources. I'm eternally grateful for this collective dedication to my dream.

An added dimension to this text is the collective experience and insight from the "guest speakers" in Chapter 11: Sheril Antonio, Sharon Badal, Michael Bonfiglio, Sheila Possner Emery, Barbara Gaines, Rich Henning, Ann Kolbell, Matt Lombardi, Jeffrey McLaughlin, Brett Morgen, Stephen Reed, Laurie Rich, John Rosas, Tom Sellitti, J. Stephen Sheppard, Valerie Walsh, Justin Wilkes, Scott A. Williams, and Bernie Young. I'm indebted to my friends and colleagues Sharon Badal, Stephen Duncombe, Evan Fairbanks, James Gardner, Rich Henning, David Irving, Jon Kamen, Al Lieberman, Lynn McVeigh, Linda Oken, Andrew Susskind, Justin Wilkes, and the Bradley-Jones team, who believe in me and in the potential and power of television and new media, and have stood by me through some dicey moments. Thanks also to Amit Das who convinced me to expand my original *Producing for TV* syllabus into a textbook. And a deep bow to Kent Cathcart, my sole touchstone in high school, whose struggles with me back then have paid off.

An integral part of the book's development process are the proposal reviewers—Don Caristi, Mischelle L. McIntosh, Mary Beth O'Connor, and Eric Scholl. Equally as helpful were the manuscript reviewers for the second edition, Alison Reddihough and Andrew Susskind. Each made significant contributions with his or her candid feedback. The folks at Focal Press, under the thoughtful guidance of Elinor Actipis and Michele Cronin, have combined their talents to make the second edition even better than the first. The graphics, charts, and photographs were imaginatively designed and photographed by Polina Khentov; all these people are partners in this book.

Producing for TV and New Media: A Real-World Approach is the end result of collaboration, experience, curiosity, a bit of good luck, and a lot of hard work—a formula that's remarkably similar to producing for television and new media. Welcome to the journey.

ABOUT THE AUTHOR

Cathrine Kellison's career as a writer/producer spans two decades, and includes an eclectic range of projects-from a CBS special to a PBS documentary, from corporate image pieces for IBM to behind-the-scenes celebrity interviews for MGM, from a kids' piece on recycling to educational films for teachers. To date, she has produced, written, and/or directed hundreds of hours of broadcast and non-broadcast programming for television and various avenues of new media.

Starting as a writer of feature-length scripts in Hollywood, Ms. Kellison moved into producing for NBC and, later, United Artists in New York City as Director of Creative Services. She then went independent, starting her own small-but-meaningful production company, Roseville Video. Ms. Kellison began teaching producing for television and film at New York University's Tisch School of the Arts in 1994, and now teaches and advises students of media studies in NYU's Gallatin School of Individualized Study and SCPS (School of Continuing Professional Studies).

Ms. Kellison works as fluently as a writer, authoring or co-authoring a number of books and articles primarily in the Affective Education domain and in mathematics education reform.

Ms. Kellison is a member of the Producers Guild of America, the Writers Guild of America, the Independent Documentary Association, and has won numerous industry awards, including two WGA awards for Outstanding Achievement. She lives and works in New York City.

INTRODUCTION

Know what you don't know.
Stephen Reed, producer (interviewed in Chapter 11)

If ever there was a succinct description of the producer's role, "know what you don't know" defines it best. To succeed as a producer, you become a lifelong learner—constantly researching, asking questions, and listening. Not stopping until you know what you don't know.

There isn't one producer in any area of television or new media who has all the answers, or has mastered the tricks of the trade, or grasps the nuances of each and every detail on the producer's to-do list. Although producers share certain skill sets, each genre in which the producer works is different. Each project requires a unique result from its producer. This book strives to lay out the producer's many roles and options, and the steps generally taken in producing quality programming. As importantly, there's an almost philosophical approach to the people skills required in producing: communication, understanding, respect, and an ongoing sense of humor.

There's no doubt that new media takes us on an exciting romp into the unknown. Its potentials and risks grow exponentially. The expansion of new media content and delivery systems is the subject of countless panels and articles, yet it's still in its infancy. We're in the vortex of what could possibly be one of the more transformative eras in human communications.

Television is the mentor of new media content, and at almost 80 years old, TV has shaped our world for generations before us. Television now is pervasive. It reaches literally billions of people around the globe; for many of them, TV is their sole source of information and entertainment. So regardless of our own viewing habits, TV has had a resounding impact on the data, the culture, changing trends, and the economics that inform our world.

Yet, TV initially was dismissed as simply a passing fancy, "an inventor's will o' the wisp." Over subsequent decades, its detractors have been harsh and outspoken, insisting that TV caters to the lowest common denominator, that it barrages us with negative impressions, controls the content and delivery of news, manipulates cultural trends, and encourages viewers to contribute to the consumer society.

But the tides are turning. Current research increasingly points to television as a vehicle that, when used intelligently, can actually make its viewers smarter. We can make thoughtful choices that lead us to navigate complex narrative plots, explore ethical issues of relationships that are central to reality programming, compare and contrast political platforms, learn a language and explore its culture, and in general, pique our appetite for further exploration.

And joining in, new media. It's fast on its way to going beyond traditional television, into uncharted territory. Within this range of viewpoints, it's indisputable that these media offer opportunities that are virtually limitless. Here's where the producer enters the picture.

TV IS THE PRODUCER'S DOMAIN

A plasma screen, a computer monitor, a mobile phone—each is simply a mechanical device that can receive digital signals. Each is similar to a blank canvas that's ready for the artist's brush. It's the role of the producer to create an image on the screen—painting that canvas. The producer can stand up to television's critics by using creative vision, technical know-how, and a rather extraordinary set of skills to produce unique programming and to open new directions.

TELEVISION LIVES WITHIN AN HISTORICAL CONTEXT

> May you be born in interesting times.
>
> **A curse in Ancient China**

Today's producer certainly lives in "interesting times." Few periods in human history have been as dramatic or as enlightening—or as uncertain. TV and the Internet are both reflecting and shaping what is happening in the world around us, and flooding us with data and impressions. It falls on the producer, and of course the viewer, to become educated about it all.

Television has over a century of creative and technical history behind it that's rich in insight and provides a foundation for programs that we watch today. In America, we can see echoes of Steve Allen's 1950s' late-night humor and hosting style in shows hosted by David Letterman and Jon Stewart. Legendary performances on the BBC and dramatic U.S. series *Playhouse 90* and *Hallmark Hall of Fame* upped the ante for superior acting, writing, and directing that is still seen every night in dozens of network series and premium cable programs. Early children's television gave us *Mr. Wizard* and *Mr. Rogers,* paving the way for *Sesame Street* and *Dora the Explorer*.

Yet television's detractors target, rightfully, the predominant themes of competition and humiliation in "reality shows," or the evening news broadcasts—once reported by courageous pioneers in journalism like Edward R. Murrow and Walter Cronkite—in which news is constricted by upper-management dictates, or focuses primarily on the sensational and shallow. Explicit music videos and adult-only channels have lowered the bar of constraint, as mature content seeps into family programming; concurrently, the vital issues of censorship and essential freedom of speech are challenged by political and economic pressures. The pros and cons of television are in constant flux, and with new media entering the arena, the debates will surely continue to flourish.

So where does it all go from here? What is television's future? Where does new media factor in? That answer is up to the producer. The producer can choose to go with the flow, or dare to divert the direction of that flow.

TV IS A UNIQUE MEDIUM

Recently, both business and academia have held the word "television" up to the light: Is television that wide-screen set in front of your couch? Or is TV what you watch on your laptop or on the hand-held device you take on the plane? They're all capable of playing the same rerun of *Seinfeld*, or tomorrow's weather forecast.

It doesn't matter. An effective producer can take advantage of the newest delivery systems or stick with traditional television, but the skills needed for producing remain constant. The producer continues to create compelling entertainment, in-depth information, or educational content. Once a stable industry unto itself, television is now smack in the middle of a radical transformation as it merges with new media.

The TV set continues to be a staple in most households. It's a familiar voice in the background; an antidote to loneliness. As with a family member, we can enjoy it, tune it out, argue with it, or laugh out loud. We don't have to leave the house, hire a babysitter, or pay the high price of admission for feature films and documentaries—we'll eventually see them on our TV set.

THE PRODUCER IS AT THE CORE

Some producers are responsible for bringing an entire project to life, from a simple concept through development to its final broadcast or distribution. Other producers work on specific areas of a project and are a valuable part of a larger team of producers. The parameters of the producer's functions cast a wide net: producing is the least understood job in television. It's also the most demanding and time-consuming of media jobs, and yet a natural-born producer loves (almost) every minute.

The skills needed to be a producer are rather like the tiny pixels in a television image. Each skill deals with detail, and each detail is important. Like pixels, it takes thousands of them to create an image on the TV screen.

This book explores each stage of producing a project:

- Stage One: The Idea (Project Development)
- Stage Two: The Plan (Preproduction)
- Stage Three: The Shoot (Production)
- Stage Four: The Final Product (Postproduction)
- Stage Five: Next Steps (Wrap Up and Distribution)

Producing isn't just about mastering the details. A producer also has a clear vision of the "big picture": the current marketplace, the changes in technology, audience demographics, the trends of the day. She or he reads the industry publications, actively watches programming in specific genres, and seeks out opportunities to learn more, to gain an edge.

PROFESSIONAL OPPORTUNITIES

According to the U.S. Bureau of Labor Statistics, "Employment in the motion picture and video industries is projected to grow 31 percent between 2002 and 2012, roughly double the 16 percent growth projected for all industries combined." Demand for content comes not only from networks, cable and premium channels, and satellite, but also from burgeoning new media, such as the Internet, cellular technology, video-on-demand, and gaming, along with nonbroadcast venues.

And the international market continues its consumption of the latest hit show or newest format idea, primarily from America and the United Kingdom, increasing its audience base and advertising revenue. As an industry, television and new media both offer a range of options to the producer—from a staff position at a national network to working with a news producer in a local television station, from segment producer to working on a network show as a writer/producer. Producers in video may opt for being freelancers, or independent with their own small companies that produce content for broadcast, corporations, documentary channels, or educational distribution. Like the industry itself, the options for a producer are expanding on a daily basis.

THE PRODUCER IN THE DIGITAL DOMAIN

Producers now work almost exclusively in the digital domain. Most of the producer's integral tools are digital—the computer with its software for writing and editing, the cameras, the formats on which to capture the image and record the sound, the editing and mixing systems, and the technology of the delivery system. Each aspect of production and postproduction processes takes full advantage of these technological advances. We now live and work in the digital domain; this book focuses on these digital tools and on the producer's relationship to them.

ORGANIZATION OF THE TEXT

The Roles of the Producer

A producer's role is as much about working with people as it is about the many phases and details of producing. The producer may have a marketable skill such as writing or directing, but the inherent role of the producer depends on collaboration with others. The strength of this relationship between the producer and the creative teams, the crew, the talent, the client, the vendors, and the dozens of other people along the way is what propels and accomplishes the five stages of production just listed.

The primary purpose of this book, then, is to look closely at this teamwork, and to explore the ways in which each individual on the producer's team functions. What does a director of photography bring to the project? Will you need a location scout? How does the script supervisor make your job easier? At what stage do you hire the editor? Should you consult an entertainment lawyer for each contract? And, most importantly, do you have the necessary "people skills" that can keep this team together?

There are five overall stages of producing, and inside this book, 10 chapters are devoted to this journey. The reader gets a step-by-step explanation of the producer's jobs, from the initial idea of a project to its final distribution process, from concept to contract.

Chapters 1 through 10

Each chapter delves into a specific area of producing, from an overall perspective on the many jobs and titles of a producer, television's history, its current state, and its possible future, to the five stages of producing a project, the details of budgets and breakdowns, legalities and rights, pitching and selling, and the ever-important people skills.

Each chapter opens with talking points that cover the highlights and main points of that chapter's material. Various anecdotes from the author, "In the Trenches," join with memorable quotes, and excerpts from the 19 professionals' interviews in Chapter 11 are scattered through each chapter, as well as commentary on the personal side of producing, "On a Human Level."

Chapter 11

This chapter offers interviews with high-profile, experienced television and new-media producers, academics, and other industry professionals. These 19 contributors talk candidly about their jobs: what they do, how they do it, the people they work with and depend on, their day-to-day functions, and the balancing act between their professional lives and the personal. Their producers' titles range from executive producers in network television to independent producers of documentaries or nonbroadcast material. Industry professionals share their insights ranging from legal issues to festival submissions.

Just like a compelling guest speaker in the classroom, or a mentor in the workplace, each shares his or her stories from the trenches. Each offers a unique perspective on producing.

1
Added Features

Throughout the first 10 chapters in the book, each contributing producer and industry professional from Chapter 11 shares pertinent information through:

- *Top Ten Lists*: The top ten aspects of professional success as noted by its contributor
- *Sound Bites*: Salient excerpts from the interviews in Chapter 11
- *In the Trenches*: Each chapter has at least one anecdote from the author's experiences
- *Let's say…*: Various "what-if" examples
- *Graphics*: Charts, formats, and maps
- *Quotes*: Some of the best global, media, and historical minds offer their thoughts

The Glossary

The words or terms of the language of television, new media, and communications are explained in the glossary. Each word in the text is italicized, referring the reader to the glossary.

2
The Web Site

Every producer uses specific forms and legal agreements in organizing and protecting his or her project. In the web site that accompanies this book, there are a variety of templates for most forms and agreements that working producers use on a daily basis. The web site also offers a variety of resources, including an extensive Books and References section, web sites, and more. The web site can be found at http://booksite.focalpress.com/Kellison. Its contents are listed in the Table of Contents.

3
Note to the Instructor

In tandem with this textbook, the Instructor's Manual offers an overview of the material, as well as a per-chapter classroom-tested syllabus, opportunities for classroom interaction and individual student projects. To access this material, contact your Focal Press sales representative, or go to www.textbooks.elsevier.com.

4
Note to the Reader

You may be a student of television and its gradual convergence with new media, and you've enrolled in a plan of study that explores the role of the producer. Or, you have an idea you think could be expanded and broadcast. Or you may be an experienced producer who is actively involved in producing content and who can benefit from an updated approach to the technical and creative aspects of producing your project.

Regardless of the category into which you fall, this book has been researched, designed, and written for you. It is the first book of its kind to fully explore both the "big picture" and the small details of producing for both television and new media. It can be part of an overall curriculum, or provide helpful creative and technical guidelines for the independent producer. This text aims to present the realities and possibilities for the producer, one who is ready to devote time, energy, and passion to producing quality programming and content in this extraordinary period of media expansion.

Put simply, this book promises to help you know more about what you don't know.

What Does a TV Producer *Really* Do?

The definition of a producer: An idealist, a realist, a practical dreamer, a sophisticated gambler, and a stage-struck child.

Oscar Hammerstein

THIS CHAPTER'S TALKING POINTS

I. The Producer's Domain

II. Defining a TV and New Media Producer

III. The Many Roles of a Producer

IV. Producers' Titles and Job Descriptions

V. The Need for People Skills

I. THE PRODUCER'S DOMAIN

Television has affected—and reflected—the culture of global communications for over a half-century. And now, the explosion of new media shows every sign of having a similar impact, as it bursts onto the scene with innovative possibilities and real challenges. Even the very word itself, "television," takes on new meaning. As we enter this extraordinary era of media transition, traditional television programming, viewing habits, advertising models, and delivery systems must inevitably change with the times.

TV and its new media offshoots must be fed, and it's the producer who feeds them. The producer is central to every aspect of a project—from the wisp of an idea to a tangible piece of work. In theory, a producer has unlimited potential to educate and entertain. But the trade-off is intensive hours, stressful demands, and myriad responsibilities.

The demands of viewers and the appetites of commerce require a continuing stream of unique programming, or *content*, for television and new media to survive. This content can range from sitcoms on NBC and TV movies on Lifetime, to internal corporate training videos for IBM, or segments for CNN cable news; from one-minute "webisodes" for mobile phones, or an intricate video game, to 24/7 content for online channels—regardless of the delivery system, each of these content formats has a producer in charge. The producer must satisfy both the client and the viewer, and utilize the talents of the cast and crew, manage the budget, possibly write the script, and master dozens of skill sets.

A producer's job description combines art with craft, commerce with technology, and leadership with collaboration. There is arguably a producer's personality and mind-set that comes with the territory; some people who want to be a producer are naturals; others may simply not be right for the job. So, whether you become a producer, or work with producers, or simply want to adopt a valuable producer's skill set, you can start by exploring the many layers of responsibility and creativity involved in producing. This chapter, as well as those that follow, examines the producer's vast domain, its benefits and challenges, and reveals what a producer needs to know about the many phases of a project's development.

> I love bringing talented people together. There's no greater feeling than standing on a shoot, sitting in an edit, or watching the final product on TV, knowing that you as the producer pulled together an incredible, hard-working group of people to create something.
>
> **Justin Wilkes, excerpt from interview in Chapter 11**

An effective producer is a multitasker, regardless of the content or its delivery system. A producer might not only research, write, and produce a program or segment, but might also shoot it, edit the footage on a desktop system, mix the audio, design and add graphics, or write and record narration or voice-over. The increasing availability and low cost of equipment, along with decreasing budgets, make these skills both valuable and necessary to the producer.

A producer's talents cover a broad spectrum—from creative to technological, from the first hint of an idea to its final broadcast, from finding finances to marketing. In this chapter and throughout the book, we'll explore the producer's role: finding, writing, developing, and pitching an idea; budgeting a script; negotiating a deal; securing financing; planning, shooting and editing; and creating a team of talented people with great attitudes.

> Producers are risk takers, who seize an idea, run with it, and convince others to follow them.
>
> **Gorham Kindem, *The Moving Image***

Clearly, this book can't cover each detail of every producer's job, although most major points are discussed. For everything you'll explore in the following chapters, there are dozens of books, web sites, and seminars that target these specifics in more detail. Each bit of knowledge adds to the producer's arsenal.

II. DEFINING A TV AND NEW MEDIA PRODUCER

> I'm a producer. I do whatever is necessary to turn an idea into a finished product. That means at different times I've been a salesman, director, film editor, casting director, creative consultant. I've even driven the bus.
>
> **David L Wolper, *Producer: A Memoir***

Without a producer, there is no project. The producer propels the project from an unformed idea to final broadcast or download. He can nurture the project from conception to distribution and might also be the writer, director, and/or the source of the financing. At various stages of production, he may bring in other producers who can help in handling the hundreds of details that need supervision or polish.

The producer is usually the first one on a project and the last one off. She is essentially the overall project supervisor. She gets the project off the ground, and then supervises every step of its development and production. Not every producer originates the idea; often, a producer is hired to work with a network or production company after an idea has been created and sold. Some producers do it all themselves, others are part of a producing team. It's work that's exciting and exhausting.

The job of a producer of television and new media is different from a film producer's job. Conventional wisdom defines feature films as the director's domain, theater to be the realm of the actor, and TV as the domain of the producer. In most cases, the feature-film producer acts as the liaison between the studio and the production, providing a support system for the film's director: increasingly, producers shepherd their own scripts or projects, hiring the director and cast, and overseeing the film's integrity, production value, and marketing.

In television and new media, the producer is the governing force who often doubles as the director, unless the project is heavily actor-oriented, like network episodics, sitcoms, and drama. The producer usually hires and fires the director, writers, key department heads, actors and other talent, crew, and anyone else needed to bring the project to life. The director in television generally makes more of a technical contribution, working with the talent and crew on blocking and lighting and rehearsing lines, or is in the control room, making camera decisions on a live or prerecorded show. But it is the producer who makes the final decisions; the buck stops there.

> I carried my tape recorder with me everywhere as a kid. I had this odd fascination with recording things and playing them back. I taped everything. As I got into school, I brought my video camera to school. It was this odd fascination with wanting to play things back for some reason. By the time I was old enough to try and figure out what I was supposed to do for a living, all I really knew was I wanted to continue this process of recording something and making it into something.
>
> **Matt Lombardi, excerpt from interview in Chapter 11**

Who and What Makes a Good Producer?

> These digital cameras now? People can make a show—make a movie. That's what I like. The industry is just so hard to get into, you know, unless you have a lot of money. Now, people that have an idea of some kind of media that they want to share can put things on YouTube—the sky's the limit now. It's wide open for people to be as creative as they can possibly be.
>
> **Sheila Possner Emery, excerpt from interview in Chapter 11**

If you're eager to meet challenges and can multitask and handle a steady stream of demands and questions, if you are slightly type A or obsessive–compulsive and like to run a tight ship while still having fun, you have the makings of a good producer. Combine those qualities with creativity and flexibility, an openness to new ideas and information, a genuine respect for all kinds of people, and an ethical and profitable approach to business—if this all sounds like your personality, you could wake up each day excited to go to work as a producer.

The majority of working producers truly enjoy their job. They like its random nature, and welcome the challenges. The job fits their personality. Some producers are calmer or nicer or more organized than others; some act badly, others can inspire. As you read the interviews with contributing guest speakers in Chapter 11, you'll see that producers tend to choose this work because it genuinely excites them.

A good producer:

- *Is a problem-solver.* A producer anticipates what's needed, and solves problems rather than creates them. He's smart and plays fair. He's a nurturer, an arbitrator, can be both a leader and a team player. He's a risk taker with contingencies for any predictable scenario—he has a plan A, plan B, and even a plan C.

- *Is the master of multitasking.* Whether the project is a low-budget documentary or an expensive weekly drama, the producer balances dozens of tasks at once. She might be an entrepreneurial executive producer who secures the financing and makes deals, or a producer commissioned by the executive producer to work on aspects of the project, such as segments, postproduction, music, and so on. She might also be working in several stages of production at once.

- *Is a middle man.* The producer who's wise enough to be on set regularly (even though he may not be needed) becomes the point person for the director, the DP (Director of Photography), the actors, and the crew members who rely on his leadership. The producer balances the needs of the network or client with the needs of the talent and cast.

- *Wants to know everything.* A good story and useful information are both at the core of a producer's craft. The world of producing changes daily so the producer researches everything at her disposal—books and magazines, the industry trade papers, newspapers, the Internet, plays, biographies, art and history, and philosophy. She looks for ideas that interest her and that might also appeal to a wide audience. Her goal is to understand where the media industries are going, as well as keep current with what is popular now. She watches TV and explores new media.

- *Enjoys the process.* The producer is comfortable doing business *and* being creative. He doesn't need to know how to do everything—like write, direct, edit, create sound design, and light and design sets—but he does know how to hire the best people to do those jobs. He creates a loyal and talented team who can all work toward a common goal—creating a compelling story.

To paraphrase Gertrude Stein, a producer is a producer is a producer. The needs of each individual job may fluctuate but the skill sets on most jobs are similar. A good producer can produce almost anything—a two-hour documentary, a half-hour sitcom, streaming online video, a 30-second commercial, a mobisode, a corporate image piece, even a music video. The projects may differ in content and length. They may require skills in producing a specific kind of program or content; but the creative, financial, technical, and interpersonal skills required are similar for all producers.

> I don't really think there is a "producer's personality," but I think there are many qualities that a good producer should have, if he or she wants to do the job well and also be able to sleep at night. Despite the clichés of what a producer acts like (sharp-dressed, fast-talking, megalomaniacs), I think that honesty is very important. Anything else will eventually come out anyway, so aside from basic ethics, there's really no point in making things up to cover your bases, or to convince someone of something that isn't true, just so you can get out of them what you want.
> **Michael Bonfiglio, excerpt from interview in Chapter 11**

III. THE MANY ROLES OF A PRODUCER

To see it from the outside looking in was always exciting to me. Anything in this business that helps you learn, to me, is always interesting. It's never *the same, it changes every day. It's not a job where you go, "Okay, I've got to do that for another eight hours." You know what's coming, and it's always about being prepared for what could happen.*

Bernie Young, excerpt from interview in Chapter 11

The producer in television and in new media has the power to educate, entertain, and emotionally move an audience. But developing a project takes time and energy—a lot of both. No matter what its length or content, each project goes through the following five stages of production, and each of these stages needs a producer.

The Five Stages of Production: From Idea to Wrap

Stage One: The idea (project development)
Stage Two: The plan (preproduction)
Stage Three: The shoot (production)
Stage Four: The final product (postproduction)
Stage Five: Next steps (wrap up and distribution)

Stage One: The Idea (Project Development)

Your idea might be a full-length script or a simple one-paragraph treatment. During the five stages of production, this idea is developed, fleshed out, and hopefully produced. In the project development stage (explored in Chapter 3), the entrepreneurial producer often, though not always:

- Either writes or finds material to option, or obtains all rights to found material. This material can be an original idea, a script, a book, a story on the Internet, a newspaper or magazine article—a producer can find material from many sources.
- Evaluates the project's initial costs, funding sources, and likely markets.
- Develops the idea, first into a story synopsis and then into a formal proposal, or pitch, for getting financing or development funds.
- Oversees the development of the idea. In dramatic programming, this might include writing the show's *bible* that covers the overall narrative arc, with plot lines and character sketches for a season of shows in a series.
- Develops a rough estimate of the budget.
- Pitches the project. Raises network or client interest. Obtains financing that covers the project's initial development or that spans the entire project. A development deal can range from simply developing the script to producing a pilot.
- Negotiates and obtains contracts for licensing fees and other legal aspects of the project's distribution or broadcast.
- Selects, interviews, and hires a director who shares the project's visions and can deliver on schedule. Not every project requires a director; often, the producer may fill this role.
- Selects and hires a writer or team of writers (staff and/or freelance) to develop the idea further.
- May consult with and hire additional producers, associate producers, and/or a production manager.

Stage Two: The Plan (Preproduction)

By now, the original idea has taken a more tangible form. It can provide a kind of blueprint for the research and hiring of the essential crew members who will take it to the next stage. In the preproduction stage (explored in Chapters 4 and 7), often, though not always, the producer:

- Is the principal point person for the financing and/or distribution group. Is involved in negotiations, contracts, rights, and union discussions. Secures rights and permits for locations, music, and other elements.
- Breaks down a script or treatment into a rough budget estimate.
- Continues consulting with the director on aspects of the script and production.
- Depending on the scope of the project, hires and consults with the line producer, location manager, director, cast, DP, production designer, postproduction supervisor, editor, musical composer, and graphics and special effects personnel, as well as essential crew such as camera operators, audio recordists, lighting designers, and other production areas such as make-up, wardrobe, props, construction, transportation, catering, and more. The director may or may not be involved in the hiring process.
- Hires and supervises legal consultants, accountants and auditors, production coordinators, office managers, script supervisors, producer assistants (PAs), interns, among others.
- Supervises the completion of the shooting script.
- Scouts and approves all locations (often with the location scout, director, and/or DP).
- Consults with the production designer on sets, construction, props, and the overall look of the production.
- Consults with the DP and director on shooting format (HD, 24P, P2, film, 4K, etc.).
- Breaks down the shooting script to prepare the overall shooting schedule, call sheets, and production report forms (usually with the line producer and/or production coordinator and/or executive in charge of production).
- Negotiates with appropriate unions on contract and fee agreements.
- Prepares all contracts and deal memos, or oversees them after the unit production manager (UPM) has compiled them.
- Signs off on the final budget.

Stage Three: The Shoot (Production)

Stages one and two lead to the actual shoot, where the vision of the project can now be captured on tape or memory card. During the shooting stage (detailed in Chapter 8), usually although not always, the producer:

- Is on set or on call, always available.
- Consults with the writer(s) and supervises any changes.
- Works closely with the line producer.
- Works with the production designer and approves all aspects of the project's overall look, tone, and mood.
- Consults regularly with the director, on-camera talent, production designer, and other key department heads.
- Screens the dailies with the director (and often the editor).
- Prepares, balances, and/or approves the daily or weekly cost estimates.
- Stays on top of any press or publicity material generated and carefully supervises what's appearing in the media about the project.

Stage Four: The Final Product (Postproduction)

The footage has been logged and loaded into the computer, and now all the pieces are ready to be joined together in the editing room and audio facility. At this stage, it's unlikely that you can reshoot additional footage, so it's up to you to make it work through careful planning for the shoot and postproduction. During the postproduction period (which you'll explore in Chapter 9), usually but not always, the producer:

- Often screens and logs all footage, and supplies the editor with a "paper cut" (see Chapters 4 and 9) that acts as a script for the editor, with notes, time-code references for footage, and reel numbers and logs. Lists all graphic elements and audio components. (Templates for these forms are available on the book's companion web site.)
- On most projects, is fully present during editing or comes into the editing room on a regular basis to review the editor's work in progress.
- Continues as the point person for the network, client, or producing group regarding issues of the final cut, timings and show lengths, standards and practices. Keeps track of all other delivery requirements.
- Keeps a close eye on the budget. Postproduction can be one of the least controllable financial aspects of the project.
- Selects, negotiates, and books postproduction facilities, such as editorial houses and editors, stock footage facilities, audio studios, composers and/or stock music supervisors, graphics houses and designers, and so on.
- Is familiar with all footage, selected takes, B-roll, cutaways, and other elements needed in the edit. May work closely with an assistant who's familiar with the footage.
- Regularly supervises the editor. Is responsible for the final cut, depending on contractual agreements.
- Works closely with the musical composer and/or stock music supervisor.
- Supervises audio sessions including narration, dubbing, ADR, foley, rough mix, and final mix.
- Works closely with the graphics designer(s) on show titles, in-show bumpers, opening and end credits, special effects, and other graphic design elements.
- May organize and conduct focus groups or audience testing and supervise any editorial changes that could result from their responses.
- Signs off on the video master of the final cut for client delivery.

Stage Five: Next Steps (Wrap Up and Distribution)

The project is edited and ready to go, whether for broadcast, online, and/or for a client. Still, the producer must deal with several vital details. In the wrap-up stage (explored in Chapter 10), often but not always, the producer:

- Pays and reconciles all outstanding invoices.
- Finalizes all legal contracts and other issues still outstanding.
- Reconciles all budget issues and submits a final report to the client.
- May distribute copies of the final product to key personnel on the production.
- May be involved in advertising and promotional campaigns, including on-air promos, online advertising and PR, print ads, Internet blogs, and grassroots campaigns.
- May consult with the network or production company on publicity, such as special events, public relations photos and artwork.
- May work closely with the network or production company on securing international broadcast, copyright issues, ancillary rights, licensing, and so on.
- May coordinate press activities by carefully controlling what material is appropriate for release to the press.

Why Become a Producer?

A producer's job demands hard work over intense periods of time. Yet most producers genuinely love their job, partially because they find its demands to be stimulating. Producers work their way up from different places—some begin as interns, others as a PA, a secretary, a production coordinator, or an assistant. Some producers make the transition from their former careers as lawyers, writers, directors, actors, agents, or managers. Still other people have the financing and entrepreneurial passion to fund projects independently.

Over the last few years, universities have recognized the value of curricula that focuses on producing for television and new media. Their classes can be excellent sources of information, ideas, and discussion; yet, as you'll read in Chapter 11, many important aspects of producing can be learned only on the job and in the trenches. Out there in the real world, television and new media continue to evolve on a daily basis.

> I do think there are a lot of creative advantages to television—the immediacy, the amount of financing, funding—making it vastly superior to film, particularly now in cable television.
>
> **Brett Morgen, excerpt from interview in Chapter 11**

Many producers started off as writers or directors or actors who had an idea for a project they wanted to see actualized. They wanted to brand their idea with their own unique voice, and because they wanted that voice to be heard, they refused to relinquish control over the development of the idea. They chose to become producers so they could protect that idea's vulnerability and actualize their original idea. They saw their vision to be rather like a fragile newborn, one who is sheltered by legal, fiscal, technical, interpersonal, and creative knowledge. Reinforced by these assets, their vision can grow and thrive.

Creativity, Clout, and Control

Every producer works toward some kind of payoff. The payoff can be financial, creative, experiential; ideally, it's all of these. That payoff is more likely to occur if the producer uses the components of *creativity*, *clout*, and *control*.

Television writers, for example, seldom have enough clout to be guaranteed that their script will be produced and aired as they originally wrote it. For the most part, writers—even the best of them—are regularly hired, used up, fired, then replaced.

But when writers can understand the producer's skill set, or even take on the producer's role, they can dramatically increase their control over their project, especially if they can develop a reputation as a strong producer who is also creative, and who can write and/or direct.

This overall concept of originating and nurturing an idea can be explored through these three very different lenses.

Creativity: Inspiration and Creative Skills

Your idea is the creative essence of your project. As its producer, you may write it yourself, or you have found an idea that's been originated by someone else. Then, after you've legally secured it, you develop it and flesh it out, and finally, you make it come alive.

Your team may be small or large, but it's a vital creative component. This team brings together the writers, actors, directors, crew, and production designers whose visions are aligned with yours. You're creating and building a team of talented people who share your passion, reflect it in their work, and bring positive *creativity* and energy into the process.

Clout: Networking and Contacts Skills

The cliché hasn't changed: it's *who* you know, plus *what* you know. Networking has become a way of life, so you can research opportunities to meet people at festivals, organizations, school clubs, openings, charity events, and dozens of other events in your locale. If nothing currently exists, exercise your producing skills by putting on networking events or organizing film/TV festivals. Create an online presence, write a blog—the opportunities to connect with like-minded people in an online world are endless, as social networking creates new visions and versions of community.

You can sharpen your producing skills when you know who's who, and who does what the best. You can follow the trends in television and new media, and research who's financing them and in what ways the projects are financially viable. When you keep on top of media industry news, follow the smart blogs, and observe the ebb and flow of current trends, you are stockpiling your own clout.

Control: Business Skills

You have a vision and it deserves to thrive. Your job is to protect it. You can research the legal requirements like copyrights, contracts, deal memos, and other forms of negotiation (see Chapter 5) that can protect your idea and the whole project that revolves around it.

You can master the numbers when you fine-tune your skills in breaking down a script, in budgeting, costing out, rough estimates, daily costs, and so on. Research budgeting software, and research online sources for shortcuts and hints on budgeting.

You also want to understand and know your audience, both domestic and global. What are their interests and their demographics such as age, income, ethnicity, and education? Who are the media companies that reach out to those audiences, and how can you form a relationship with them?

In this era of technological revolution, research the changing equipment in production and postproduction—they're both vital to your project. Although the delivery systems that include broadcast television, mobile phones, cable, the Internet, and video gaming systems are increasing exponentially, they all need content to go out to the viewer—as a producer, that's where you come into the picture.

IV. PRODUCERS' TITLES AND JOB DESCRIPTIONS

Unlike other areas in television, such as writing, directing, or acting, the producer doesn't fall under the protection of a union in the same way that a writer, director, and/or actor does because the producer is generally in charge of the project, rather than at the mercy of higher ups. The producer determines and maintains the budget, negotiates with these unions, and adheres to their guidelines.

Although the Producers Guild of America (PGA) offers benefits to producers with varying titles and levels of experience, their contractual and legal parameters aren't currently comparable to those in the traditional unions such as WGA, DGA, and SAG.

Producing historically has attracted the entrepreneurs and the rebels, people who tend to be risk takers and self-directed, along with a few control freaks here and there. Most producers are genuine—hard-working and passionate. And there are also the wannabees—those who crave the title but don't do the work that goes along with it.

This title of "producer" becomes a negotiating tool, and often is given out freely as a reward. It's not uncommon for a so-called producer to know very little about the intricacies of producing. Instead, he may be a major investor—or a minor con artist—who wants to flaunt his credits without doing the hard work. Because there is no official governing union that controls the assignment of the producer title, a network or production company can bestow it on actors, agents, managers, or anyone else who has had some part in putting the deal together. However, the PGA has taken on the watchdog role over the allocation of producing credits; the desired outcome is a more stringent control over who gets what credit and title.

Producers' Titles

In both nonscripted and scripted television, and in new media, producers can also be writers and/or directors. From show to show and genre to genre, producers' titles and their job descriptions can vary considerably.

> **Author's Note:** As is often the case when it comes to producing, the rules change on a regular basis. These titles can vary from show to show, but generally fall under the following definitions.

Following is just a taste of producers' titles.

Executive Producer

This is the murkiest of all producers' titles because it covers the gamut of descriptions. It generally designates the person who makes the deals, finds the finances, and/or puts the package of writer, director, actors, and/or crew together. Usually she sets up and controls the budget. She may hire various crew and cast, and can be in charge of other producers for one or more projects. There may be several executive producers and co-executive producers on a single project. For example, one may be the liaison between the network and the press, another deals directly with talent and creative, a third with budgets and business planning.

On a financial level, the executive producer might have single-handedly financed the project, even mortgaged her house to develop it, or she may have had just one brief meeting with an investor who said yes. She may be actively on the set and in the office every day, or may show up only at the wrap party. The lead actress could demand the executive producer credit as part of her contract, and so could her husband or manager.

> **The Top 10 Things you Need to Be a Good Executive Producer**
>
> 1. Loyalty to the host and show that borders on insanity
> 2. A long fuse
> 3. A small ego
> 4. Attention to detail
> 5. Organizational ability
> 6. Ability to make a split-second decision
> 7. Learn to take a joke
> 8. Pick your battles
> 9. Good listening skills
> 10. Snappy dresser
>
> Barbara Gaines, *The Late Show with David Letterman*, excerpt
> *from interview in Chapter 11*

Showrunner

The term *showrunner* is informal, and not credited as such. The showrunner is responsible for the overall creative direction of a series, and often he may have the title of executive producer. The showrunner may be the original creator of the show and/or the writer of the show's storyline overview, "the bible." He is usually the primary writer, and/or manages and guides other writers in creating the scripts; he often may rewrite scripts and make sure they're delivered on schedule.

The showrunner on a reality show, talk show, news, specials, and so on may not always be as involved in the writing, and may be more involved with generating, selling, and/or managing ideas. He may also be very involved in pitching a new show idea to a network, casting the actors, and staying on top of a very long list of elements needed to produce a weekly show. Most important, the showrunner maintains the essential vision of the show. A showrunner can be a writer, a producer, or both, and has the power to hire or fire, shouldering the burden of the show's success or failure.

Producer (Senior Producer, Supervising Producer)

She can be an entrepreneurial producer or a producer commissioned to come in at any stage to work on the project. Either way, she starts the ball rolling, usually from concept to broadcast, by initiating ideas and hiring and coordinating crews. She can also be the writer and/or the director, or hires them; casts the talent; and supervises and controls the budget and the technical and administrative aspects throughout the project. This producer oversees contracts and negotiations, and may receive a percentage of the final profits, if any, as well as a regular salary.

Integrated Producer

The integrated producer is a new breed of producer who has a decidedly interactive focus. He can create and manage interactive content for the web, gaming, mobile, and newer systems, and is equally adept at directing teams of producers and designers. He is able to draft project goals, schedules, and budgets, has mastered most software programs, can shoot live action, and deals easily with both vendors and clients.

Associate Producer

Also called the co-producer or assistant producer, she is the producer's right hand and does specific jobs that the producer assigns. Her work can be on the creative side, such as helping to set up interviews on a talk show, and can also lean toward administrative tasks, such as making production schedules, allotting budgets to departments, booking talent and/or crew, research, interviewing talent, finding locations, and more.

Line Producer (Production Manager, Unit Production Manager, Producer, or Co-Producer)

The nuts and bolts of producers, the line producer is most involved in the day-to-day operation from the beginning to the end of the project. He keeps budgets on track and compares estimated costs to actual expenditures. The line producer represents the administrative side of television, and turns ideas into reality by figuring out the logistics of a project. He keeps the production on schedule (set constructions, props, wardrobes, talent releases, etc.), breaks down the script into a storyboard and its components for production, and decides the sequence of shooting that's most cost-effective. He works closely with the producer(s) in various aspects of location scouting, transportation and lodging, and dozens of production details. It's a vital job—the line producer helps the executive producer, producer, and director do their jobs much more smoothly.

Staff Producer

Generally hired on a permanent or per-project basis, the staff producer works in a network or production company as an employee with benefits. Her job usually involves producing an ongoing aspect of the show that's assigned to her—it could be her task to interview potential guests, research stories, track down licensing information, secure locations, and more.

Segment Producer

In magazine format shows, news broadcasts, talk shows, and reality-based programming, he is assigned to one of several stories aired within the program and may produce his own segment. Some shows may have several teams comprised of a producer, PAs, a camera operator, and an editor who work together on their segment. He may also be one of a growing group of producers—the producer-editor, or *preditor*—who research, shoot, and edit their own pieces.

Independent Producer

Also called *independent contractors* or *freelancers*, she may own her own company with a capable infrastructure, and work on projects for a network, another production company, or a variety of clients. She might have a complete staff, or hire on an as-needed basis. She usually pays her own insurance, benefits, taxes, and other expenses like overhead and equipment.

Field Producer

This area of producing refers to a producer who is "in the field" or at a location some distance away from the primary producer. Many companies in New York or Los Angeles, for example, have a roster of field producers who are located around the country or abroad. He can be on the scene faster and less expensively, and can work flexibly in a variety of fields like sports, entertainment, and news.

Session Producer

Often a producer is needed to supervise and produce a recording session, an interview, a voice-over recording, a satellite feed, or other producing necessities. She keeps it on track, is aware of the time used, the length of a shoot or recording take, and generally maintains close quality control.

Postproduction Supervisor

As a producer in the postproduction stage, he is familiar with the footage to be edited, and keeps logs of where the footage is and on what reel numbers. He may create a paper cut or storyboard of the editing order of the shots, with their time code and reel locations. He keeps track of the graphic and audio elements; supervises all edit, graphic, and audio sessions; and works closely with the editor and later, with the sound designer throughout the final stages of postproduction.

V. THE NEED FOR PEOPLE SKILLS

Balance? I've heard of that... It comes and goes. There are times in television when you're completely overwhelmed. You've got to pump it out every eight days, and it's not always great. You get scripts thrown back at you by the networks sometimes. You get a ton of notes at all times. You're having to please a lot of different people, and you have fights, but you have to pick your battles.

Scott A. Williams, excerpt from interview in Chapter 11

A producer's creative and business skills are essential to the success of a project. And so are vital people skills—they are an equally compelling facet of a strong producer's approach to the job. It can't be emphasized enough: A producer can do nothing without a team. The producer builds his team on the talents of writers, directors, crew, actors, editors, composers, and so many more. Without these people to actualize the project, a producer is useless. He needs people skills not only to attract qualified people to the project, but to keep them motivated and collaborative.

A strong producer relies on the following skills while working with dozens of people involved in bringing a project to life:

Collaboration. A strong producer embraces collaboration and encourages teamwork by supporting each member of the team, and encouraging open discussion.

Communication skills. These skills are vital for effective relationships. Without them, you risk misunderstandings, even chaos in your project. Communication is either *verbal* (the choice of words as well as the tone and volume of our voice) or *nonverbal* (facial expressions, body language, gestures).

Verbal. Is *what* you said the same thing as *how* you said it? You say you're not mad but your tone of voice says otherwise. Say what you mean.

Nonverbal. Do you look at people as you talk or listen, or are you distracted? Does your body language say that you are nervous or inattentive, or calm and in control?

Conflict management. Conflicts happen all the time, especially in the high-stress world of media. No matter how hard we try to solve them, some conflicts are inevitable and can't be resolved. But most conflicts can be *managed* effectively if you can grasp the cause of the conflict and deal with it. As the producer, you are also the peacemaker. Not everyone has to like one another, but they're professionals, who have a job to do. Sometimes it's up to you to mediate.

IN THE TRENCHES...

A large production company in New York brought me into a project that required building six interior locations, a host for each location, a specific color palette, props from the 1940s, among other details. Plus, I researched and wrote the script and scheduled the shoot. It was great fun, we hit very few brick walls, and it involved the hiring of a lot of people for a range of jobs. Busy, busy, each day, with fires to put out and quick decisions at every turn. At a lunch break in our third week, one of the gaffers came up to me, rather shyly. "Sorry to interrupt, but...were you ever a kindergarten teacher?" I hooted out loud, but I could see he genuinely meant this question. "No, but why do you ask?" He took a deep breath, then he said something like this: "Well, you always make sure people eat their lunch, and the snacks and meals are totally cool. You let us do our jobs and you don't interrupt us to ask what we're doing. When you're listening to us, you kind of bend over to hear us better. You like to hear our stories. You say please and thank you. And you're funny." To this day, years later, it's maybe the best compliment I've ever gotten. Totally true story.

~*C. Kellison*

Emotional intelligence (EQ). In this growing field, initially developed by Daniel Goleman, a person's emotional strengths are considered as important as his or her intellectual abilities. A high EQ is measured by a producer's ability to show genuine empathy, respect, positive leadership skills, and sincerity for the team.

Learning styles. We are seeing impressive research over the last few years that focuses on how we learn, both cognitively and emotionally. Researchers have identified over 20 different ways that people absorb information and learn. They're all effective. When you can understand the different ways in which each member of your team learns, you can strengthen the bonds of communication.

Most of us have one predominate way in which we absorb information:

Visual. This person learns best by reading or looking at information, and then creates a mental picture from the data.

Auditory. In this case, a person absorbs information better when it comes through hearing the spoken word or audio. The auditory learner generally has strong listening skills and verbal abilities.

Kinesthetic. To the kinesthetic learner, information is best conveyed through ways that are physical, spatial, or sensory, such as charts and 3-D modeling.

Each of us tends to be either one or the other:

Analytical learner. The analytical learner understands information best when it's presented as sequential, linear, organized, and delivered one step at a time.

Global learner. The opposite of the analytical learner, this person sees the big picture first, then breaks it down into smaller and more manageable details.

Here, too, we tend to fall into one of two categories:

Goal-oriented. This type of person tends to stick with a task, with no breaks or lulls, with an almost single-minded focus until the job is done.

Process-oriented. Here, the process and the journey of reaching the goal can be as engaging as the goal itself.

Multiple intelligences. This originally was researched and revealed by distinguished Harvard professor, Dr. Howard Gardner. His research reveals at least a dozen distinct predominant intelligences that each of us can claim, such as a strong musical, mathematical, spatial, or athletic intelligence.

Listening skills. The ability to simply listen to another person is a real skill that can work wonders. Being attentive, not interrupting, and acknowledging that we hear the other person can be a real challenge for some people. As we suspend our own need to talk and control, we can genuinely listen, and make people feel truly valued.

Leadership skills. As the team's leader, the producer recognizes that the team is made of individuals. Each member of the team has his or her own emotional needs, learning styles, problem-solving strategies, communication approaches, and personal issues that can influence professional function. Leadership comes with the producer's territory, so treat the position with respect for those you're leading.

Leadership has a harder job to do than just choose sides. It must bring sides together.

Jesse Jackson

The producer benefits—as do the team members—when the needs of the team are taken into consideration. With a goal of creating harmony, the producer models behaviors and viewpoints that set a tone for the project and all its stages of production.

Some of the essential leadership skills and ideals that the producer can embody are:

Commitment. If you don't believe in your project, don't expect anyone else to. Stand firmly behind it.

Credibility. Though you want people to respect you, don't let your need to be liked get in the way of getting things done.

Delegation. Hire the best people you can find, and learn what they do. Then, leave them alone to do their job. Check in regularly to confirm that the project's vision remains intact.

Motivation. Producers don't expect praise (and seldom get it), but they know how to lavish it on their team when it's genuinely earned. Find ways to show your thanks.

Ethics. The value of *ethics* in producing is more about strength of character than a spiritual or religious mandate. A producer who assesses his or her own ethical framework is more likely to create a project that's under control, stimulating, and a positive experience.

Accountability. Because you're in charge, you're accountable to your team. It's their project too. Keeping up with changes in technology, creative trends, and the business of the TV industry is also part of your job.

Honesty. Your word is solid enough to build your reputation upon it.

Objectivity. You can listen to criticism without taking it personally, and can hear all sides of an issue.

Patience. Respect the fact that people work at different rhythms with varying working styles.

Personal balance. The demands of the job can take over your "other" life. With the right perspective and determination , you can have a professional *and* a personal life.

Will power. Stress during production can result in producer burnout caused by too many long hours, too little sleep, a diet of junk food, and the temptations of smoking, alcohol, drugs, and negative relationships. Save your energy.

Relationships. You can cultivate new friends who share your passion for producing while staying close to your most important supporters: friends and family.

Daydreaming. Occasionally, make the time to take a walk, a mental break, and a few deep breaths. Find a source of peace: meditation, painting, yoga, laughing.

I've found in life that when you refuse to settle for anything but the best, you very often get it.

W. Somerset Maugham

ON A HUMAN LEVEL . . .

As the producer, you are at the core of a project. You encourage collaboration and provide strong and balanced leadership. You know when to step back and let people do their job. You model patience, humor, and a clear vision of the project, supplying creative direction while balancing the pressures of the budget. You are generous with your flexibility and encouragement, while staying connected to the realities of the budget and time constraints. In spite of the long hours and often grueling situations, you're focused and relaxed—or at least appearing to be.

SUMMARY

A good producer knows about the elements of producing. He or she might also be talented as a writer, director, or editor. As a storyteller, an entrepreneur, a risk taker, a producer has strong leadership skills and works well with a team. Another sure sign of a skilled producer is an understanding of the larger context of television and its offshoots, including its past history, current status, and future potential. You'll learn about all three in the following chapter.

REVIEW QUESTIONS

1. How do producers in TV and new media differ from film producers?

2. List three important skills and traits of a good producer. Explain why each is helpful.

3. List one role the producer plays in each of the five stages of a project's development.

4. Define "clout" in producers' terms.

5. What does the line producer do? How is this job different from other producing titles?

6. List two reasons why "owning" your emotions can help in managing conflicts.

7. What areas of producing might be impacted by a failure of leadership? A failure of ethics?

8. Define three learning styles outlined in the Learning Styles section that best describe your own, and give examples.

9. How can delegation skills contribute to the execution of a project?

10. What have you learned so far about being a producer? Has it affected your interest in producing?

Television: Its Past, Present, and Future

There's nothing on it worthwhile, and we're not going to watch it in this household, and I don't want it in your intellectual diet.

Philo T. Farnsworth, the Father of Television, to his children

THIS CHAPTER'S TALKING POINTS

I. Television Is a Unique Medium

II. How Television Works

III. The Impact of Human Vision on Television

IV. The Creators of Television

V. Television's Evolution

VI. Television's Transitions: From the 1920s to the Present

VII. Television Merges with New Media

I. TELEVISION IS A UNIQUE MEDIUM

Television is our culture's principal mode of knowing about itself.

Neil Postman, *Amusing Ourselves to Death*

Television wields an undeniable impact on the lives of literally billions of people around the globe. Clearly, it influences how we view and shape our culture, an influence that can be very positive or deeply distressing. Yet media historians would be hard pressed to name another medium of equal importance—the printing press, perhaps, though printed matter was limited to those few elite who could read and write. Morse code, the telephone, the radio, the cinema, the computer—each medium incorporates and improves upon what preceded it.

Television arguably embodies a compilation of the best of these earlier media—access, affordability, interactivity, the aesthetics of film's look and sound, the imagination of radio, the reach of the telegraph. The content range is diverse enough to appeal to any viewer; the technology constantly improves upon itself; and its fiscal viability attracts all aspects of commerce—in short, TV rules.

TV is more everywhere than ever before. It's accessible in the remotest areas—just bring a simple generator and a portable satellite dish into an isolated village, for example, and suddenly the world opens up for people who have had little exposure to the outside world and fewer educational opportunities. Television in urban settings offers hundreds of channel options; it commands a place in corporate boardrooms, classroom discussions, and hospital operating rooms—the venues are endless.

Since the 1950s, television has been recognized as the primary global catalyst for social and political dialogue; its convergence with the Internet and other venues compound its potential as an agent for change. And ever-lowering costs of digital technology and ease of use have had a visceral impact on how we learn and communicate.

Virtually every American home has at least one TV set, and more than 40% of Americans own three or more. Now, people around the world can also "watch TV" on their laptops, iPods, mobile phones, gaming devices; the list of gadgets keeps growing. This transferal of delivery systems on which we can watch TV is referred to as "place shifting." We have shifted from just watching our TV set at home, to now seeing whole episodes of our favorite series on our computer, or webisodes on our mobiles, or news and weather in a taxi cab TV or on iPods, or a game box. It's a whole new game.

But TV still lives primarily at home base. It is a facet of our day-to-day lives that we can enjoy alone or with a group. We can plan parties around it or ignore it completely. Its presence in the background feels like a source of human contact, another member of the family: familiar, frustrating, inspirational, somehow comforting. With its combination of intimacy and immediacy, television is, for many of us, a primary connection with the world.

TV provides us with a unique environment in which to entertain ourselves. We can choose from hundred of options on our media menu: from drama to comedy, endless movies, from sports to news to do-it-yourself. We may get this content via transmission towers, cable, satellite, and now, cyberspace. The quality and production values of what we watch can vary from superior to truly mediocre, but the choices are ours to make, and for the producer, this flexibility creates vast opportunities.

In the past, a viewer was captive to the clock: if a favorite show aired at 9 P.M., the viewer rushed to the couch to catch the show before it began. This was "appointment viewing"—keeping track of what favorite shows were airing and on what channel, day and time, then having to be there at that exact time. The only option, until recently, was to record it onto a VHS tape, then consign that tape to the growing pile of dusty tapes

Now, that's all changing, and very rapidly. The phenomenon of "time shifting"—saving our favorite programs by using DVR devices like TiVo—is radically replacing appointment viewing.

These two recent trends—place shifting and time shifting—are creating real waves of excitement, as well as gloomy moments of uncertainty. We can no longer depend on the traditional business model of television that focused primarily on the confluence of ratings and advertising dollars. As television and new media expand their reach, and run parallel and even converge, these old models of commerce and creativity are radically changing.

Yet the new models of success have short track-records and most remain speculative. Will television remain the same, with the pluses of interactivity? Or, will TV somehow morph into solely Internet, with TV-quality content? How will it become financially viable? What is the new advertising matrix? Will the novelty simply wear off after awhile, with just one or two victors?

That's the thing about TV: if we're lucky enough to have a show, you
have to go with it—because as an independent producer, it's like now, the
money is here now, but when we're done, then what?

Sheila Possner Emery, excerpt from interview in Chapter 11

Television provokes contention and controversy. Its critics argue that the full potential
of television as the great communicator may never be reached, or that the fiscal control
that media conglomerates hold over television programming prevents objective news
reporting, or that entertainment programs pander to the lowest common denominator.
Ultimately, the validity of these arguments rests on the shoulders of the producer with
the skills and the passion to put these criticisms to rest.

II. HOW TELEVISION WORKS

Television: "the art of distant seeing...the possibilities of the new art are
as boundless as the imagination."

David Sarnoff, 1927

We all watch TV, yet we're seldom curious about how it works. Television *content*—what
is seen on our sets—comes into our TV set via broadcast signals. These signals hold
data—images, sounds, graphic art, electronic lettering—all reconfigured inside our TV
set as clear visual and aural impressions. There are four broadcast signals. Each signal
separately controls the:

- Brightness of the image
- Color of the image
- Audio from the image
- Synchronization of the transmitter and the receiver (a TV set)

Broadcast signals are transmitted through virtually the same radio waves that deliver a
radio show. These waves travel through the atmosphere at the speed of light, and can
accommodate vast amounts of information. Television's video signals are heavier, don't
travel as far, and use about 1000 times more *bandwidth* (channel space) than the transmission of an audio signal. Now, with the advances in today's technology, programming can be transmitted by discrete digital signals delivered via fiber optics, opening up
potentials for interactive use.

III. THE IMPACT OF HUMAN VISION ON TELEVISION

Watching TV—how complicated is that? You'd be surprised. Watching TV involves several steps. First, as we look at an image on the screen, this picture stays imprinted on
our retina for just a fraction of a second. This phenomenon is known as *persistence of
vision*; as we watch a sequence of rapid images at the right speed (30 frames a second
for video, as compared to 24 frames a second for film), an illusion is created of a complete and uninterrupted picture.

Lines and Pixels

In early television, scanning was the key principal: scanning wheels created a picture
by scanning an image slowly, line by line; the blurry images on the earliest sets were
comprised of only 48 scanned lines. Now, modern color sets reflect a picture made from
several hundred scanned lines. These lines contain over 100,000 rectangular or square
picture elements known as *pixels*, a short version of "picture elements." Our TV screen
is coated with fluorescent compounds consisting of millions of miniscule dots that give
off light as they're hit by electrons at high speed.

For an image to be transmitted and broadcast by electronic impulses, this image is first broken down into tiny pixels using a scanning process. Thousands of these pixels form lines that are rapidly transmitted, one line at a time. Even though the TV screen never has more than one pixel displayed at once, the electron gun scans the screen so quickly that we see a complete picture, not the separate elements from which it's made.

Each of these tiny pixels is made from three colors: red, green, and blue (*RGB*). The pixels are combined on a phosphor screen, close enough together that they appear to be just one color. These lines, in order to be seen by the viewer, must be reproduced one by one and rapidly reassembled into the original image. This whole process happens in a microsecond, and results in a clear video signal.

NTSC, PAL, or SECAM?

Modern television sets in America as well as several other countries receive programming that has been transmitted as 525 rapidly scanned lines. Most other countries broadcast in 625 lines, which gives their picture a higher resolution, resulting in a clearer picture. Early mechanical TVs could broadcast only a 48-line image; the electronic *kinescope* boosted the count to 60 lines. NBC broadcast 120-line images in 1931 and then improved their system to 240 lines two years later. By 1940, NBC had televised a 507-line picture, and one year later, the National Television Standards Committee (NTSC) adopted what has remained the American broadcast standard ever since: a 525-line, 30-frames-per-second picture called the *NTSC format*.

As the map in Figure 2.1 shows, the NTSC standard shares the global stage with two others—PAL and SECAM. They both have a 625-line scan at 25 frames-per-second, differing from NTSC's 525 lines.

When a video camera is pointed at an image, the camera's shutter opens and allows that image to enter the camera, just like a film camera. But the way TV captures that image is different than film; here, images are captured on film stock coated with an emulsion that's chemically treated to be sensitive to light. It must be developed in a film lab before it can be viewed. In television, the image is transposed electronically—either to videotape or to digital storage—and can be viewed immediately.

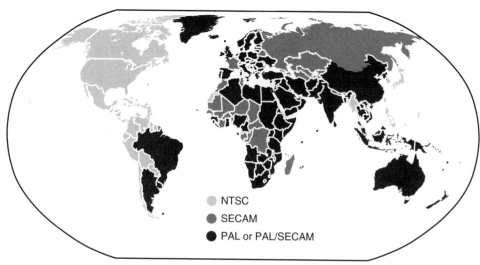

FIGURE 2.1 World Map of PAL-NTSC-SECAM

Aspect Ratios: 4:3 versus 16:9

Since 1941, standard American TV sets were designed to display an *aspect ratio* of 4:3, with its familiar almost-square shape that is a bit wider than it is tall. More recently, *high-definition television* (HDTV) has vastly improved our enjoyment of viewing television. An HDTV set has a larger aspect ratio of 16:9 that better accommodates the way our eyes naturally see an image. With HDTV, we see more of what is in our field of vision. It gives the image a finer resolution, with more clarity of detail and about twice as many pixels and lines (1080) than traditional NTSC images.

Regardless of how or where we watch it, television is firmly established as part of our daily culture. TV is no longer confined to the living room; now, it's in the office, the super-market, dentists' and doctors' offices, a bank line, on airplanes, trains, and in New York City taxis. In order to really explore this phenomenon called television, let us visit its rich and tumultuous history.

IV. THE CREATORS OF TELEVISION

If it weren't for Philo T. Farnsworth, the inventor of television, we'd still be eating frozen radio dinners.

Johnny Carson

The Battle over Television's Paternity

When we explore television's first wobbly steps, determining the "truth" of its ancestry can be as fuzzy as its first broadcast images of Felix the Cat. For instance, there is the question perennially debated by TV historians and aficionados: Who can legitimately claim the title of The Father of Television? These are the primary contenders:

- In 1884, German engineer **Paul Nipkow** designed the primary component of early mechanical television systems called the *scanning disk*. The disk was punched with holes that created a spiral from the outside into the center, and each hole vertically scanned one line of an image. Each line was then transmitted to a selenium cell, transferred to an electronic signal, and recreated in the receiver by a similar disk. Nipkow called his early conceptual design an "electric telescope," although he never actually built the device itself.
- In 1897, German physicist **Karl Braun** invented the first cathode-ray tube, which forms the basis of most modern TV sets.
- Russian **Boris Rosing** was also exploring the cathode-ray tube by 1906. He has been credited with discovering the theory for electronic television via wireless transmission in 1911 by using the Braun tube and the research of other scientists and engineers. One of Rosing's students was **Vladimir Zworykin**, with whom Rosing created "very crude images" and whose work would be integral to the advancement of television.
- Often called the pioneer of mechanical television, **John Logie Baird** was a Scottish entrepreneur with an engineering background who was the first to transmit a moving image using a mechanical television system in 1925. His public showing of "television" in Selfridge's Department store in London was viewed as only blurry silhouettes. Three years later, Baird had so improved his system that the BBC (British Broadcasting System) adopted it for the broadcast of experimental programs. By 1930, the British public could either buy Baird kits or ready-made TV sets to receive these broadcasts.

- Widely crowned as the "true" father of electronic television, American **Philo T. Farnsworth** was a Mormon teenager who conceptualized the technology of television while plowing his rural fields. By the age of 21, Farnsworth had designed the first all-electronic television system, patenting it in 1927 and holding its public premiere in 1928, broadcasting a short film. His "Image Dissector" camera pick-up tube recorded moving images that were coded through radio waves, then reconfigured back into a picture on a screen. Farnsworth's invention in tandem with Zworykin's "Iconoscope" (see later) combined to create all-electronic broadcasting in 1939, although bitter litigation between the Radio Corporation of America (RCA) and Farnsworth's company historically has eclipsed his essential contributions to television.
- Another contender for the title was **Charles Francis Jenkins**, whose wealth and intelligence enabled him to develop "radio movies to be broadcast for entertainment in the home." In 1925, he broadcast a toy windmill as a moving silhouette over a five-mile distance to Washington, D.C. His "Radiovision" depended on Nipkow's scanning disk as its basis.
- **Vladimir Zworykin** was a highly educated Russian immigrant whose research was financed by the powerful RCA and who is often credited with the Father of TV title over Farnsworth. His research contributed to RCA's domination of the infant television market by first manufacturing TV sets, then setting up the National Broadcasting Company (NBC) to provide programming that could be viewed on these TVs. Zworykin's efforts resulted in the *Iconoscope*, an early electronic camera tube that he patented in 1923, as well as an all-electronic TV receiver that utilized a picture tube, called a *kinescope*.

The work of these early inventors and scientists clearly shows television to be the result of continuous experimentation, labor, and the passion for realizing their vision of "distance seeing." Yet, the possibility of communicating ideas via images has intrigued thinkers throughout human history. In ancient Greece, Aristotle was convinced that we were surrounded by invisible particles that combined to form images of matter. He was unable to prove his own theory, yet this vision has propelled over two millennia of experimentation, and television stands as one concrete actualization of Aristotle's curiosity.

Today, the programs that we watch seem effortless in their execution—the acting and writing and image and sound all appear seamless and easy to duplicate. We could write *this* show ourselves! How hard could it be to make a show like *that*? Yet the making of any program relies on a complex system of factors: a program needs a good story, and it needs producers, writers, directors, actors, and a complete crew. It requires money to finance it and time to complete it and hopefully a guarantee that it will air or reach the desired end-user. A TV show depends on camera and audio equipment to videotape the image and record the audio, and then relies on technology to transmit the picture and sound. It must have satellites, cable, electricity, and hundreds of other components to complete the broadcasting process.

This broadcasting process that we viewers take for granted has been the result of the labors of some extraordinary and driven people, as you'll see in the next section.

V. TELEVISION'S EVOLUTION

As far as I'm concerned, you can't say you love a field and not have any interest in its history, its evolution, its mistakes, and its accomplishments. You can't be cutting-edge or do anything new if you don't know what came before. You have to be curious about how things worked years ago, how they work in other countries, what traditions and formats were used, and why. Being informed is being serious about what you are doing.

Sheril Antonio, excerpt from interview in Chapter 11

Guglielmo Marconi played a key role in the invention of television. A bright and wealthy Italian inventor, Marconi discovered a method of transmitting Morse code over limited distances by using electromagnetic waves. In 1896, Marconi's "wireless" telegraph crossed the globe soon after he first telegraphed the letter S, in Morse code, across the Atlantic Ocean, over 2,000 miles away; he claimed responsibility for *the broadcast*—a transmission of sound waves that could move in all directions, follow the earth's curvature, and be picked up by a receiver on the other end.

An ambitious young Russian immigrant named **David Sarnoff**, who worked as an office boy at Marconi's company, astutely realized the potential of Marconi's growing company. Taking engineering classes at night, Sarnoff quickly mastered this new technology; in just a few years, he became a governing force at RCA and is now known as one of the founding fathers of NBC.

The dawn of the twentieth century ushered in the concept of "distance vision" at the 1900 World's Fair in Paris. During the First International Congress of Electricity, a Russian named **Constantin Perskyi** was the first person known to bring the word "television" into the public's consciousness. This dim concept was already taking root in the minds of other inventors and scientists around the globe.

Early Television and Commerce

Television was the most revolutionary event of the century. Its importance was in a class with the discovery of gunpowder and the invention of the printing press, which changed the human condition for centuries afterward.

Russell Baker

In America, the television industry began with the radio. At the end of World War I, General Electric joined forces with three powerful companies—AT&T, Westinghouse, and United Fruit—to form a company known as the Radio Corporation of America, or RCA. As the popularity of radio took hold worldwide, the initial goal of the alliance was to manufacture and sell radio receiver sets. Although the original company eventually unraveled, RCA survived as an independent company.

In 1926, the National Broadcasting Company (NBC) became a wholly owned subsidiary of RCA. The overwhelming popularity of the NBC radio audience soon necessitated a second radio network; the two networks were soon dubbed NBC-Red and NBC-Blue. By the early 1930s, RCA was gathering more resources and power with its manufacture of radios and two networks of radio programming along with a growing number of national stations. More significantly, RCA controlled the talent contracts of the most popular radio stars, writers, and producers of the era. NBC ruled the airwaves. Yet as NBC gained supremacy, Columbia Phonograph Broadcasting System (CBS) was formed. Now NBC and CBS were rivals, and the concept of network competition was born.

Television was taking hold in other countries as well, most significantly in the United Kingdom and Germany. In 1925, both John Logie Baird in London and American Charles Jenkins held public demonstrations of television. By 1929, Baird Television Ltd. (via the BBC) transmitted primitive images through mechanical television, scanning a scant 30 lines. That same year in Berlin and Potsdam, Germany,

Fernsehsender Paul Nipkow experimented with transmitting pictures, and eventually broadcast from 1935 until 1944.

VI. TELEVISION'S TRANSITIONS: FROM THE 1920s TO THE PRESENT

Television began as a TV set, the product of technology; the entertainment and programs followed later. In labs around the globe, talented scientists, engineers, and inventors were driven by their vision and passion to design components that would ultimately be brought together as television.

Television's Early Systems: Mechanical versus Electronic Television (the 1920s)

Television: Greek (*tele*, far) and Latin (*video, videre*, I see) = Far I see

Early television was primitive, with limited audio and an image that was small and blurred; transmission was erratic at best. It was based on a *mechanical* system with a rotating scanning disk as its basis. An image was first scanned mechanically, then transmitted mechanically. The transmitted image was received on a set—again, mechanically. The design for the scanning disk had been invented by Paul Nipkow 40 years earlier, and became the foundation for other mechanical television systems being explored by inventors like Baird, Jenkins, and others.

Charles Francis Jenkins successfully transmitted an image that was mechanically scanned in 1925, the same year that **John Logie Baird** transmitted pictures in his lab. Two years later, **Dr. Herbert Ives** of Bell Telephone Labs introduced his television research program by transmitting an image of a tap dancer on top of a New York skyscraper, which was carried through phone wires.

Another engineer, **Dr. E. F. W. Alexanderson**, demonstrated a television system that operated on revolving mirrors; in 1928, his first regular broadcasts on W2XB began in Schenectady, New York. Unfortunately, very few people owned the Alexanderson TV sets that were necessary to watch the telecasts. That same year, Baird Television proclaimed the first all-mechanical television system, in color. This system appeared to be satisfactory at the time; it would be several years before investors would fund research for a better way to capture, transmit, and receive an image by using electronics and moving away from the cumbersome mechanical system.

By the end of the 1920s, there were at least 15 experimental television stations in America that transmitted limited programming via the mechanical television system. In fact, all television stations in America were called experimental until a commercial licensing system began in 1941. But when the crash of Wall Street in 1929 devastated the country, most research into television came to a dead halt.

Although groups of engineers and scientists continued trying to refine the mechanical television, research into *electronic TV* was energizing television technology. The basis for this new all-electronic system was the cathode-ray tube, originally explored by early inventors such as **Boris Rosing** in Russia and **A. A. Campbell-Swinton** in England.

But ultimately, it was **Philo T. Farnsworth**'s extensive work with his Image Dissector, along with **Vladimir Zworykin**'s Iconoscope, that converged as the genesis of modern television. Millions of research dollars were invested by RCA; with the entrepreneurial genius of **David Sarnoff** behind it, RCA victoriously developed a television system that was powered by electricity. By the late 1930s, both the camera and the receiving TV set were electronic, making mechanical television a thing of the past. The first all-electronic TV set had a 14-inch tube and was manufactured by DuMont in 1938. It was called "The Clifton."

Although television could now be transmitted and viewed in a few limited areas in America and England, radio continued growing in popularity; television was barely a speck on the public's horizon. Live radio shows and their beloved stars were wildly popular; as a business venture, radio was inexpensive to produce, transmit, and receive. Television was still considered a speculative venture. Its costs were high: TV facilities had to be built and programs written, cast, produced, and paid for. TV sets were not only expensive, they were hard to find and only limited programming was available for viewers.

Yet the *idea* of television was thrilling: an image could actually come into our homes—no longer were we limited to the movie theatre. Television was like radio, but with a picture. This TV ideal was offset by its primitive reality. The images were blurry, the audio was scratchy, and the picture barely visible on available 2- or 3-inch screens. Many sets even came equipped with an attached magnifying screen.

In 1928, NBC's experimental TV station—W2XBS that later became WNBC—debuted with its broadcast of a blurred image of Felix the Cat, made of papier-mâché, rotating on a slow turntable. CBS followed a year later with what could generously be called the first television "spectacular," which featured George Gershwin playing the piano, New York mayor Jimmy Walker, and singer Kate Smith. But television continued to be cynically regarded by most Americans as just a passing fancy.

Television's Experimental Steps (the 1930s)

> Television is the newest and most controversial wonder child of modern science and industrial ingenuity, and because it appeals to both the eye and ear simultaneously, television may make the greatest possible impression on the human mind.
>
> **Eleanor Roosevelt**

On the other side of the Atlantic, television was making similar inroads. In 1930, John Logie Baird installed a television set in the Prime Minister's official residence to premiere *The Man with a Flower in His Mouth*, Britain's first TV drama. TV in the United Kingdom had its official launch in August of 1932 with the beginning of BBC One when Baird's company merged with the BBC, although Baird TV had begun regular transmissions three years before using BBC transmitters. A television revue called *Looking In* was broadcast in 1933 by the BBC, although as in America, the limited scan lines made the image a chore to watch. But Baird and the BBC continued their efforts. In 1936, regularly scheduled programs were being transmitted from Alexandra Palace in London to less than a thousand people in the immediate vicinity. Even though by 1939 TV viewership had grown to almost 40,000 homes, the escalation of World War II forced broadcasters to shut down operations for several years.

In other parts of Europe, Germany and France began limited broadcasting in the 1930s. German television began as electromechanical broadcasts in 1929 but transmitted without sound for five more years. And France's first official channel debuted in 1935 at a primitive 60 lines, though by the end of the year, the channel was broadcasting from the Eiffel Tower in 180 lines. The tower's transmitter was sabotaged, and French television was subsequently seized by the German occupying forces in 1940. The Germans' 441-line system merged with Vichy radio, resulting in the formation of Fernsehsender Paris; it resumed limited programming until August of 1944 when both Paris and its television channel were liberated by the Americans.

In Canada, the Canadian Broadcast Company (CBC) was formalized in 1936, eventually adopting the NTSC 525-line standard of its American neighbors. It was not until 1952, however, that the CBC began television broadcasting; its Montreal station transmitted in both French and English, and its Toronto flagship station in English.

Elsewhere around the globe, other countries were making their own approaches into the myriad possibilities of television: Poland in 1937, was still convinced that mechanical television was the route to take, and by then, France had switched over to an electronic system. A year later, the Soviet Union began limited transmissions; by 1939, Japan, Italy, and Poland were all broadcasting primitive pictures using the all-electronic system. Mechanical television was officially obsolete.

Behind the scenes in the United States, the government was reviewing the technical advances and the ethical ramifications of both radio and television. They measured their effects not only on the public but also on business. In 1934, Congress established the Federal Communications Commission (FCC), whose purpose was to patrol the airwaves with the understanding that because the airwaves were essentially owned by the public, all private businesses that controlled and owned radio and television stations must be regulated and issued licenses in order to use these airwaves for profit.

A landmark breakthrough came in 1936 with the introduction of coaxial cable. This transmission device was constructed of a hollow tube enclosing wires that transmitted electrical impulses of different frequencies without combining them. This prompted the FCC to create the NTSC (the National Television System Committee). Comprised primarily of engineers, the NTSC researched and recommended a comprehensive set of standards for electronic television that was adopted in 1941; the majority of these original guidelines are still in effect today.

As it had with radio, RCA expanded its energies into building and selling television receivers, or TV sets, and then created programming that consumers could watch on the sets they purchased. The theme of the 1939 World's Fair in New York City was "The World of Tomorrow," and it was an ideal forum for NBC to be the first network to broadcast a head of state, President Franklin D. Roosevelt. Although television had been pushed into the background by radio for over a decade, the World's Fair provided RCA with a promotional spotlight that planted the desire for television firmly in the country's consciousness.

Television in the Trenches (the 1940s)

I believe television is going to be the test of the modern world, and that in this new opportunity to see beyond the range of our vision, we shall discover a new and unbearable disturbance of the modern peace, or a saving radiance in the sky. We shall stand or fall by television—of that I am quite sure.

E. B. White

While the war in Europe was intensifying, and dominated everyone's attentions, people stayed glued to their radios; it ruled every waking hour and connected Americans to the battlefields with an urgency that diminished research into television. Increased war efforts forced TV stations to make cutbacks in spite of early hopes for television's advancement.

In 1941, the Federal Communications Commission sanctioned the broadcast of commercials on television, but soon were forced to reduce commercial TV's air time from

15 hours a week to four hours. At the time, stations primarily transmitted sports events, news and live theatre, as well as war-related information and training. There were fewer broadcasts as employees went to fight in the war, and available programming was reduced drastically; many stations stopped transmission altogether. Even manufacture of TV and radio sets was halted from 1942 until 1945.

Radio still ruled the airwaves. NBC had become so popular that the company was forced by the FCC to divide its extensive radio shows (and limited experimental TV programming) into two networks, the Blue and the Red. The Blue network transmitted programs that were more cultural in content like drama, music, and thoughtful commentary, whereas the Red network favored entertainment and comedy. Eventually, almost 250 stations across the country received programs on NBC's two networks. Fearing the possibility of a monopoly, the FCC ruled that one company could no longer own more than one network. RCA was forced to sell its Blue network in 1943, and shortly after its sale, it was renamed the Blue Network Inc. A year later, it became the American Broadcast Company (ABC) but would not be seen as a viable television network until the late 40s.

In 1941 both CBS and NBC officially became what we now call "commercial television," replacing their former titles of "experimental" stations and allowing the broadcast of TV commercials. Television advertising was born when Bulova watches produced the first TV commercial. But these sets weren't cheap. In 1941, a brand-new four-door Chevy sold for $895, and an 8" × 10" RCA set cost $395.

The fledgling DuMont Television Network had also begun limited broadcasting, and by 1942, it was one of the few sources for TV programming as the Big Three (RCA, ABC, and CBS) cut back. This innovative network from New York City, formalized as a network in 1946, was the creation of Dr. Allen B. DuMont, one of the original pioneers in electronic television who had premiered his innovative and high-quality TV set at the 1939 World's Fair alongside RCA.

DuMont was equally as creative in his programming directions as he was in his technological advancement of television sets. The DuMont Network was determined to provide comedy and entertainment for Americans that could help to combat the stress of war by introducing many of early television's legends, including the brilliant comedian Ernie Kovacs, ventriloquist Paul Winchell with his dummy/sidekick Jerry Mahoney, and Fred Waring's famous Glee Club. However, because the network had been forced to broadcast on a lower UHF frequency than the standard VHF, the growing popularity of the other three networks finally forced the DuMont Network off the air in 1956 after 10 memorable years.

Television after the War

Finally, World War II drew to a close. Research that had focused on television's potential benefit to the war efforts ultimately thrust the United States into the forefront of technology and creative programming. America's major competitors at the time were England and Germany, both of which essentially had stopped all research during the war years. American companies were exploring and refining color TV; CBS developed a color disk that could be placed over the black-and-white image. But ultimately it was NBC that perfected the technical ability to make a TV set "compatible," meaning that a color broadcast could also be watched on a set that was a black-and-white receiver.

By the mid-1940s, the country's nine original commercial (nonexperimental) TV stations had expanded to 48 stations and in 1948, sales of TV sets had grown by over 500%. Most viewers, over one million of them, still watched TV in public places like bars, restaurants, and hotels, or in stores that sold TV sets. Shows like *Howdy Doody* and *Meet the Press*—still broadcast today—debuted on NBC in 1947, and the first televised World Series was broadcast on both NBC and the DuMont Television Network.

As the chaos of the war settled down, television research reemerged in earnest in other parts of the world. In 1946, the Soviet Union launched commercial television, and Nicaragua became the first country in South America to transmit television. Three years later, Cuba became part of the global television broadcasting linkage in 1949. The BBC resumed broadcasting and rather than becoming a commercial entity, chose to charge all owners of TV sets a licensing fee. BBC broadcast the 1948 Summer Olympics and a year later, premiered *Come Dancing*, which ultimately would have a 46-year run.

In spite of radio's ongoing popularity, it was clear that TV was rapidly catching up. It offered the additional sensory advantage of seeing images as well as hearing them, giving viewers the ability to watch and hear sports and dance and music in action, to experience news as it happened, the beauty of scenic locations, works of art, the facial expressions of an actor, the pratfalls of a comedian, and a politician's eyes.

TV played up radio's lack of visuals with the introduction of image-based shows such as *The Texaco Star Theater* with Milton Berle, in the fall of 1948. "Uncle Miltie's" energy, unique humor, and famous guests revolutionized television programming and vastly expanded the number of people buying TV sets. At the time, the average cost of a television set was $500, though an average annual salary was less than $3,000. In 1946, only 10,000 TV sets were in use; by 1948, more than 400,000 homes in America had sets; and four years later, 19 million TV sets were in active use. By 1956, 85% of American homes had sets.

Television's Golden Age (the 1950s)

Recipe for an Average TV Program
1 cup of Sponsor's Requirements—sift gently
2 tablespoons of Agency Ideas, carefully chilled
Add ½-dozen Staff Suggestions, well-beaten. However fresh and flavorful, they will curdle when combined with Agency Ideas, so they must be beaten until stiff.
Stir together in a smoke-filled room and sprinkle generously with Salesmen's Gimmicks.
Cover the mixture with a tight lid so that no Imagination can get in and no Gimmicks can get out, and let stand while the costs increase.
1 jigger of Talent—domestic will do.
Flavor with:
Production Problems
A pinch of Doubt
And, if you have any, a dash of Hope.
Fold ingredients carefully together so they can get into a small studio. This requires a very light touch as the slightest jolt will sour the results.
Line the pan with Union Regulations—otherwise the mixture will stick.
Place in oven with your fingers crossed.
Sometimes it comes out a tasty delicacy, and, sometimes, it's just cooked.

Mrs. A. Scott Bullitt, President of King Broadcasting Co., *in a speech given in 1952*

The 1950s justifiably has been called The Golden Age of Television—in retrospect, that phrase is almost an understatement. It was a magical time in television's transition from scratchy images and wispy potential to a solid undeniable force.

On the heels of Milton Berle's show, which ran until 1956, came Sid Caesar and *Your Show of Shows*, a 90-minute weekly comedy show that featured groundbreaking humor, clever writing, satire, sketches, and acting. Although its final episode was broadcast in 1954, its influence has rippled indelibly through eras of television humor in shows like *Laugh In* and *Saturday Night Live* decades later.

Ed Sullivan was a rather stiff master of ceremonies with a dry delivery, yet his early show, *Toast of the Town*, and later, *The Ed Sullivan Show*, made entertainment legends of young talent such as Dean Martin and Jerry Lewis, Elvis Presley, Ingrid Bergman, and the Beatles.

The Birth of Madison Avenue

Advertisers recognized television's value as a marketplace with which to sell products. As they began to invest their revenues in the creative aspects of this new medium, the technical designers and engineers were keeping pace by building sound stages, facilities, and transmitters. Radio stations, fledgling television stations, and newspapers were lining up to buy TV licenses, while producers, directors, and writers were busy creating the next big show.

It was virgin territory for engaging personalities like Faye Emerson, Perry Como, Gene Autry, William Boyd, and hit shows like *The Lone Ranger*, *Hopalong Cassidy*, *Howdy Doody*, *Meet the Press*, John Cameron Swayze's *Camel Newsreel Theatre*, and *Kraft Television Theatre*, which aired on both NBC and ABC. Television's Golden Age had begun.

With the end of World War II, the economy essentially had recovered and stabilized, and television became so popular that magazines regularly featured articles on home decorating with the TV set as the centerpiece. The dining room table had been replaced by frozen dinners on a TV tray, and *TV Guide*, launched in 1953, was on the American coffee table.

The Era of Creative Drama and Breakthrough Comedy

TV producers and writers freely adapted their ideas from radio and traditional theater. For example, TV news consisted of the anchor simply reading the newspaper and news wire reports into camera, with none of the visuals and sound effects in today's news broadcasts. CBS and NBC created legendary dramatic television with innovative anthology programming such as *Kraft Television Theatre*, *Studio One*, *Playhouse 90*, *Philco TV Playhouse*, *General Electric Theater* (hosted by Ronald Reagan for eight years), and *The United States Steel Hour*. By the mid-1950s, there were 14 live-drama series from which to choose. Early television was transmitted live, broadcast from the studio directly to the viewer with all its visible glitches and mistakes—there was no censoring capacity of a 7-second delay or possibility of a second take.

As programming boundaries expanded, television shows and the creative minds behind them got bolder. Brilliant young comedic minds like Ernie Kovacs and Sid Caesar wrote witty and irreverent material, and used TV's technology to produce special effects that played with the material at hand. Television was moving away from simply adapting traditional radio formats to creating innovative programming concepts that were tailor-made for TV broadcast.

Yet with all its creative departures, the technical limitations of live broadcast prevented the production and transmission of a show from any location other than television studios in New York City. This changed with the introduction of videotape in 1956; it allowed programs first to be taped, edited, then broadcast from a wider range of locations, and viewers experienced much clearer sound and picture.

Videotape made it possible to record and archive programs; it was electronic, more flexible, and less expensive than film. Prior to videotape, the only way to record a broadcast had been to place a film camera in front of a television set and actually film the live broadcast. The result was called a *kinescope*. The first broadcast use of videotape was a segment in color on the eccentric, taboo-breaking *Jonathan Winters Show*.

The Wide Reach of Cable

Coaxial cable, which originally had connected only New York and Philadelphia, eventually worked its way to the West Coast. Its cross-country completion was celebrated in the fall of 1951. NBC could now broadcast coast-to-coast over its 61 stations. The same year, the first experimental color TV transmissions were attempted, but were a failure because black-and-white sets still couldn't pick up shows that were transmitted in color. Although CBS had developed a color disk that could be placed over the black-and-white image, it was NBC who ultimately perfected the technical ability to make a TV set compatible, making NBC synonymous with "compatible color."

The creative borders of television continued to expand, as the dramatic long-form productions gradually took a back seat to shows like Jackie Gleason's *The Honeymooners* and *I Love Lucy* with Lucille Ball and Desi Arnaz. These shows captivated viewers with their familiar and lovable ongoing characters. *I Love Lucy* was also the first show to have "repeats," introducing the lucrative concept of *syndication*, where repeats of a program could be sold and rerun on various stations. By 1960, only one of the original drama series was still broadcasting, as the sitcom genre dominated the air waves.

Quiz shows were another popular genre in the 1950s. Shows like *Twenty-One*, *Tic Tac Dough*, *The Big Surprise*, *You Bet Your Life* with Groucho Marx, *What's My Line?* and *The $64,000 Question* swept the ratings, as Americans enthusiastically played along with the contestants. Then, a contestant on *Twenty-One* admitted to being provided with the answers to the questions. The genre was permanently tainted and mutated to milder shows such as *Queen for a Day* and *Let's Make a Deal*. As an antidote to the scandal, strict FCC regulations were put in place that are still enforced on similar shows today.

The FCC Steps In

The overall technology of television was getting more sophisticated and significantly cheaper. As the sales of TV sets flourished, movie theaters and the Hollywood studio system felt threatened by this burgeoning medium. Television's explosive growth alarmed the FCC, too. The mounting technological sweep and TV's ethical questions hadn't been anticipated, and the establishment of monopolies was only a matter of time. In 1948, the government stopped issuing any additional broadcasting licenses. Instead, they focused their resources on harnessing the rapid expansion of television as a powerful business and cultural force to be reckoned with.

It took the FCC four years to draft and finally agree upon a statement of principles that would govern television and the standards by which it operated. In 1952, TV's political and electronic complexities were regulated by a set of guidelines that set new standards for flourishing areas of television, as well as for future media advances that then were only theoretical.

The FCC guidelines included the assignment of *very high frequency* (*VHF*) and *ultra-high frequency* (*UHF*) channels. These new standards for engineering and technology applications defined public service and educational programming, and dedicated certain channels to be used only for educational and public access. It took the FCC over a year to review the various color systems that were still experimental, finally agreeing on one color system that could be transmitted by all the networks and received by all color TV sets.

As television's popularity increased, its reach was still limited, so cable TV was launched in 1950 as an effort to provide television to homes in rural areas that were unable to receive broadcast signals because of their distance from major transmission towers. And when cable TV finally provided the programming, television dealerships in these rural areas grew exponentially.

The Battle of the Big Three: NBC, CBS, and ABC

In 1951, the merger of ABC with United Paramount Theatres created a huge leap in creative programming that catapulted the young station into direct competition with NBC, CBS, and the renegade DuMont—who in the long run couldn't survive the competition and went off the air in 1956 after 10 years.

The remaining Big Three networks battled for domination, vying for advertising dollars, viewer ratings, and programming originality. This competition led to the development of the "network system" that included production services for writing and producing programs, sales and distribution of these programs to the network affiliates as well as to their *Owned and Operated* (*O&O*) stations, and generating advertising dollars with which to subsidize the network.

Television's Early Influence on Politics

The first political TV ads had an explosive effect on television viewers, and could well have changed the outcome of a national election. In 1952, presidential candidate Adlai Stevenson bought 18 half-hour time slots, hoping to get his political message across to the American people. But a half-hour proved to be way too long and tedious for most people to watch, and viewers got angry when his speeches interrupted their favorite shows. His rival, General Dwight D. Eisenhower, wisely made his TV ads short and sweet, brief 20-second spots that aired before or after popular shows like *I Love Lucy*. The sway of these ads is speculative, though Eisenhower did win the 1952 presidency.

It was during the 1952 political convention that the term "anchorman" was first used, describing Walter Cronkite's convention coverage for CBS. His intelligent and thoughtful observations on the political arena won him the title of "the most trusted man in America." Cronkite's nightly broadcasts emphasized television as a source of trustworthy news and information for most Americans.

TV bore witness to another breed of politics called McCarthyism. The House Committee on Un-American Activities (HUAC) had begun their investigation of the film industry in 1947 as part of their sweep for "Communist infiltrators." This witch hunt soon spilled over into the television industry. Dozens of writers, producers, actors, and directors suspected of having left-wing tendencies were fired and blacklisted, preventing them from being employed anywhere. CBS required its employees to sign an oath of loyalty, yet it was that network's esteemed journalist, Edward R. Murrow, who ultimately broke the back of McCarthyism. In 1954, Murrow exposed Senator Joseph McCarthy with the legendary quote: "His mistake has been to confuse dissent with disloyalty." Within months, McCarthy was censured by the U. S. Senate. Television had effectively ended his reign.

The Glitter of the Golden Age

The Golden Age of 1950s television saw the creation of *I Love Lucy* in 1951. This was the first sitcom shot with the now-standard three-camera setup, along with family shows such as *The Adventures of Ozzie and Harriet* and *Father Knows Best*. In 1952, Dave Garroway hosted the new *Today Show*, the first magazine-format program. One year later, *TV Guide* began publication. The country's first "adult western," *Gunsmoke*, began in 1955 and ran for 20 years. *The Mickey Mouse Club* put ABC on the map as a youth-oriented network in 1955. The teen hit of the decade was *The Many Loves of Dobie Gillis* with Warren Beatty and Tuesday Weld; and Rod Serling's sci-fi series, *The Twilight Zone*, aired from 1959 to 1964 on CBS—the first network to introduce 30-minute soap operas rather than the traditional 15-minute dramas; both *As the World Turns* and *The Edge of Night* began airing in 1956. *Broadway Open House* with Morey Amsterdam was the first late-night variety show, setting the stage for *The Tonight Show*, *Late Show with David Letterman*, and many others.

Television's International Expansion

Globally, television gained real momentum during the 1950s; the exposure to international culture and politics opened borders that previously had been ignored or closed. The establishment of television stations in Mexico and Brazil in 1950, and Argentina a year later, gave South America an international presence. European television in 1951 expanded to Denmark and the Netherlands, and TV transmission returned to Poland. In 1957, Portugal and Finland were transmitting programming, and by the end of the 1950s, more than 60 other countries would establish their own television broadcasting.

Canadian television adopted several aspects of American television when the Canadian Broadcasting Corporation (CBC) began transmission in 1952. It chose the U.S. NTSC standard of 525 lines, for example. Its first two stations premiered within two days of one another—one in English-only, the other in both French and English.

British television launched the BBC version of *What's My Line?* and premiered a delightful variety of original programs, from *The Flowerpot Men* and *Hancock's Half Hour* to *The Sky at Night*, *Quatermass and The Pit*, *Blue Peter*, *Grandstand*, and an adaptation of *1984*. The establishment of ITV brought commercial television to the United Kingdom in 1955, with *What the Papers Say*. And in 1953, over 20 million viewers in England alone joined the rest of the world as they watched the coronation of a young Elizabeth II.

The First Television Society (the 1960s)

Sock it to me !!!

Rowan & Martin's Laugh-In, *NBC, 1968–1973*

By the 1960s, Americans had become the first television society. Both the subtle and overt influences of television visibly permeated the culture—over 90% of American homes had at least one television set. The three networks—NBC, CBS, and ABC—transmitted to around 200 affiliate stations, most in major metropolitan areas.

The networks produced the vast majority of their programming in their Los Angeles and New York studios, seldom subcontracting any productions out to independent producers or filmmakers. The network system included the program sponsor (soap products, automobiles, cigarettes) along with an advertising agency that created the commercials designed to sell these sponsors' products.

By 1960, there were 640 *community antenna television* (*CATV*) systems that delivered all available channels from nearby metropolitan centers to more isolated areas. These fledgling independent and public television stations were new and inexperienced, and made little impact on the big networks that targeted their programming to a mass audience.

An Era of Firsts

The first television satellites to transmit transatlantic images in 1962—Relay and Telstar One—heralded a new kind of immediacy in news gathering, and delivered the news of the world to the world, like the assassination of President John F. Kennedy and the Vietnam War. Seven years later, more than 600 million people around the globe were transfixed as they saw the first TV transmission from the moon on July 20, 1969. People everywhere realized they could now be connected in real time, experiencing events as they happened.

In the United Kingdom, the BBC transmitted a diverse range of program offerings to its viewers, from game shows and soap operas to drama and innovative comedy. Known affectionately as "The Beeb" and "Auntie," the BBC had only one significant competitor, the commercial station ITV. The night that its sister station BBC2 was scheduled to be launched in 1964, a fire in a power station caused a citywide power failure and delayed the premiere by a day. The original BBC TV later became known as BBC1. Because BBC2 was the first British channel to use UHF and 625-line pictures, its picture delivered a much higher picture resolution than the previous VHF 405-line system.

British programming in the 1960s was innovative and memorable, reinventing some genres and creating others with shows such as *Monty Python's Flying Circus*, *Doctor Who*, *Top of the Pops*, and ITV's *Coronation Street* and *The Avengers*.

Television as a New Business Model

Globally as well as in America, the television industry attracted producers, writers, directors, and actors who had previously worked only in film. There were many advantages to working in this medium: the exposure of TV was much wider than that of the average motion picture; millions of people watched TV regularly and seldom went to movies, and it was more cost-effective to produce programming for television than for film.

Particularly in Hollywood, the major film studios saw the potential of television as the next logical step for their films after a traditional theatrical release, and channeled money into building departments that could develop projects exclusively for TV. On Madison Avenue, advertising agencies had become a remarkable creative force, funneling huge sums into creating television campaigns, slogans, and commercials for television.

It wasn't until 1964 that the FCC finally approved RCA's color system in America, opening the airwaves for broadcasting programs in bright, highly refined color. Although CBS had first originated the color system, RCA quickly flooded the market with black-and-white sets that could also receive programs (in black-and-white) that were broadcast in color. By the mid-1960s, NBC was producing the majority of its prime-time programs on color film.

Television's Technological Firsts

The 1960s produced some technical elements that we now take for granted:

- **Electronic character-generator.** Also known by its brand name of *chyron*, it could create opening and closing *credits* as well as superimpose words over a picture and *lower-thirds* that can spell out the speaker's name, occupation, and/or location under his or her picture on the screen.

- **Slo-mo.** The ability to first record a picture (say, of a baseball play), and then replay it in slow motion, repeatedly.
- Other equipment and technology, such as color videotape machines, videotape cartridge systems, portable small cameras known as "mini-cams," and remote-controlled operation of radio and TV stations' transmitters.

Television Shapes the Political Landscape

The growing influence of television was incontrovertible. When a charismatic, articulate John F. Kennedy debated an unshaven and shifty-eyed Richard Nixon on television in 1960 in the "Great Debates," the disparity between the two men was obvious, magnified by a new special effect called a *split screen* used for the first time during the debates. Interestingly, audiences who only listened to the debates on the radio picked Nixon as the winner.

Television featured prominently in national tragedy as well. Almost every American, 96% of the population, and much of the world, mourned the death of JFK by watching his funeral on television after his assassination in 1963. Days later, when Kennedy's suspected assassin Lee Harvey Oswald was murdered on live television by Jack Ruby, its stark immediacy stunned the world.

TV Reveals the Horrors of War

The Vietnam War was the first war we watched almost as it was being waged. The first satellite link to Asia revealed the harsh truths of the front lines, and fanned the flames of American and global dissension. When CBS aired a report that exposed the cruelty of a group of U. S. Marines in a Vietnam village, President Lyndon Johnson angrily attacked the network as being unpatriotic. In a brave counterattack, Walter Cronkite produced a documentary in 1968 on the state of the war, saying: "It is increasingly clear to this reporter that the only rational way out will be to negotiate." A defeated President Johnson reportedly said, "If I've lost Cronkite, I've lost middle America."

TV Boldly Reaches Out

The relevance of the TV documentary broke new ground in the 1960s, with intelligent and courageous exploration of issues from civil rights to communism. One memorable example was NBC's *The Tunnel*, the filmed escape of East German refugees who had carved tunnels under the Berlin Wall. Other 1960s highlights included the debut of ABC's *General Hospital* in 1963 and rival soap *Days of Our Lives* on NBC in 1965. The Beatles made their legendary first appearance on *Ed Sullivan Show* in 1964, and a year later, Bill Cosby became the first African-American actor to costar in a continuing drama, *I Spy*.

Congress created PBS (the Public Broadcasting System) in 1967, which, two years later, debuted the iconic *Sesame Street* for children. In 1966, NBC became the first all-color network; it premiered the made-for-TV movie genre with shows like *Columbo, McMillan and Wife*, and *McCloud* that featured continuing lead characters. Humor got a needed boost with shows like *Rowan and Martin's Laugh-in*, *That Was the Week That Was*, and *The Smothers Brothers Comedy Hour*. Each reflected the chaotic era of the 1960s, using bold satire and irreverent wit that pulled no punches and challenged the censors.

Over the span of this decade, more than 70 countries established their own networks and transmission systems. Massive countries such as People's Republic of China and smaller ones such as Haiti, Iceland, Israel, Ireland, and Uganda all now had access to the world around them.

Television in Transition (the 1970s)

I've always had a feeling that any time you can experiment, you ought to do it. Because you never know what will happen.

Walt Disney

In the wake of Woodstock and the Vietnam War, television grew bolder in the 1970s. Programs reflected the social and emotional changes of the Woodstock Generation, outspoken and outrageous. In 1970, the networks cancelled at least 30 series that had been hits in the 1960s and replaced them with a new approach to programming that was targeted directly to a younger audience.

All in the Family was the first prime-time sitcom to bring hotbed issues like racism, bigotry, and sexism into America's living rooms. *The Mary Tyler Moore Show* proved that a single professional woman could succeed on her own, addressing pertinent issues facing the working woman in the workforce. *Bridget Loves Bernie* was not only a forum for ethnic comedy, it also showed its stars in the bedroom. *The Partridge Family* added popular music to the sitcom genre.

A new genre of programming emerged in prime-time drama, as viewers entered the professional and personal lives of doctors, lawyers, cops, and detectives in shows such as *Kojak, Starsky and Hutch, Baretta*, and *M*A*S*H*. The genre of the "super woman" forged new icons in the 1970s with *Charlie's Angels, Police Woman, Wonder Woman*, and *The Bionic Woman*. Their characters reflected the burgeoning woman's movement, as sitcoms *Laverne and Shirley* and *Phyllis* provided working women with a playful dimension of fun.

The 1970s ushered in a new level of immediacy in news reporting. Sony developed the Portapak video camera that revolutionized *electronic news gathering* (ENG) with its portability and low cost, and combined with satellite relay and distribution systems to transmit footage directly to the news stations.

This decade also saw the emergence of cable channel services that offered more specialized *niche programming*: movies and specials on HBO, children's shows on Nickelodeon, live broadcasts from the House of Representatives on C-SPAN, sports on ESPN, and Ted Turner's "superstation," WTBS. Cable television became increasingly popular for specific events like baseball and basketball games and hockey in areas with a loyal fan base. By 1971, New York cable, for example, had over 80,000 subscribers.

Television in the 1970s heralded such classics as *M*A*S*H*, which first aired in 1972 and ran for 11 years, and the mini-series *Roots*, which focused on African-Americans and their ancestors, attracting a record-breaking audience of 130 million viewers. PBS, created in 1967, unveiled unexpectedly popular hits such as *Upstairs Downstairs, Masterpiece Theatre, Nova, Crockett's Victory Garden*, and *The French Chef with Julia Child. Mork and Mindy* unveiled the whirlwind who was Robin Williams, and in 1979, *Knots Landing* brought the steaming sex and ongoing intrigue of daytime soap drama into prime time. *Saturday Night Live* and *The Phil Donohue Show* became programming models, actively relevant today. During this time the FCC ruled that shows broadcast during the Family Hour (7 to 9 P.M.) must be "wholesome" for family viewing.

Technology Marches into the 1970s

Advancing technology resulted in a consumer-friendly *video cassette recorder* (*VCR*) in 1972, followed four years later by Sony's Betamax VCR (selling for about $1,300). By the next year, RCA had introduced a competitive standard, VHS, which eventually would dominate the market and push Betamax into obscurity. The improvements in fiber-optic cable in 1970—delivering 65,000 times more data than copper wire—vastly improved television delivery to American homes.

Although television by now was considered part of the everyday world, another 30 countries joined rank and adapted broadcasting to their own transmission standards. Africa saw more of a media presence as stations were established, including those in South Africa, Tanzania, Lesotho, and Swaziland. The Middle East launched stations in Qatar, Bahrain, Oman, and Brunei among others. In Japan, the show *Abarembo Shogun* was launched, a series that would prove successful for 25 years.

Television was solidly an international mainstay, but most programming came from America or the United Kingdom. British audiences lost *Monty Python's Flying Circus* in 1974 but gained *Fawlty Towers* a year later. The range of BBC and ITV programs continued to expand with popular shows like *The Goodies*, *Open University*, *Last of the Summer Wine*, and *Grange Hill*.

Television Merges with Electronics (the 1980s)

Television! Teacher, mother, secret lover.

Homer Simpson, *The Simpsons*

With the widespread popularity of VCRs, viewers could now buy and rent movies, or record their favorite program on VHS tape and watch it at their leisure. Video stores popped up in every neighborhood with movies and video games to rent. This translated into the gradual evolution of television from a passive medium to a more aggressive, interactive device. The impact of the VCR was especially harsh on advertisers who grew apprehensive—now, viewers could completely tune out Madison Avenue's expensive commercials with a push of the fast-forward button.

Creatively, producers tuned into television's potential to reach an audience with innovative programming that was enhanced by special video effects, sophisticated video editing systems, and eye-pleasing uses of texts and fonts, moving logos, digitized backgrounds, page turns, multiple pictures on one screen, and layering pictures on top of one another. At first, the editing costs were high and time-consuming, but by the mid-1980s, these video effects became easier to produce and less costly.

The Impact on the Youth Market

Competition between the networks increased in the 1980s with the emergence of popular new cable outlets. Ted Turner founded the Cable News Network (CNN), an all-news channel, in 1980, and eight years later, Turner premiered TNT. Bravo was the first cable network dedicated to film and performing arts. In the fall of 1981, MTV went on the air with the defiant logo, "I want my MTV!" It was the first station specifically targeted to the growing youth culture, showcasing the new music video format, that promoted recording artists and their labels, and influenced the creation of programs like NBC's music-centric *Miami Vice*, airing in 1984.

The Expansion of Social Issues in Television

The smash hit of the 1980s featured an upper-middle-class African-American family, the Huxtables. *The Cosby Show* ran from 1984 to 1992, and like *All in the Family* a decade earlier, the show used humor to examine racial and gender differences, bigotry, values, and family dynamics. It not only brought NBC back to Number One in the ratings, it ushered in an era of African-American sitcoms, like *A Different World*, *The Fresh Prince of Bel Air*, and *In Living Color*.

The Oprah Winfrey Show in 1986 became the first major talk show to be hosted by an African-American woman. And sitcoms with underlying cultural issues were ratings bonanzas—shows like *Roseanne*, *Saved By the Bell*, *Growing Pains*, *Three's Company*, *Who's the Boss*, *Facts of Life*, and *Diff'rent Strokes*. *Live Aid*'s 16-hour global satellite broadcast of musical artists and cultural icons raised millions of dollars for famine relief.

The theme of "independence" ran through the television industry in the 1980s. The birth of a fourth network called Fox Broadcasting Company challenged the iconic Big Three. Because of complex differences between its structure and that of ABC, CBS, and NBC, Fox was able to slide under the radar and create its own singular identity.

Independent production companies on both U.S. coasts broke away from programming stereotypes and developed episodic drama that was thought-provoking and examined real issues through dimensional characters and multilayered plotlines. Shows such as *Hill Street Blues*, *Cheers*, *St. Elsewhere*, *Cagney and Lacey*, and *L.A. Law* stunned and provoked audiences, and paved the way for more intelligent and mature programming, along with higher network ratings.

Television competition in the United Kingdom heated up in the 1980s when Channel 4, Sky Television, and S4C joined the solid ranks of BBC1, BBC2, and ITV. *EastEnders* on BBC1 began in 1985, and *Doctor Who* ended after 26 years on the air in 1989. Both *Thomas the Tank Engine & Friends* and *The Bill* premiered on ITV in 1984.

Global television made inroads into lesser-known countries and territories in the 1980s. Vatican City, for example, started broadcasting in 1983, the same year as Andorra, Nepal and the Seychelles. Another 20 stations were launched in areas such as Western Samoa, Belize, Burma, and South West Africa.

> The strength of our attachment to television is reflected in a *TV Guide* poll in the mid-1990s in which one out of four Americans declared that even if they were given one million dollars, they wouldn't give up their TV.

Television Moves toward Digital Technology (the 1990s)

Cable and satellite gave people more accessibility to global events happening in real time. In 1991, the world watched the Persian Gulf War unfold as America dropped "smart" bombs on Baghdad. Three years later, millions of viewers were riveted to cable news stations, watching the saga of O. J. Simpson—from the white Bronco freeway chase to the infamous final verdict.

The popularity of cable had a direct impact on the major networks as Fox and two new stations—UPN and the WB—reached wider and younger audiences in 1995, using improved cable technology and direct-broadcast satellite (DBS).

As competition grew between cable and networks, the focus of television program-ming became increasingly unconventional and volatile. Talk-show hosts, such as Jerry Springer, Jenny Jones, Maury Povich, and Ricki Lake, explored raw topics with confrontational guests, and watched their ratings soar. Cable sex shows and adult cartoons were in sharp contrast to a more sophisticated crop of made-for-TV movies dealing with mature issues like changing family values, gender bias, AIDS, homosexuality, and domestic abuse.

In response to increased violence and sex on TV, the public and subsequently the government forced the broadcasting industry in 1996 to adopt a rating system for every show: TV-Y, TV-Y7, TV-G, TV-PG, and other ratings labels. Newer television sets were equipped with a V-chip, which could be programmed to block those programs the set owners thought were unsuitable.

The Potential of High Definition Television

The emphasis on *high definition television* (*HDTV*) grew substantially in the 1990s. The broadcasters saw that images transmitted in digital HDTV were sharper and clearer than traditional *standard definition television* (*SDTV*) transmitted by analog signals; HDTV sets were bigger, with a 16:9 rectangular shape, and more than twice the cost of SDTV sets.

The inevitability of HDTV was confirmed in 1997 when the U.S. government allotted $70 billion worth of broadcast spectrum to its TV broadcasters. This gave each broadcaster an extra channel to transmit programs in digital high definition along with their analog signals. The goal of totally phasing out SDTV broadcasting was originally set for 2006 (later extended to 2009), by which time all broadcasts would be totally digital. The mandate also required that after this cutoff date, all broadcasters must give back their original channels (extra broadcast spectrum) to the government.

As personal computers became more user-friendly and less expensive in the 1990s, the popularity of the Internet illustrated the potential of interconnectivity between computers and TV, creatively and economically. Experiments in digital audio and video, fiber optics, and HDTV moved from theory to actuality, and digital technology promised to energize the TV industry's future.

The Big Three Continue to Dominate

In the 1990s, NBC dominated the ratings with shows such as *The Cosby Show*, *Mad About You*, *Seinfeld*, *ER*, *Cheers*, *Friends*, *Veronica's Closet*, *Golden Girls*, and *Frasier*. CBS offered popular programming with *Murphy Brown*, *Murder She Wrote*, and *Everybody Loves Raymond*. And ABC aired popular shows like *Home Improvement*, *NFL Monday Night Football*, *The Practice*, *NYPD Blue*, *Who Wants to Be a Millionaire?*, and *Roseanne*, which featured the first "gay kiss" on television.

Other shows like *Ellen* and *Will and Grace* challenged sexual stereotypes. Each major network had its own version of a news magazine—*Dateline* (NBC), *20/20* (ABC), and *60 Minutes* (CBS). PBS debuted *Charlie Rose*, and Bravo premiered *Inside the Actor's Studio*. Both became iconic classics and consequently targets of late-night comedians. The *X Files* and *Star Trek: Deep Space 9* brought hard-core sci-fi fans back to television.

British television in the 1990s added Channel 5 to the growing roster of stations. Programs from the United Kingdom would eventually be adapted for U.S. and other international audiences, with shows like *Who Wants to Be a Millionaire?* In 1992, *Absolutely Fabulous* saw its debut on BBC One, and two years later, 20 million people tuned into the *National Lottery Live*.

Recently, I produced a project for a major global corporation that involved creating a breathtaking six-minute visual opening for a live international conference, attended by 8,000 people and accompanied by a full orchestra and a five-piece rock band. The challenge for me was the size of the piece: the screen on which my piece was to be projected was 80 × 17 feet. Think about it—80 × 17 *feet*! All the many images and graphics had to be in high definition, or 2K and 4K scans—a monumental technical undertaking, with a lot of creative appeal.

The week after that job finished (the audience cheered, btw...), I started another project for a nonprofit organization in which I interviewed dozens of school kids, their teachers, and their parents. After the research, scheduling, legal releases, shooting, and editing had been completed, the interviews became the centerpiece on the nonprofit's web presence. The size of these online interviews was roughly 3 × 6 inches. Two projects, one the size of a New York City block, the other like an index card—and both projects had one producer in charge (yours truly...) who used similar skills in each project.

~C. Kellison

The Transformation of Television in the Twenty-First Century (the 2000s)

What is the purpose of life? To be the eyes and ears and conscience of the creator of the universe, you fool ....

Kurt Vonnegut

Television in the dawn of the 21st century reflected the unimaginable reality of terrorism with the attacks of September 11, 2001, and in the weeks and months following. Cable and network news covered the ensuing wars in Afghanistan and Iraq, as well as the increase of international debate on the rights of America's involvement in world politics. News broadcasts relied more heavily on graphic elements, musical effects, and added a running "ticker tape" below the anchors to cover additional news not included in the broadcast itself.

TV Gets Smarter, Funnier, and More Cynical

Comedy is a welcome relief in times of political crisis, and shows such as *Everybody Loves Raymond*, *Friends*, *Cheers*, *Frasier*, *Sex in the City*, *The Simpsons*, *Will and Grace*, and *Whose Line is it Anyway?* appealed to all age groups. Episodic series such as *The West Wing*, *ER*, *Lost*, *Boston Public*, *NYPD Blue*, *Desperate Housewives*, and *24* continued to broaden political and cultural themes and storylines. HBO saw a dramatic increase in subscribers and in Emmy awards with *The Sopranos*, *Six Feet Under*, *Deadwood*, and an impressive roster of quality documentaries. Talk shows reached out to broader audiences and topics with *The View*, *The Rosie O'Donnell Show*, *Ellen DeGeneres*, *Sharon Osbourne*, *Oprah*, *Dr. Phil*, and *The Martha Stewart Show*.

Roughly 25% of American viewers under the age of 24 got their primary news and information from the satirical "fake news" show, *The Daily Show with Jon Stewart*. The lines between political parties blended and blurred with *The Colbert Report*, and Bill Maher and Dennis Miller continued their rants against the establishment. Social satire stayed alive and well with *South Park* and *Saturday Night Live*.

Children's television targeted diverse audiences with dimensional writing and production value on Nickelodeon, Noggin, and PBS with shows like *Zoboomafoo*, *Dora the*

Explorer, *Zoom*, and *Sesame Street*. Advertisers were attracted to sponsor shows aimed at the growing market of "tweens," teens, and young adults with shows like *Buffy the Vampire Slayer*, *Ally McBeal*, *Hannah Montana*, *Gossip Girls*, *The Hills*, *Dawson's Creek*, *The O.C.*, *Felicity*, and *The Real World*. "Format" shows that started in other countries came to America, reconfigured as *American Idol*, *Survivor*, and *Big Brother*.

The Onslaught of Reality Programming

Arguably, the most influential and contested genre in the 21st century has been the reality show, also called unscripted programming. Shows such as *Trading Spaces*, *Dog Whisperer*, *The Apprentice*, *The Bachelor*, *Road Rules*, *Fear Factor*, *Survivor*, *Extreme Makeover: Home Edition* and others have been ratings bonanzas. The seemingly global appeal of reality programming intrigues television scholars, and the considerably lower costs of producing these shows delights broadcasters. It has spawned several all-reality channels, and at least 250 reality shows have aired, are scheduled for air, or have left the airwaves in less than a decade.

The unparalleled success of the reality genre over the last few years once again illustrates the power of the consumer. The TV viewer can be fickle and highly discerning, with tastes and loyalties that shift with each season. A program that feeds water-cooler conversation one week can be old news the next week, easily replaced with a better show. Networks give their shows only a limited time to succeed, and cancel them if they don't perform well in their first few airings. Unlike the networks, cable and premium cable stations have more latitude in creating targeted programming that appeals to specific demographics and interests, though their budgets are lower. The changing horizons of television content in both broadcasting and "narrow casting" give producers new areas to explore in the future.

The Surge of Delivery Systems

And now, new media adds new dimensions of possibility: the delivery systems, new programming ideas, technology advances, and changes in the ways this all gets paid for—everything is new, and nothing is really known. Not yet. In many parts of the world, for example, the Internet will take a while to catch up, whereas television is firmly established in their cultures.

One thing *is* clear about television's future: No one has a clue. Even the word "television" is now in question: Is watching a show on our computer or mobile phone or game box the same as watching the identical show at home? Are all these experiences still called "watching TV"? Is television defined by what mechanical device we watch it on, or by the show we're watching?

In fact, television currently exists in a convoluted state of excitement, panic, invention, uncertainty, and innovation, and its equilibrium is constantly shifting. Almost 100% of American homes have at least one television set; most homes have two or more, and there are over two billion TV sets around the globe.

It's estimated that the average American watches around 32 hours of TV a week. We can watch our hours of TV on our laptops, iPods, mobile phones, or game boxes; though TV sets are everywhere. In almost all parts of the civilized world, most countries have dozens, even hundreds of channels, received via cable, satellite, the Internet or an antenna on the roof. Most international cities also offer programming through terrestrial mobile phones, DVR, video on demand, pay per view, television on the Internet, and straight to DVD.

And the technological momentum is only picking up speed. The merge of television, film, the Internet, and digital speed is coming together in dynamic ways that are both exhilarating and challenging to producers.

Technology is increasing the ways in which a television image can be transmitted—although even in mid-2008, some 13% of American homes were still using rabbit ear antennas to receive their programming.

Those transmission services include:

- **Broadcast towers. (or sources, also called terrestrial).** Traditional method of delivering analog, and now digital television signals.
- **Satellite dishes.** Large dishes that pick up video signals and transmit them to receivers. The systems depend on frequency modulation (FM) to send the video.
- **Direct satellite system (DSS).** Smaller dishes receiving transmissions operate at a higher frequency and whose signals are converted to digital data.
- **Internet.** Video, film, and graphic materials can be transmitted and viewed or downloaded online.
- **Mobile phones.** As with the Internet, video transmissions and user-generated content can be viewed, saved, and/or forwarded via mobile phone.

The traditional television business models of the movie studio system and the Top Three networks have essentially been replaced by consolidations between big business and film and television powerhouses, often called the *conglomerates*. Entertainment, news, and information content is voraciously demanded by, and fed to, the international markets, and the end result is a vast entertainment industry worth billions, in any currency.

The control by these few powerful conglomerates spreads over vast domains: from television stations and theme parks to movie studios, from newspapers to home video and publishing, from motion simulator rides to sophisticated video games and Internet networks. They're all connected through commerce, with real consequences on our expanding culture. The implications of the conglomerates' influence on the viewing public have sparked vigorous debates, and it is a vital subject for more exploration and study by a committed student of television. Additional resources can be found in the appendix contained on this book's web site.

VII. TELEVISION MERGES WITH NEW MEDIA

Two words: branded entertainment. When TV first started, each program was sponsored, like General Electric Theater. I think we're going back to that now as a result of TiVo, which is going to open a lot of doors for producers.

Brett Morgen, excerpt from interview in Chapter 11

Over the last seven decades, television has traditionally involved watching our favorite programs at a specific time on a TV set in our homes. But traditional TV was then, and this is now, an era of time shifting, place shifting, and unique and varied content – thousands of programming hours are at our disposal.

Television now is controlled by the consumer. TV is totally flexible, can be searched, manipulated, stored, and accessed at the viewer's whim. It is multichoice, able to be customized, and has almost total interactivity. It can be watched when and where the viewer chooses. The viewer is now in control.

The future of television relies in part on emerging trends in technology, but the primary function of television always comes down to storytelling. The stories it tells may range from the harsh reality of a news broadcast to the narrative fiction of episodics and sitcoms; a compelling and engaging story will always trump technology, no matter how cool or revolutionary the handheld device, or gadget, or size of the screen.

The Transformative Trends in Television

Regardless of how good or bad the storytelling, digital technology is evolving at an exponential speed. What was considered visionary a year or two ago is, in some cases, already out of date. But as of the writing of this second edition, we can look at technological advances that show real promise in transforming the horizons of television and new media.

Digital TV (DTV). Is transmitted via an aerial tower, phone lines, or cable into either a box on top of the user's TV or through a decoder built into the set itself. One of the distinct advantages of digital television is that, with the same amount of bandwidth, five times more information can move through a digital signal than an analog one (the current transmission standard). A digital signal can transmit more data than an analog signal and stays consistent over wide distances. Digital transmission can also deliver data that gives our TV sets the potential to be interactive—we can vote, shop, or order specialized programs. The high quality of HDTV sets have vastly improved digital sound capacity with its 5.1 channels of audio.

Digital images, for the most part, are sharper, have deeper color and are more immediate than those in analog. HDTV can be broadcast over digital or analog signals. According to FCC regulations, all U.S. broadcasters must have made the transition from the traditional one-channel analog signal to digital signals by February 2009 (moved from its original date of 2006). Although it can be expensive and time-consuming to modify the technology and replace the equipment, the broadcasters, advertisers, and producers are convinced it will pay off over time.

Interactive TV (ITV). Involves a digital signal that can transmit a multitude of images and sound as well as graphics, games, forms of information, and whatever available data a broadcaster wants to add to its signal. It achieves a real convergence with computers and the Internet because digital TV can implant interactivity within the signal. An impressive number of TV viewers are now simultaneously surfing the Internet, and virtually everyone involved in media is researching ways to unite the two.

The future of television is by definition almost all interactive. It includes downloading TV shows from networks, channels, and independent producers onto our computers and mobile phones; putting our own user-generated content (UGC) onto spaces like YouTube, MySpace, and video blogs; using our gaming devices such as the Xbox 360 to play sophisticated games and connect them with the Internet; and using the computer, the Internet on television, and more. Networks air their shows with an Internet component of "Enhanced TV" that encourages viewers to play along with game shows and to watch the short ads that either play in the shows or are embedded.

Multicasting. Broadcasters who transmit their programming via digital signals can send out one high-quality, high-definition picture—or, by using the same amount of signal, they can multicast four regular, standard-definition pictures. For example, during the day, a broadcaster might offer four standard-definition programs such as a documentary on one channel, a kids' program on the second, global news coverage on the third, and a gardening show on the fourth channel. But in prime time, the same broadcaster airs just one program in high definition, such as an original drama with high production value and a stellar cast of actors.

Video on Demand (VOD). A system that gives its user a variety of ways in which to watch video, film, and user-generated content. It searches, selects, stores, and screens content, either by downloading it to a set top box to watch at the user's convenience, or by streaming it in real time. American VOD systems can also deliver content to computers and mobile phones, on-demand and virtually instantaneously.

Digital Video Recorder (DVR). Also called personal video recorders, or PVRs in the United Kingdom, DVRs and devices like TiVo allow the user to time shift. They can be programmed to record several programs, which are then stored onto a hard drive so that the user can choose when to view them. DVR is generally combined with a digital TV service and can be accessed, played, rewound, and paused at will. DVRs also provide menus and guides that tell the viewer how to access a program, and usually supply specific facts about each show, like actors, director, tag line, and other facts.

All these technologies may expand exponentially, or may die a quick death in the shadow of another more powerful system. At the core of it all, ultimately, they must survive fiscally.

Can It Make Money?

The traditional advertiser-supported television business models are clamoring to keep up with the rapid changes in technology. Networks like ABC, NBC, CBS, Fox, and the CW, as well as many cable networks, are all supported by commercial advertisers. Yet increasingly, viewers are using their DVRs to fast-forward through these commercials. This threatens advertisers and sponsors, who are all scrambling to monetize their Internet presences: banner ads, imbedded ads, even preroll—10-second ads that come before a program and can't be turned off—each shows some success. Few sites have been able to charge a subscription fee; most Internet users will only pay for access to limited sites, like those for downloading movies or music, or for online learning.

The ratings systems are changing rapidly as well, and though they will eventually pinpoint every demographic, interest area, age group, gender, and each individual viewer's watching and buying habits, they are still in early stages of experimentation. The role of the audience is vital; the viewer is the end user and essentially sponsors the TV and new media industries. The traditional Neilsen and Arbitron audience measurement matrix is being replaced by new ways to understand just who is watching, and what they want to see.

Narrow casters, like cable and satellite channels, offer niche programming targeted to special interest groups like do-it-yourself, sports, all-movies, and dozens more. They are financially supported by subscription fees or commercials, and their advertisers' products closely parallel and reflect the viewers' interests and buying habits. But there are hundreds of them, literally, and the competition for even limited viewership is fierce.

This era is one of genuine transition—many of the old rules no longer apply, but the new rules have yet to be established or formalized. Everyone in the television medium, and those in related new media industries, are scrambling to outthink their competitors. New strategies, innovative tactics, and visionary thinking will inevitably trample the old model of conducting business as usual.

> The illiterate of the 21st century will not be those who cannot read and write, but those who cannot learn, unlearn, and relearn.
>
> **Alvin Toffler**

ON A HUMAN LEVEL . . .

You've explored the facets of television's evolution—as a storytelling medium, and its technological and cultural growth—and you've also imagined its potential. You could parallel the growth of television with your own development as a producer: each step you take depends on the step you took before it, how well you understood it, what lessons you learned, and how you choose to apply it all to your own progress, professionally and personally.

SUMMARY

This chapter has barely touched on television's rich past, its transitions, and the unlimited possibilities of the medium's future. Within its short life span in human history, TV always moves forward, and at such a rapid rate that even its definition is now being re-examined. As you explore the plentiful resources for further study, each adds more depth to your resources as a producer, and arms you with the experience and wisdom of TV's early pioneers as well as its visionaries.

In the following chapter, you will begin to focus on the essential core of any project— its story.

REVIEW QUESTIONS

1. What do you consider to be the most pivotal events in television's early experimental years?

2. Define *persistence of vision* and *pixels*. What is their connection?

3. Choose three of television's creators and discuss their contributions to television.

4. Choose one decade in television history. In your own words, discuss its progress, the risks taken, and the technical and creative advances that specifically characterize that era.

5. Choose one highlight in TV history that you feel is significant.

6. What is the FCC? The NTSC? What roles do they play?

7. Compare the NTSC, PAL, and SECAM systems.

8. Pick one fact from each decade that may have contributed to your desire to be a TV producer.

9. Identify one of your favorite programs and trace its ancestry back to earlier television programs.

10. What are your own speculations about the future of television technologically? Creatively? Economically?

The Big Idea: Script and Project Development

A need to tell and hear stories is essential to the species Homo sapiens—second in necessity apparently after nourishment and before love and shelter. Millions survive without love or home, almost none in silence; the opposite of silence leads quickly to narrative, and the sound of story is the dominant sound of our lives, from the small accounts of our day's events to the vast incommunicable constructs of psychopaths.

Reynolds Price

THIS CHAPTER'S TALKING POINTS

I. Think It

II. Write It

III. Develop It

I. THINK IT

I don't think art alone changes people, but consciousness, the life of the mind, is a critical force for change and art helps the shaping of consciousness.

Tony Kushner, playwright

The thinking, researching, soul searching, criticism, doubt, recognition, quiet victory— it's the process behind the story. The story is king. Always. This principle applies to a dramatic series or a sitcom on a major network, a cable news show, a mobi-sode, podcast, a short film on YouTube, a video blog, even a 30-second commercial— storytelling is always at its core. All genres want to tell a story that is compelling and engages the viewer.

The markets for story ideas are proliferating. Traditional TV venues are expanding into hundreds of channels and networks, running parallel to new formats for content that are introduced into the marketplace—VOD, DVD, the Internet, mobile phones, and video games, to name a few. Add to this an impressive market for such nonbroadcast areas as corporate image and training videos; DVD sales presentations; domestic and global video conferencing; teaching tools in education, medicine, and science; do-it-yourself videos; and satellite media tours. This massive market can only be satisfied by producers and writers with ideas.

Producers in television stay in touch with what is currently airing on TV, and what might be aired in the future. They watch television, they read the regular publications and industry trade magazines that deal with the TV business (see the web site that accompanies this book). Producers who work in new media are aware of constantly evolving directions by reading online sites and blogs, attending conferences, subscribing to magazines and weekly trade papers, and joining online communities that share information. As you begin to put the many pieces together, the intricacies of TV and new media become clearer and more accessible. And more fun.

The Global Demand for Content

America and the United Kingdom traditionally have supplied the majority of programming for the global marketplace. More recently, many international markets have become less dependent on this content, and are producing more shows locally. But the viewing public can be fickle—shows could be a hit in one country and a flop in another, or can make much more money internationally than in a country of origin. In some cases, hit programs are syndicated or repurposed; in other instances, the idea for the show, known as a *franchise*, can be a huge seller, as in the case of *Survivor* and *American Idol*, both of which began in the United Kingdom.

The very nature of a producer's job requires constant updating and lifelong learning. Producers increase their worth by researching and watching international television and other forms of online media; whenever possible, they'll view it in its original language. This adds a considerable depth to their abilities as a producer, and as a writer as well.

The Harsh Reality of the Marketplace

The metamorphosis of your rough idea into a tangible end-product can be a real challenge. The research can be daunting, the writing itself often agonizing, there isn't always a positive payoff, and the competition is intense. The majority of television shows are written by seasoned television veteran writers—they not only have the experience and understand the necessary nuances of writing for television, but they are trusted and familiar entities to the executives with whom they work on a daily basis.

Very few TV shows come from the minds of beginning writers. This often translates into business as usual for the viewer, and it is comfortable for the executives. The following statistics vary from year to year, but they're accurate enough to test your commitment to writing and developing your idea:

- At least 100,000 scripts are written each year and very few are good; most are written quite badly.
- Of these 100,000 script ideas, only about 10,000 get pitched to people in a position to develop them for broadcast.
- Maybe 250 to 300 of these 10,000 get to the finished script development stage.
- Fewer than 10 percent of those 250 to 300 are ever shot as pilot episodes.
- Depending on whose statistics you believe, maybe half of these pilots get aired and even less continue on as series.

New Media's New Frontiers

As discouraging as these statistics are, they are just that—statistics. Hundreds of shows over television's history were huge hits in spite of opposition from critics, executives, investors—*Seinfeld*, or *Lost* and *Ugly Betty* were considered real risks at first. Their triumphs remind us that passion and talent is hard to quantify or consign to a spreadsheet.

And as importantly, the potential of new media is challenging and breaking the rules laid down in television. In this new media frontier, the producer is encouraged to expand the boundaries, share unique ideas, and carve out new territory.

Ideas for Programming are Everywhere

There is no wasted job, no wasted time for a writer. Life experience is everything. Without it, what is there to write about? If you're working at a McDonalds and you're an aspiring writer, you can write the greatest story about the French-fryer that anyone ever wrote. When I was in my 20s, I was in a very big hurry—I wanted to succeed yesterday. But what I know now is "get a life," continue to work out there in the world, continue to write, and know that everything you do is material for your work.

Scott A. Williams, excerpt from interview in Chapter 11

Maybe you have what you think is a saleable, viable idea for a TV show, or a clever piece that is perfect for an online series. Or maybe you have strong writing skills, but haven't yet found an idea that engages you. Here are just a few sources to help inspire some exciting programming ideas.

- *Friends, family, colleagues, or fellow students.* Some have great ideas but can't write. Adapt their ideas into tangible formats.
- *Total strangers.* People you meet on a plane or at a party; everybody has an interesting story.
- *Newspapers and magazines.* Big city or small town papers report rich stories from real life.
- *The Internet.* Hundreds of web sites focus on how to write and pitch scripts, plot suggestions, as well as links, blogs, chat rooms, social networking sites—all are rich with ideas.
- *Libraries.* Find out what books or plays are not restricted by copyrights and are in the *public domain*, such as works from authors such as Jane Austen, Charles Dickens, and Shakespeare. Adapt them, or "borrow" freely.
- *Book expositions and fairs.* Publishers large and small promote their books and authors; find ideas among them. Option the ones you think you can develop. (There's more information about your legal options in Chapter 5.)
- *History.* Truth is as interesting as fiction. Write an imaginary character in an historical situation, and imagine what could have happened if….
- *Biographies.* Why are famous people interesting? Read biographies for story ideas. What techniques and skills made them succeed?
- *Let genius inspire you.* Read great books, both narrative and nonfiction, and see if they inspire any ideas in you. Something a character does or says might compel you to take a different direction that becomes your own.
- *Your creative well.* Inside your active brain is a whirlwind of ideas. Tap into your own dream world, for instance. Try some techniques, like giving yourself a creative suggestion or story problem to solve, right before you go to sleep. Keep a notebook or tape recorder with you and jot down ideas, not only

after dreaming, but while walking and working. Listen for snatches of interesting conversations, a sight gag, or an incident you see on the street. The more you tap into this fountain of riches in your brain, the more ideas are available to you.

- **Listen to your "running tapes."** Founded in semiotics, we each have them: these attitudes or beliefs about our appearance, health, fashion, entertainment, politics, aging, race. As a writer, you can emotionally or ideologically tie yours into a viewer's "running tapes" and create a convincing connection.

Successful businesses have mission statements; a dimensional producer has a *vision* statement. Author Laurie Beth Jones calls this "...a picture of how the landscape will look after you've been through it. It is your 'ideal.'" Whether the idea you want to write about is your own original concept, or one you acquired from someone else, your vision statement helps you define the effect you want make on a viewer.

> You have to have the willingness to collaborate, and definitely the ability to tell a story. At the end of the day, you're telling stories. You have to be able to structure a story so that someone knows what you're talking about. In the news field, the challenge for a news producer is that nine times out of 10, you are writing a story for someone else's voice. One of the functions of a news producer is to write a story and collaborate with the on-air talent. If you don't have the writing skills to write a story and collaborate with someone who may have a different vision for that story, you're not going to be very happy.
>
> **Matt Lombardi, excerpt from interview in Chapter 11**

II. WRITE IT

> The difference between the right word and the almost-right word is the difference between the lightning and the lightning bug.
>
> **Mark Twain**

The television industry has been built on a strong foundation of producers who started as writers—each had an idea they were passionate about, one important enough to nurture and protect. They wanted it ultimately to reflect their passion and weren't willing to give up control to a production company or network that could destroy it. These writers adopted the skills of a producer so they could protect their vision.

Increasingly, new media is attracting TV and film writers and producers. They're creating projects and innovative ideas for the Internet; for elegant, sophisticated video games; and for mobisodes. They are taking chances, redefining the aesthetic language of new media, and exploring the financial pros and cons.

The Writer/Producer

In the entertainment industry, the writer/producer can be a major player. He is known as a *hyphenate*—a creative person with two (or more) specific skills who, as a result, can do twice as much work (and often earn twice the money). The title and the job can change with each show and its circumstances. As you learned in Chapter 1, the producer's titles can range from executive producer or showrunner, to co-producer or associate producer, to line producer or consulting producer—each depends on the individual project.

As the public's demands for new programming and content keep changing and evolving, producers are challenged to find bright new ideas. They capitalize on popular formats and topics that can satisfy viewers' demands.

In addition to spinning a tale, the script serves several other purposes. Producers, directors, actors, and crew members all depend on the script as a blueprint to provide the structure for the construction or creation of their part of the project. The producer also needs a script to create a budget, breaking it down into specific departments, or accounts, as you'll see in Chapter 4.

Writing for TV versus Film

Whether you're writing the script yourself or working with a scriptwriter, you want to know what elements make a script work. Writing for television is not the same as writing for film. One essential difference is the people at the core of the story. In a feature film, the characters and their storylines are introduced, the story begins, peaks, ends, and everything is resolved. When the movie is over, so is the story.

Yet in most genres of TV programming, the characters and their storylines continue—both are ongoing and familiar to the viewer. TV writers capitalize on that endurance by first creating strong storylines and then constructing lasting characters, writing plots around them, building on their reactions, and constantly testing them. Viewers rely on this familiarity with the characters and their storylines. The audience gets to know them well, and brings their own cumulative memories and experiences of the show to each episode.

Art theorist, Steven C. Pepper, has called this phenomenon "aesthetic funding," adding that "a late perception in a series … carries to considerable degree the results of previous perceptions as its constituents." Simply put, an episode of *Lost* that we're watching now is enriched and added to by previous episodes of *Lost* that we've seen already. Each viewing adds to the experience, and is part of the viewer's aesthetic fund. It provides a meaningful context for the intimate details and character traits, and gives every aspect of the show an extra significance.

> In television, I find it more rewarding, because you write something and it's being shot in a couple of weeks. It's a great, great feeling to write and rewrite and create with real live actors and directors and technical people on a real live set. And in a few more weeks, it's airing on television—so your rewards are more immediate.
>
> **Scott A. Williams, excerpt from interview in Chapter 11**

Television and New Media Programming Genres

As a producer, you may be interested in developing a project in any of the following genres of either television and nonbroadcast programming, or for the growing number of delivery systems:

- *Reality/nonfiction.* Documentary, make-over, competition, biography, nature, travel, "making of," interviews, how-to
- *Sitcom.* Family, teen, smart, silly, spin-off characters
- *Episodic drama.* Police, law, forensics, medical, firefighters, family, political, edgy, young adult
- *News.* Local and national news, entertainment, politics, weather, magazine format, special news reports
- *Children's.* Cartoon, educational, puppets, classroom
- *Talk.* Daytime, late night, women's issues, sports
- *Soaps.* Daytime, primetime, novellas
- *Sports.* Event coverage, games, playoffs
- *Game and quiz shows.* Words, numbers, trivia, all competitive
- *Movies of the week.* Network and cable, multipart or one-off

- **Infomercials.** Cable and nonbroadcast, from weight loss to makeup to vacuum cleaners
- **Corporate.** Corporate image, training, industrials, promotional, conferences and conventions
- **Advertising.** Commercials, trailers, promos, DVD added value and special features
- **Music videos.** Broadcast, point of purchase, special features
- **DVDs.** Commercially released films and TV series, do-it-yourself, specialty, events, games
- **Webisode.** Web episode, usually short, of a TV show that's streamed or downloaded
- **Mobisode/podcast.** Generally a one- to three-minute broadcast of a TV episode made for mobile phones and portable media players
- **Video game consoles.** Games that are either streamed, downloaded, or on DVD

The purpose of art is to lay bare the questions that are hidden by the answers.

James Baldwin

From Idea to Script

A script translates an idea into a specific format that can act as a blueprint for production. It includes many or all of the following components:

- **A strong story.** One that grabs the viewer's attention and holds it.
- **An amazing hook.** Something unique about the story: a character, a location, a texture is edgy and different, and stands out from the others.
- **A protagonist.** The traditional hero who is somehow unique yet familiar, vulnerable yet courageous, someone about whom the viewer can care.
- **An antagonist.** A bad-guy role, the villain, someone who creates conflict, tension, and challenges the good guy or the overall plot in some major way.
- **A buddy.** The main character has a friend, colleague, or sibling who's a sidekick or performs essential functions, like the conscience, the helper, the smart one, the comic relief—often, the character who's sacrificed in the end.
- **A challenge.** The character(s) must confront a challenge and either wins or loses in the process.
- **A conflict.** The character must make moral choices and each option has consequences. Plus, the conflict must be resolved in a way that convinces and satisfies.
- **A contradiction.** A situation that seems good but turns out to be bad, or vice versa.
- **A demon.** Something that happened to the character before the story starts (in the back story) that haunts and influences his or her actions now.
- **A heartstring.** Romance, vulnerability, and sex all help the viewer understand and bond with the characters and their lives.
- **An "up" ending.** Happy or resolved endings sell, regardless of how real life is lived; they often show some form of redemption or measurable growth of the character that satisfies the viewer.

Length

In commercial television, the scriptwriter must also factor in commercial breaks. These breaks include regular commercials, promos, and other material supplied by the national and/

or local station affiliate. Depending on the station, a one-hour show actually consists of only about 44 to 48 minutes of programming, along with 12 to 16 minutes of breaks. The script is generally about 50 to 55 pages long. A half-hour show runs 22 to 24 minutes with 6 to 8 minutes of commercial breaks. The traditional guideline is that one script page equals one minute of action, although this can vary with the genre.

Commercial Breaks

When a show goes to commercial, that interruption needs to be seamlessly integrated into the storyline without losing action or suspense or pacing, while still maintaining the plot's thread. The same applies to coming back into the story from the commercial. Unless you're writing for noncommercial television, these breaks come with the territory. Count the number of breaks in a TV show that's similar to yours. How often do they come? How long are they? How does the story line move in and out of the break?

Dramatic Plotlines

Starting with the genius of classic thinkers like Aristotle, and continuing through to the postmodern teachings of dramatic writing, the big idea of the story is what's most important. This action is more important than the characters, and is what determines who they are and how they react. A compelling story revolves around action that's bigger than life and greater than its players.

A plotline has two distinct movements, according to Aristotle:

> By Complication I mean all from the beginning of the story to the point just before the change in the hero's fortunes; by Denouement, all from the beginning of the change to the end.
>
> **Aristotle, *Poetics***

The Complication. This involves all that's happening in the plot along with any kind of back story that connects to the plot. It starts as the plot's beginning until something changes in the hero's fortunes.

The Denouement. From that moment of change until the end. It develops as a cause-and-effect of the complication, takes time to unfold, and continues to the very end.

Most dramatic series, and many comedy series, rely on the ABC structure, shown here, and interweave three story lines.

- **The A story.** Propels most of the episode's primary storyline, or main idea.
- **The B story.** Focuses on primary and/or supporting characters; often they carry over into subsequent episodes.
- **The C story.** The comic or soft-hearted relief that deflates tension.

Acts

> …a whole is that which has beginning, middle, and end.
>
> **Aristotle, from *Poetics***

Aristotle's *Poetics*, the classic primer on the elements of dramatic writing, mandates that for a story to be compelling enough to arrest the audience's attention, it must have a beginning, a middle, and an end.

- **Beginning.** There is an event or action that sets the plot in motion. It's initiated by the hero/protagonist or the villain/antagonist, and it happens early. There may be a back story—what Aristotle calls the *prologue*—involving what happened before the story begins and connects that to the action in the beginning. This back story might set a tone, introduce characters, and reveal a location.

- **Middle.** Here, the event or action in the beginning results in the direct cause-and-effect of that early thing. In the middle, the hero—or sometimes the villain—must make moral choices; relationships and characters develop; we see increased conflict. The middle motivates the plot to come to a specific change in the hero's fortunes or misfortune. This becomes the turning point that leads to the end.
- **End.** The pace picks up, vital questions are answered, conflicts get resolved, and the story comes to a climactic and usually viewer-satisfying end.

In television and in much of the content created for new media, the main story does follow Aristotle's advice for a beginning, middle, and end—but there are also subplots and themes that run throughout the life of the series. These may or may not be addressed in each episode, and don't always end.

Having a beginning, middle, and end to a story doesn't necessarily mean the same thing as having three acts. Though most half-hour TV shows are divided into three segments, and the majority of one-hour shows into six, some forms of programming might be spaced into four or five parts: a teaser and four acts, or it could run to five acts. Some shows may add a short end tag, too.

- **The teaser.** Three to five pages, with a plot set-up that hooks the viewer
- **Act 1.** 13 to 15 pages (the beginning)
- **Act 2.** 12 to 13 pages (the middle)
- **Act 3.** 11 to 12 pages (more of the middle)
- **Act 4.** 11 to 13 pages (the end)
- **Tag.** One to two pages (wraps up a plotline or teases the next episode)

IN THE TRENCHES...

A very bright, very successful screenwriter who created and wrote for a half-dozen hit shows once told me: "Don't **say** it if you can **show** it." What brilliant advice.

~C. Kellison

Sitcoms

Generally, sitcoms tend to open with a funny teaser and have two or three, even four acts. A few sitcoms break this mold and use the A-B-C structure, earlier. Other sitcoms might devote their half hour to one main story. *Seinfeld* was quite a unique concept in that each episode usually featured four plotlines that resulted in one conclusion and satisfied all four conflicts.

Script Formats and Styles

Most writers prefer to begin writing their scripts by first outlining their overall Big Picture idea into acts or segments. Then, they might expand that into a treatment form before they finally flesh out the story in a full script format.

Outlines are shorter than full scripts, and can provide a clear map for the writer to follow. It can also help to highlight story problems early on. An outline is usually one to three pages, almost a sequential laundry list of the show's beats that is used by the writer as a basic guideline. Some writers use 3"×5" index cards, pinning them on a cork board, to help them organize their scenes, then translate that to an outline on paper.

A **treatment** traditionally is written in a narrative form rather than in script form. It might run from three to 10 pages, sometimes longer. In most cases, development executives read the treatment only for the nuances of the primary story idea. If they are interested in what they read, they'll ask for a full script. You can find more information about treatments in Chapter 6.

A **script** should be easy to read, should follow a very specific script format, and is written with language that is sparse but interesting—many scripts are a delight to read. These formats have been agreed upon as industry standards; if you decide to use a different format in the hopes of appearing innovative and unique, you're only branding yourself as an amateur. Several software programs are widely used by writers, like Final Draft and Movie Magic Screenwriter, and some shareware is available online.

The basic guidelines for writing a script are:

- It is neatly typed with no erasures, scribbled notes, or correction fluid.
- Each page has 1½-inch margins and paragraph separation.
- The paper is simple 20-pound, white, and 8½ ×11 inches.
- It's printed on only one side.
- Each page is divided into frequent paragraphs so the words don't run together.
- Scripts are usually typed in Courier New or Times New Roman, with a 12-point font. Avoid other fonts that are overly busy or pretentious, another sure sign of an amateur.
- Each page is numbered with a numeral followed by a period in the upper right corner.
- Each page is double- and triple-checked for spelling, punctuation, and grammar.
- The finished script is bound in plain card-stock covers with brass brad closings.

Formatting Your Script

A script for a film or television show generally follows the rule of one script page per one minute of on-screen action. That's not always the case but it's close. There are a few other commonly agreed-upon elements in formatting a script to keep in mind:

- *Story Title.* You want your project to be noticed and remembered; its title is a big part of creating a good or bad first impression. When possible, keep it short and descriptive. Your title can say a lot about the show, either directly or in its nuance: think *Desperate Housewives, Lost, 30 Rock, Rescue Me, Heroes, Mad Men*. It can also signal the show's tone or direction.
- *First Page.* There is no one rule for the format of the first/title page, though usually the title is written in all caps, and centered in the upper third of the page. Under the title, type "by" the original author, which also is centered. Subsequent writers may receive credits in descending lines. There might also be the contractual mandate that "Based on the novel by…" follows. Generally, the date and the color of the script's revisions pages are listed; in the lower right corner might be the author's representative, with a contact phone number and/or email address. In the lower left corner, type the copyright symbol, the year, and the author's name. The WGA web site provides additional updated information.
- *Formatting. Film or A/V Script?* A script for television, new media, and nonbroadcast is usually formatted in one of two basic styles, depending on its content, its genre, and its delivery system(s). It can follow the traditional **film screenplay** format used in writing films and television dramas (as seen later), or it can be in **A/V** (audio/visual) format (see later), using two, three, sometimes four vertical columns.

Here's a short scene from a TV drama that uses the **traditional film script format**:

FILM SCRIPT FORMAT

FADE IN:
INT. LUXURY CAR - NIGHT

Two men sit in grim silence in the back of a cruising limo.
The lights of passing cars flit across their faces, revealing that
MAN #1 is the much older alpha dog, over stuffed, while
MAN #2 is clearly afraid of him.

MAN #2
(a whisper of quiet desperation)
Dad... you gotta pay her back! She's dying, Dad!

MAN #1
(ignores him)
...you eat yet? You look real bad, kid. Green.
(taps on the dividing glass in the limo window)
Hey, you. Boy! Pull over to the next burger joint.
Doc says I gotta eat regular meals. My ticker...

INT. FRONT SEAT OF LIMO - NIGHT

The LIMO DRIVER'S eyes look back from the rear view mirror.
They shine with hate. PULL BACK to see the driver barely
able to hide his anger. His right hand moves down to a pistol on
the seat. He caresses it as his left hand guides the wheel into
the burger joint parking lot. He steadily chews gum, humming
"Amazing Grace" under his breath. [END SCRIPT BOX]

This descriptive header sets up each scene for the reader. It is always capitalized. It tells where the scene is taking place (the luxury car) and reveals that the scene is either inside (INTerior) or outside (EXTerior,) and when: DAY or NIGHT.

The first time a character is introduced, his or her name is ALL CAPS. Indent character names.

Describes emotion.

Describes action.

Camera direction, in ALL CAPS.

The same idea written as an **A/V script** is formatted in landscape format rather than portrait, with at least two columns. This format is used in many television shows, commercials, corporate image, music videos, games, how-to, and other programming genres:

AUDIO/VIDEO SCRIPT FORMAT

AUDIO	VIDEO (or VISUAL)
	Two men sit in the back of a cruising limo. Light on their faces. MAN #1 is older, MAN #2 is afraid of him.
Sounds of Passing cars	
Man #2: Dad, you gotta pay her back! She's dying, Dad!	
Man #1: ...you eat yet? You look real bad, kid. Green. Hey you. Boy. Pull over at the next burger joint... Doc says I gotta eat regular meals. My ticker...	Man #1 taps on the limo window
	The limo driver looks back into rear view mirror. His eyes blaze hatred. He touches the gun on the front seat, steers the car with the other hand into a drive-in burger shack. He's chewing gum with slow deliberation.
Soft hum of driver humming. "Amazing Grace."	

You can add other information to this format. Some producers prefer the format with the two vertical Audio and Visual columns, so they can add other columns for graphics information (lower thirds like name, location, title), transitions (a dissolve or wipe), and time duration (the length of a sound bite, narration, or visual action). Any voice-over or narration is written in the Audio section.

Camera Angles

Few writers add written descriptions for camera angles (such as CU for Close Up) or directions (such as Camera Pulls Back) except when it accomplishes a specific story-related action. This use of camera angle description usually lies within the realm of the director, worked out just prior to the actual shoot.

If you do want to prepare a shooting script, however, it's not difficult to grasp the language of camera angles and directions; by using these terms correctly in your script, you can convey the texture and feeling that you want your script to invoke. You can explore this in more depth in Chapters 4 and 8.

Script Components

A strong script provides the reader with a clear format and brief descriptions of the action. Your script also includes dialogue that reflects the characters and their part in the main storyline. Good dialogue gives important plot information, reveals characters' motivations, and propels the flow of the story line. Following are a few components of compelling dialogue.

- Dialogue should create the illusion of reality, not reality itself. Conversation in real life can be tedious and boring.
- Each word and every line advances the plot, explains the character, or provides further story exposition.
- When dialogue is used sparingly, less can be more. Pure silence at the right time can be eloquent.
- One perfect adjective is better than two or three that are not.
- Adding action to a character's dialogue creates momentum and is usually preferable to talking heads that don't move. An actor can be talking or yelling as he jogs. Sitcoms, for example, tend to place their primary sets in a living room in front of a staircase and/or the front door (think the *Cosby Show* and *Two and a Half Men*). This provides more momentum—a set with multiple entry and exit points allows for characters to inject more action into the comedy.
- By knowing your characters and how they speak, you can add nuance with speech patterns, or unique phrases that only he or she would use.
- Read your dialogue out loud to yourself. Record it into a tape recorder. How honest does it sound to your ear when you listen?
- An honest writer is a rewriter. Even the most seasoned will rewrite until they're satisfied. They can usually sense when it works—it's a gut feeling. By trusting your own intuition and pushing your ego and over-think aside, you can more authentically review your work. If you're still not sure, show it to another writer, a professor, or someone who can be totally honest with you.

The Spec Script

Some writers have gotten into the entertainment and media industries by writing a *spec script*—a script written on speculation, one with no guarantees of being seen or bought. Its primary purpose is to showcase your writing talents—if it sells, that's icing on the cake. Most spec scripts are written for a current program or show that is popular; one that you like and watch regularly. Your lawyer, agent, or an inside connection who—if it's positively received—then sends it to development executives or other producers or partners who may be looking for writers with talent and innovative ideas.

A good spec script can be a major factor in a hiring decision. In writing a spec script, the writer is first a researcher. If you're writing a script for a specific show, you want to know that show inside and out. Study the characters, their histories, and how they speak. Watch at least a season of the show and you'll get its overall perspective and its nuances. What is the rough format of each episode? How many story arcs and commercial segments in each episode?

Create a plotline that has not been used before on the show but that remains faithful to its overall story line and its characters. If you decide to send a spec script for a specific show to an executive who works on that show, keep in mind she is familiar with each of the show's elements and will quickly spot any story flaws that are unfaithful to the show.

Working with Other Writers

Writers in television take various approaches to their work. Some work best alone and prefer the solitude, and others write better with one or more partners. Many writers are on staff in a show and are a part of larger writing teams, usually from six to 10 writers. Finding the writing style that fits your personality is integral to your creativity and to your own brand of discipline. As you'll see throughout this book, virtually every aspect of television involves other people. Television is a highly collaborative medium, so by talking to other writers and producers, joining a writers' group or starting one, taking a class, and reading books about writing for television and emerging media, you can expand these vast creative horizons.

Writing with a Partner

Having a partner with a different viewpoint can be a stimulating combination. You bounce ideas off one another, experiment with dialogue, and discover plot counterpoints and narrative beats. Often one person originates the dialogue and another acts as the word-smith. Writers have varying skills, and when they're combined collaboratively, the results can be exciting.

A script is a valuable commodity. If it sells, you can both be paid—sometimes, paid a lot. But before you pitch your idea, you and your partner must discuss the pertinent details of your partnership. For example, talk over how you'll share writing credits, future percentages and profits, and who's doing what aspect of the writing process. Write these details down in a deal memo (a process you'll explore in Chapter 5), and sign it. This can prevent hard feelings or disagreements between you and your partner in the future.

IN THE TRENCHES...

Before I started producing, I wrote several feature-length film screenplays with a partner. He was the Big Idea man, while my strengths were more about format and dialogue and structure. He would pace the floor, spouting rapid-fire ideas. I'd type as he ranted, put my own spin on the story, and eventually, I'd turn out a finished script. We happily collaborated like this for four screenplays, pitching them and hoping. But when a Hollywood producer expressed a strong interest in one of our babies, my partner turned traitor. He claimed credit for the majority of the script's ideas and dialogue, and insisted that the producer pay him much more than me. When I objected, the producer pulled out—nothing scares a producer more than partners who don't get along. None of this would have happened if we'd simply put the details of our partnership in writing. And no...I haven't spoken to him since.

~C. Kellison

Working with a Writing Team

A writer can be hired as a staff writer on a specific TV show, or can be a member of a group of independent writers. In both cases, a successful writing team creates the script from the many details contributed by each writer. On most established shows, the writing team is closely supervised by the showrunner who acts as the head writer and team leader throughout the life of the series.

As a staff writer on a show or series, you are likely to enter into a contract situation that spells out the parameters of your pay, credits, time frame, responsibilities, length and genre of the show, and so on. The WGA web site (www.wga.org) can give you specific pay scales for various writing situations. If you're working on spec with an independent team of writers, clarify everyone's specific responsibilities within the group and put together a deal memo between all the contributing writers. You can find further information about deal memos and other contracts in Chapter 5.

Working with an Agent

Professional writers usually have an agent. This agent may be from a boutique agency and represents the writer, promotes and either options and/or sells the writer's work, pitches scripts or ideas to producers, negotiates contracts and subsidiary rights, and looks for other possible venues for the writer's work.

Another form of talent agency is the larger, more powerful packaging agency; these represent actors, directors, often producers, as well as the writer. They put together whole creative packages that ideally bring all these talents together: a great script, just the right actor, and the director who can pull them all together. An established talent agency, such as CAA or ICM, acts as the middleman between buyers and sellers.

Each kind of agency has its advantages and its drawbacks. But the bottom line is that your agent believes in you and your material, and can provide essential access to the right people. Agents usually take a commission of 10 percent, sometimes more, for their services, which can include finding a buyer for your script, getting you a writing job, and/ or negotiating final deals.

Yet finding an agent can be a frustrating catch-22 for new writers. Typically, an agent is interested in representing only established writers, so how can you establish yourself without an agent? If you already have some kind of track record, have sold a script, or have the promise of a sale, agents will pay more attention to you. You can research literary agents through the WGA and online.

If you strongly believe in your project, research agencies, or specific agents, then use polite persistence to make contact with an agent you think is right for your project. It can be challenging to get an agent to read your script and hopefully represent you, but it isn't impossible. Many a writer has gotten an agent by not giving up.

Working with an Entertainment Lawyer

Lawyers who specialize in entertainment and media are aware of the current trends in the television industry, and can see the potential payoff from emerging media and their new delivery systems. Because they have strong connections with producers, directors, actors, and other writers, as well as domestic and global market opportunities, they're in the position to bring these elements all together, similar to the packaging agency.

As you'll see in Chapter 5, lawyers can charge by the hour or by the project. These fees can vary significantly, depending on the lawyer and the project's demands. Some lawyers may stay with a project from start to finish, and are a permanent *line* in the project's budget. For a low-budget project, producers can often find reasonable or free legal advice from organizations of volunteer lawyers, university law departments that offer programs in entertainment law, on the Internet, and from sources listed on the web site that's mentioned throughout this textbook.

> Do you really need a lawyer? If you are making a $15,000 movie as a thesis project, then maybe not. But if you have any notion of ever doing anything with it beyond showing it to the department, then you probably will need to get a lawyer involved at some point because nobody will distribute it unless they know that you have all the rights that you need, or all the clearances that you need and there won't be a bunch of claims flying in as soon as this thing ends up on television somewhere.
> **J. Stephen Sheppard, excerpt from interview in Chapter 11**

Working with a Manager

The same way that agents and lawyers are well connected, managers are skilled in networking. Unlike agents, however, managers are not required to adhere to the same restrictions that regulate legitimate writers' agents. If you have a manager who makes a deal for you, you'll still need a lawyer or agent for final legal negotiations. Managers generally charge a 15 percent commission.

III. DEVELOP IT

The script development stage refers to the early phases of a project in which you and/or a writer can polish your rough idea into a treatment, proposal, and/or script format. During the development stages, a producer considers potential directors, crew, talent, and the overall budgetary issues within the project.

This **development phase** can have several scenarios. Here are three of the most common:

1. You are developing an idea that is either your own original premise, or it belongs to someone else and you have legally optioned it for a period of time.
2. A production company or a network has put up development money for a writer(s) to develop and flesh out your idea.
3. A private investor sees the potential of your idea, gives you partial or complete funding, and expects a cut of any profits.

Each **development phase** has its pros and cons:

1. In the first scenario, above, you own the idea or have optioned it; no one else controls it. You may have control, but you're also financially responsible for its ownership.
2. In the second example, someone else's money is involved, which gives them more control, but at least you're not using your own money.
3. In example three, investors have little assurance that the script or project will sell. They may demand a high return on their investment often two to three times the initial investment. But it may be worth it for the security that their investment provides.

The phrase "development hell" refers to a script's development getting stalled at various stages, languishing for months or years, and often not getting made—or changing drastically over the course of its development. Sometimes these delays are caused by a conflict of ideas, the sudden firing of an executive, a cut in the budget, an actor who demands a bigger part, or simple dissipation of interest.

Protect and Control Your Idea

Before you fully commit yourself to developing a project, you must first legally protect it. If you are not legally protected, you could be wasting your time developing an idea for which you have no rights. Submitting an idea that you don't legally own can invite a lawsuit. In Chapter 5, you can find more information on the following legal issues:

- If the idea belongs to you, protect it.
- If the idea belongs to someone else, option or buy it.
- If a book, short story, article, or other material is the basis for your story, get the rights from the author or his or her legal estate. This doesn't apply if the work is in the *public domain*—meaning the book or play is no longer protected under copyright. Authors such as Brontë, Dante, Shakespeare, Dickens, and hundreds of others all wrote great ideas that are now in the public domain, and can be freely adapted.

Ownership and control are both important concepts for a producer. Let's assume you have an original idea that you think can be developed into a program concept. After you have fleshed it out into a treatment or script format, your next step is to legally protect it.

If you're understandably concerned that your idea could be plagiarized, you can legally protect it. Most companies to whom you would submit your project will insist that you sign a submission release (an example can be found on the web site) before they will read or consider it. You can find more information in Chapter 5.

- *Copyright it.* Go online for forms at www.copyright.gov or call the hotline (202) 707-9100. In either the end titles or on your cover page, list the copyright notice; for example, © 2009 CKNY Productions. (The date indicates the year of first public distribution.) Send the paperwork, which is a nonreturnable copy, with a check or money order via certified mail. You will receive a certificate of registration and a registration number.
- *Register it.* You can register either your treatment or script by mail, with Writers Guild of America or online at www.wga.org. You'll be charged a reasonable fee to register it, and WGA holds the registration for five years. You can reregister it then for another five years.

If It Is Someone Else's Idea, Buy or Option It

Let's say... a colleague of yours has written a script that has real potential. You may be considering producing it, or at least developing it further. But first you must either buy the full rights from your friend, or agree on an *option agreement* that gives you the exclusive rights to develop and pitch the idea, and possibly, to purchase these rights. An option is taken on a script for a period of time, usually six months to a year, during which time you are the only person who can legally develop and pitch the idea.

If you have found a short story, novel, magazine article, Internet story, or another source for your script or project, determine who holds the copyright and negotiate any rights involved. You can option the rights to adapt it, or purchase these rights completely. If you can't find the original writer or copyright holder, an entertainment lawyer or professional copyright search company can help you locate the owner of the copyright. You must be satisfied that no one else has optioned it. Be sure that there are no outstanding liens on the work.

Find the Best Market for Your Idea

The potential markets for your program and project ideas are expanding rapidly in this digital revolution. Traditional television networks and cable are being eclipsed by online networks, cellular markets, home entertainment options, DVD, videogame consoles, and more. Nonbroadcast demands are rising too, for material in the fields of corporate training, education, advertising, how-to, and industrials, just to name a few. The venues for your content are endless.

But you've got to sell the idea first. Breaking into the business of entertainment and media can be a real challenge. Yet, every successful writer and producer did it somehow—why should you be an exception?

These industries continue to evolve, and though there are no set formulas, the following descriptions give you several directions in which you can go:

- Every network, movie studio, cable broadcaster, and most production companies have at least one executive, if not an entire department, devoted to development. They're looking for ideas: treatments, scripts, books, articles, news stories, short films that can be made into a series. Then, they work with either their own production department, or with an independent production company, to further develop the idea.
- Networks, cable broadcasters, and other buyers of content often develop and/or produce their own programs in-house. For example, NBC Universal may produce a show through their own production arm. Often, they may buy a property and then repurpose it for one of their other media branches, such as Bravo or MSNBC. They might make a short version of it for release as a webisode or mobisode, sell it to an international syndicator, or release it on DVD or VOD.
- The network or cable channel may rely on independent production companies with whom they have a strong relationship and lucrative history. These companies work closely with the development executives to script, cast, shoot, and do postproduction for sitcoms, episodic dramas, reality, animated, streaming and downloadable content, and more.
- The frontier of new and emerging media is still wide open. One direction is that of talent-owned Internet content companies. Spurred on by the 2007–2008 WGA strike, a number of professional writers turned away from TV and film and moved over to the Internet to create new kinds of programming. Here, the writers generally own the copyright, and can go anywhere they want with the content. A show, for example, might debut on the Internet, supported by advertising or subscription. It creates a real viral buzz and gets enough hits to warrant taking it over to network TV. The writers form the company and own a stake in any future profits.

When pitching your project to a specific venue, be certain that it is the right fit. You wouldn't bring a soap opera to a sports channel, or a music video to an all-news channel.

- If you want to interest a production company in your idea, make sure that company has experience in, and enthusiasm for, projects like yours. You can locate production companies by watching shows you like or that are similar to your own idea; look at the show's opening and/or closing credits for the production company's logo, and then research it. What is its history? What's their success rate? Read *Variety* or *Hollywood Reporter* or go to several online resources to see what shows are in production—they list the names and addresses of the production companies involved. You can also go to www.wga.org and click on the TV market list.

- If you want to pitch your idea to a specific network or cable broadcaster, watch the programming shown on that channel. Be aware of what they may be developing for the future as well as their current programming. And if you do find an "in" to pitch your project, be really sure that your idea is well-suited to their programming history and their audience.

- If you want to create a project that engages your audience, understand who that audience is. Research projects that are similar to yours. What were their overall ratings? Who were the show's advertisers? What was the breakdown showing male/female, ages, backgrounds, incomes, education, spending habits, and other statistics? Compile real data showing that your project can generate revenue.

- Most content buyers who do agree to read your idea or take a pitch meeting will ask you to first sign what's known as a *submission agreement* or a release. This protects them from any claims you may have later if you think they've stolen your idea. Each organization has its own regulations. And very few will accept unsolicited material; most accept proposals or take a pitch meeting only after they have been contacted by an agent or lawyer. You can find a sample of the submission release on this book's accompanying web site.

Getting a Pitch Meeting

One consistent thread runs through most traditional development departments: they almost always work only with writers who are known commodities. These writers (and producers) have experience and credits, are usually members of the Writers Guild of America, and are reliable. Many also have specialties—one writes beautifully about family drama, another knows the worlds of medicine or the law or politics. When one of these established creatives (writer, producer, director) has a promising project idea, he or she usually:

- Calls an agent, an entertainment lawyer, or an executive in the development department of a network, a studio, or a production company for which the idea is best suited.

- Sets up a pitch meeting (see Chapter 6) in hopes of convincing everyone to commit to further development.

- Pitches the idea verbally in the meeting.

- Gives the executive a *leave-behind* fact sheet about the project (see Chapter 6), including story synopsis, the creative team, potential talent, and more.

- Hopes that the development executive likes the idea enough to take it to an executive further up the ladder who either approves it for further development or rejects it.

- Understands that if it is approved for development, the executive in charge works with the producer and/or writer on refining the idea. It helps if the producer is also the writer, but if not, the executive and the producer find a writer they both like. Sometimes, a showrunner is brought in at this stage to help guide the vision and hire writers.

- Is emotionally prepared if the project hits a brick wall. As part of the process, the project details are discussed by the top executives. Some might be the development heads, and others are in charge of their shows that are currently airing. These executives could have deals with producers around these existing shows that include guarantees of future buys. This means that the executives may have promised to buy more programming from the same producers who are producing their current shows. To make sure they have enough content for each TV season, they tend to overcommit to these suppliers. This translates to fewer available time slots or less money for developing new projects. But economic pressures are changing the old models; fewer pilots are being commissioned and less development money channeled toward traditional television. Instead, all eyes are looking forward to producing content for the new delivery systems.

Getting in the door to pitch your project often depends on your connections. An agent, manager, lawyer, or referral from a colleague or friend can provide an opportunity for a pitch meeting or at least a phone call. Or, you can take a chance. By researching the network, cable, or studio, or the production companies and who they produce for, you could find the right person to approach with your idea. If you send it, if he or she reads it, and if your idea is right, it could signal success. If not, focus on other opportunities for your project.

Potential buyers and development executives seldom have the autonomy, interest, and/ or funding to *green light* (agree to start developing) ideas from producers or writers that don't have a proven track record. However, there are venues that are more receptive to innovative projects. The recent proliferation of new markets and delivery systems has created a demand for programming that can be supplied by independent producers and production companies with exciting and compelling ideas—ideas that generate revenue.

The Role of a TV Pilot

Seeing a pitch evolve into a TV pilot can be a producer's dream come true. But the statistical chances of that pilot getting picked up to go to series are as slim as the pilot getting made in the first place. Traditionally, a pilot for a one-hour series can cost from $3 to $7 million, so out of the hundreds or even thousands of pitches heard annually by each network's development executives, only about two dozen are finally produced by each network. And of these, just five or six pilots ever make it to broadcast.

Traditionally, network and cable executives followed a programming routine: ideas usually were pitched in the fall, then rewritten, scrutinized, and recast, and the pilots finally shot in time to be presented with grand hoopla to the networks affiliates' meetings during the May "up-front" presentations. The ones that made it through that gauntlet went into full-time summer production, filling the order just in time to premiere in early fall.

Over the last few seasons, however, all that has been changing. Some series have reversed the old order, and now debut during the summer months, or at the beginning of the new year. Many cable channels and some premium channels hear pitches, develop and shoot ideas, and air their pilots all year round. It's steadily moving toward a 52-week programming schedule.

And in today's global economy, most networks and cable channels are no longer investing significant development money into expensive pilots, going instead with short demos or animated storyboards to present their story ideas. These demos, or presentations, focus on the actors and the writing, and are a fraction of what a traditional pilot costs.

Many companies are changing the way they've always done business, limiting their orders for pilots to one or two, cutting back on their extravagant up-fronts in May, and investing more money into developing content for new cellular and online media.

The Impact of Budget on an Idea

TV is all about business. It is an industry driven by advertising or subscription revenue, and must have significant profits to survive. Although cellular and online content is still testing the waters about how best to be monetized, billions of dollars, pounds, Euros, and yen are being pumped into new media. Your idea may well translate into a business opportunity from which these content providers can profit. No matter how creative or innovative your project is, it is also a vehicle for profit.

If your project idea is expensive to produce, that's already one strike against it. A vital part of the producing process is maintaining your creative vision while operating on a tight budget. For example, if you hire union actors, you wouldn't write speaking lines that aren't necessary: an actor with a spoken line costs more than hiring an extra who says nothing. Minors under 18 must have a tutor on set, which involves extra money and paperwork. A virtual set can cost a fraction of what it takes to build and dress a real set. Each aspect of your project costs money, so look for ways to cut costs without sacrificing the quality of your story.

Basic Budget Categories

As you write and develop your idea, these main categories with their many departments are part of most projects' budgets:

- Screenplay and/or story rights
- Talent
- Crew and equipment
- Director
- Producer(s)
- Legal rights and contracts
- Locations and sets
- Wardrobe and makeup
- Special effects
- Postproduction
- Music
- Miscellaneous items like overhead, contingencies, insurance, finance charges, etc.
- Advertising and marketing costs

Experienced writers keep their plotlines simple. Unless they have the luxury of a large budget to play with, they try to avoid storylines with complicated locations, extravagant sets, expensive stars and large casts, explosions, stunts, expensive postproduction concepts, and other extras that expand the budget. A solid story line can usually survive without them.

> You've got to write what you want to produce, or at least the first few shows, because otherwise, it will pretty much be taken out of your hands. Even if you don't have the desire to be a writer, take writing classes because you should know how a script is put together, even if you are the postproduction supervisor.
>
> **Valerie Walsh, excerpt from interview in Chapter 11**

ON A HUMAN LEVEL . . .

The writing process is painful for some people, exhilarating to others. Taking a vague idea all the way through to a producible script is a triumph when it's finally done, yet that journey comes with pressures and uncertainties. You worry that when it's read, people may not understand it, or may respond with rejection, or worse, apathy. Your calls and query letters go unanswered. It seems endless.

But just turn on your TV set, or laptop, or cell phone, and you'll see a program or show or commercial—behind it is a producer and a writer. Every project went through some form of development process and most everyone survived, intact, and only mildly bruised.

SUMMARY

Throughout this chapter, you've weighed the harsh realities of developing an idea against the promises of success that lure writers and producers into producing for television and new forms of media. In the next chapter, you will explore how these ideas translate into the real world of budgeting.

REVIEW QUESTIONS

1. Devise a comprehensive strategy for informing yourself of current trends and producing deals in the television and new media industries.

2. What are four good sources for story ideas?

3. Write a vision statement for your life and another for a project idea you have. In what ways do they connect?

4. Compare writing for television and writing for online video channels.

5. What is your favorite television genre? Why?

6. Write a sample five-minute scene for any genre, using a professional script format.

7. Name five components of dialogue that you find compelling. Why?

8. Would you rather write alone, with a partner, or as part of a writing team? Why?

9. What is the importance of legally protecting your idea? How can you protect it?

10. Name six major story components that could impact your budget. What are some low-budget alternatives?

CHAPTER 4

Connecting the Dots: Breakdowns, Budgets, and Finance

The TV business...is a cruel and shallow money trench, a long plastic hallway where thieves and pimps run free, and good men die like dogs.

Dr. Hunter S. Thompson

THIS CHAPTER'S TALKING POINTS

I. Break Down the Idea

II. Budget the Idea

III. Find the Financing

I. BREAK DOWN THE IDEA

There is a crack in everything...that's how the light gets in.

Leonard Cohen

Budgeting is most every producer's nightmare. Mistakes get made, blame gets tossed around. Making a budget for your project obligates you to predict the future. It requires you to examine each aspect of your project, give it a face, and assign it job descriptions and a set of parameters. Without a realistic budget, your project faces confusion and failure. Budgeting can be daunting, even for seasoned producers, yet with time and some practice you can understand and eventually master the budgeting process. As a guideline for this process, you can refer to the comprehensive budget template on this book's web site, or research budgeting software programs like Movie Magic Budgeting and EP (Entertainment Partners).

Designing a budget is a process during which the producer evaluates the project's vision, and then translates that vision into time and money. Costs for any aspect of a budget can have an enormous range. If a dozen producers were to budget the same script, each would come up with different totals and calculations. One story can be told in many ways, and the best budgets emerge from solid research and cost comparisons, studying other producers' budgets, talking to people with budgeting experience, and practice. Lots of practice.

The now-classic television series *Friends* first started with six unknown actors who were paid modest salaries. But by the time the show left the air, each actor had become a big star, earning a million dollars per episode. Although these stars boosted the audience and advertiser appeal, the talent budget alone was six million dollars per episode. Other costs rose too, as producers created new swing sets and added guest stars. Ultimately, its high ratings, and subsequent sales to syndicators and international markets, justified NBCs' increased costs. Because money is *always* at the core of every television show, the producer's job is to achieve the best quality for the lowest cost and highest profits.

Understand the Big Picture of Production

> You have to be flexible. You have to be willing to roll with the punches, you have to believe in what you are doing and believe you can do it. If someone is telling you something is impossible, it is usually not. Anything is possible. There are some things that are impossible for budgetary reasons, but there are always compromises and ways to make your vision come to life.
>
> **Tom Sellitti, excerpt from interview in Chapter 11**

The producer works closely with people who can transform script ideas on paper to a dimensional finished product. The producer may work with a small two-man crew, or might build a large team with other producers, writers, director, actors and talent, a substantial production crew, heads of key departments, and others outside the immediate team such as lawyers, insurance agents, accountants, public relations, representatives. The list can be impressive. Regardless of whether the production is large or small, the producer (or a team of producers) is at its core, delegating, supervising, supporting, and making decisions throughout the project.

Create a Production Book

A good producer has a high regard for organization. Producing is all about details, and keeping those details in order makes the job easier. An essential tool in that organization process is called a *production book*. Producers generally keep a separate production book for each project, a three-ring loose-leaf binder with tab dividers for each section. It includes most, if not all, of the following categories:

- A contact list including names and phone numbers for producers, talent, crew members, director, catering, vendors, and other essential contact information
- The script and all versions and revisions
- Daily shot lists
- Shooting schedules and call sheets
- Production reports after the project wraps up
- Scene breakdowns
- Storyboards
- Props and art breakdowns
- Wardrobe, hair, and makeup breakdown
- Transportation details
- Meals and craft service plans
- Location agreements and shooting permits
- Releases and clearances for talent, locations, art work, etc.
- Deal memos with crew
- Insurance information
- Budget (optional—most budgets are confidential)
- Inventory (video stock, props, wardrobe, etc.)
- Equipment list
- Miscellaneous

Break Down Your Script

The script is the blueprint for your budget. And whether you've got a full shooting script for a sitcom, or just the bare bones of how you'll shoot a documentary, it's the source of your budget.

- Allow yourself or your writer(s) adequate time to develop your script. You don't want to frantically rewrite it on set, when time and money is at a premium.
- Most scripts must get final approval from development executives or clients, which can result in additional changes to the script or overall project restructure. The time required for the writer(s) to complete any rewrites is an added budget item. Most scripts require some tweaking and several revisions. Include money in your budget to cover an outline, a treatment, and at least two rewrites before you start shooting

The Breakdown

Every script is a compilation of scenes, and each scene has certain requirements that cost money. Does the scene call for three actors or only one? Is the scene being shot with multiple cameras and lighting, or just one hand-held camera using available light? What props or greenery or furniture are in that scene? Every component has a direct relationship to the budget and the shooting schedule. A *breakdown sheet* helps the production staff to understand what is needed in each scene. It can be compiled by hand or by using special software. (An example is provided on this book's accompanying web site). It makes the process easier, and provides a concise blueprint that helps to make the scenes work.

The breakdown is fully explored in Chapter 7, and includes any or all of the following categories:

- The scene number and name
- The date of the breakdown sheet
- The project title
- The page number of the script
- Location (on set or on a real location)
- Interior or exterior (shooting inside or outside)
- Day or night
- Brief scene description (one or two lines)
- Cast (with speaking parts)
- Minors (often require tutors, overtime, etc.)
- Extras (no speaking parts, either in the scene or in the background)
- Special effects (this ranges from explosions to blood packs to extra lighting)
- Props (anything handled by a character in the scene, like a telephone or pencil)
- Set dressing (items on the set not handled by the character)
- Wardrobe (any details that are pertinent to that scene, like a torn shirt)
- Makeup and hair (special effects, like wounds or aging, wigs or facial hair)
- Extra equipment (jibs, cranes, a dolly, steadicams)
- Stunts (falls, fights, explosions requiring a stunt person and stunt coordinator)
- Vehicles (picture cars or other vehicles used by characters in the scene)
- Animals (any animal that appears in the scene comes with a trainer, or *wrangler*, who takes charge of the animal during production)
- Sound effects and music (anything played back on set, like a phone ringing, music for lip-syncing, or music the actor is reacting to)
- Additional production notes

Storyboarding

Storyboards are not necessary in each project, but they can be useful organizational tools. *Storyboards* are simple, cartoon-like sketches of each scene in a script. They're numbered boxes with a drawing inside; each box refers to a scene or shot number from the script. When the image or camera angle changes, so does the content of the box.

Each sketch is a rough portrait of the scene being shot: the location of one character in relation to another, the framing, the surroundings, the colors or lighting in a scene. Storyboards can be a real advantage to a production as a kind of shorthand for the director, producer(s), Director of Photography (DP), art director, production designer, and others. See Chapter 7 for an example of a storyboard.

Prior to the shoot, the producer, line producer and/or UPM go through the script. They make a rough sketch of each scene (often with the help of a storyboard artist or storyboarding software) that details every camera setup in that scene. Usually storyboards contain minimal black-and-white line drawings, although they can be in full color photography, or even animated.

For unscripted programs, storyboards can help the production team to visualize and structure a location so that it looks natural but includes optional spots to place cameras or microphones.

Storyboards can be excellent visual tools for presenting an idea for a project—producers often pitch and sell their project ideas by using imaginative storyboards as persuasive selling tools. You can find a storyboard format on the web site.

Shooting Schedule

Let's say… your show costs around $5,000 a day to shoot and you have a 10-day shooting schedule. Easy. You need to budget $50,000. But what if the lead actor breaks his foot? Your shooting schedule goes off course and extends to 15 days, and now you've got a $25,000 difference to come up with. You can prepare for this kind of emergency by padding your budget whenever possible, adding an extra 10% contingency to your budget, and/or giving yourself extra shooting days in your overall schedule.

The shooting schedule is a key component in creating a budget. It isn't unusual for the cast and crew of a one-hour TV drama series to work 16 hours a day; some shows shoot as many as 12 to 18 script pages each day. This translates to shooting a feature-length script in two weeks—an incredibly tough schedule. There are additional fine points about structuring shooting schedules in Chapter 7.

Cross-Boarding

Several prime time television shows, both narrative and unscripted/reality, now shoot with a method known as *cross-boarding*. Using this approach, the producer shoots scenes, consecutively, from two or three different episodes that all take place on the same set or location. In other words, in Episodes 110, 113, and 117 of *The XYZ Show*, Tommy and his kids are in the kitchen. Their lines are different and so are the wardrobe and the story lines, but they all take place in the kitchen set. It is much more cost-effective to keep the crew in place and the set dressed and lit so that all three scenes can be shot in the one location.

II. BUDGET THE IDEA

There are no wrong answers in producing, only answers that will cost you a lot of money.

Valerie Walsh, excerpt from interview in Chapter 11

Each producer has his or her own approach to budgeting. Some television producers divide their budgets into three main categories: *preproduction, production*, and *postproduction*; and others distribute their costs into two sections: *above-the-line* and *below-the-line*.

Producers also factor in *indirect costs*, like legal fees, accounting services, insurance premiums, taxes, and a contingency that covers unforeseen costs. Some charge a direct *markup fee*, which is a percentage added to the costs that cover office and personnel overhead. Other producers might hide their profit margin in other ways, such as inflated crew costs and facility rentals. The overall goal is to make a profit in the long run, or at the very least, not to lose money.

Larger productions tend to have budgets extensive enough to require budgeting software and spreadsheets; smaller productions might need only a page or two to keep track of their costs. As the producer, you'll look for the right budget template that works best for each project, or work closely with the production manager or the line producer in keeping track of daily costs and the overall budget.

Budgeting Costs: Two-Part versus Three-Part Formats

The budget form that a producer uses to keep track of the production's costs is a personal decision. There are several formats, and some excellent software. Most fall into one of two categories:

- Three-part budgets: Preproduction, production, and postproduction
- Two-part budgets: Above-the-line, below-the-line

Three-Part Budget

Most television and new media producers find it easier to look at their costs by dividing their budget items into three major categories:

- Preproduction
- Production
- Postproduction

Budget Costs: Preproduction

Costs tend to be lower and more controllable in this first stage of a project. Budget items usually include the producer's fee for either writing or working with a writer; taking meetings; hiring crews; casting actors or talent; coordinating stunts; planning the shooting schedule; booking hotels, meals, and travel; and generally planning the project's overall development. In larger projects, the producer supervises other producers who deal with many of these details.

The script is an essential component of the project, which calls for the producer to work closely with the writer(s) in the preproduction stage. Budgeting for a writer can be done in several ways. For example, the producer and writer might agree on a flat fee that covers all aspects: developing the idea, writing the script, and any revisions. A writer might also be paid in stages, such as 30 percent of the agreed-upon fee after signing a contract, 30 percent with the first draft, and the remaining 40 percent is paid after final acceptance. In this case, the fee may include a specified number of revisions. If that number is exceeded, additional fees for extra revisions may be negotiated as part of the contract. Writers may also require the assistance of a researcher or other resources as part of the story development.

Other preproduction costs can include designing storyboards, consultant fees, casting fees (casting director and facilities), space for talent rehearsals, production staff and production assistants along with a coordinator and/or manager and an AD staff, office rental, location scouting, messengers and shipping, meetings, and meals. Any sets must be planned, constructed, painted, and moved to a sound stage that needs to be scheduled, and paid for. If the shooting is in a foreign location, research each country's requirements for locations, permits for shooting, currency exchange, and more. Careful preproduction planning is vital, and saves money and time for the overall budget of the project. You'll find more details about preproduction in Chapter 7.

Budget Costs: Production

When the producer has thoroughly mapped out everything needed to shoot the project, the production phase can be the quickest and least problematic part of the project. The script has been researched and finalized, the crew and equipment have been hired, the talent cast, the key departments heads have submitted their department's requirements, with estimated costs for production, contingency money has been put aside, and the many other details have been finalized so that the actual shoot can begin. In the following section, under Budget Lines, the majority of production crew members, equipment, and materials are outlined. Chapter 8 also explores the many specifics of production, too numerous to list in their entirety here.

Budget Costs: Postproduction

This is traditionally the most challenging area for producers to accurately budget. As you'll learn in Chapter 9, there are many factors in the postproduction process to consider. These include the many hours of footage that need to be screened, logged, and loaded into the editing system; the skills and style of the editor, and the costs for the editor, editing facility, the audio mixer and the audio facility; any graphics, artwork, animations, text, captioning, credits, and other design effects; music, narration, voice-over, sound effects, sound design, and even foreign language translation.

Two-Part Budgets

Not all producers like the three-part budgeting system. In some television projects, commercials, and more elaborate, big-budget television series or specials, the producer might use a format that's similar to a feature film budget. This format divides the production costs into two areas:

- Above-the-line
- Below-the-line

Above-the-Line Budget Costs

These costs are project-specific fees or salaries paid to the creative personnel (producers, directors, writers, and actors, depending on multiple factors including union affiliation, time required, special perks, and star power). Above-the-line fees are paid in several ways:

- **Union fees.** If the writer is a member of the Writers Guild of America (WGA), that fee is stated in the WGA contract with the producer. The same applies to a director who's a member of the Directors Guild of America (DGA) and to a Screen Actors Guild (SAG) actor.
- **Daily or weekly fees.** The personnel agree to a fee to be paid daily or weekly.
- **Flat fees.** Often a producer agrees to pay a fee to an above-the-line creative in installments: one-third upon signing a contract or deal memo, one-third on completion of principal photography, and the final one-third when the project is completed.
- **Producer fee.** Because the producer is usually the person deciding how fees are paid, this fee can vary. The producer(s) generally takes the project from start to finish, and works longer than most everyone involved. Some producers take daily or weekly fees, others work on a flat per-project fee. A producer might also *defer payment* until the project is sold, in exchange for a bigger fee at the back-end of the deal. More experienced, savvy producers can structure their contracts to earn extra profits or bonuses in addition to their salaries if the project succeeds.

Below-the-Line: Budget Costs

These costs tend to be more predictable, covering the technical crew and their equipment, resources, and standard expenses such as overhead, insurance, and more. Below-the-line personnel can be union or non-union; this depends on whether the company behind the project is a *union signatory*—the production company has agreed to adhere to all the unions' regulations. There are several unions that cover professionals such as writers, directors, actors, camera operators and audio engineers, grips and gaffers, makeup and hair, wardrobe, and others.

A note about unions: Membership in a union doesn't necessarily imply quality or experience, nor does it mean the opposite. It does mean that union members are protected by strict rules that include hours worked, overtime, meals and breaks, benefits, and pension and welfare (P&W). Non-union members can be more flexible with the hours they will work, they aren't paid benefits, and their rates tend to be more negotiable than union members who often are bound by rate scales. Non-union members can be as qualified as union workers, and often, union members will work on non-union jobs.

Costs: Estimated versus Actual

In addition to using one of the two previous formats, the producer(s) keeps a separate budget that shows at a glance two aspects of spending the project's money:

- Estimated costs (what the producer *thinks* a budget item will cost)
- Actual costs (what the item *actually* ends up costing)

On some budget templates, the "estimated column" might be called "budgeted costs." Many budgets add a third column to the right of the first two that lists the "plus or minus" amounts (also called "over and under" or "the variance"). This figure represents the difference between the estimated costs and the "actuals." This plus or minus column provides an instant readout on the running costs, and lets the producer know if the budget is on track or if adjustments need to be made to keep costs in line with the budget.

Estimated Budget Costs

In the early stages of developing your project, you may be asked by a potential buyer or investor for an estimated budget that details the predicted production costs. Drawing up this estimate and putting specific figures on a still-sketchy idea can be a real challenge, especially for a beginning producer. Often the script hasn't been written yet, and there isn't enough hard information as a basis for a budget. If you need to create a rough budget estimate, consider one of the following options:

- Ask about the client's financing parameters. Most are experienced enough in the business, and have an amount in mind that they're willing to spend. For example, they may have only $300,000 to spend, but your budget estimate is $350,000. You might be able to trim your budget down by $50,000, or you can justify the reasons behind your estimate and convince them to raise their offer by $50,000.
- Give the buyer choices: a Plan A budget that reflects everything on your production wish list, and a Plan B budget that covers fewer extra effects, locations, and other items that add to a budget.
- The buyer may be willing to give you a small development fee for expanding your script, research, location scouting, or doing a script breakdown.
- A buyer may be so dedicated to your project that he or she can find additional money from other budgets; others may feel passionate but genuinely not have the funds. Often their commitment to your project can motivate you to pare down your budget as much as possible and to somehow make it work.
- Don't be afraid of walking away. If, for example, a buyer won't budge from a $200,000 offer and you're quite sure that your budget of $300,000 is realistic and professional, you can politely refuse their offer and look elsewhere. The skills of negotiation can be developed over time; meanwhile, an agent or entertainment lawyer can be a tremendous asset in deal-making.

Actual Budget Costs

On this book's web site, you'll find a sample project budget that has several columns. One is labeled "actuals" and the other is labeled "estimated." The figures in the actuals column represent what was *actually* spent, rather than what was originally *estimated* (seen in the other column).

Consider the example of a producer who budgets enough money to cover a three-day shoot on a beach. Suddenly, an unexpected storm shuts down the entire production for all three days. The production has stopped, but the talent and crew are still receiving full pay, by contract. After the storm passes, the producer shoots the necessary scenes for three additional days. In this example, the original estimated costs called for three days of shooting while the actual costs were for six days. This extra time and salary have to be covered in the budget, somehow. Sometimes other areas are padded, or a 10 percent contingency is added to the overall budget.

> You have to know what things cost, because you have to know when you can say yes and when you can say no. We've got $30K to do this, and $30K seems like a lot but then you realize that $30K must cover your travel, your crew, three days of shooting, your transfers, expenses, editing, the mix…you have to know what is in the budget. What is allocated for what portion, and realistically, can it be done?
>
> **John Rosas, excerpt from interview in Chapter 11**

Researching Budgets Costs

Putting a budget together relies heavily on research. The producer must make phone calls, research online sources, compare prices, talk to other producers, and keep up with the industry trends. It also helps to look at other producers' budgets to see how they have calculated their costs.

Almost every item included in a budget can have a low-to-high price range. Say you plan to shoot a TV documentary with a small two-person crew that includes one video camera, various microphones, and their operators. The costs for a professional crew could range from $1,000 to $50,000 per day—literally! In this case, the lower costs would cover a crew that specializes in shooting news, interviews, and documentary material. In the world of high-end commercials and episodics, these costs can be considerably higher.

While budgeting any project, the producer takes all these variables into consideration, with the goal in mind of creating the highest quality product for the least amount of money. He or she finds the best people, equipment, services, and locations, and makes it all work within the budget.

Creating a Working Budget

When you break down your script or your treatment to determine specific factors that contribute to a realistic budget, look for these components:

- Number of preproduction days: To develop the script, scout locations, interview/hire talent and crew
- Number of shooting days: On set and/or on location—what sets are needed, what locations and where, your *shooting ratio* (how much material shot compared to what's actually used in the final version); which talent and crew are working on what days, their costs, equipment rental charges
- Number of postproduction days: Log and screen footage; notes on editing script; plan and complete graphics; overall sound design; edit; the final mix

Budget Templates

An effective budget outlines each and every category involved in every phase of the project. Each category in the budget is known as a *budget line* and each item has its own line on that budget. There's a line for a producer, for props, for equipment rental, for every item.

There is no one standard budget form that's used by all producers but there are several programs (such as EP Budgeting, PointZero, QuickBooks, Movie Magic Budgeting, etc.) that make it easier to budget. Depending on the project, a budget could be under a page, or up to a hundred pages. As previously mentioned, some budgets are separated into above-the-line and below-the-line costs; other budgets are divided into preproduction, production, and postproduction categories. But all budgets must clearly specify what money gets spent, and where.

The Top Sheet

Most longer form budgets begin with a *top sheet*—a brief summary of the project's costs in each department. It gives the producer a valuable overview of the budget at a glance. A blank top sheet, known as the Project Costs Summary form, can be accessed on this book's web site.

The Detailed Budget

A *detailed budget* addresses every aspect of the project's production. Each detail in a script or project translates into a cost that's part of a key budget category, or *account* or *account line*. These accounts include all the departments and all their expenses—salaries, material, equipment, overtime, and more. Budgets tend to be confidential, seldom distributed to anyone but the producer, director, line producer, and/or the production manager. A detailed budget varies in length, depending on the project.

Budget Lines and Categories

When creating a budget for a project, you might include any or all of the following categories:

- **Producers.** Each project has at least one producer with specific responsibilities. The primary producer is usually at the helm of the project from day one, and gets paid until the project is completed. His time must be budgeted for meetings, pitches, and day-to-day development in the beginning, all the way through production and postproduction, and continue through consulting on marketing and distribution at the project's end.

- **Screenplay and/or story rights.** If the script isn't the producer's original script, then she pays for the rights to use someone else's story, script, article, book, or idea.

- **Writer(s).** Regardless of the source of the idea, a writer or team of writers is usually hired to flesh out the idea or refine an existing script.

- **Director.** If you're producing an actor-heavy dramatic project, you may hire a director to work with the actors, similar to a film director who has experience, vision, patience, and the ability to work fast. He may be expensive but can save you money over the long run.

- **Casting Directors and expenses.** Casting involves both principals and extras; expenses involve casting space, taping and equipment, meals, PAs, etc.

- **Actors.** Well-known stars can escalate a budget, but their names attract viewers and sponsors. Unknown actors charge less, and with the right script, director, rehearsal time, and network promotion, they can create a hit show. Minors require extra fees, including on-set tutors, overtime, and other perks. Agency fees are also part of the budget to consider. For union talent, you'll need to add roughly 30 to 35 percent for pension, health, and welfare, FICA, Medicare, FUI, SUI, Workers Comp, and fees for the payroll service company.

- **Talent perks.** Stars often demand extra benefits such as a personal makeup artist, a wardrobe stylist, a physical trainer, special trailers, travel accommodations, secretaries, and nannies.

- **Crew.** A crew can consist of one or two people, or hundreds. It depends on the project as well as any necessary union regulations. Basic personnel might include camera and audio operators and their assistants, a director of photography, assistant director, a prop master, wardrobe designer and supervisor, producing designer, electricians (gaffers), grips, a stylist, a script supervisor, scene artists, set designers, carpenters, still photographers, a location scout, craft service, stock and materials, ambulance or paramedic/nurse on call, a tutor for children, choreographers, stunt coordinators, parking coordinator, catering crew, and others depending on the project. If you're paying the crew through a payroll service rather than as independent contractors, include an additional 18 to 22 percent for each crew member's check for fringe benefits.

- **Staff.** The project usually employs production secretaries, administrative staff, production assistants (PAs), and interns who are assigned to areas in which they're needed.

- **Locations.** Costs for locations can include scouting fees, transportation, hotels for cast and crew, meals, location and permit fees, and equipment rentals. A location can be less expensive than building a set, although locations can have their own challenges: audio problems that can't be controlled such as airplanes, and air conditioners or inadequate electrical power for cables and lights. Foreign locations create additional costs such as varying personnel rates and wages, travel expenses, taxes, and currency exchange rates. However, these costs, when compared to domestic costs, might still be less expensive.

- **Set construction.** Sets can be elaborate and handcrafted, they can be computer-generated, or they can be minimal and simple. Set design can require a production designer, set designer, construction costs, and personnel such as artists, painters, carpenters, and others.
- **Hair and makeup.** The needs of this department depend on the project's talent requirements and size of the cast, including supporting characters, children, and extras. Special effects, such as fake blood or wounds, toupees, hairpieces, or wigs are also taken into account.
- **Wardrobe.** The clothing and costume needs of each actor—from principal actors to background extras—is carefully designed, maintained, and kept track of. This can require a wardrobe designer, supervisor, and often assistants.
- **Period pieces.** Recreating another time period automatically increases the budget in virtually every below-the-line area including locations and sets, wardrobes and props, researchers, and production designers.
- **Special effects.** This category includes extra costs for things like explosions, stunts, smoke, special lighting, car chases, gun shots, and rain. This category might also include animals and picture cars used in the shoot. Additional insurance is also part of the cost.
- **Music and sound effects.** Most programs include show themes and filler music that has been composed especially for the program, as well as additional sound effects and voice-over narration. Occasionally, a sound track or theme song can become a popular hit. For lower budgets, stock music is an excellent alternative.
- **Transportation.** Hauling equipment, cast, and crew from one location to another requires trucks, vans, and other vehicles, along with tolls, parking, gas, insurance, and vehicle maintenance.
- **Equipment.** This general category might include camera and audio equipment, cranes and jibs, walkie-talkies, generators, lighting, fans and air conditioning, tape stock, gas and electric, etc.
- **Meals.** Keeping everyone fed and energized is essential to any production, large or small. Make sure there's at least one full-sized healthy meal per day. Keep a table stocked with healthy snacks and fresh fruit or veggies, a bit of junk food, and refills of coffee, tea, and plenty of water.
- **Security.** In many cases, a production needs security guards to protect equipment, keep talent isolated from fans, for crowd control, and generally to keep an eye on everything.
- **Postproduction.** This area can be cheaper when producers and directors know how to shoot less footage by editing "in their heads," to log and screen their material, and have a game plan for the edit room. Costs include tape transfers, downloading into an editing system, the edit system, the editor, music and sound design and audio mixes and engineers, and graphic elements.
- **Animation.** If a show contains animated portions, or is entirely animated, this budget line can be complex, and might include artists, designers, colorists, software operators, and a variety of other personnel and equipment. Animation studios located in other countries can keep costs down.

Additional Budget Lines

The producer also factors in expenses such as office overhead, petty cash, finance charges, insurance and special riders, and payroll, accounting, and legal costs. Additional expenses could include music licensing, stock footage, stock music, and research fees, transcriptions, and foreign translation.

- **Office overhead.** Whether you're renting an office space or using your apartment as a production office, you've got daily operating expenses. They include rent, electricity, telephone (cells and land lines), faxes, high-speed Internet, copy machines, a DVD and monitor for screening demo reels and your own footage, and basic supplies like paper, pens, and staples. Shipping and messengers can add up, too. The standard overhead fee is 8 to 10 percent, depending on your location.
- **Petty cash.** Get into the habit of keeping track of petty cash. By using a Petty Cash Report form (like the example found on this book's web site), you can keep track of your costs (and receipts) for meals, taxis, tolls, copying scripts, and various odds and ends that can inflate the budget.
- **Finance charges.** If you're paying for anything with a credit card, remember to factor in the monthly interest. That 4 to 21 percent can be significant on a large monthly bill. The same goes for production loans, car leasing, and other costs.
- **Payroll services.** When you make your budget, you'll factor in fringe benefits for crew and talent payroll. You can pay them in one of two ways: the first is through a payroll company who will take out fringes like taxes, workers compensation, and other fees, and charge a payroll service fee. Or, you can pay people as independent contractors. You don't take out any money, and they're paid on a W9.
- **Accounting fees.** Often a production hires an accountant or accounting service to keep track of all daily and weekly costs for the production, and issue regular reports on the budget's progress. The accountant regularly pays all personnel, takes out taxes when necessary; pays the accounts for union costs, agents or managers' percentages, pension and welfare; and pays any other costs.
- **Legal fees.** Attorney fees can be nominal, or they can be significant. Almost all productions require releases and contracts with the creative teams, the talent, the crew, and other personnel, as well as negotiations with sound stages, facilities, and other businesses needed in a production. Although producers can often handle these areas, a lawyer may be brought on board to take care of more complicated issues. Many contracts are simple enough to be drafted by the producer using a deal memo, such as the Crew Deal Memo found on this book's companion web site, as well as additional information in Chapter 5. More complex contracts and negotiations require consultation with an entertainment lawyer. A lawyer can bill by the hour or ask for a flat fee that extends over the project; legal fees generally account for 2 to 3 percent of the budget.
- **Music licensing.** Costs for music can be prohibitive. They could include a composer, lyricist, musicians, and recording studio costs. Factor in licensing fees with the music publisher and the recording company. This can be a real test of patience for the producer; you'll find more in-depth information in Chapter 5 on music rights clearances.
- **Stock footage.** To save the costs of an original musical composition or pre-existing music, producers often rely on stock music that is royalty-free and cost-effective. The same applies for stock film or video footage that has been bought by a stock footage company and can be licensed. You'll find more information in Chapter 9.
- **Research fees.** Depending on the project, a researcher or team of researchers might be an integral part of the process, especially in the case of fact-based programming, documentaries, news, and some reality shows. A researcher can be a staff member or a freelance professional, depending on the complexity of the research needed. Sometimes interns can help—and they're free.
- **Transcription.** Many producers prefer to work with written transcripts of interviews and documentary footage that are word-for-word transcriptions, often with

time-code references. In some cases, a translator may be needed who's also a transcriber.

- **Translation.** Certain projects might require a separate audio track for translating the dialogue into another language. This requires a translator to do the actual translation, a narrator to read it, a director or producer to oversee the audio session, and often subtitles.

- **Advertising and marketing.** Both paid and free publicity is vital to the success of a show. This could include a still photographer to take publicity shots, as well as a publicist to make sure the stills are featured in articles or ads for the project. Other costs could include promos, printing and distributing posters, flyers, direct mail, online, newspaper and magazine advertising, as well as hosting screenings, and entering festivals.

- **Contingencies.** Most productions run into a problem somewhere: the location could fall through at the last minute, an actor gets sick, or the tapes are lost. A professional budget builds in a contingency amount of roughly 10 percent of the budget.

- **Insurance.** As the producer, you must absolutely protect your production and yourself with insurance. It's a necessity: you could lose everything from one lawsuit. All independent producers and production companies protect themselves with a Comprehensive General Liability insurance policy that includes liability and workers' compensation.

In most U.S. cities and states, a Certificate of Insurance (COI) is necessary to get a shooting permit. Often, a one million dollar minimum is required. Insurance coverage can cost from $3,000 and up per year, depending on what and where you're shooting; some entertainment insurance companies are willing to insure a production by the day or for the duration of the project. Globally, insurance costs and legal requirements for insurance vary considerably. Insurance for your specific project could include:

- **General liability.** Protects you against claims of bodily injury, property damage, and vehicular damage that's additional to auto insurance. You might also add riders or special coverage for stunts, explosions, cast insurance, props and sets, extra expenses, third-party property damage, equipment loss or damage, faulty stock, faulty cameras or audio equipment, excess liability, union insurance, animal injury or death, and more.

- **Workers' compensation.** Covers temporary or permanent loss of cast or crew (whether they're hired on a temporary or permanent basis), and pays for hospital and medical, disability, and possible death benefits. The rates depend on the nature of the work.

- **Entertainment package.** In addition to the insurance policies, producers can also cover their project with extra insurance riders that protect against bad stock, lost or damaged camera masters, video or film processing, lost or damaged props, sets, equipment, wardrobe, extra expenses, and third-party damage. Other coverage includes bad weather, demands by an actor, excess liability, aircraft and watercraft, animals, vehicles, political risks, and unique sets or props.

- **Errors and Omission insurance (E&O).** Insurance that protects the production against lawsuits involving authorship and copyright issues such as plagiarism, unauthorized use of ideas, characters, titles, formats, or plots. It also covers invasion of privacy, slander, libel or character defamation, and copyright infringement. It defines a clear chain of title: who wrote what, and when, and who ultimately owns any rights to any aspects of your project.

- *Institutional and educational insurance.* In some cases a college, university, or public or private school might provide insurance coverage for enrolled students' class productions. This includes general liability insurance, as well as insurance for video and audio equipment and third-party property. This insurance seldom covers a project that is shot in a foreign location, uses explosives or moving vehicles, depends on stunts, or other liability-prone components.

> There is a bundle of insurance coverage that a picture needs. It needs liability insurance, it needs property insurance, general liability if you smash your camera through someone's plate glass window, or if someone trips over a cable, or if you've rented a car and have an accident during production. Then, there is producers' liability, or Errors and Omissions, that protects against claims arising out of the content and copyright trademark, and libel and privacy claims. Insurance is a big item.
>
> **J. Stephen Sheppard, excerpt from interview in Chapter 11**

Hiring Union versus Non-Union Talent

There are pros and cons to each option. **Union members** are generally assumed to be professionals with experience. However, unions dictate specific rates and rules for working conditions to which producers and the union member must adhere. There is also extra paperwork, and payments such as P&W, benefits, and other costs.

Non-union talent and crew can be as experienced and professional as union members without the restrictions of a union governing their work. Producers often pay their non-union crew the same rates as they would pay a union member, without having to deal with paying benefits or doing extra paperwork.

Often, union members will work on a non-union production, although they can be in violation of their union depending on the situation. There are several unions that a producer may deal with, depending on the circumstances of the production. These unions can be found on the Internet, and include:

- Writers Guild of America (WGA)
- Directors Guild of America (DGA)
- Screen Actors Guild (SAG)
- American Federation of Television and Radio Actors (AFTRA)
- National Association of Broadcast Employees and Technicians-Communications Workers of America (NABET-CWA)
- International Alliance of Theatrical Stage Employees (IATSE)

III. FIND THE FINANCING

In some projects, it's up to the producer to bring in the financing. It can be challenging for even a veteran producer to secure enough money to develop and complete a quality project.

Possible Sources for Funding Your Project

Once you have created a rough budget for your project, you can now focus on raising the funds you need. As you'll learn in Chapter 6, one of the more effective tools is a solid *business proposal* that you can offer to potential financing sources who could include:

- *Private investors.* You can approach people you know—friends, family, coworkers, fellow students, neighbors. Or, you can find business people you've never met who see the economic promise in your idea, are looking for tax advantages, or simply an ego boost. Ideally, your project will be successful, and your investors can see a return on their initial investment. But you don't want to promise anything that can't be delivered. Assure investors that you will do your best to pay back their good faith in you, if not their monetary investment. Some investors are happy simply to be on set and watch the shoot, or to get a small walk-on part in return for their investment.

- **Grants.** Grants are a source of money that could prove beneficial in funding phases of your project, such as the initial research, writing, and/or postproduction; some may cover the entire budget. Grants are awarded by public and private foundations. You'll find more information on grants in Chapter 10 and on this book's web site under Grants and Funding.

- **Public foundations.** Various categories of financial aid and grants are given out to filmmakers, depending on the nature of their project. Organizations like the National Endowment for the Humanities (NEH), National Endowment of the Arts (NEA), the National Science Foundation (NSF), and the American Film Institute (AFI) are better-known sources, though each state and local government also offers funds for projects that fit their grant's requirements. These sources are listed on the web site.

- **Private foundations.** Most large corporations earmark specific funds to support projects in the public interest, and not by accident, to elevate their own public image. They may fund part or all of a project, or underwrite projects that they want to be associated with. Public television might air a special or a series that is partially or fully sponsored by a public or private foundation.

- **Bank loans.** Avoid investing your own money if you can. However, if you're determined to make your project, and you know that you can pay the loan back later with interest, it might be possible to get a bank loan if your credit allows. If not, the bank will require a cosigner or collateral such as a car, house, or something else of value that you own.

- **Credit cards.** You may have a healthy credit rating and can afford to take out a cash advance to pay for production costs. But before you do this, add up the extra interest costs on the advance, and be sure that you can cover the payments. You don't want to lose your valuable credit rating if you can find another financing source.

Options for Self-Funding

Depending on the project you're developing, you may choose to bypass the more traditional approaches and produce it yourself, owning and controlling it. This approach is risky, of course. It could deplete your savings and ruin your credit. Or it could be a risk that totally pays off.

Producers can subsidize their projects with their own money. Or, they can find investors, corporate sponsorship, foundation grants, bank loans, donations, barter goods, or exchange services. For smaller budgets, producers put together fundraisers and online auctions, sell stocks, throw keg parties, and come up with imaginative and creative ways to pull together the money.

Make a list of the people who could help you. Be clear about what you need. You may want them to finance your entire project, or simply to cover development or postproduction costs. Maybe they can donate their services (like set construction or seamstress) or give you food to feed the crew, or props or wardrobe or transportation.

In many cases, people will exchange goods and services for a courtesy credit or special thanks at the end of the show. You can also offer *deferred payment*, giving them an agreed-upon sum if your project hits a specified profit point down the line.

Your list of potential contributors could include any of these people or organizations:

- Family and relatives
- Friends
- Other writers and producers
- Fellow students
- Former elementary or high school students
- Coworkers
- Independent TV/film/new media volunteer organizations
- Writers
- Directors
- Producers
- Lawyers
- Agents
- Managers
- Investment brokers
- Actors
- Restaurant or deli owners
- Local stores
- National chains
- Social networking sites

Bartering, Clever Negotiation, and Tips to Save Money

An effective producer can call in favors when necessary, knows how to negotiate and barter, and cuts costs wherever possible while still maintaining quality. Here are just a few creative directions you can consider as alternatives to spending real money.

Negotiation

A producer can often negotiate better rates. Few unions will agree to lower the rates for their members, but there may be exceptions. Sometimes non-union actors, crews, writers, and directors, as well as equipment rental houses and postproduction facilities may be willing to negotiate. Offering them the employment security of several days or weeks of work can provide an incentive for reduced daily or weekly rates, or a flat fee for the duration of the project. Some people are willing to work for half-day rates. Another potential area of negotiation involves product placement, in which a product is placed in such a way that it's visible to the viewer, and integrated into the scene. A fee is paid for this service.

IN THE TRENCHES...

As anyone can attest who's been working in this business for awhile, it ain't what it used to be. Back in the day, there was generous money for budgets, more relaxed shooting schedules, nice perks we could count on—a free lunch, if you will. Now, in our current economy, every client expects more work for less money, shorter shooting schedules, adjustable to all delivery systems, and an end product that's brilliant.

And as a professional, it's my job to do all that with a smile. So I do a lot of negotiating, haggling, and gentle wheedling. I talk to editing facilities and sound stages and equipment rental companies to negotiate a better deal, while looking for alternative companies with even lower rates. If I'm working with unions, I bring the truth to the table and try to reach common ground on fees, fringe benefits, hours and days, and

(Continued)

other areas I could save money on. In hiring crew and talent, they're told right away that we're not rich, here's the fee I can offer, though we enjoy our work, have a good time and are always fed. I'm not afraid to ask—politely and respectfully—while being totally prepared that they might well say 'no.' It has been my overall experience that, in almost every situation, there's a middle ground on which we can all feel financially and ethically comfortable. In the rare situations in which there is a more generous budget, I always make sure it's distributed to the people who deserve it.

~C. Kellison

Deferred Payment

A project may have a modest budget but everyone involved wants it to succeed. To save money, a producer might offer a *deferred payment* to some or all of the people involved. This means that when (or if) the project eventually makes money, all who agreed to defer their salaries are paid when it makes money later, often with interest or bonuses on top of their original salary agreement.

Courtesy Credits

A producer can often negotiate with airlines, hotels, restaurants, and other providers of goods and services, simply by giving them an acknowledgement in the end credits of the program. For example, you might see "round trip travel provided by British Airways," or "hotel accommodations provided by Marriott Hotels." These are known as *courtesy credits*.

Money Back

Occasionally, after the shooting has been completed, a project may end up with items that can be sold for cash, returned for refunds, or exchanged for services. Items might include unused stock, wardrobe, props, furniture, plants, equipment, building materials, wall hangings, furniture, and more.

In-Kind Donations

An inventive producer can save substantial costs in the budget by asking for donations of goods or services. Some classic examples of *in-kind* donations that are offered either at a lower rate or for free include no-fee locations, food and beverages from a restaurant or grocery store, vehicles, software, supplies, film or digital stock, and more. Legal and accounting services, databases and computers, telephone and Internet, and postproduction facilities are other in-kind services. This generosity is traditionally rewarded with a *courtesy credit*, which acknowledges and thanks the contributors by listing their names or businesses in the project's closing credits.

Student Budgets and Resources

Many students can take advantage of resources their school offers, either as part of full-time tuition or for a single continuing-education class. These resources might include video and audio equipment, allotments of video stock, editing equipment, graphics tools, music libraries, and possibly extra student labor.

A student can often benefit from the school's tax-exempt status and liability insurance. Students might also qualify for lower student rates that could apply to van or car rentals, travel, and meals by joining various filmmaking collectives and organizations that offer student membership rates. Several professional unions, like SAG, Actors Equity, and AFTRA may give students concessions on rates for student projects made under the auspices of an accredited school. Many editing and audio facilities and businesses provide student rates for software programs, as well as original music, or stock music and stock footage.

Usually these resources for students come with specific guidelines, and must be made only for use in the classroom or to be shown in student festivals. A SAG actor, for example, may work on a student film under special union exemptions, but if the film is purchased for broadcast or offered for sale, the rates must be renegotiated at a professional level.

Students can often benefit by affiliation with:

- School-sponsored grants, awards, and sponsorships
- Private investors like friends and family
- Professional business investors
- Festivals
- Public and private foundation grants

ON A HUMAN LEVEL . . .

Feeling comfortable with the budgeting process can be daunting, especially in the beginning. Your original idea seems to pale in the dark shadow of a dollars-and-sense scenario. The reality of money can dampen your initial enthusiasm and even create an urge to back off the project altogether. It's common to have "math anxiety" over budgets, or to become impatient. Refine your organizational skills and understand the value of details. Stick with it, and know that even the most experienced producers, no matter how good they are, share your feelings.

SUMMARY

The only thing more challenging than finding the money is managing it, once it comes in. Creating a budget and sticking to it takes discipline, ingenuity, experience, and patience. Each project brings its own requirements and frustrations, and mistakes. Yet each also brings you closer to mastering the skills of budgeting. As you become more familiar with the budgeting process, your next challenge is to explore the legalities of the project. The next chapter guides you through the legal odyssey.

REVIEW QUESTIONS

1. What is the first element of "reality" that you must consider when developing a project?

2. What is the purpose of a production book? A breakdown sheet? A storyboard?

3. Define *cross-boarding*. Give an example of its use.

4. Identify the key differences between hiring union and non-union crew employees.

5. What are estimates versus actuals? Why is it helpful to track both throughout a project?

6. What is a budget top sheet?

7. What are three areas in which a lawyer can be of assistance to your project?

Welcome to Reality:
Legalities and Rights

Let us never negotiate out of fear. But let us never
fear to negotiate.

John F. Kennedy

THIS CHAPTER'S TALKING POINTS

I. Own It

II. If you Don't Own It, Get Permission to Use It

III. Protect It

IV. Double-Check It

I. OWN IT

Your idea is a precious commodity. For it to develop, thrive, and ultimately succeed, this idea must be protected. It's the producer's responsibility to provide this legal protection. With a common-sense understanding of entertainment law, and an awareness of the contracts, agreements, and rules that are integral in each stage of producing your project, you can provide this protection. A deal can start with a hearty handshake and a verbal promise, but ultimately you want to make sure it's backed up with solid legal documentation.

This chapter explores the legal side of producing. Its purpose is to offer many of the legal basics that every producer should know. However, it is simply a guide, and a beginning producer should also consult other sources for backup or additional information: an experienced entertainment attorney, books and resources, publications, the Internet, or a legal aid service for further in-depth legal and business information. This book's web site also provides a number of resources, including an assortment of templates for legal agreements and releases.

In this chapter, we explore the primary legal aspects involved in producing—owning or optioning the story material in your project, protecting the many components of your project, and then double-checking all these elements. When you've done all this, you have given your idea, and yourself, legal protection and the freedom to move forward.

IN THE TRENCHES...

As a producer, I'm always looking for a good idea—either of my own or from someone else. So when I received a DVD that had been recommended by a respected colleague, I popped it into my computer. Right away, I saw that it was pretty damned good. The producer had traveled into the bowels of the NYC subway system and interviewed dozens of buskers, musicians who make their living performing in the subway. He shot footage of them playing, talking to their fans, relaxing at home. It was well-lit, sounded really good, the musicians were fascinating and driven, and the edit had a flow to it. I saw some real talent here. My excitement was palpable—I'd already decided who to pitch this to, maybe developing it into a longer piece, even a series. I called the producer, a bright young man who clearly had passion for his project. "So, you've cleared everyone, right?" Long pause. "Excuse me?" he said. "You got signed releases from everyone on camera, right?" The answer was No. He'd never thought of it, didn't know it had to be done. Without those releases, his piece was dead to me. Maybe he could track everyone down to have them sign releases retroactively, but probably not. In spite of his enthusiasm for his vision, he had failed to protect it.

~C. Kellison

The Entertainment Lawyer

Whether you are new to producing or have years of experience, you want a strong alliance with an entertainment lawyer. He can help protect you and your project before you enter into any kind of binding agreement. Entertainment law is highly specialized, and a certified entertainment lawyer is not only competent in state and federal law, but is also familiar with the complex wording of contracts, releases, agreements, and dozens of other legal documents.

In addition to reviewing the legal documents involved in your production, some entertainment lawyers can be a big help in pitching projects or making valuable connections with financing sources, production companies, directors, even talent. She can open doors for you by sending an introductory cover letter to the networks, studios, and production companies. Most executives won't take a pitch unless they know that you have legal representation. And if your agent or other representative sells your work, the lawyer subsequently drafts and coordinates the contracts.

Lawyers get paid in several ways: by the hour, by the project, for a flat fee, or as an ongoing line in the project's budget. Some lawyers might take a lump sum up front, either as a *retainer* (not used toward any fees; this money is paid simply to retain the lawyer), or as an *advance* that the lawyer works off on an hourly fee basis. Discuss the fee structure with your lawyer at the beginning of the first meeting, and come prepared with a list of questions. Each minute you waste costs money. Whatever the amount, sound legal advice is worth the investment and could save your project significant costs down the line. In many ways, the entertainment lawyer could make the difference between your project's success and its failure.

If you can't fit the cost of an entertainment attorney into your budget, look for a legal aid organization in your area. You might consult with universities that have legal departments, or contact groups such as the Volunteer Lawyers for the Arts. There are boilerplate contracts available in books, articles, and information online; many can be customized for your project. There are also contract examples, and web site resources listed on the web site for this book.

Intellectual Property Law

For producers, virtually every project involves an aspect of intellectual property that is covered by a set of laws. Any product of the human intellect—a creation of the mind—that is unique and has some value in the marketplace falls under the term, *intellectual property* (or IP). This includes literary works, music, sculpture and art, inventions, images and symbols, and unique names, as well as publicity rights, unfair competition, and misappropriation. In essence, intellectual property rights allow an artist the freedom to be creative with the promise of ownership that protects his or her work from being used by others without compensation or recognition.

It's important to understand that each country is bound by its own IP laws. Just because one country operates under a specific set of laws by no means assumes that other countries follow suit. There is no sole worldwide copyright law, for example; each country has its own set of laws. And because the laws vary widely from country to country, we focus primarily on American laws and on some British law in this book. Readers living in other countries can consult their local legal experts and sources. In America, intellectual property law includes:

- *Copyright law.* Protects creative or artistic expression of an idea
- *Trademark law.* Protects distinctive symbols used in relation to services or products
- *Patent law.* Protects inventions

Copyright Law

Maybe you've got a great idea for a TV show: some college kids live together; their daily experiences are filled with fun, romance, and conflict. OK. So far, it's just an idea, and not a particularly original one. Anyone can use it. This rough idea is the *core creative concept* at its most basic.

But when you define the number and gender of the students (three British guys, two American girls and one Indian girl), give them specific names and background stories and individual characteristics, put them in a four-bedroom converted carriage house in Camden Town in north London, and then write a defined script that fleshes out these details, you've created the *expression* of this core idea. It's this expression—the script with its details—that is protected by copyright.

A copyright protects works that have been created and preserved in any tangible form of expression—such as written works, video and film, photography, music, multimedia, software, drama, pantomime, choreography, motion pictures, and sound recordings. It's a right that is granted to the author or creator of "original works of authorship," and includes having the exclusive rights to exploit his or her copyrighted work, with the sole privilege of multiplying copies, publishing, and selling them.

Copyright Protection

Essentially, once you have translated your idea from your mind onto a fixed medium, like a piece of paper, a canvas, computer, photograph, videotape or tape recorder, it's automatically copyrighted; it doesn't necessarily require official copyright registration to protect rights of the copyright holder. The advantage of officially registering a copyright (see later) is that it provides specific evidence of its valid exact copyright dates and ownership, and gives the copyright holder (the artist) an advantage in seeking statutory damages, loss of profit, and/or attorney's fees.

Copyright Symbol

The symbol of a copyrighted work is © and should be affixed to anything you write, produce, draw, compose, and create. A copyright forbids only actual direct copying. If a writer or musician creates work that has an idea similar to, but not an exact copy of, someone else's, it will generally not be considered an infringement of someone else's copyright. It can only be the actual expression of that idea that's protected.

Copyright Terms

The terms of most American copyrights now last for the lives of the authors plus 70 years after their death. Most films and stills that are less than 95 years old are also copyright protected—the best way to verify a copyright is to do a copyright search with the Library of Congress. Copyrights that have expired allow those works to fall into the *public domain* (meaning they are no longer protected by copyright law and can be freely adapted). Many producers and writers have adapted or overtly copied the works of major writers, artists, and musicians available from this rich repository—the public domain.

However, not everything can be copyrighted. Only the expression of a creative or artistic idea can be protected. Ideas, titles, themes, or general concepts aren't protected by copyright law until they are written down, videotaped, painted, or somehow made tangible. Facts are also unable to be copyrighted. You can't copyright the facts of a person's life or an historical event, but you can copyright your *expression* of that idea—the script you have written about the person or the event. Rights are usually not necessary when your project involves a public or historical figure, although there are always exceptions.

The area of copyright law is a complex one, riddled with legal potholes, so should you have any doubts about who holds the copyright to a work you're interested in, it will save you valuable time and money—and potential lawsuits later—to verify its legal rights holders early in the process.

Work-for-Hire Clause

In both America and the United Kingdom, a producer or writer or other creative who is employed by a network, a production company, or other media employer is usually working under a *work-for-hire* agreement. This states that the employer owns the copyright to the work that the employee developed while in their employment. This is the usual trade-off when the employer does the hiring and pays the bills. In some cases, the producer can negotiate for revenues from foreign broadcast rights, syndication, home video rights, merchandising, books and publishing, and other possible bonuses, depending on the terms of the employment contract.

Once a work has actually been created, and translated into tangible form (book, film, portrait, still), it is considered legally protected. When a copyright notice © is attached, this requires that anyone wanting to use your work must contact you for licensing fees and permissions. To copyright your work in America, call the U.S. Copyright Office in Washington, D.C. at (800) 688.9889, or register your work online at www.copyright.gov. The fee to register is under $50.

Copyright in the Digital Age

We suddenly find ourselves in the midst of the digital age. We are not only producing our programming digitally, we're also transmitting it through a multitude of digital delivery systems. We're no longer limited to traditional television broadcasting in thinking about ways to express ourselves through digital media.

People who were previously satisfied to just be passive viewers, are now actively contributing their ideas in tangible form to the thousands of online sites that feature *user generated content* (UGC). The legal parameters for online material are being closely studied and scrutinized by lawyers, producers, traditional networks and cable channels who are setting up online tributaries, music providers, and others. This rapid expansion has created new and challenging legal scenarios for both content providers and content deliverers; at the moment, several factions of legal experts, seasoned filmmakers, and producers are looking closely at best practices for these intellectual property laws and their applications in these new digital territories.

Fair Use Defense

Under its terms, the Copyright Act allows for some legal exceptions to U.S. trademark and copyright laws, situations in which copyrighted material can be used without the copyright holder's permission. This clause is known as *fair use*. When a producer uses another person's copyrighted material—like a film clip or video footage, art, photographs, or music—in specific circumstances, the producer isn't required to have the copyright owner's permission. The producer can claim the defense of fair use, which declares that the work has been used in a reasonable, "fair" manner that poses no competition to the copyright holder's finances or reputation.

The fair use defense is generally claimed when the public interest is served. This can apply to news reporting, review, analysis and criticism, teaching or scholarship, or as commentary. One example is the use of a short music segment or a film clip in a documentary or a news piece. Fair use often applies in parodies of material, either to make a social comment or for humorous effect; it's usually considered fair use if it's clear that the parody is just that—a parody.

But fair use may not always apply, and it can easily be misused or misinterpreted. As included as part of the Copyright Act of 1976, there are four determining factors under which the fair use defense can be considered. These factors include:

- The purpose and character of the use, including whether such use is of a commercial nature or is for nonprofit educational purposes
- The nature of the original copyrighted work
- The amount and substantiality of the portion used in relation to the copyrighted work as a whole
- The effect of the use upon the potential market or value of the copyrighted work

Fair Use for Documentary Filmmakers

In November of 2005, a statement of best practices in fair use was released after long discussion, debate, and research. The study was compiled by an impressive group of legal experts, scholars, filmmakers, universities, and media-based organizations. *Documentary Filmmakers' Statement of Best Practices in Fair Use* (centerforsocialmedia.org/fairuse) was born of the frustration felt by documentarians who, when they finally located the right footage that could best tell their story, weren't legally allowed to use it. Either the copyright holder would not give permission, the licensing fees were exorbitant, or the copyright holder could not be located, despite all efforts.

This group organized their thinking around four classes of situations that filmmakers consistently deal with in every phase of production. In each case, it's possible to apply the fair use defense; they include:

- Employing copyrighted material as the object of social, political, or cultural critique
- Quoting copyrighted works of popular culture to illustrate an argument or point

- Capturing copyrighted media content in the process of filming something else
- Using copyrighted material in a historical sequence

Fair Use in the Digital Domain

The previous statement provided succinct guidelines for documentary filmmakers. In 2008, another statement was released by the Center for Social Media and the Program on Information Justice and Intellectual Property that provides similar situations of the fair use defense for online content producers.

This study, called *Recut, Reframe, Recycle: Quoting Copyrighted Material in User-Generated Video*, outlines its methodology and research results, including in-depth details and provocative examples of the nine categories in which the fair use clause might apply. The easy-to-understand study can be found at centerforsocialmedia.org/recut along with specific examples for each of the following nine categories in which fair use can be considered, under the U.S. Copyright law itself, to encourage the production of culture:

    I. Satire and Parody
    II. Negative or Critical Commentary
    III. Positive Commentary
    IV. Quoting to Trigger Discussion
    V. Illustration or Example
    VI. Incidental Use
    VII. Personal Reportage or Diaries
    VIII. Archiving of Vulnerable or Revealing Materials
    IX. Pastiche or Collage

Fair Use in User-Generated Content

As the name suggests, UGC (user-generated content) is produced by amateur filmmakers, with a smattering of professionally produced content, and is contributed to an online UGC site by anyone with the skills, time, and the right equipment. Another description for UGC videos is viral videos—videos that are clever, evocative, edgy, informative, or in some way have spread virally, by word of mouth and email. There are literally billions of UGC videos spiraling through cyberspace and being shared in every language and in every country.

In the fair use study, the nine elements have the potential to help cover all UGC with the fair use defense. For example, the viral video "If Dick Cheney Was Scarface" is cited as an example of copyrighted content used for satirical purposes—that protects it as fair use. The famous "Evolution of Dance" viral video is cited as an example of copyrighted music and dance footage being reused for illustrated purposes, protecting it under fair use as well.

Avoiding Copyrighted Material

To protect themselves against possible copyright or trademark infringement, some producers insist on blurring out recognizable logos, artwork or posters on the wall behind an actor, brand names on a T-shirt, or products with obvious logos. If they're given a choice between one piece of footage or music that is copyrighted versus a better one that isn't cleared, producers might take the safer legal route. Their understandable paranoia often constricts their creative and narrative reach, yet they feel they must play it safe. Quality and passion for the project is sacrificed as a result.

Because fair use is an area of the law that's consistently ambiguous, it's currently under close scrutiny by producers and broadcasters. It raises important issues of free speech and creative freedom, especially in the United States in relation to the concept of Free Speech. Fair use is actually a defense to a finding of copyright infringement, an assurance that the defense is valid and legal. It's always prudent to consult an entertainment lawyer who has experience with issues of fair use; she can often negotiate rights for a lower fee, or can assure the network or insurer that your fair use claim is valid and legal.

The concept of fair use can be speculative. Most U.S. networks, distributors, and Errors & Omission (E&O) insurers require that the producer provides documentation that protects them from possible lawsuits or copyright infringement arguments. Insurers aren't risk takers by nature, and if there's litigation, it's up to the producer/defendant to prove that the use of the copyrighted material was indeed fair, and not a copyright infringement. The cost of legal fees can be so exorbitant that it dissuades producers from using material that legitimately falls under the fair use defense.

Conversely, taking risks can prove successful, and much cheaper than paying research fees and licensing costs. The nature of our litigious society can be daunting, and the creative rights of artists, filmmakers, composers, and others linger in a legal abyss as dedicated people with true conviction on both sides battle it out. An increasing number of filmmakers are willing to test the limits of fair use in order to preserve their freedom of expression.

The Digital Millennium Copyright Act (DMCA) was passed in 1998. Its intent is to monitor, filter, and protect online platform providers (such as social networking sites and user-generated content sites, later) from litigation, allowing them to promptly remove content if its copyright has been infringed upon.

Currently, two Internet areas in particular have attracted great attention, and both deserve closer scrutiny:

> ***Social network sites.*** These online sites provide a forum for social networking, connecting people with one another via pictures, music, video, blogs and video logs, message boards, and music. Facebook.com and MySpace.com are currently the two most popular sites.
>
> ***User-generated content sites.*** Content that is either the original creation of someone, or has been re-edited from other sources, makes up the majority of user generated content sites, such as YouTube and hundreds of others that pop up each week on the internet.

Let's say... that you videotape your best friend dancing to the hit song of the week, recorded by a world-famous pop diva. Then you place that video on your MyFace page without getting the diva's permission. Bingo. You've violated this song's copyright laws. If the diva should be browsing your MyFace page and sees that you've used her song without permission, she has the right to contact her lawyer, who then contacts the designated agent for MyFace. The lawyer provides information that proves the diva's rights, and MyFace removes your content, advising you that your video has been removed due to copyright infringement. You can protest their decision, and the diva has 10 to 14 days to file a lawsuit. If she decides to let it go, MyFace may then put your video back up on your MyFace page. Or, you start all over at the new YourPlace network and bring your friends along with you.

Trademark

The overall purpose of a trademark is to protect the consumer—to distinguish one product and/or service from another. An organization, individual, or other legal entity may choose a name, a word, a phrase, a symbol, design, logo, image, or combination of any of these components and simply use it. It can also be filed with the U.S. Patent and Trademarks Office, which further protects the holder in any formal procedures. When it is registered, the holder can use the symbol, ®. You can check this out further at http://www.uspto.gov.

The indication of a trademark is the symbol connected to it (™). A trademark includes any word, symbol, name, or device that distinguishes certain products, services, or items from another like it. Trademarks serve as a source of origin: you may prefer Heinz catsup, or Kellogg's cereals, or Cadbury's chocolates—each is identified with an aspect of quality assurance. Brands, consumer goods, even buildings and well-known landmarks can be trademarked. So can a movie title. In almost all cases, you don't need permission from the trademark holder if a trademarked item appears in your piece. If, on the other hand, you plan to refer to this trademarked object in a negative or derogatory way, they may pursue legal avenues to either make you stop, to charge licensing fees, or to slap you with a lawsuit. To check if something is trademarked (or patented, as discussed next), check with the U.S. Patent and Trademark Office.

Patent

When the U.S. Patent and Trademark Office grants a patent to an inventor in America, it gives the right to the inventor to prevent other people from making, using, offering to sell or selling, or importing the invention. It can be a machine, a process, manufactured article, and must be new, inventive, useful, and/or industrially applicable. The term of a U.S. patent is usually 20 years from the date on which the application for the patent was filed. Patent laws and clearances are seldom an issue in television or new media production.

Public Domain

After the U.S. copyright of material expires, it usually falls into a free use area known as the *public domain*. There is an appreciable amount of available literary material, music, photography, and other artistic expression that is no longer protected by copyright and can be freely used by producers. This material includes works by literally hundreds of authors, artists, composers, lyricists, and others.

Public domain material is appealing to producers and broadcasters because the rights to use it are free. However, although the material itself may be in the public domain, it may have been adapted or used by someone else, and that expression of the original work has been copyrighted. For example, the music of Chopin is in the public domain, but if the London Philharmonic Orchestra records it with their arrangement, their musicians, and their unique interpretation, they own the copyright and their recording cannot be used without their permission. Your option is to record the music of Chopin with your own musicians, only paying them and not the composer. Make sure any work you might be considering falls completely and legally within the public domain status. You'll usually need to show documentation of this clearance as a requirement for getting production insurance.

Orphan Work

A producer isn't always able to locate the holder of the copyright for a film clip or piece of music. Sometimes, it isn't clear if the material actually falls into the public domain category. This kind of undeclared material is known as *orphan work*, and creates a legal nightmare for the producer. There is potential risk in using this material without permission, but if the producer has genuinely pursued all avenues available to find the copyright holder—and provides clear documentation and backup of all efforts and intent—that can be strong proof of diligence if there are legal ramifications later.

Writers Guild of America Registration

Producers and writers often protect their work by registering it with the Writers Guild of America (WGA), the primary union for television and film writers. Registering thousands of scripts each year, the WGA registration establishes the completion date of a literary property, which includes written treatments, outlines, synopses, and full scripts that have been written for radio, theatrical, television, motion picture, DVDs, video cassettes/discs, and interactive new media. The registration provides a dated record "of the writer's claim to authorship" of the registered literary material. WGA, similar to copyrights, cannot protect a title. This registration is valid for up to five years, and it can be renewed for another five years. A non-WGA member can register a script for a small fee. Check the organization's web site, www.wga.org, for more details.

Poor Man's Registration

In this scenario, a writer finishes her script, puts it in an envelope and seals it, takes it to the post office and sends it to herself via registered mail, keeping it unopened. She's now confident that she can prove when, and where, she established the origin of her work.

Wrong. This is an urban myth, and U.S. courts don't recognize this method of proving ownership or date and time of its origin. To prevent any litigation, you're best to register your project at www.copyright.gov. In some countries such as the United Kingdom and the Netherlands, however, this "poor man's registration" has a bit more legitimacy and is recognized in some courtroom dealings. A copyright is a better alternative.

II. IF YOU DON'T OWN IT, GET PERMISSION TO USE IT

In the course of the life of a project, you have to start dealing with third parties, with other people. If a book, for example, is going to be the basis of a movie, or if there is somebody's story, somebody's life rights, or if you need to get particular access to a building or certain circumstances, these are all obvious triggers for a conversation with a lawyer. When you start dealing with third parties, you have to make arrangements with them, and you have to get certain rights or permissions or clearances from them. That's when it probably makes sense to start talking to a lawyer and make sure that you are getting what you need and that you are not getting more than you need—not getting taken to the cleaners.

J. Stephen Sheppard, excerpt from interview in Chapter 11

If you didn't create your project idea, it is owned by someone else. If you want to use it, you first have to get permission. Permission to use it might be granted for free or for a fee, and for a specified amount of time. This applies to almost every aspect of your project: the script, the music, clips, images, photographs, products with brand names, props, and more. It is the job of the producer to legally protect every single component with some form of permission attached.

Licensing

When a body of work—a screenplay, a drawing, a piece of music—has been copyrighted, the rights to use it in a project must be either paid for outright or *licensed* for a fee. The producer (or the producer's employer) pays a fee for the right to use this copyrighted material. The financial involvements and legal aspects of licensing are highly complex; they cover artist representations and credits, copyright, promotional approvals, and much more. We will explore some of the primary areas of licensing, next, as you continue to research updated information and changes, even consult with legal experts, in the ever-evolving landscapes of digital and new media.

Brand licensing can also be a highly lucrative opportunity for a producer. A cooking show, for example, sells the license of the show to spin off other shows for its host, cook books, cooking magazines and web sites, a line of food items or cooking tools—all bearing the brand of the cooking show.

However, the area of licensing is a highly specialized area. It requires specific contracts, including elements of exclusivity, duration of use, definition of media, insurance, and more. In addition to talking with an entertainment lawyer, producers can consult with a company that specializes in rights and clearances. Both are experts whose advice is almost mandatory when considering the area of licensing.

Literary Rights and Clearances

Your storyline might rely on the use of material such as books, online research material, manuscripts, articles, treatments, outlines, newspaper columns or stories, and biographies and autobiographies, as well as adaptations, theatrical plays, or public performance rights. If you don't control all the rights involved in your project, you have no legal foundation upon which you can develop it. You will need to either:

- *Option the rights.* Negotiate for exclusive, limited rights to the project in return for a fee or agreement.
- *Buy the rights.* Negotiate to buy and permanently own all ownership rights.

> **Let's say…** that you have a novel you want to adapt into a two-hour network broadcast special. Your first step is to contact the author's publisher, agent, or attorney, or, if the author has died, the representative of the author's estate. Then, you'll write a compelling letter that outlines your project and the significance of the requested material to your project. You may want to option the material for a limited period of time (six months to two years, for example) so you can generate interest, raise funds, and develop the project. Or, you may want to buy it outright, in perpetuity, and hold worldwide rights for all media. Both options are open to negotiation and require discussion between you, your attorney, and the holder of the copyright.

Music Rights and Clearances

Most producers thoroughly appreciate the impact that music can have on a project: an identifiable theme for the show's opening credits, mood music through the show itself, end music for the closing credits. Music can inject suspense or humor or sorrow, and is yet another expression of your creative vision.

But music can be legal quicksand for a producer. Unless you are using original music that has been scored especially for your project, you must get *clearance*, or permission, for *a license* that grants you the right to use any preexisting musical compositions and recordings that are owned by someone else. If your music hasn't been licensed, it could mean delays, lawsuits, and even the possible termination of your project. For music rights clearances, by all means check either with an entertainment lawyer or with a music clearance service.

In almost every country, music falls under that country's specific copyright protection. It falls on the producer (or a music clearance service or lawyer) to determine who owns the copyright, to negotiate for permission with the copyright owner to use it, and to pay the fees that are necessary to get the clearances. Some of the larger networks and cable channels have blanket license agreements, though these agreements don't cover each and every piece of music; each still needs to be researched.

Music Licenses

There are two kinds of music licenses in the United States. Most pre-existing and/or recorded music requires that you get both:

- *A Sync (synchronization) license.* Gives you the right to "sync up" or match a song or music to your visual image. The publisher represents the composer of the music (the person who wrote and/or arranged the music) and the song-writer (the person who wrote the lyrics, if any). The publisher owns and grants the right to include the actual composition or piece of music that is synchronized to the picture. The songwriter(s) of that composition assigns his copyright to the publisher who shares any royalties; the songwriter(s) might also retain rights to grant the license. Some compositions can also have multiple publishers who own portions of it. These all need clearance.
- *A Master Use license.* Gives you the right to play a specific recording in your content. The record label owns the actual audio recording—the performance of the song the way it was recorded in the studio. The label owns and grants the right to include a specific recording of the composition in timed relation to the picture or image. The artist(s) might also need to grant a separate license. Some recordings may include "samples" of other recordings that also require clearances.

Music License Fees

The range of fees you'll pay to use licensed music can boggle the mind, and strain the budget. From free to a couple thousand for a documentary, all the way to hundreds of thousands—dollars, pounds, Euros or yen or rubles—for the license to use a popular song in a car commercial airing worldwide.

IN THE TRENCHES...

For a documentary, I wanted to use a 12-second excerpt from a popular song under the opening credits. I contacted the publishers and the record label, and talked to specific departments that deal exclusively with reviewing requests for licensing. They required information from me in these categories:

- Detailed information about the project
- A synopsis of the project
- Its genre and length
- Its overall budget including the music budget
- The creative team (the producer, director, actors, and narrator)

- Any funding or donors
- Profit or nonprofit status
- Any distribution plans
- Information and address for the licensee

And this was all before they dropped the crushing blow of just how much it would cost me. When I found out, I thanked them politely, and the next day, hired a couple of freelance composers who gave me great original music for half the price of the licensed music.

~C. Kellison

Music Cue Sheets

Producers—and anyone else involved in the process of music licensing—use a form known as a *cue sheet* for listing each time and place that music appears in the program. This is necessary to calculate fees that must be paid either to ASCAP (American Society of Composers, Authors and Publishers) or to BMI (Broadcast Music Incorporated), who use these cue sheets to identify the publishers and composers who are to be paid and what percentage of the royalties they're entitled to receive. An example of a music cue sheet can be found on this book's web site.

A music cue sheet lists:

- The title of each composition
- The use and timing of each music cue
- The composer(s)
- Publisher(s)
- Their performing rights affiliation

Music Venues, Geographical Territories, and Time Periods

Both the publishers and the record labels want to know how you plan to use their music. It's how they can assess the rights and fees involved. For example, fees charged for music used in a network primetime broadcast are different than those for music used in an educational nonbroadcast venue. One fee amount might be charged for use, say, on a PBS show, but if that show goes to DVD, additional fees and rights issues could apply.

Publishers and record labels also want to know what geographical territories the rights cover, such as only North American rights and/or world rights, and for how long you want to retain the license (a specific time limit or for perpetuity). Publishers require the title of the composition, its writer(s), and its publisher(s); and record labels require the title of the recorded track, the performing artist, and the source of the recorded track.

Live Music Performances

If you have plans to shoot a performance where live music might be played, or if there is any inclusion of a song's lyrics in the script, make sure you have all the necessary clearances before you shoot the performance. Before you go into the postproduction phase, clear all music you intend to use in your opening main credits, montages, background songs, musical underscore, end credits, or anywhere else in the program. The Internet is an excellent source for access to performers, recording artists, songs and compositions, publishers, and recording labels. In some cases, you can actually submit your request for clearances over the Internet.

You may find, after all your research and negotiation, that you are denied clearance to use the musical composition or a recording. The Copyright Law gives the final say to the owner(s). If you choose to move ahead without clearance, you're liable for copyright infringement and possibly other claims as well. Both ASCAP and BMI regularly monitor television and film as well as other media looking for potential copyright infringement. Their job is to protect the composers, artists, publishers, and record companies from being deprived of the benefits they're entitled to.

Alternative Sources for Licensed Music

Original Music

It often makes sense for a producer to totally bypass the expenses involved in buying licensed music, and instead, hire a composer to write and record original music. A talented composer often owns his or her own studio and equipment and can work closely with you to create a music track that compliments your vision and production. Many universities have departments for musicians and film and television composers. Young composers are often eager to get experience and projects to add to their demo reel; they can provide a real energy and originality to your project for much lower fees. In certain cases, a student can work on your project as an independent study for which she can get school credit.

You can consider hiring a composer on a *work-for-hire* basis. Here, all publishing and recording rights for any music composed specifically for your project by the composer belong to you. In exchange, you'll pay a fee and work out your contract details, including screen credit, soundtrack residuals, and other details that could be involved down the road. If you do have music composed specifically for your project, you want to avoid any music that could bear a strong resemblance to a well-known piece. Even this might attract a lawsuit.

For any of these options, work closely with an entertainment lawyer and/or a music clearance company. Both have established links with licensing departments who can navigate the system quickly and legally. For more complex projects involving music rights, you can hire a music supervisor whose job it is to find the right music and to then research clearances.

Stock Music

A viable option to licensed prerecorded or original music is *stock* music—also known as *production* music—that has been composed and recorded especially for a stock music house. It's considerably cheaper and is generally *royalty-free*. This means that the producer usually pays a one-time fee for a one-time-only use or for an unlimited use of stock music, depending on the terms agreed upon. The music's rights have been cleared for sale. The prices tend to vary, depending on the music's end use—a nonbroadcast one-time use is much less expensive than use in a prime-time network drama, for example.

The variations of available stock music are impressive, covering all genres, emotions, rhythms, and timing. As technology gets more sophisticated, composers can simulate the sound of any instrument, from an entire classical orchestra to a single acoustical guitar. Most music libraries also provide sound effects, which are often referred to as *needle drops*. The range of available effects is staggering—from different bird and cricket sounds, to engines, gunshots, footsteps, screams, laughter, applause, and thousands of other choices. In most cases, they are quite reasonable to license.

Stock Footage

Similar to stock music, *stock footage* includes photographs, film, video, images, animation, and clip art that has been catalogued and archived, and available for a fee. Depending on its end use, the footage can be licensed and often can be purchased and/or come royalty-free, from hundreds of organizations that sell:

- ■ *Archived footage with an historical focus.* Usually shot in 16 or 35 mm film, footage includes historic events, old newsreel footage, documentary material, clips or whole programs from early films and television.
- ■ *Stock footage specifically shot for resale.* Generally shot in high-quality video or film, stock footage can be an excellent and inexpensive alternative to costly aerial shots of cities or landscapes, time-lapse footage, or establishing shots such as the front of Buckingham Palace or the Hollywood sign.

Stock footage can also provide a realistic-appearing background for blue-screen backgrounds, used in creating virtual sets. You can research other resources about stock music and stock footage on this book's web site.

Network Footage Clearances

For your project, you may want to use a clip of footage you've seen in a network or cable show, in a movie, a news broadcast, or online. To get the legal right to use this footage, contact the Rights and Clearances (R&C) department from the broadcaster; this department focuses on rights and clearances, and handles requests by producers to license their footage.

The R&C department first considers the source of the request, how the clips will be used, what fees to charge, and the details of the licensing agreement They also determine that the clips are not denigrating their company in any way, and that they own the legal rights to the material.

Some networks or production companies can charge as much as $200 per second or as little as $25, depending on the exclusivity and content of the material. Other fees can be considerably more, or a lot less, and occasionally might even be free. This depends on several factors: Will this footage be used for broadcast or nonbroadcast? Online, in DVD sales, or for corporate training? Is the request coming from an educational, nonprofit source, or from a rival broadcast network that might profit by featuring the footage in a program? What geographical territories does the use cover? For how long is the footage being licensed? The combination of answers to all these questions will determine your final fees and rights.

The Right of Publicity

This area of the law addresses our basic right to prevent someone from using our name, our image, or our voice for commercial purposes, or for any reason, without first getting our permission. Even a celebrity look-alike or sound-alike can be fertile grounds for a lawsuit. Although the right of publicity usually affects celebrities who have been exploited without their permission in advertising or in some other form of media, it can apply to any of us.

Producers are especially diligent in this area, knowing that each state has its own laws. You'll get written permission (a talent release) from every person you may be shooting or recording, from regular citizens, to politicians and well-known public figures. Make sure that this release is easy to understand. You can find examples of release forms in this book's web site; look for the form that's most appropriate for your needs.

III. PROTECT IT

> The most important thing is to know your audience, and also know that probably any idea you have, there are a hundred other people with that same idea and you'd better have something unique and special about your particular take on it. There is not an original idea—there hasn't been since I've been around. There are just reinterpretations of things, and particularly nonfiction, where you can't copyright an idea.
>
> **Brett Morgen excerpt from interview in Chapter 11**

In the world of ideas, new projects can simultaneously erupt from different pockets of the collective unconscious. Your sitcom pitch about modern-day pirates, for example, may be unique to you, but the network has already been developing a similar idea for months. It happens all the time.

Both Sides of Plagiarism Protection

Because of their understandable aversion to plagiarism lawsuits, the group or network that you're pitching to will ask you to sign what is known as a *submission release*, especially if you aren't represented by an agent or lawyer. Essentially, this release says that you are the legal owner of the material you're pitching, that you have given them your permission to read and consider your pitch and share it with others in their company, that they are under no obligation to use the material, and that if they are in the process of developing a project similar to yours, it's a coincidence. You can find an example of a submission release form on the web site.

First the Pitch, Then the Protection

This group, after hearing your pitch, may decide to green light it, and you shake on it. After you've celebrated, get back to reality and get every detail between you and the interested parties in writing. An agreement between professionals is more resilient when it's detailed on paper. If you don't have a written contract, it is almost impossible to receive any kind of compensation if the details are later questioned.

A traditional contract between a producer and a client specifies:

- how much time you all agree that it could take to develop, write, shoot, edit, and mix your project
- how much money that time is worth

In most cases, the client prepares the contract. The onus is on you and your lawyer to ask for explanations or changes.

Before you consider drafting any contracts, agreements, deal memos, or releases, talk first with your entertainment lawyer. If you don't have a lawyer, research similar agreements in books, on web sites, or talk with experienced producers. Find the format and wording that you can understand, adapt it to your specific project, and keep it short and to the point. Brevity can prevent misunderstandings.

> The ultimate goal of a contract is to articulate to the parties what the understanding is between them in such a way that you never have to look at it again. It's to describe the understanding between the parties. It's a very valuable process. What happens in drafting contracts is that I will write something down and send it to the client or to the other side, and very often they say, "I can't agree to that," so it's a very good thing that we wrote it down that way. So then we change it to what you can agree to or what you think you are agreeing to. It's the same with warrantees: when you sell something, you have to warrant to the guy that it is yours to sell and you are not actually selling somebody else's property. That is what a contract is.
>
> **J. Stephen Sheppard, excerpt from interview in Chapter 11**

Most Common Contracts

The following contracts are those you'll most likely encounter during various stages of producing. As with any legal aspect of entertainment and producing content for media, you can benefit by consulting with a lawyer. In time and with experience, you'll understand contracts and their contexts; until then, look for specific examples of contract templates in this book's web site. For more in-depth information on other contract formats and templates and union regulations, research the listed reference texts and web sites:

- **Deal memo.** This is the most common legal deal-making document, used by most producers in most circumstances. It is short and sweet, written in more casual language as a one- to three-page letter between the producer and whomever she's hiring. It outlines names, job descriptions, fees, start and stop dates, any mutual expectations, county and state of legal jurisdiction, any additional pertinent information, signatures, and dates. A longer, more formal agreement is sometimes used, called a *letter of agreement*.
- **Long form.** When a deal memo isn't sufficient, as for a license agreement or distribution deal, or for a more complicated negotiation, the project may require a long form. It is usually a long 20- to 70-page document, written in formal legalese, and attempts to present the positions of all concerned participants.
- **Literary releases and options.** A clearly defined outline of the assignment of any literary rights from the copyright holder to the producer, the project, and/or its major participants.
- **Writer employment.** This agreement is between the producer and the writer(s) and outlines the writing and/or revising of a final script for a specific project. It usually follows the WGA contract formats.
- **Director's employment.** Similar to the writer's contract, terms of the director's employment following DGA guidelines are outlined.
- **Pay or play clause.** An added clause, usually part of a deal memo between the producer and the actor(s), writer(s), and/or director. It is a guarantee that the producer will pay all agreed upon fees, even if she or he is taken off the project or the project is cancelled.

Contracts for Television and New Media versus Film

TV is a fickle business. I'm only good for the length of my contract.

Tom Brokaw

In signing a contract for a film project, the producer makes a commitment to work on that one project. Put simply: when the film is completed, so is the contract. It's seldom the case in TV. By contrast, television and new media contracts usually require a commitment to the entire run of a series unless your project is a one-off program, which is often the case with pilots. You may start a TV project with a short deal memo that details the essentials of your deal—such as compensation, screen credits, the duration of the project, and so on. A more in-depth, long-form agreement may follow as the success of the project becomes apparent. Contracts for employment on a series and in most aspects of network and premium cable negotiations can be complex and most rely on long-form contracts.

Fees and Compensation

Financial compensation for the producer, especially for the independent producer or production company, is obviously an important issue to consider. The range of financing can be considerable; for example, a major network pays more money than a premium cable station, which pays more than a standard cable channel, which pays more than a start-up online or other new media format. Is your project a single documentary, a multipart reality series, or a sitcom? A movie of the week, or a one-camera attempt at creating user-generated content? Each has varying costs and profit margins, and each pays the producer fees and profits based on different fee structures.

Each project has its own budgetary parameters. Compensation for the producer depends on overall budget costs like foreign locations, big stars, complicated rights clearances, animation, and dozens of other elements that are then balanced against any revenue that could be generated through ancillary opportunities. There is no set fee structure, and each deal is on a per-project basis. Some deal structures promise bonuses, others a fee for coming in under budget, or ahead of schedule.

The Three-Phase Deal

For smaller independent producers and production companies, the client—like a network, cable channel, or other end user—first agrees with the producer on an overall total estimated budget. The client then divides the total budget into three distinct phases of payments to be made to the producer over the life of the project.

- *Phase One.* When the initial contract is signed by the producer and the client, one-third of the budget goes to the producer to allocate to the project's needs.
- *Phase Two.* After all principal photography has been completed, the client gives the second third of the budget total to the producer.
- *Phase Three.* When the job has been completed, and all guarantees satisfied, the producer receives the final third.

The Step Deal

Sometimes, it's not feasible to guarantee a writer that she will be the writer of choice for the duration of a project. Sometimes the script just isn't taking form, or the form it's taking isn't what the producer is looking for. So the writer is replaced, or additional writers are brought in to add dialogue or action or to develop a subplot or theme. It's commonplace for the producers to protect themselves and their project by entering into a "step deal" with the writers.

The step deal process divides the fixed payments into various steps, or phases, of developing a script. Each step along the way allows for review and evaluation, and gives notice to the writer that the producer can put an end to the relationship after any step. It's not uncommon for more than one writer to be working on one idea simultaneously; all the writers are working under this similar step deal. All the details of any on-screen writing credit(s) are negotiated on an individual basis.

This is a general overview of the step deal process, though each deal has different requirements:

- *Step One.* Here, the writer usually authors a **synopsis** of the idea. He is paid, whether or not his idea is bought. He may or may not be asked to take part in the next step.
- *Step Two.* The writer completes a full **treatment** of the story, and is paid for her work whether it's accepted or not.
- *Step Three.* Generally, one writer is given the go-ahead to develop the **script**. In some cases, additional writers may be paid to write dialog, relationships, or other elements.

Fees and Funding, Rights and Territories

Often a network, cable channel, or other end user/client gives the producer the full budget amount needed to complete a project and bring it to broadcast or distribution. The producer negotiates a license fee with the buyer that outlines how much they will pay, how many runs they get, and so forth. If there is not enough money to make the project, or if the network is contributing only a percentage of the budget, it's up to the producer to find the remaining money.

Coproduction financing is an example of one funding source. Though this doesn't apply to all projects, the producer sometimes grants the license for specified rights to the end user, who can then transmit the program or content domestically, over a certain time period, and in clearly defined territories. The producer still owns the project and retains all the rights connected to it, other than those granted to the domestic network.

The producer can then negotiate with broadcasters or end users in other countries for additional monies to fill the budget gap. This gives the broadcasters the rights to air the project, but only for a specific time in defined territories. Coproduction financing can be a complicated process. Everyone involved wants as much as possible out of the deal, like home video rights, new media rights, extensions of territory and broadcast time periods, and net profit splits. This is another area where an entertainment lawyer or coproduction specialist is an essential component of the producer's team.

Most Favored Nation

Some projects are works of genuine passion and commitment, but they have a bare-bones budget. The project's success is more important to everyone involved than their salaries, especially in documentaries and independent productions. Joining the pack are ventures into new media and delivery systems. All the players—the producers, actors, writers, directors, and financial participants—value the importance of the creative direction and story content enough to take equal salaries.

When, for example, the casting of a project is based on a *most favored nation* (MFN) clause, this ensures that equal opportunities are extended to all parties involved. Everyone has agreed to receive the same salary, and get equal treatment in terms of work conditions. They might also agree to alphabetized on-screen credits rather than ranking their names by star power and/or salary levels. Everyone gets the same amount and shares equal parity. Salaries under most favored nation generally tend to be union scale plus 10 percent. MFN can also apply to a soundtrack; when one artist agrees to take a specific fee for use of a song, all other artists also agree to the same fee for their songs.

Insurance Coverage and Policies

In the same way that the producer protects her project legally, she also wants to protect it financially. This is where insurance comes in to the picture. Because producing for television and new media can be an expensive proposition, and often in the firing line of possible litigation, insurance is always included in the costs. This, like entertainment law, is a complex aspect of producing; most producers consult with professionals who specialize in this financial arena.

One form of protection is a *completion bond*, a form of insurance sometimes required in television, corporate, and new-media production. The bond guarantees to the parent company or client that you can complete the job, and that you will fulfill all the requirements of delivery. Bond holders can legally take over much of a project's control. They can fire the crew and do whatever else they feel will bring the project back on track.

After the producer submits the shooting script, the budget, shooting schedule, the financing plan, and the bios of key production personnel, the bond company reviews them and meets with the producer and director to discuss ways the project will be produced. The primary requirement by the completion bond company mandates that the producer and the team bring the project in, on or under budget and by a specific date. The costs for the completion bond usually runs around 3 percent of the budget's total.

Other insurance coverage could include *workers' compensation* and *liability insurance*, as well as extra insurance riders that might cover a variety of contingencies, like stunt work, foreign locations, equipment, and other aspects of production. Although this is more common in filmmaking, some networks or distributors require this extra protection. You'll find more detailed information in Chapter 4.

IV. DOUBLE-CHECK IT

Reviewing and checking each legal document is a vital part of the producer's job. Some documents require extensive research and review by an entertainment attorney, although the majority of contracts, releases, and clearances are standardized forms that are preprinted or available on software program templates. Many are included on this book's web site; check with the web site's Table of Contents in the front of the book.

Find the Right Attorney

You want an experienced attorney who is reputable and knowledgeable, and respected within the media industry. Using a lawyer simply because he or she is inexpensive can cost you in the long run. Deal directly with any legal challenges in the beginning of the process, rather than ignoring them until it is too late. Any delays could result in stunningly expensive court fees.

If you don't have access to an attorney and instead rely on shareware template forms, make sure they are current with legal rulings, relevant to your specific needs, and written in language that you can follow.

Review Releases, Clearances, and Permissions

If you haven't gotten a signed release from an on-camera talent or a signed location agreement, or have neglected to obtain permission to use a film clip that your program depends on, your project could be terminated, or the magnet for a lawsuit. It is the producer's responsibility to cover all these bases, whether you are an independent producer or on a work-for-hire contract. You can find examples of talent and extras release forms on this book's web site and other online and published sources.

Check All Production Contracts

Each specific job requires a new set of contracts. Double-check the details in an often wordy contract between the producer and the production company, network, or end buyer before it's signed and finalized. Make sure that it is accurate, and that it mirrors the deal you think you have agreed on. If the wording is unclear or ambiguous, consult with a lawyer for clarification.

Location Agreements

Because owning a studio or location can be an expensive proposition, producers generally lease or rent spaces in which to shoot. They rely on location scouts to find and secure locations to avoid studio costs; they may need locations like a private home, a public museum, a restaurant, school cafeteria, a city street, a country meadow, a senior citizens home. Using this site that's owned by someone else requires a location agreement between the owner of the property (or the owner's agent) and the producer.

Agreements with Unions

If you—or a production company you're working with—is a *signatory* to any of the media-related unions (described in the following) this means that you have agreed to use only active dues-paying members of that union in your project. It also means that you can't use *creatives*—writers, actors, directors, crew, or other union members—who are not union members; you as the producer face possible fines or other repercussions.

Unions are the bargaining agents for the on- and off-screen talent in television, film, and some new media. The major unions are:

- The Screen Actors Guild (SAG)
- The Directors Guild of America (DGA)
- The Writers Guild of America (WGA)
- The National Association of Broadcast Employees and Technicians–Communication Workers of America (NABET–CWA)
- The American Federation of Television and Radio Artists (AFTRA)
- The American Federation of Musicians (AFM)
- The Producers Guild of America (PGA)
- IATSE

These guilds and unions provide specific services to their members. They take care of payments of residuals, based on a contractually agreed-upon percentage of a project's profits; they also make payments to the members' pension and health plans. They have established specific rules and regulations around their members' work rules, timetables, and work conditions; they also take part in negotiations and arbitrations on the part of their membership. This is all good news to the union member; it's less fun for the producer whose project's costs and paperwork load are considerably higher when unions are involved.

As you'll see in Chapter 7, the producer's focus is delegated to negotiating with unions and drafting and signing various agreements that outline the terms of the project, job descriptions, fees, contracts, and schedules—just a few of the project's ongoing details. Know the union rules and follow them. When you're hiring, be very clear about your status as either a signatory company or a non-union shop.

On-Screen Credits

Every deal memo or contract outlines the union member's specific screen credits at the opening and/or closing of the show. Negotiation for proper screen credit might include how the credit is phrased, proper spelling, font style and size, how long it stays on the screen, whether the person's name is by itself or part of a group of names, among other contractual details. This also applies to any advertising on posters, on-air promos, and so forth.

Most programs give screen credits that might include: produced by, film by, directed by, story by, written by, and composed by, as well as credits to executive producer(s), and associate producer(s). There may also be extra attention to the opening logo(s) of the production companies, the presentation credits, the executive producer(s), and a longer list in the closing credits that include a "special thanks" section that gives courtesy credits to people and companies who have contributed goods or services, copyrights, and other legally-mandated information. You can see examples of credits lists by watching programs similar to yours or by checking specific union-related web sites.

Ancillary Revenues

The producer seldom gets rich from ancillary revenues, partially because the formulas used to make the overall calculations are intentionally obtuse and vary with the network, channel, production company, or other end user. The producer's financial participation is usually based on net profits, a tricky area that can be difficult to pin down or audit. Although there are exceptions to this "formula," here is how it works in most cases:

1. The network/end user adds up all revenues from the project, as well as any extra sources of income that total the net profits. Networks and most end users are experts at "creative accounting," so net profits are seldom profitable to anyone but them. The producer is wise to get as much money as possible up front, in salaries, lines on the budget, and other *perks*; whatever extra money comes at the back end is icing on the producer's cake.
2. The network/end user deducts a distribution fee from this net profits total. This fee is paid to itself or an outside distributor for home video, foreign sales, and other ancillary licensing. All production costs, which could include each phase of production, insurance, overhead, services, costs for promotion, and more, are also deducted.
3. The network/end user divides any profit that might still be left between the producer and themselves. The producer usually receives a much smaller percentage than the network, but over time and with experience, producers can negotiate deals that benefit them as well as the network.

Making the Deal: A Final Check List

- *Get it in writing.* Protect yourself with ample documentation. Follow up an oral promise with a written memo or email version of the points made and agreed upon.
- *Take notes.* In a meeting or on the phone, take notes and date them.
- *Keep a paper trail.* Even in this electronic age, keep hard copies as well as computer backups of correspondence and memos sent and received, and dated. Keep each draft of any screenplays. If you've made some form of contribution to the story, follow that up with a brief memo outlining that contribution—dialog, story line, theme, subplot, location, etc.
- *Register your work with the WGA.* This is a valuable verification of your ownership; register it before you begin to pitch it around.
- *Check out potential buyers.* Be objective and realistic about excited interest in your project. It may be wonderful, but the people may not be. Check them out thoroughly—search the web, ask other filmmakers, do a credit check.
- *Don't make the first offer.* See what the other side has to offer first. And never sign any binding contracts without thoroughly dissecting each point with your attorney.
- *Keep each promise you make.* If you can't keep it, don't make it.
- *Don't be afraid of negotiation.* In most cases, it is expected.
- *Always try for a win-win.* In this ideal scenario, everyone is happy, and no one sues.
- *When in doubt, hold it out.* Should you suspect that you may not get paid what you originally agreed upon, you can consider holding onto all video, film, or digital material until you've cashed—and cleared—their check.

ON A HUMAN LEVEL . . .

As an effective producer, you understand the value of making everyone feel that they are being treated fairly—and that includes you. Yet the pressure of making everything fair, and legal, can create an emotional detachment from the people with whom you are making the deal. Stay conscious of this: being a good producer requires being empathetic, involved, and emotionally balanced, as well as staying objective.

SUMMARY

The legal component of producing is as important as the creative, technical, or budgetary needs of your project. In many ways, it is the *most* important part. We live in a litigious society, and an overlooked detail can lead to production delays, even lawsuits. But you can't be expected to know everything, especially as you first embark on your career in producing. So, it's worth the investment to have an entertainment lawyer—and an arsenal of legal textbooks, resources, and templates—on your side.

Now, with all the legal aspects taken care of, you can move more knowledgeably into pitching and selling your idea, coming up in Chapter 6.

REVIEW QUESTIONS

1. Why is legal documentation important to a producer?

2. What are the responsibilities of an entertainment attorney?

3. What are three areas of intellectual property?

4. What's the difference between a copyright and a trademark?

5. How can you legally protect your own project idea?

6. What are the steps you'd need to take if you wanted to use a Top Ten album or single as music for your project?

7. Pose an imaginary situation in which a favored nation clause could benefit your project.

8. Name three types of production insurance.

9. What's the primary difference between a contract for a film and one for TV or new media?

10. Why are screen credits included in a contract?

Pitching and Selling the Project

If a story is in you, it has got to come out.

William Faulkner

THIS CHAPTER'S TALKING POINTS

I. Pitching and Selling: The Big Picture

II. Research the Pitch

III. Create the Pitch

IV. Pitch the Pitch

V. Keep Pitching

I. PITCHING AND SELLING: THE BIG PICTURE

Your idea for a project is great. You're confident that it's a perfect fit for NBC, or HBO, or maybe it could be a breakthrough online series. But you have to sell it first, and selling your project is a real challenge. Because getting the green light might depend entirely on your pitch, this pitch process can be stressful for even a seasoned producer.

In reality, a pitch is just a sales job: you're appealing to someone in a position of power who can approve your project, possibly fund it, and who stands to benefit from its success. In most cases, a pitch has two parts:

- *A written pitch.* Also called a proposal, prospectus, or pitch on paper (POP). In some cases, it includes a detailed business plan, put together by a professional.
- *A verbal pitch.* A face-to-face, in-person meeting where you get a chance to share your idea, project your confidence, and confirm your ability to produce it.

Before you translate your idea to paper and rehearse your pitch, take a moment to explore the bigger picture of both television and new media.

It's All about Business

TV and new media can both offer a wealth of creative rewards and opportunities for the producer. But commerce is always involved—profits must be the bottom line whether it comes from advertisers, a subscription base, or from an expanding range of other revenue streams. You want your project to be a business opportunity for other people as well as for you. Can it generate high ratings, online hits, advertising or subscription revenue, critical acclaim, ancillary markets, and an international reach?

Know the Market

When pitching your project, you want to be sure you're pitching it to the right place. Is the network, cable channel, production company, online site, or other end user the right venue for your project? Research everything you can about the person or organization to whom you're pitching—their current programming, the company history, what they've paid for similar content, and other details that tell you if this is the right fit for your project.

You benefit by keeping in touch with current projects that producers have sold, and to whom. Read publications and research online sites that target the television and new media industries such as *Variety, TV Weekly, The Hollywood Reporter*, and others. When you first start out, it can be overwhelming—the sheer number of names, companies, broadcasters, production companies, and online sites and delivery systems, but you'll soon recognize names and companies that appear across many of these publications. You can find resources on the Internet that focus on new online sites and ideas, the TV business, chat rooms, and blogs.

Don't ignore the rest of the world. The majority of international markets depend primarily on American and British programming. Some shows that might do only moderate business in their originating country can generate significant profit from international markets. Although the trend is moving toward more programming being locally produced in these markets, they still depend on outside providers. Watch programs produced in other countries, and research the global marketplace: it's a potential goldmine for your project.

II. RESEARCH YOUR PITCH

> I will study and get ready, and perhaps my chance will come.
>
> **Abraham Lincoln**

Writer Dashiell Hammett once advised another writer, Raymond Chandler, to "make it sound fresh." As a producer, you want your project to be unique and have a hook, an originality, that appeals to a viewer. Even if it bears some similarities to an existing show, you want your idea to have its own voice and to offer a solid business opportunity. There are few original ideas anymore, merely their unique reinterpretations. But these interpretations can take on a life of their own with an inspired and capable producer behind them.

When you give your pitch, the development executives or clients are paying attention to your idea but they're also looking just as closely at you as its producer. They want to see your professionalism, your passion, and your potential to follow through on the project. Do they want to spend months, even years with you as you all develop the project together? Do you convey confidence and enthusiasm for your project, or could you be seen as a loose cannon who's not capable of collaboration or taking criticism? You want your image to be that of a professional, flexible producer who can be both passionate and realistic.

Pitch to the Right Place

You want your project to be a comfortable fit with the end user's branding, programming schedule, public image, overall vision, and financial capabilities. You wouldn't, for example, pitch a children's cartoon show to a documentary channel, or a sports show to a classic-movie channel. You also don't want to pitch a big-budget high-concept idea to a low-budget online startup or public access channel.

Do your research before you go into a pitch meeting. You want to know their brand, their logo, their mission statement, the demographics of their audience, their primary advertisers or subscribers, and their budget range.

> I think the most important thing for young television producers is to understand that you can take the same pitch to about nine different places, but you need to alter that pitch for each place. When people come up with ideas, it's really helpful to know to whom you're pitching. Know which networks serve what audience. Is there a way to change certain aspects of your pitch so it appeals to different networks?
>
> **Brett Morgen, excerpt from interview in Chapter 11**

Get Your Pitch in the Door

After you have researched where you want to pitch, your next step is to find the right person working there to whom you can direct your pitch. There are no set rules or protocol about who will or won't take a pitch. Some people will take a pitch based solely on someone's recommendation. Others might see your written pitch material, and ask to see your *demo reel* as the next step. On occasion, your emailed or faxed pitch might reach the right person who'll ask you to send follow-up material, even the script.

Following the traditional scenario, television development executives usually take a pitch meeting *only* if your lawyer or agent has paved the way with a note or phone call. This assures the executive that you have representation and some credibility. Generally, you'll be asked to sign a *submission release* (see more on this in the previous chapter and an example on this book's web site) before they will read the pitch or meet with you.

But the traditional model is changing. Now, independent production companies, large and small, are more often the development vehicles for new projects. They have the valuable connections with the networks and bigger cable channels; they also have the in-house resources to produce a project. Newer, younger cable channels and online channels are more open to taking a "cold" pitch, looking for exciting and edgy material. And in the more adventurous and informal world of new media, guidelines have yet to be established. Stay tuned!

Who Do You Know?

Make a list of the people you know or the people they might know who could connect you to an insider for a pitch meeting, or an investor who might help fund your whole project or at least its initial development. This list might include:

- Family and relatives
- Friends and colleagues
- Fellow and former students and professors
- Actors
- Writers
- Directors
- Producers
- Lawyers
- Agents

- Managers
- Investment brokers and accountants
- Professors
- Other professional and creative people

Maybe you've already given a pitch but the project wasn't picked up. Or you may live in an area far from the offices of a network or cable channel. In both cases, you do have options. For example, you can approach an independent production company that has produced projects similar to yours that might air on the channel or site you have targeted. If the company likes your idea, it may agree to act as an "engine" for your project, pulling your project behind their established working relationships. You can find the names of these production companies in the opening and/or closing credits of a program and research them online.

Potential Markets

Our current media climate involves the gamut of delivery systems—from traditional television to the revolution in digital new media—and the result is an almost unlimited marketplace. TV and its many formats, the Internet, video on demand and DVD, cellular technology, portable media players, video games—the list grows exponentially. And each one requires content.

Each market has its advantages and its drawbacks. As a producer, your job demands ongoing self-education: finding in-depth technical, creative, legal, and fiscal information; researching books and online information and articles; talking to producers, professors, and international producers and buyers; taking advantage of classroom instruction; and attending professional conferences and seminars that focus on television and new media. Producers interested in succeeding are lifelong learners—it comes with the territory.

Motion Picture Studios

In addition to producing motion pictures, the major film studios produce television programming. They're also developing a strong web presence, and exploring other delivery systems for their content. Ideas for programming might start with the studio's executives, or could come from independent producers or production companies, or from packaging agencies, or a number of other sources.

A network, in most cases, pays a *license fee* to the studio for producing the series for them, and gets the exclusive rights to broadcast the first run of the series along with limited reruns. The studio traditionally retains ownership of the property and can eventually sell it to cable, syndication, or to other markets. Often, a studio and a network, such as Sony and F/X, will coproduce a project with one or more independent production companies.

The guidelines for monetizing online content are far fuzzier. The advertising and business models are all over the map in this young digital era, while the studios, networks, and production companies negotiate with the major unions and discuss among themselves just how best to proceed.

Major Broadcast Networks

By selling your idea to a broadcast network, such as NBC, CBS, ABC, Fox, or the CW, you are likely to be well paid because your program reaches an audience of many millions. However, networks are under pressure by advertisers to bring in high audience ratings and to adhere to certain constraints and formulas, so each network has a

Standards and Practices department with strict guidelines that dictate parameters for a program's themes and creative risk-taking.

Cable Channels

Cable channels such as Discovery, The History Channel, A&E, National Geographic, or MTV are also advertiser-supported, yet tend to have lower production budgets with more creative leeway for the producer. Ratings play an important role, but they are measured in much smaller increments than those of the networks. Advertisers tend to create their ads around specific niche interests and demographics; they can object, or withdraw ad sales if they disagree with programming content. Cable's creative latitude allows for storylines that incorporate more sex, violence, and adult content than the networks.

Premium Cable Channel

Creative control is a key benefit to most producers. You're more likely to have that control from premium cable channels, like HBO and Showtime. Although their budgets tend to be lower than the networks', they don't have advertisers to harness them. Their subscriber base is a loyal one, and their ratings aren't as big a concern as they are for the networks. There are few boundaries on adult content or complex themes, and a series like *Weeds* or *Dexter* can attract a large audience base that stays loyal to the channel beyond the life of the series.

Public Television

The traditional role of public television has been to air educational and entertaining programming via independent, noncommercial, local and national public television stations. Public television is funded by individual memberships, private corporations, and grants, as well as city, state, and/or federal funding. A station can acquire programs that have been independently produced, or it can partially or fully fund and develop a project. Budgets are generally medium to low, and each station adheres to specific standards for the programs it broadcasts. Many producers find that if their project is aired on a local public television station, it can subsequently be picked up by other local or national stations.

Production Companies

A network or broadcaster might have its own in-house production arm, though most also work closely with independent production companies that produce programming for them. These recognized producers are trusted by their clients, and act as the engines for smaller production companies and independent producers. They can usher your project into the network, and also offer their experience, staff, and facilities after you have mutually agreed on your involvement, credits, payments, and ongoing interaction with the project. Production companies might be small, local companies, or larger businesses that are listed in the opening and/or closing credits of a television show, the Internet, or in *Variety* or *The Hollywood Reporter.*

Local Television Stations

Most local and regional television stations have limited budgets, and depend primarily on preproduced programming supplied by a network, a syndicator, or producers of paid-programming infomercials. Many stations produce their own programming—children's shows, daytime talk shows geared mostly to women's interests and social issues, home shopping, local weather, how-to shows, news, traffic, and information. A producer can often raise funding from local advertisers that pays for the entire cost of production; this adds an extra appeal to any smaller station to consider your idea more positively.

Syndication

Most programs in syndication have already been broadcast on the networks and now air on local stations. Frequently sold in five-day-a-week *strips* by syndicators, they are usually classic favorites such as *Friends* and *I Love Lucy.* Shows can also be designed and produced for the syndicated market, airing on local stations in whatever time slot the station chooses. Occasionally, a show starts in syndication and is popular enough to get picked up by a network or cable channel. Budgets for syndicated shows vary considerably, as do the sources of funding.

DVD

Some programs are first broadcast on a network or cable station or online, are aired a second, maybe a third time, and then go into syndication or reruns. Now, entire seasons of most hit shows are repackaged and sold in DVD sets. These rights may be solely for home video, with other rights belonging to airing online or other repurposing of the material.

VOD

VOD, or video on demand, is available everywhere. Perhaps it's a recent film on your cable delivery system, like Comcast; it can be the latest episode of *24* downloaded from iTunes or Netflix and viewed where you choose; you can download thousands of choices directly into an Apple TV or Xbox. Some viewings are free, others are inexpensive to rent or buy.

Direct Mail

This is a growing market for producers who have raised enough money to produce their project through grants, private investors, or other sources but cannot find a broadcast venue. The project may be too politically inflammatory, or it has an adult theme or a specific niche market like home improvement or exercise. Look for online sites and distribution companies that specialize in selling specific projects and genres to clearly defined markets; they can help sell your project. Research the company, making sure they're legitimate and their contracts valid.

Self-Distribution

By far the most ambitious option for selling your project involves distributing it yourself. With the potential reach and marketing possibilities of the Internet, it's possible to reach a tremendous audience. Your how-to play golf DVD, for example, can be promoted, ordered, paid for, and tracked, all online. If you're willing to allow users to download your project for a fee (or free) the Internet takes care of it all. You might also find advertisers to place banner ads on your web site, or embed short commercials.

But this method can be time-consuming, and it requires not only an entrepreneurial mindset but an initial startup fund, a lot of research, and infinite belief in your project. You could see results—and even profits—if you can navigate the duplication, marketing, mailing lists, and networking, along with the packing and shipping, accounting, and phone calls. Explore successful models of self-distribution before you take the plunge.

There are many phases of a program's potential revenue stream, and each should be spelled out in the contract between the producer and the buyer. Some independent producers create projects specifically designed to be sold to a home video distributor who then markets and sells directly to home video markets like video stores and online sites.

The emerging areas of new media continue to expand, and although they vary tremendously in technical scope and accessibility, they all relay on content—an out-of-home ad in the back of a taxi; a mobisode on your cell phone; an alternate reality for a video game; a short film on your portable media player; an ongoing online series. The delivery systems vary, but the integrity of the content is the same.

Understand the International Marketplace

A solid project has the potential for two rounds of audience exposure and income. The first round begins with domestic broadcast or market, and the second extends to the global marketplace. Europe, Latin America, Japan, and Australia are a few of the larger markets who regularly license or buy American and British episodic drama, comedy, children's TV, family shows, and a range of documentaries and reality shows. These markets are generally managed by specialty distributors.

However, there has been a shift in this traditional approach to the international market over the last few years. With advances in technology and increased programming demands from a more sophisticated international audience, local producers and investors are being attracted to creating programming for their specific local and regional needs.

Countries that once acquired programs and series from the United States or the United Kingdom are now producing their own programming. The popular trend is to adapt American and European hit shows that are packaged and sold as formats to fit local protocol, tastes, language, and subtle change. In some cases, local broadcasters may "borrow" key elements as they produce their own version. They create a loyal audience base with shows produced in their own language that are entertaining and reflect local cultural and social issues.

American producers often choose to shoot their projects in other countries such as Canada, where tax incentives and strong currency exchange rates are offered. Several television movies and series use the excellent facilities and experienced crews in places like Prague and New Zealand. Animated shows routinely send their complicated illustration work to Korea and China. The phrase *runaway production* describes the cost-cutting approach taken by American productions to go outside the country for shoots and locations, production personnel, services, and facilities.

The international marketplace continues to fluctuate. The emergence of new media and the merging of large media companies; the presence of the Internet; the mercurial environments of advertising and sponsorship; domestic and international political shifts; economic downturns—these can all affect the sale of your project to the foreign market. With research and time, and by consulting experts in this field, you can evaluate, and hopefully master, the global market.

III. CREATE THE PITCH

> Words are, of course, the most powerful drug used by mankind.
>
> **Rudyard Kipling**

The pitch on paper reflects the tone and face of your project. Its graphic format is the first impression the reader sees, and its words and ideas become the "voice" the reader hears.

The Cover Letter

A cover letter generally introduces your pitch. Sometimes known as a *query letter* that accompanies your proposal, it's the recipient's first impression of you and your project, and it plays a strategic role in enticing a potential buyer to consider your proposal.

In some cases, the cover letter can be a stand-alone sales vehicle. It can convince a client, development executive, an independent producer, or an investor to read your proposal. It might excite them enough to take a pitch meeting with you, prior to seeing anything more fully developed in writing.

Anyone to whom you might send a proposal probably receives dozens of similar pitches every week, so you want your cover letter to be brief. You also want it to stand out and reveal several things about you and your project that the proposal doesn't:

- The cover letter sets a tone for the attached written proposal.
- It tells a potential buyer why he or she should be interested, financially and creatively.
- It creates enough interest for the reader to read your attached proposal.
- It gives selected highlights of the proposal, like a short promo.
- It reflects *you*: your personality and your voice, your passion for the project.

You want your cover letter to reflect your professionalism and confidence as a producer, and as importantly, your own personality. Like its author, each cover letter is different but most follow these simple guidelines:

- If you've been recommended or referred by someone important or known to the recipient, say that right away. Mention in your opening sentence that he or she was kind enough to recommend you.
- Make your first paragraph an attention-grabber, just like a good novel. But overly dramatic is a turnoff.
- Reduce your complex ideas into simple, brief sentences. Each word counts.
- Keep the letter to one page, maximum. Avoid distracting fonts or amateur graphics.
- Allow for margins and open white space, don't crowd your words. Make it easy to read—not everyone has young eyes. Use 12-point Times New Roman or another simple font.
- Use good paper, professional letterhead quality.
- Use a high-quality printer for your copies.
- Make sure you've spelled the person's name and company correctly. Confirm his or her title if you're using it in your letter.

IN THE TRENCHES...

While I was writing the Great American Screenplay, I freelanced for United Artists as a script analyst, reading manuscripts, books, galleys, and treatments, searching for the next big blockbuster for the studio. I read hundreds of these submissions, and although very few story ideas have lived on in my memory, what I do recall, vividly, are the dozens of embarrassing mistakes made by writers. Many were professional screenwriters, but if they only knew how these gaffs made them appear to be total amateurs.

A misplaced apostrophe, misspellings, bad grammar, a pretentious adjective rather than an expressive one, the F-word on every page when a descriptive word could work....I was a lowly story reader, but if I didn't like it, it went into the circular file. My first impression **was** the last word, at least for these writers. Obviously, if the story embedded in the bad or sloppy writing was genuinely good, I'd recommend it. But I'd also caution that the writer not rely only on a spell checker; ask someone trustworthy to double-check it all; value using one right word rather than lots of wrong ones. And keep telling good stories.

~C. Kellison

Writing the Cover Letter

Some producers compose their cover letter before they actually start on the written pitch. Others do the opposite, taking the tone of the pitch and echoing it to some degree in the cover letter. Here is a sample cover letter.

Your letterhead [Your name, address, city, state or region, country, zip code; email, fax, phone, mobile]

Date

Ms./Mr. [development exec buyer, investor, etc.]
Title
Company
Address
City, state or region, country, zip code

Dear Mr./Ms. ___,

At the suggestion of [So-and-So], I'm enclosing a proposal for my television show [*or other content*] called **It's a Hit!** [*title*], a half-hour [*or other length*] program about two teenage golf caddies who use their tips to form a rock band in the clubhouse basement [*the show's one-liner*]. The Chaos Brothers have expressed strong interest in playing the lead roles. [*Emphasize any talent with name value attached to your project such as stars, writers, directors, etc.*]

The story's theme of teenage joys and relationship demons expressed through music [*very brief synopsis*] bears some similarity to your excellent documentary series on boy bands [*make reference to the development exec's former track records*] last year. Your production company [*or studio, network, independent producer*] could be the ideal group with whom to partner in making **It's a Hit,** well, a hit.

As the producer [*and/or writer and/or director*] of this project, my background complements the project because [*your very brief bio and connection with the story*]. I feel strongly that it's highly marketable, appeals to [*your project's main target group*], and can result in profits and satisfaction for all concerned.

I'm honored that you're taking the time to consider my project. I look forward to hearing from you at your convenience [*and/or to having an opportunity to pitch you in person*].

Sincerely [cordially, respectfully, best regards],

Signature
Printed name
Title (if any)

The Written Pitch

Imagination is more important than knowledge.

Albert Einstein

The professionally written pitch reflects certain industry standards—its basic format is short and sweet, dramatic, and direct to the point. It is selling your idea.

Your pitch is a direct reflection of your project. Also called a *proposal, prospectus*, or the *pitch on paper* (POP), this written pitch is a powerful tool. It can make the difference between your project fading away or being successfully produced. Most importantly, a good pitch gives an investor, development executive, end user, or online entrepreneur good reason to trust you with their money.

As with the cover letter, a good pitch attracts the reader's attention and reflects your professionalism. It avoids fancy confusing fonts and complex graphics, and instead, follows the "three font rule" by using no more than three fonts throughout. Any graphics — such as photos and art work — illustrate an important character or theme, emphasize the words, or show a product. Its pages are bound by a spiral or stapled. Some producers print their proposals using the landscape format, rather than the upright portrait format. This approach makes it easy to hold and use as a great presentation tool during your verbal pitch.

The Basic Elements of the Pitch

- Unlike the cover letter, don't personalize your written pitch. Avoid using the phrases "I think" or "I want to accomplish."
- Write it in the present tense: "the project **is** an exciting exploration of college life," not "the project **will be** an exciting exploration."
- Look for creative ways of infusing the pitch with your ideas, vision, and passion without overworking it.

Each project is different and each producer takes a unique approach to writing a solid, strong pitch. Most producers integrate any or all of the following components into their written proposals, and infuse the document with their own individual styles of presentation. The basic elements of a pitch are as follows.

The Title Page as First Impression

This first page tells a mini-story. The title is usually in the largest font, followed by words in smaller font:

- The title
- Genre and length
- The log line
- Author(s)
- Graphics if any
- Name and contact information of agent/lawyer/representative
- WGA registration and/or copyright notice

The title. A good title can create a memorable impression. It can reflect a genre or mood of your project. *Survivor* and *Ugly Betty* and *24* – each title is short, memorable, sets a tone, and often tells a story in itself.

Genre and format. Is it a sitcom? Reality show? Episodic drama? Is it a half-hour or one-hour series, or a one-off that airs just once? The page that follows the title page repeats the title at the top, and quickly moves to genre, format, and log line.

The log line. (one-liner) Your log line is a mini-version of your story. It explains the plotline — or parts of it — in just a few words. It can be a snappy appetizer that grabs people's immediate interest. *TV Guide* is an excellent source of log line examples, so are movie and TV ads, promos, movie trailers, and user-generated content sites. Countless shows have been green lit from a simple but dynamic log line.

Star value. If a well-known star, director, writer, or producer has shown any interest or a real commitment to your project, highlight that fact in your proposal. If you own exclusive rights to a book, or have rare access to a real-life story, this is also valuable information to include as an extra attraction. Your project could also be right for a specific actor who may have his or her own production company. Research this information and approach the company with your proposal. Convince them: you have something no one else has.

The synopsis. A well-crafted synopsis is easily read and understood. It gives some character detail, but not too much. It gives a direction of the story arc but doesn't digress. It also moves the reader's emotions in some way—anger, sorrow, hope, humor. A synopsis, when done right, confirms that there's a good story at the core of your project.

The Synopsis as Storyteller

The synopsis provides one chance to impress its reader. A couple of narrative paragraphs must reveal the dimension of character, the arc of the story, the clarity and passion of Aristotle's "single issue." The synopsis brings your story to life; it also gives a glimpse into your writing skills. You want the story elements to be organized, and flow smoothly from one segment to the next. As outlined in Chapter 3, you can write your synopsis in the classic three-act format, just much shorter.

> **Let's say...** you're weaving your synopsis almost entirely around a character who is a cop. Now what? Is the cop a man or a woman? Is this cop a tough cop, a crooked cop, a gay cop, or religious, or sensitive, or old, or respected, or a drunk? That one right word can flesh out a character and paint a more subtle picture of who that character is.

The Presentation of Information

You've designed your title page and written a synopsis. Now what? You still have other information that's integral to your project and are genuine sales points. But there are no rules about what order you present them in.

Ideally, after your title page you want to present your story—pull in the reader with the power of the narrative. Then follow with the other components that bring the story to life. Here are some components of a project that you may or may not want to include in your pitch.

Connection to the project. Are you the producer, the writer, or both? Did it grow from your personal involvement in the story? Maybe you once worked for the FBI and now you want to create a series based on your own stories and experiences from that job.

Comparisons. Producers often compare their project idea to hit shows—maybe they say their project is just like *James Bond* meets *Desperate Housewives.* But what does this really mean? It says derivative, copycat, and safe. Too many preexisting images block a new impression. But if you say something like, "Five women escape the suburban slump and charter a yacht. The fun really starts when they meet the sixth passenger." Give your idea its own identity. Occasionally, you can simply imply a resemblance; for example, "in the spirit of…" or "in the tradition of the timeless classic…." Your idea should be strong enough to speak for itself, and to have its own log line.

The cast list. Talent or hosts who are well-known can lend credibility and quality, as well as appeal to international markets in which the talent is popular. If they're unknown actors or a real-world cast, flesh out his or her character and each relationship to the others.

Style. Emphasize your project's unique stamp. Talk about production design, lighting, the elegant designer wardrobe, and exotic locations. Or stress its realistic approach and edgy noir look.

Research. Is your project reality-based, a documentary, or does it requires extensive research? Are rights clearances involved?

History of the project. Your project may have its genesis in a book, a stage play, a friend's real-life adventure, or your own creative epiphany. Sometimes, how it started isn't important enough to include in the proposal.

Production schedule. Provide a short breakdown of your production schedule, including the proposed number of days or weeks needed for preproduction, production, and postproduction; how and where you'll shoot; locations and/or constructed sets; and a general project overview.

Creative team. Devote a brief sentence or paragraph to each key person involved in making your project come to life. As the producer, your own bio should reflect your experience, jobs, awards, professional affiliations, education, and people who can be contacted as references. If you are a student, mention any experience you may have had in television, film, or new media, as well as your course of study, pertinent classes, internships, study abroad programs, and independent studies that have added to your skills as a producer. Mention areas that make you more unique, such as fluency in other languages, computer skills, athletic abilities, and travel experience. All this being said, keep it short!

Demographics and market description. Create a need for your show. Look for projects like yours that are already on the air and making money, or conversely, provide evidence that there *isn't* anything like your project out there, with convincing arguments for why there should be. Use industry publications, newspapers, and the Internet for credible resources.

Global markets. International sales can be impressive, and vital to a project's potential sales. Does your project appeal to other cultures' customs, views, and traditions? Can it be dubbed and/or subtitled in other languages? Audiences in every country have their own tastes, so research the markets that routinely buy American or British products as well as the show genre you are pitching.

Budget top sheet. The top sheet, or *budget summary*, represents a brief overview of your more detailed, estimated budget. It's a general idea of what your project could cost. Neither the top sheet nor the budget should be included in the proposal unless it specifically has been requested. If you do make a deal, most end users rework your initial budget to suit their company's financial parameters.

The financial benefits. Though the financials are seldom included in a pitch, they can be vital when seeking investors. Financials might include a distribution plan, an in-depth financial statement, any tax breaks, projected profits, and the means of transferring funds from an investor to the production account. This area is best handled by an attorney and/or an experienced accountant.

IN THE TRENCHES...

Remember, this is a sales pitch—it's not your life story. It's brief, and cuts to the chase, while still being eloquent and unique and compelling. Every choice is made thoughtfully—from the choice of your font to the use of graphics, from your choice of the right word to the paper stock to the binding. Each detail reflects your project, and reflects you as a professional.

~C. Kellison

The Video Pitch

Some producers choose to make a mini-version of their project to use as a sales pitch. They'll shoot one pivotal scene from their script, or produce a five-minute "trailer" that paints a portrait of the project. But there's a caveat to taking this approach: It must be good enough to showcase your creative vision and technical abilities. Don't expect people to depend too much on their imagination and look for something that just isn't there in quality of acting, lighting, production values, and especially, in the story.

Each pitch is unique. Each takes its own approach. You can weave any of these elements into your pitch, either by using a bullet-point laundry list approach, or in short paragraphs accompanied by graphics. There is no single template that is used by everyone, so without going too far outside the professional box, make your pitch reflect the voice and tone of your project.

> Now for the pitch itself. We're big fans of not sending materials ahead of time and instead showing up with a simple, but well art-directed pitch book that takes the reader through the concept. We'll usually talk through the pitch and refer to the book as we go. Occasionally we'll use a piece of video or still photos to capture the essence of what we're presenting. The power of a pitch book shouldn't be underestimated. Basically, until your show is produced, the pitch book *is* the show. Everything from the overall look and feel, to the writing, to the design should be reflected in the book. It becomes a great presentational tool and a great way to solidify what your own vision of the project is.
>
> **Justin Wilkes, excerpt from interview in Chapter 11**

Next Steps with Your Pitch

When you've finally finished your pitch, and before you show it around, legally protect it. Although a document technically is protected by copyright the moment it is written, you can also register your copyright by filing the proper forms with the copyright organization in your country, or register your treatment or script at WGA, either online or by mail. You can review how to best protect your work in Chapter 5.

You may have legally protected the ownership of your project, but most development executives or other end users will insist that you sign a *submission release form* (see Chapter 5) before they'll agree to read your proposal, especially if you aren't represented by an agent or a lawyer. This document protects them from any plagiarism charges you may bring against them later.

Let's say... that you've got a terrific idea you want to pitch to a major youth-oriented network who wants an online series to increase its presence in the under-25 market. Your story focuses on modern-day pirates who rob from rich yacht owners and give the booty to the poverty-stricken in Cuba and Haiti. It's funny, adventurous, and a great star vehicle. But the network execs insist that you first sign a submission release—unbeknownst to you, they've got a couple of projects already in development, with pirates as their centerpiece. They don't want you to come back later and accuse them of stealing your idea, but they also don't want to lose your idea if it turns out to be better than the ideas they're developing. There just aren't a lot of brilliant and original ideas out there, and often, bright minds truly do think alike—and at the same time.

Other executives will accept a pitch only from your agent or entertainment attorney, though a few may take unsolicited material that is mailed or hand-delivered and will give it to their readers first. Having an "inside contact" is also an effective way to by pass the usual requirements.

IV. PITCH THE PITCH

> Whatever you can do or dream you can, begin it.
> Boldness has genius, power, and magic in it.
>
> **Goethe**

Without the ideas and motivation of producers, there would be nothing on television, little to watch online, and most Internet and television executives would have no product to sell. So, these buyers stand to profit as much as you do—probably much more—when they can buy, develop, and transmit your project. Your goal is to prove that your project is viable, and that, as its producer, you are focused, passionate, and competent to produce it. Your goal as producer is to inspire confidence, all around.

The media world is a small one; everyone knows someone who knows someone else. Seasoned producers know that today's secretary can be tomorrow's big shot who doesn't forget how you treated her back in the day. The guy who answers the phone might also make decisions for the boss, field calls, give feedback, and often write script coverage to see what makes the next round and what gets tossed. How you treat all these people now can get you work later when they've got their boss's job. If you don't give them respect, they can make sure you never get another chance with that company again.

Your intuition and sense of timing is also important. Certain times of the year are death for getting a pitch meeting, or an answer to your query letter. Winter holidays, the summer months, and religious holidays can be dead zones for an aspiring producer to try scheduling a pitch. Instead, ask the assistants or secretaries what times and dates they can suggest. They know their boss's schedule and moods better than anyone.

The Verbal Pitch

Having your written pitch is the first half of the producer's sales job. The second half is your verbal pitch, and it's just as important. The verbal pitch can effectively convey your passion, your professional skills, and your ability to handle the project.

After you've finished your synopsis, begin thinking of it as a script for your verbal pitch. Shorten it into a few punchy sentences: describe your main plotline, the hero and anti-hero and their journey, the conflict, the resolution. What are your important back stories, and what can you leave out of the pitch? Knowing these basic elements makes it easy for you to succinctly tell a story—an excellent skill for a producer.

The average pitch meeting is short and sweet, with only a few minutes for you to make your sale. The most effective pitches immediately grab the attention of the person or group you're pitching. If they like it, you may be asked to give a longer version that expands on the short pitch or to answer specific questions.

However, not every producer is comfortable giving a verbal pitch; this skill is a unique gift, one that can be a natural gift, or one that's developed. Following are a few approaches to the fine art of pitching.

Prepare Your Elevator Pitch

The elevator pitch is a metaphor for your ability to "own" your project so thoroughly that you can pitch it easily and convincingly, any time and any place—even in an elevator.

Let's say... that your 20-minute short has been accepted at an edgy festival, and it's generated a lot of buzz. You got a haircut, your shoes are cool, and you've memorized and practiced your verbal pitch a dozen times. You're in the elevator, on your way up to the screening, when you realize that the other person in the elevator is the new head of development at The Cool Channel, the perfect home for your project. But the elevator is moving toward its destination, and you've got only a few seconds to pitch your short. You are fully prepared. Your pitch is a clear and compelling synopsis, uncomplicated by back stories, ideals, or irrelevant quirks. Your pitch totally grabs her attention, and by the time the elevator door opens, she's gotten your business card. An elevator, a festival, a party, crossing the street—there are people everywhere who might be just the right person to hear your pitch. And to buy it.

Energize the Pitch

Anyone who's in a position to green light your project has heard hundreds of pitches, so you want your pitch to shine and to stand out. You want to capture their attention with your idea and with your presentation. As you work on developing your verbal pitch, concentrate on your communications skills, starting with eye contact. Find a balance of enthusiasm and calm in your voice. Keep your body language loose and relaxed even if that's not how you really feel. Focus on your breathing, and keep it deep and regular.

Memorize the pitch so you can give it without notes, but speak naturally and clearly. Use a timer as you practice to keep the time in mind. You want to keep it down to two to three minutes, even less if possible. Your genuine enthusiasm and confidence can control the meeting when people are as comfortable with you as they are with your project. Forget about yourself, and think about the people who are listening to you as fellow human beings.

There are several approaches you can use in the actual pitch meeting. You can simply talk it through, be direct, and be yourself, occasionally referring to graphics or ideas from your written pitch book. Maybe you act out a short scene, or use a storyboard presentation, or screen a short demo piece, or even use a few well-chosen props. However you choose to deliver your pitch, do what fits the project and your personality. But remember that this is all about selling your idea—so sell it. Don't give it away.

IN THE TRENCHES...

I once pitched a guy who was infamous for his remarkably short attention span. He would fiddle with his pencil, look at his watch, avoid eye contact, check his text messages. I saw this as a challenge, so I got a few friends together and asked them to hear me pitch. One agreed to play the guy, and he was great—he put up barriers like distracted yawning, answering the phone, gazing out the window, and generally just wasn't there. The others friends were assigned to watch my every move. Each time I gave them my pitch, I got better. Little nuances here, good body language there, making it as much of an act as it was a sales pitch. I was having fun. And when I gave the real pitch to the real guy, it felt natural and exciting. The rush was from excitement, not nerves. I got the job because I got his attention.

~C. Kellison

Sometimes, your idea really IS good, and the pitch was equally as successful. But the executive isn't interested because the company has tried a similar idea and it tanked. Or they don't have the budget, or the right scheduling slot for the type of show you've pitched. You can always ask them if they're looking for other ideas, and have some ready to pitch, just in case. You don't want to be known as a one-idea producer, but as one who's a source for many project ideas.

Work with a Partner

If you're pitching with a partner, practice who will be doing and saying what, and in what order. But keep it natural. It doesn't have to be like a Las Vegas routine unless taking that approach is genuinely relevant to your project. Rehearse your roles before the meeting, and come in relaxed, respectful, and enthusiastic. You can have fun with this without draining the energy in the room.

Remember: You may have come to pitch only one idea, but sometimes the people you're pitching may not like your original idea, or they're already in development on something similar. Have one or two ideas ready to pitch, just in case. And you can always entertain the possibility that they might also be interested in you as a producer (and/or writer) for other projects.

The Follow-Up

If you do get a pitch meeting, or even a courtesy phone call from someone in power, email them or send a brief thank-you note for their time. Ask them for any useful feedback they may have from the meeting. If you're not sure if they're interested in working with you, follow up with a phone call or email. You can be respectfully assertive, but not aggressive. Don't come off as a stalker by calling every other day. Know when to move on to the next possible buyer.

V. KEEP PITCHING

Nothing in this world can take the place of persistence. Talent will not; nothing is more common than unsuccessful people with talent. Genius will not; unrewarded genius is almost a proverb. Education will not; the world is full of educated derelicts. Persistence and determination alone are omnipotent. The slogan "press on" has solved and always will solve the problems of the human race.

President Calvin Coolidge

The people you pitched usually know what they're looking for, and their suggestions are valuable; they could improve your idea or propel it toward a possible development deal. They can also help you sharpen your pitching skills, or give you valuable references to other buyers.

If the people you've pitched to continue to say no, they usually mean it. Even if they initially seem to be receptive, don't get too excited—this could easily change and often does. If you haven't heard from someone who expressed interest, let a few days pass before you call to check in. Some producers let a week or two go by. It isn't personal. These are busy people who are swamped with work and are considering other producers' pitches and ideas. But if your weekly calls go unreturned for several weeks, take the hint.

Every project you see on TV, online, and on other new media formats represents a deal that was agreed on by a buyer and a seller. The producer may have taken the first deal that was offered, or pitched the project to several other places before finding the right one. The negotiations may have been straightforward or highly complex.

The producer is often tempted to hold out for a better offer, believing that you should never accept the first offer or that a sweeter deal could be waiting in the wings. How do you know that the first offer isn't the best? Ask other producers, your attorney, or an accountant. But act on the offer, one way or another, while it is still active and fresh in a buyer's mind.

The Demo Reel

Most producers leave their demo reel at the end of a pitch, or send it out to multiple sources when they're looking for work. They edit, and regularly update, their demo reel, which is a composite of their best work, with short clips and excerpts skillfully edited together into a demo reel. It can be on DVD as well as posted on the Internet, and helps form an overall impression of a producer's ability, experience, and creative approach. Most demo reels don't exceed five minutes, 10 at the very most. The first couple of minutes should be good enough to keep the viewer from fast-forwarding or hitting the stop button.

Networking and Connections

In most situations, real success depends first on *who* you know. *What* you know comes next. Most producers' jobs or project financing comes through connections, colleagues, friends, or friends of friends—ultimately, your reputation backs up their recommendations. You may be smart, creative, and motivated, but you're somewhat hindered if you don't have contacts.

Get to know people who are in the position to help you in as many ways as you can. As you'll see in Chapter 10, you can expand your sphere of connections, and experience, when you:

- Offer to work on student films or independent projects
- Find internships or apprenticeships
- Search the Internet for the newest sites and online channels
- Join media-oriented social networking communities
- Start your own blog and talk to other people on theirs
- Volunteer for and/or attend television and film festivals
- Go to media-centered panel discussions and social mixers
- Join TV-related organizations
- Subscribe to industry journals and publications
- Attend continued education programs that focus on TV, new media, and media studies

I really have to be in love with each and every show, and I think that one of the reasons that I've been successful is because that's what I look for. I look for something that I'm going to love and something I'm going to laugh at after 18 months of the same jokes that I laughed at to begin with. It's a really hard business because you burn out. You're expected to work one day for eight hours and the next day is 14, and to keep your energy and enthusiasm up day after day, year after year.

Valerie Walsh, excerpt from interview in Chapter 11

ON A HUMAN LEVEL . . .

Selling your project can feel a lot like selling a part of yourself, and it can be easy to confuse the two. Expect to encounter rejection along the way but don't take it as a personal affront. Each time that you hear "we've decided to pass on your idea" should motivate you to try even harder the next time. And when someone does give the green light to your project, stay objective and centered. A swollen ego just gets in the way when you have work to do.

SUMMARY

Pitching your project is a vital part of the producing process. There are countless stories of producers whose pitch won enthusiastic kudos from development executives, and got made—or were never heard from again. Yet every time you turn on your TV or computer or game box, it's clear that hundreds of shows did get made. Each went through the preproduction stage, as you'll see in the next chapter.

REVIEW QUESTIONS

1. Define "the pitch." What are its important components?

2. Why is it necessary to research the network, cable channel, online channel, or production company to whom you are pitching your idea?

3. List five potential venues to which you could pitch one specific idea. How are they similar? Different?

4. Discuss the benefits of the global marketplace.

5. What is a query letter? Why do you need to write one?

6. Describe the synopsis element of a written pitch. Write a brief example, using an existing script or your own project idea.

7. What is a demo reel? What are some of the ways it can benefit a producer? How might it be detrimental?

8. Define an elevator pitch. Why is it advantageous to have one ready?

9. List five possible venues that can help you increase your breadth of networking connections in entertainment and media industries.

10. Look at your own positive personality traits, and identify those that you can maximize when you give your verbal pitch.

The Plan: Preproduction **7**

> The producer is like the conductor of an orchestra.
> Maybe he can't play every instrument, but he knows
> what every instrument should sound like.
>
> **Richard Zanuck**

THIS CHAPTER'S TALKING POINTS

I. The Script

II. The Talent

III. The Crew

IV. Scheduling the Shoot

In the preproduction phase, hundreds of details come together to form the big picture, like pixels on a TV screen. These details are the essence of production. They add dimension and texture to your project. When you devote attention to these preproduction details—researching, double-checking, and making dozens of careful decisions—you can often save costly mistakes. Planning ahead is easier than going back and trying to cover your mistakes. You can find an in-depth preproduction checklist on the web site for this book that summarizes the many details that you'll need to be aware of as you plan your shoot.

I. THE SCRIPT

If you are shooting a narrative script, like a dramatic series or online short, you ideally want the script to be completely finished before you start shooting. The late delivery of shooting scripts can limit everyone's preparation time, and slow down the production itself. You do *not* want to realize as you're shooting that an essential story element is missing, requiring a last minute rewrite and stopping production, even though you're still paying everyone to wait. The more time you can give to your preproduction planning, the better your chances for a seamless shoot.

Maybe you've got a full script that can serve as a blueprint for your preproduction planning. Or perhaps your project is reality-based and you've only got an outline for who and what you hope to shoot. Yet in both cases, you'll carefully review each element before you begin shooting. Both extremes, and every kind of project in between, require preproduction strategies.

> **The Top Ten Things a Producer of Documentaries Should Know**
>
> 1. There's no substitute for a good story.
> 2. Working with great people is better than working with a lot of money.
> 3. How to write.
> 4. How to use as much of your production gear as possible (just in case).
> 5. How to budget (and stay within it).
> 6. If you're traveling with equipment, show up really early at the airport.
> 7. If you're going on location somewhere, it's best to have someone local on the crew.
> 8. It's never going to be the way you expect it to be.
> 9. It's okay to ask for advice.
> 10. Everything takes longer than you think it will.
>
> **Michael Bonfiglio, excerpt from interview in Chapter 11**

Script Breakdowns

Chapter 4 explored the budget ramifications of your project by breaking the script down into specific categories. You can now apply this same breakdown process to preproduction planning.

A breakdown sheet is a valuable tool that helps you organize and categorize your production details—the crew, on-camera talent, locations and sets, props, wardrobe, stunts, explosives, and more. There's a sample breakdown sheet form on this book's web site that can help define each element in your script (or storyboards) that you'll need to shoot.

Each scene requires its own breakdown sheet, and includes any or all of the following components:

- The script's title and scene number
- The date of the breakdown sheet
- The page number of the script
- Location: A constructed set or a real location
- Interior or exterior: Shooting inside or outside
- Day or night: This determines choices of equipment and gear
- Brief scene description
- Cast with speaking parts
- Extras: Any nonspeaking people in the scene or background
- Special effects: From explosions to blood packs to extra lighting
- Props: Anything handled on-camera by a character in the scene, like a telephone
- Set dressing or furnishings: On-camera items on set not handled by the character
- Wardrobe: Any clothing pertinent to a scene, like an outfit or torn shirt
- Makeup and hair: Normal makeup and sfx, such as wounds or aging, wigs or facial hair
- Equipment: Audio and video equipment and extras, grip, electric, cables, etc.
- Special equipment: Jibs, cranes, a dolly, Steadicams
- Stunts: Falls, fights, explosions; may include a stunt coordinator
- Vehicles: On-camera cars or other vehicles in the scene or as background
- Animals: Any animal that appears in the scene comes with a trainer, or wrangler, who takes charge of the animal during production

- Sound effects and/or music: Anything played back on set, like a phone ringing, music for lip-syncing, or music the actor is reacting to
- Additional production notes

Production Book

All productions involve details—hundreds of them. As you saw in Chapter 4, organizing these details is easier when the producer uses a *production book*. The traditional production book is kept in a three-ring loose-leaf binder, with dividers for each section. On a small project, the producer keeps her own book, and updates it regularly. On a larger production, usually a production assistant (PA) or production coordinator is put in charge of making multiple copies of production books for the key production personnel, giving everyone the same updated information. Refer back to Chapter 4 when compiling your own production book.

Equipment List

Each member of the crew either provides his or her own equipment as part of the contract at an extra rate, or gives an equipment request to the producer, prior to the shoot. Special production equipment needs to be arranged in advance of the shoot, and might include:

- Cameras and lens, screens, tripods, batteries, video stock, etc.
- Sound, extra mics, mixers, booms, windscreens, lavs, wireless bodypaks, etc.
- Grip and electric with cables, extra power sources, generators, cords, gaffer's tape, etc.
- Walkie-talkies
- A dolly and tracks
- Additional cranes and jibs for cameras
- Steadicam mounts
- Explosive devices
- HMI and other lights, gels, stands, and neutral density gels
- Camera cars
- A video monitor for each camera
- Teleprompters

The Look and Sound of Your Project

After you have organized these components, you can begin to explore the more aesthetic dimensions of your project.

Your *visual approach* provides important clues to the viewer. A narrative drama can reflect a moody noir texture requiring sophisticated lighting and a single-camera film technique; sitcoms are brighter, use more color, and usually take the traditional three-camera approach. A reality show might depend on three or four hand-held cameras; an online show can be shot in close up with one video camera. Elements such as lighting, camera lenses and angles, video or film stock, wardrobe, makeup, props, and set design all contribute to the overall visual aesthetics.

Shooting original footage is not your only option. Producers of all programming genres make clever use of components such as stock footage, still photos, archival or historical footage, text, documents, or graphics in postproduction either to augment or replace original footage. These elements can also add visual and audio effects and textures to the overall look.

The **audio impressions** you create are no less important. Sound can create subtle, even subconscious effects; though an audience isn't always conscious of what they hear, they get an audio impression. The clarity of dialogue and the ambient background sounds such as birds, traffic, a voice on the radio, a humming freezer, background conversations, all adds nuance to the story. The many elements of sound can be designed and enhanced in postproduction. Sound design can contribute to your essential narrative beats, or it can be distracting if it's not done well. A professional sound designer is a real asset to your production.

Storyboarding and Floor Plans

The next step is to plan out how you're going to shoot each scene. A scene, for example, might call for one long shot, or it might require master shots, individual close-ups, pans, two-shots, and cutaways. These shots are planned to fit together later in the editing process. By the time you actually shoot each scene, you will have totally planned it out.

Depending on the producer and/or the size of the project, there are a couple of ways in which to plot out each step of the production.

Storyboards are sketches in numbered boxes that illustrate the details of the scene to be shot. They can be simple hand-drawn cartoon-like sketches, or elaborate pictures generated from storyboard software. Each drawing represents a scene or shot number from the script (see the storyboard form example on this book's web site). When the image or camera angle changes, so does the content of the box.

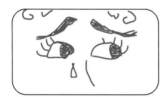  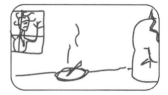

Before the actual shoot, the producer reviews the script, often with the director, UPM, and/or line producer. They storyboard each scene. They detail every camera setup in that scene. Does the camera go in this corner and shoot in that direction? Is it a close-up or a two-shot? Does the shot work in the overall edit sequence? Where are the actors placed? Do any set, prop or wardrobe details in the shot need special attention?

Most storyboards are minimal black-and-white line drawings, although they can be full-color illustrations, photographs, or even animation. They save time and money by providing a visual synopsis of the scenes to be shot, the look and the feel of the set or location, the location of one character to another and their actions, and even the colors, textures, and mood of a scene.

All these aspects are essential to an art director, production designer, director, producer, the director of photography (DP), and others involved in production. However, not all projects can be storyboarded; many reality-based shows are shot with little or no advance knowledge of the shooting circumstances. And in many television dramas on a tight schedule, the camera coverage can't be planned until the scene is blocked for the camera on the actual day of shooting.

IN THE TRENCHES...

Storyboards, if they're imaginative and descriptive, have proven to be great tools for selling an idea or project. I've often pitched project ideas with just a set of storyboards. They can be on strong boards or paper, or as a PowerPoint presentation. This way, the clients get a clever glimpse into what my project could look like, without my having to shoot a scene or a trailer for a lot more money.

~C. Kellison

Floor plans provide an overhead view of what you plan to shoot, as well as the space around it. In complex, highly detailed projects, a floor plan can augment or replace the storyboard. It shows where the cameras and microphones are placed, as well as the lights, the actors, furnishings, set walls, and more. A floor plan helps the various department heads see what's needed for that scene, like props, furnishings, and set design. Because a floor plan shows the camera placements and shooting angles, it helps the DP plan how to best block the actors. Floor plans and storyboards both illustrate the shoot and make it easier for everyone involved to visualize the project's vision.

Shot List

When the producer carefully studies the storyboards, she can then put together a *shot list*. This is a detailed list of each shot that's part of a scene or specific sequence. Most shot lists are made on set after a blocking rehearsal; when time allows, they're ideally put together prior to the day of the shoot. The shot list is distributed to the camera and audio crew, as well as to other crew members who are directly involved in the shoot.

The shot list uses a specific language that everyone understands to describe the shot that is needed:

STORYBOARD SHOTS

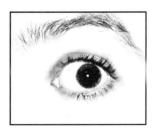

EXTREME CLOSE-UP

CLOSE-UP

MEDIUM

MEDIUM WIDE

WIDE

EXTREME WIDE

- **ECU:** Extreme close-up (eyes or mouth, or part of an object)
- **CU:** Close-up (the whole face or entire object)
- **MS:** Medium shot (an upper torso or an object in part of its surroundings)
- **MWS:** Medium wide shot (most or all of a body or group of objects) that's framed between a medium shot and wide shot
- **WS:** Wide shot (an entire body or larger grouping of objects)
- **EWS:** Extreme wide shot (many bodies or shots of horizons, buildings, sky lines, etc.)

Production Meetings

No matter where your project will eventually end up—on a major network, online, on a mobile phone, in a short film festival—your team is a vital part of making it all come together. You want to encourage good communication and collaboration during the production; one approach is to schedule daily or weekly production meetings.

Production meetings generally include the key people like the producer(s), director, line producer, production manager, and whoever else you want to be involved. Prior to the meeting, you'll create an agenda and make copies of documents or plans to be discussed, including the script or shooting schedule or myriad other details. Two areas stand out as particularly important, regardless of the size of your production.

- The production meeting is called by the producer, and invites any key positions (the gaffer, key grip, DP, sound mixer, production designer, wardrobe, AD, etc.), even if your production is a small one. Go through the schedule together, step by step, and discuss.
- If your project is scripted, or benefits from rehearsal time, do a read-through of the script with the cast and crew.

Everyone's encouraged to give notes or comments, while you listen, set priorities, delegate jobs, and generally take care of business. After the meeting, send out a memo and outline what was said and agreed upon. Production meetings can be an excellent forum for complimenting those people who are doing their job well in front of everyone else. If, on the other hand, you have a problem with a specific person, the production meeting is not the place for discussion. Do that later, in private.

> I love bringing talented people together. There's no greater feeling than standing on a shoot, sitting in an edit session, or watching the final product on TV, knowing that you as the producer pulled together an incredible, hard-working group of people to create it.
> **Justin Wilkes, excerpt from interview in Chapter 11**

II. THE TALENT

The word *talent* covers quite a range. Talent can apply to a world-famous actor, an on-camera news anchor, a game show host. Or, talent can mean real-life subjects in a documentary who have never been on camera before, the man on the street, children, animals, and extras.

Regardless of the genre you're producing, it's virtually impossible to have a project without on-camera talent; he or she is the backbone of your story who can give your project credibility and energy, and provide connection with a viewer.

Casting Talent

Finding on-camera talent—who are talented—can be a full-time job, especially when your project is especially dependent on acting talent, or a clever talk show host, or a gifted professional for a how-to show, or real people with a compelling story. Here are the steps that a producer can take to find just the right person.

Casting Directors and Agencies

Specialized talent agencies and casting directors work with producers and directors to help them find the right face, voice, or special skill for a project. Some casting professionals work only with actors, others specialize in casting "real people" or extras for a crowd scene or atmosphere.

Casting directors keep files on their clients: the actors' resumes and headshots, possibly a reel with examples of their work, and make sure they're regularly updated. Casting directors are familiar with their clients' skills, what other roles they've played, and their work ethic. A good casting director maintains solid relationships with talent agents, other casting directors, and talent managers, and can often help in negotiating overall talent fees and work conditions.

The producer first contacts the casting director and outlines the project's needs. Then the casting director calls agents, places ads, and/or posts notices for a *casting call*. Audition space is rented and times set up. Auditions are held in a rehearsal or casting space; the producer may shoot video and/or stills and reviews them later when he's making final casting decisions.

Guerilla Casting

You may not have a casting director at your disposal or the money to hire one. For low-budget projects, you can post your own notices and hold casting auditions in spaces that are inexpensive or free. So how and where can you find good talent?

- Write a short description of the part(s) you're casting, the audition date, time, and location, and a phone number or email address to get more information.
- Advertise your casting call in local newspapers and community penny savers.
- Many towns and cities have web sites with cultural links. Surf these sites for possible venues to post your audition notice or to find talent.
- Attend local theaters, high school and college plays, churches or synagogues, or youth groups that put on plays. Look for talented actors who stand out. Ask for permission to post a notice on their bulletin boards.
- Post an audition notice in local film, television, and new media schools.
- If you want "real people," your local grocery stores, health clubs, block associations, PTAs, or hardware stores might have a bulletin board for posting your audition notice.
- Consult with other producers and directors who work regularly with talent.

Casting Calls and Auditions

You've posted the casting notice. Now, you can begin to cast the parts. Because auditions tend to attract a lot of people, you want a system that helps you to keep track of who shows up, how well they read the part, and how to locate them. In an audition, you and/or your casting director will:

- ***Find a comfortable space for auditions.*** The room should easily accommodate you, possibly a director, assistant producers, and the talent. Check the room temperature, the acoustics, the amount of light, and its overall comfort factor. If needed, set up extra lighting. Supply water and enough chairs. Assign someone other than the producer or director to read any additional parts with the actor. You also want an ample waiting area outside the audition room. Assign a "people person" to the waiting area to keep the talent relaxed. Provide water and snacks.
- ***Schedule the audition.*** It helps if you time the reading yourself—read the part(s) and see how long it takes to read it a couple times, then add five to 10 minutes for conversation before and after. Consolidate the auditions by scheduling each actor for a specific time. Build flexibility into your plan; working actors often have several auditions a day, and some readings go longer than others.
- ***Keep a log of those auditioning.*** List their name, agent (if any), phone number, email address, and the part they're auditioning for. Keep track of the talents' photographs (headshots) and their resumes.

- *Make the script available.* While they're waiting to read, give actors the pages from the script that they'll be reading (also called *sides*). This gives them time to get comfortable with the audition material. Or ask them in advance to prepare a monologue for the audition.
- *Videotape the audition.* A taped audition gives you a chance to review an actor's performance later, and to compare it with other actors' performances. Take close-ups of facial expressions and wide shots for the overall performance and body language. After each actor leaves, make notes and label each headshot and tape to avoid confusion.
- *Be patient with children.* They can be a casting challenge, regardless of their age or professional experience. Children get tired, hungry, grumpy, and nervous. Keep the environment calm and provide games, crayons, and books. Assign at least one PA to keep the kids occupied and the parents calm.
- *Arrange for callbacks.* After the auditions, you've hopefully found actors or talent who you want to see again for a second reading; these repeat auditions are known as *callbacks*. It's not unusual to call an actor back two or three times. The general rule, especially if the actor is a member of SAG, is to pay the actor a fee after three call-backs. When you've narrowed your choices down, audition potential cast members together for a reading. The chemistry between actors can make or break a project.
- *Actors deserve respect.* Any talent you have rejected are worthy of a polite phone call or personal email. They may not have been right for this project, but could be perfect for another one in the future.

IN THE TRENCHES...

Auditions can be rushed and nervous-making. Stay focused. It's a real challenge to keep auditions from being repetitive for those of us who hold them. Few actors are comfortable in auditions, so help them out. Introduce them to key people in the room, and make eye contact, make a joke. You'll encourage a much better performance when you treat the talent with respect.

~ *C. Kellison*

Hiring Talent: Union or Non-Union?

The category that covers "talent" is a broad one. It includes actors with major and minor parts, on-camera hosts, narrators, background extras, children, animals, magicians, stunt people, jugglers, nonprofessionals and "real people."

Many are members of a talent union, though not all good actors are members of a union, and not all union members are good actors. But most experienced and professional actors belong to unions such as SAG, AFTRA, and Actors Equity for theatre, that impose specific rules under which the actors work. The producer must honor them or risk hefty fines from the union.

A low budget can limit producers, often requiring them to work with non-union talent, thus avoiding the additional salaries, expenses, paperwork, residuals, pension and welfare, and other regulated working conditions that talent unions require.

On the other hand, an independent producer, production company, network, or studio may take the steps necessary to become a *union signatory*, meaning they've agreed to comply with the guidelines and regulations of the union. And because a well-known actor can be the biggest selling point for your project, it's often worth becoming a union signatory and paying the actor's much-higher fees in exchange for the benefits you'll see at the box-office.

Becoming a union signatory involves taking a realistic view of its impact on your budget. There must be enough money to cover union talents' wages as well as *fringe benefits* (payments that include payroll taxes, pension, health, and other union and/or employee benefits). Each union's web site provides the most current and up-to-date information on these costs.

Each talent union has its own guidelines, but most will work with you. Some may make special concessions for student productions, low-budget shows, and affirmative action contracts, as well as multimedia, new media, some educational projects, and Internet projects. The agreements generally include lowering the pay scales and allowing more flexibility in the overall working conditions. You can find in-depth information on this complex aspect of production in the Books and References section in this book's web site as well as by going to the web site of the specific union.

Union Actors

Talent unions such as SAG and AFTRA have listed their guidelines, pay scales, and other regulations on their web sites, along with the producer's role in honoring these requirements. Most producers work closely with the unions and can negotiate the requirements which usually include:

- *Rate of pay.* Daily, weekly, or per-picture rates.
- **Per diem.** When on location and away from home, a daily allowance to cover meals, transportation, and other production-related expenses.
- **Speaking lines.** All on-camera parts with or without lines have their own pay scale. Additional recording and rerecording time may also be required at a later date.
- *Screen credit.* The actor's credit itself, its placement on the screen, the order of the name's appearance among other actors, and other union or contractual agreements.
- **Turnaround time.** Usually a 12-hour break of time between the end of one shooting day and the call time for the next day. Check the union's web site.
- *Meals and breaks.* Talent must have regularly scheduled breaks to eat and to relax.
- *Wardrobe stipends.* A fee paid to actors who provide their own wardrobe.
- *Specific requirements.* Child actors work fewer hours than adults, and if they are absent from school, require a tutor, parent, or social worker to be with them at all times.
- *Benefits.* Additional monies paid to an actor for things like P&W (pension and welfare) and worker's compensation.
- *Travel.* There are specific guidelines detailing an actor's flying status, such as first class only, or no red-eye flights.

Often, there may be a SAG representative on the set. He or she is employed by the union to resolve any contract disputes or member complaints, and deals primarily with the producer on a day-to-day basis in this regard. In some cases, you can work with the talent unions for waivers on wardrobe requirements, turn around time, stipends, benefits, and other areas.

Non-Union Actors

Actors who are not members of an actors' union deserve the same respect and base salary, whenever possible, as those actors who are protected by their unions. Producers are not required to pay them union benefits, and there are fewer restrictions for on-set hours or turnaround time. Producers do have an ethical responsibility to treat everyone fairly, regardless of their union status.

Real People

The popularity of reality-based programming, and the comparatively low costs of these shows, has increased the demand for talent who are "real people"—couples, singles, old and young. Most have never appeared on-camera and are therefore not union members. In such cases, it's up to the producer to play fair, go over all deal memos and contracts with the talent involved, and avoid any complications or potential claims later on.

Stunt Actors

Some actors do their own stunts, but most use a stunt double for dangerous action like a fall from a building or a fist fight. If a stunt is dangerous or complicated, a stunt coordinator is hired to plan and oversee the stunt actor's work. Most experienced stunt performers belong to stunt associations covered by SAG.

Extras and Background

Most programs feature people milling in the background, walking on a street, getting into buses, driving cars, eating at other tables in a restaurant scene. These *extras* add a layer of dimension and credibility to a shot. Depending on the scene, extras can be professionals in SAG, or are hired by casting agencies or nonprofessional locals—even friends and family can fill in as background. Extras are scheduled and rehearsed just like actors with larger parts.

Actors' Staff

An actor might bring his or her own people into a production. In certain situations, the production pays these salaries and provides accommodations and workspace. These extra personnel might include:

- *Hair and/or makeup.* Knows the cosmetic (and emotional) needs of the actor.
- *Wardrobe designer or stylist.* Maintains the talent's specific wardrobe "look," keeps track of clothing, and mends and cleans the clothing needed.
- *Wrangler.* Has expertise in training or managing talent, and might be a wrangler for an animal or a child actor.
- *Personal trainer.* Often a necessity when the part calls for an actor's overall health, sex appeal, or specific physical demands of a part.
- *Secretary or personal assistant.* Handles requests for personal appearances, correspondence, and phone calls, as well as production-related details.

Rehearsals

Rehearsals can be viewed as a costly luxury in some budgets, but whenever possible, the producer looks for ways to afford rehearsal time. This valuable time not only gives actors an opportunity to fine-tune their part, but it also serves the director, director of photography, audio engineers, and lighting director in *blocking*, or planning, their shoot. This saves valuable time on set when the shoot begins.

Rehearsing Scripted and Narrative Content

In actor-driven projects, rehearsal time gives the talent an extra advantage. Actors can get more comfortable with the script, the camera blocking, and fellow actors' individual styles and rhythms.

Depending on the project, the producer either hires a director who works directly with the talent, or rehearses and/or directs the actors himself. Not all projects require or have time for rehearsals before shooting, and not all actors want to rehearse; each has his or her own approach.

In most narrative dramas, commercials, or sitcoms, some directors give actors the freedom to interpret their roles; others prefer to "direct" the actors. Directors know what they want in a performance, and it is their job to motivate actors to explore their character's back story, create a specific regional accent, or use distinctive body language to explore the range of their roles.

Rehearsing Unscripted and Reality-Based Content

Whenever possible, documentaries, reality-based shows, talk shows, and sports and live events can often benefit from a technical rehearsal. For example, in planning to shoot a documentary, a producer might go to a location prior to shooting and rehearse her camera positions and moves, and decide where the microphones should be placed in relation to the talent.

Many nonscripted shows depend on special sets such as Tribal Council on *Survivor,* or on *The X Factor* and *American Idol.* The producer employs his "dream team" to run through all the possible challenges they might encounter during the actual shoot. And in most talk shows, producers often rehearse with stand-ins, or run through special demonstration segments, musical performances, fashion shows, and the like. Before the show begins taping, the producer does "look-sees" of every component of the show: "host entrance," "guest entrance," "desk cross," and other aspects of blocking and rehearsing.

Blocking

Once the action of the actor or "real person" has been determined, the next step is *blocking* the scene. Blocking looks at the camera's placement in relation to the actors (or their stand-ins) and their sequences of steps and actions: it's like choreographing a shot and involves the DP, director, camera operator, the lighting director (LD) and lighting crew, the audio engineer, and usually the producer.

Blocking considers furniture, props, or greenery in the scene, the relationship between one actor and another, and how the camera can capture it all. Blocking decides what the camera is shooting and from what angle, and spots for cameras and actors—called marks—are usually marked with masking tape on the floor or wall as reminders.

III. THE CREW

Although the actors may reflect charisma on-screen, it's the crew who creates the real magic behind the scenes. Your project may require only a small two-person crew, or you might need several camera and audio operators, as well as lighting designers, DPs, set designers, and wardrobe and makeup specialists.

Hiring a full crew can be challenging to both novice and seasoned producers alike. You may have had some experience working on productions where you met professionals whose work you liked. If not, look for creative options. Ask other producers or filmmakers for their recommendations. Contact local production crews or national crew-booking companies (check this book's companion web site) and ask for crew reels to screen; these reels reveal a visual or aural approach that could be similar to your vision. Research television, new media, and film departments in universities that may have talented students who are eager for an opportunity to augment their experience, and may work for lower fees, even academic credit.

> The essential point is that you have to try to gain the trust and the confidence of the client, and all the other parties—from all the audio people, from the staging people, the artist, all the parties involved in this event. You have to gain their trust, that you understand what their issues are, and bring them on board to be on the same team for the overall good of the project.
> **Stephen Reed, excerpt from interview in Chapter 11**

Regardless of the size of your crew, each crew member has his or her own area of specialty. Over time, you'll build your team of experienced, talented, and collaborative crew members who can be trusted and who share your vision. They are, quite simply, your lifeline.

The Key Production Department Heads

Whether your project is large and ambitious, or small and controlled, union or non-union—certain areas in every production need at least one person to cover them. In lower-budget projects, one person may cover several of these areas. The key people the producer hires for almost every project are:

- The director
- The director of photography
- The production manager
- The assistant director
- The production audio engineer
- The production designer
- The postproduction supervisor

Director

As discussed in other chapters, television—and now, new media—is the producer's domain. So, the producer can also be the director, or hires the director, or maps out the desired look and creative approaches of the production.

If a director is hired, she may fill the traditional film director's role, working with actors, the crew, and the producer in visualizing scenes. The director can be a strong creative force in the production, supervising the writing, the casting, rehearsing the actors, and crafting the overall aesthetic approach.

Or, the director might be the technical director (TD) who, in a studio setting, works out of the control room. She is generally assigned to multicamera shoots, such as talk shows and live events, and among other responsibilities, directs each camera and "calls the shots" as they come into the control room, often creating a line-cut, or rough edit, in the process.

Under the Directors Guild of America (DGA) guidelines, the director, the AD (see later), and the technical director fall into a separate fee category and pay scale. Although each project is unique, it thrives when the producer and director cohesively and collaboratively work together.

Director of Photography

The DP is often the first key position to be filled. The DP brings the creative vision of the producer and/or director to life. Whether he actually operates the camera himself, or supervises the camera operator(s), he's mastered the essentials of lighting, formats of video and film, and the use of cranes and dollies. He can bring his own experienced people into the production, and helps outline a shooting schedule. The DP often owns his own equipment or has relationships with equipment rental companies.

Production Manager

The role of the production manager (PM) or unit production manager (UPM) varies in each project, depending on its size and budget. Hired by the producer, the UPM might be in charge of breaking down the script, and creating a schedule and budget from that breakdown. She keeps track of costs and deals with paying the vendors. She might also negotiate with and hire crew members, supervise the production assistants, arrange for equipment, and cover a range of essential details. Depending on the project, she monitors the daily cash flow; makes the arrangements for travel, housing, and meals; applies for shooting permits; oversees releases and clearances; and generally supervises the production activity. In a smaller or low-budget project, the producer or assistant producer doubles as the production manager.

Assistant Director

The assistant director (AD) is the on-set liaison between the director, the producer and/or production manager, the crew, and the actors. He typically plays "bad cop" to the director/producer's "good cop," helps to create the shooting schedule, and keeps the crew in sync with the day's schedule. The AD might also be responsible for timing shows or segments during taping. If there are scenes in which extras appear, he is often in charge of directing their actions.

Production Audio Engineer

The subtleties of sound design can get lost in preproduction planning, so a savvy producer hires an audio engineer who can capture the clarity of dialogue, background sounds, special on-location audio (sirens, birds, traffic, muted conversations), and other ambient audio. She knows how to place and monitor microphones (mics) like booms, wireless, small clip-on microphones (lavs), and windscreens for minimizing wind, air conditioners, fluorescent lights, and other sounds that can cause interference. She either owns her audio equipment or can lease what's needed for the project.

Production Designer

The aesthetic texture, design, the mood and tone are essential elements in every project. From creating elaborate sets, to simply rearranging set furniture, the production designer creates a design for the overall look of the show, and works closely with the producer and director to create an environment for the action. By finding out what camera shots and angles are planned, he designs what will be seen in the camera's framing. As always, the budget has an impact on these choices, although a clever production designer can improvise and plan carefully. He may do all the jobs himself. Or, he may hire an art director whose job it is to take charge of building and painting the sets, and/or to modify existing locations. Often, a set decorator is also needed to locate items for the set such as furniture, lamps, wallpaper, and rugs. The production designer and/or the art director also decide on carpenters, greens specialists, prop masters, painters, and other support crew.

Postproduction Supervisor

Whenever possible, a producer hires a postproduction supervisor. Her overall responsibility is to be well-prepared for the postproduction stage, consulting with the producer in making early decisions about postproduction details—the choice of editor and the editing facility and the software program that's best for the project; the sound designer and the audio mix facility; the graphics designer and facility; and other postproduction elements.

In some productions, the postproduction supervisor comes on board during production and sets up systems for screening the dailies, and organizes, labels, and stores the footage and audio elements. She understands the professional standards for editing, including nonlinear editing (NLE) systems as well as online systems and when they can come in handy. She's aware of the many video, audio, and graphics needs, and can coordinate them all together. More postproduction information can be found in Chapter 9.

Key Players, Key Teams: The Script, and the Visual, Aural, and Support Teams

Depending on the size of the production, most if not all of the following positions are hired in the preproduction phase.

The Writing Team

Writers and revisions. During the writing process, the original script writer(s) might be teamed up with new writers, replaced because of "creative differences" with the producer or writer, or leave the project because of prior commitments. The initial concept of the project can change as part of the creative process, or the client or network makes demands the writer isn't willing to make. Script revisions are generally agreed on in the writer's contract, either following WGA guidelines or on a fee-per-revision basis.

Researcher. Most projects require some degree of research. An historical storyline, for example, involves details in architecture, costume, or speech mannerisms. A reality-based show hires a researcher to look for background material, find interesting ideas and real-life characters. A quiz show depends on researchers to investigate subject areas for questions and correct answers.

Researchers are valuable components in news or fact-based programs for double-checking sources or backgrounds. They might be professionals, academics, or consultants who specialize in specific areas of knowledge, or who are adept at problem solving. Researchers can also be production assistants or other administrative staff who are assigned to specific research needs.

The Visual Team

Storyboard artist. Working with the producer or director, and examining each scene of the script, the storyboard artist translates the visuals onto paper, either by hand or using a storyboarding software program. These sketches are generally simple and cartoon-like, and show at a glance what needs to be created by the production team.

Lighting director. The LD works with, or doubles as, the DP. In some cases, the LD is known as the key gaffer or chief lighting technician. He designs the lighting for the production, plans where the equipment is best placed, and decides the best lights to use and their wattage. On set, the LD supervises the rigging of the pipes and the hanging of lights, and also recommends scrims, gels, and patches for various lights.

Camera operator. Either working *with* the DP or *as* the DP, the camera operator shoots the scenes, works with blocking and framing, lighting, and lenses for each shot. She also works closely with the audio engineer to make sure that the best audio goes into the camera and onto the video tape or into digital storage.

Assistant camera operator (AC). The AC helps the camera operator, keeps camera batteries charged and available, changes and maintains lenses, and sets up and breaks down the camera equipment. The AC also slates each take, works closely with the script supervisor, is in charge of keeping track of tape/film stock, and completes the camera reports for the editor. Some duties may be given to the second AC if one is hired.

Still photographer. The photographer takes a number of still shots during rehearsal and behind the scenes, as well as on set, for purposes of providing publicity stills as well as creating a photographic archive of the production.

Gaffer. This lighting specialist works closely with the DP and cameras to set up lights, adjust them during the shoots, supervise and install various *gels and gobos*, and supervise the electric power sources or generators.

Best boy. An assistant to the gaffer, the best boy (often a female) works specifically with electrical cables and ties them in safely to a power source or generator.

Key grip. This main grip works with the physical aspects of setting up the shoot, which includes rigging light stands and C-stands that hold up silks or *cycs* (hanging background fabric or paper) and installing special equipment such as a dolly and dolly tracks, camera jibs and cranes, and more. The key grip is also primarily responsible for overseeing safety procedures on set, especially in the presence of stunts and pyrotechnics, and supervises the crew of grips.

Grip. A grip's responsibilities include pushing the dolly, operating cranes or camera cars, helping with other equipment needs, and setting up, adjusting, and taking down lights.

The Audio Team

Boom operator. In the audio department, the boom operator works very closely with the camera operator and aims the *boom* (a long flexible pole with a microphone fixed to the end) at the audio source without getting into the camera's frame. Each camera has its own mic and boom operator. A boom can also be a large wheeled stand with a moveable arm from which the mic hangs.

Audio mixer. There are often several sources of audio in production. The audio mixer operates the console and separates each source onto a separate audio channel for postproduction mixing. The mixer might also "live mix" the sound as it comes into the console; this can make the postproduction audio mix easier or, in some cases, unnecessary.

Audio assistant. This member of the audio team keeps track of all audio equipment, changes and labels audio tapes, separates the microphone and audio cables from electrical cables, places mics on set or on talent, and often tapes the cables down either to hide them from the camera or to prevent people from tripping over them.

The Production and Administrative Team

Production secretary. As the liaison between the cast, the crew, the producer, and the UPM, the production secretary is often in charge of distributing paperwork such as call sheets, contacts sheets, schedules, paychecks, and other duties assigned per project. On smaller projects, the production secretary can also double as receptionist, PA, even handling the catering.

Script supervisor. A vital asset to the director, the script supervisor checks that all the planned shots in the script have either been shot or deleted. She is the watch dog for *continuity.* For example, when an actor wears a red tie in one shot, he needs to be wearing the same red tie in another shot that follows it in the script. Taking continual notes during the shoot, the script supervisor describes each shot in each scene and keeps notes on all takes. She notes gestures or movements (like a hand on someone's shoulder) that need to match another shot. She looks for matching dialects and dialogue, details in wardrobe, hair, and makeup (like matching a bleeding wound from one shot to another), and what lens is used. The script notes also provide important references and directions for the editor to use later in postproduction.

Location manager. The location manager looks for and secures locations for the production, negotiates the location agreements and rates, takes care of shooting permits, parking, on-location catering, and makes sure the location is in good condition after the shoot has wrapped. He's the liaison between the location and the producer.

Catering manager. She is in charge of providing water, coffee, tea, and snacks at all times, as well as arranging for a healthy hot meal at least every six hours. The catering manager sets up a table, cart, or vehicle for serving food as close to the production action as possible. This area is often split up between *catering* (meals) and *craft services* (or *crafty*) of drinks and snacks.

Transportation manager. The transportation manager (or a key driver called the transportation captain) is in charge of moving the cast, crew, and equipment from one location to another. The production may require the transportation manager to rent the proper vehicles such as mobile dressing rooms, *honey wagons* (portable bathrooms), trucks, or vans for equipment as well as keeping them operational and ready to move. This is a union position, strictly available to the Teamsters.

2nd assistant director (2nd AD). This crew member, when needed, assembles the call sheets, sets the call times for the cast and crew, and tells the cast and crew where to show up and at what time. She may also direct any action in the background involving extras.

2nd-2nd AD. If a situation calls for traffic or crowd control, he may be in charge. He also secures the set in whatever ways are necessary and works with the production secretary to coordinate the actors for their arrival on set.

Production assistant (PA). A necessity in all departments, the PA can be a tremendous asset who contributes both physical labor and administrative help. Most productions have a pool of PAs, assigning them on set, in the office, on location, or wherever help is needed. PAs are on set first, and they leave last. They're available to help in all departments, to do whatever needs doing. Most location PAs must be able to drive, often large equipment trucks, understand local parking restrictions, and be trusted to guard expensive equipment. Office PAs keep track of budgets, copy and distribute the latest script revisions, help with auditions, take care of talent needs, and often go back and forth between the set/location and the main office.

Interns. Often college or high school students can work for a semester on a production for school credit, while learning in the process. Few interns have worked in television production before; they require an intern supervisor to make sure they're doing their assigned tasks and are also getting a positive and organized learning experience. Interns are paying for their internships in school credits, and their energy is important to the production. Like PAs, they're assigned to areas where help is most needed.

The Top Ten Most Important Tools for PAs and Interns

1. **Mobile phone.** Use it as a good communication tool. Get everyone's cell and office number, so you can contact them in emergencies. Don't stay on the phone more than you need to. Make sure you've got text and GPS capacity.
2. **Walkie-talkies.** Even better in certain circumstances than mobiles.
3. **Meals and snacks.** Feeding people is important, and it makes them like you more.
4. **Driver's license.** You could drive for hours, on errands and runs. Have a current license; make sure your company covers you with its insurance. Avoid parking tickets, get to know the area you're driving in, and be comfortable with the vehicle. Keep everything locked up, no matter what.
5. **Paperwork.** Write everything down. Carry a notebook with you, and put everything down that you're told to do. Keep copies of everything to avoid problems later.

(Continued)

The Top Ten Most Important Tools for PAs and Interns—Cont'd

6. **Computers.** Several software programs are standards on a production, such as Excel, Word, Final Draft, and Movie Magic, among others. Learn how to use them!
7. **The Internet.** Know how to search for things you need, like equipment, vehicles, venues, and a dozen other things you'll be asked to find out about.
8. **Attire.** Pockets in pants and jackets are important for holding phones, pens, stop watches, and other things. Wear comfortable shoes when you're standing or walking a lot, and layer clothing because it gets really hot or very cold on set.
9. **Maps.** Get familiar with the city or location you're working in. Know the streets, public transportation, and how to get around easily and quickly. Get a portable GPS system or have one on your phone.
10. **Production book.** Get as organized as you can. You'll have lots of information to deal with so when it's organized into one production book, it's all right there, in one place.

Jonna McLaughlin and Becky Teitel, *production managers and former PAs*

The Production Design Team

Set designer (construction coordinator). Works with the production designer and creates blueprints for the set(s), hires the crew to construct it, and supervises the assembly of sets, floors, ceilings, or moveable set pieces.

Set dresser. Finds, transports, makes, and/or paints all furnishings, including tables, chairs, appliances, or other furnishings that are part of the action on a set or location. May require working in advance of the next day's shoot, and being on call during the shoot.

Prop master. Supplies all props that are handled as part of the shoot, such as a paintbrush for a home makeover show or a tissue in a crying scene. He works closely with the script supervisor to maintain continuity.

Assistants. Depending on the project, each of the preceding may have one or more assistants working in various capacities.

Wardrobe designer or stylist. Designs the wardrobe "look," as well as coordinates all wardrobes needed for the shoot with the production designer, buys or rents the wardrobe, measures and fits the talent, keeps all wardrobe elements in the order of the shooting schedule, and regularly cleans and repairs the clothing or costumes. She may sell the wardrobe items after the shoot has wrapped, or handles all wardrobe returns.

Dresser. Works with the wardrobe department to keep track of clothing. Helps the talent change clothing when needed. Some productions may require several dressers who often "swing" between wardrobe, makeup, and hair, unless they are members of a union with regulations that prohibit this multiple workload.

Hair stylist. On set during any scenes that involve talent. The hair stylist may create elaborate high-concept hair styles, design and maintain wigs, or simply be on hand for touch-ups to maintain continuity from one scene to the next.

Makeup artist. Covers a range of needs from applying traditional cosmetic on-camera makeup to creating special effects such as wounds, prosthetics, facial hair, and more. The call time for makeup precedes the shoot time and requires an artist to have an on-set presence.

Additional Production Specialists

Your project might require the hiring of other specialists such as a stunt coordinator, a choreographer, crane and Steadicam operators, on-set tutors, animal wranglers, explosive experts, a teleprompter operator, florists and greens specialists, an on-set nurse, security personnel, and more. Many productions might also call for production support from an accountant, an entertainment lawyer, publicists, and marketing consultants.

> *The visual effects team.* Your project might need a visual effects designer who can create extraordinary effects ranging from magical flying characters to subtle background enhancement. You might want animation or special graphic design for screen credits and a program title, or the illusion of a city blowing away in a tornado. As the producer, you'll make an assessment of your production needs, and then consult with the designers prior to the shoot.

> I used to think that being a producer was being the brain because you have to have knowledge of what is going on in all of the other areas. Now I think it is a lot of different peoples' brains put together. But at times I have thought, am I the only one who is responsible for keeping track of this? Because it seemed like everyone was always coming to me. Then I realized that you *do* have to delegate. It will make your life so much easier, finding the right people who can take care of things for you.
> **Valerie Walsh, excerpt from interview in Chapter 11**

IV. SCHEDULING THE SHOOT

You've chosen your crew, and your script or shooting outline is clear in your mind. Now you're ready to map out your *shooting schedule*. By using storyboards and sometimes a scheduling software program, the producer can calculate what gets shot, when, and where. The end result is a concise, clear schedule that everyone involved can understand and follow.

A realistic shooting schedule seldom lets you shoot in the exact same sequence as the script—it's too expensive. Unless the project specifically follows one action from beginning to end, most content is shot out of sequence. How a shoot is scheduled has a direct impact on the budget.

The size of your production crew depends on what you plan to shoot. A high-profile sitcom or multiple-location mini-series or episodic requires a larger, more complex crew structure. A documentary or reality-based show, on the other hand, might need only a compact crew that can move quickly and whose members can competently assume multiple duties.

Before you actually shoot, you'll revise your shooting schedule often, based on the following components that are factored into the production's overall structure.

Shooting Format

Producers today can choose between a provocative range of shooting formats. Some commercials and high-concept TV shows are still being shot on 35 mm film, then transferred to digital storage and downloaded into and edited with a nonlinear edit (NLE) system. Most other television shows and new media content are being shot on some format of digital video (DV), including *24P* and *high def* (high-definition television). The question of shooting in digital versus analog seldom applies in today's digital video world. Most all broadcast-quality cameras now shoot a digital signal, which is then fed into an NLE system. More details of shooting and editing are discussed in Chapters 8 and 9.

The rapid expansion of technology in the production of content for TV and new media makes almost anything possible. You can download your video onto the web with a simple click, and can download video from the web into your computer. If you want to project your finished video piece onto a theatrical screen, the final master can be transferred to a film print. Yet, because this technology is continually evolving, some formats are not yet compatible with other systems. Some formats and systems will soon be obsolete, and others are already poised to take their place. Your DP or director is an integral part of the format discussion.

Sets, Sound Stages, and Studios

Your project could call for a complex set, built on a sound stage with backdrops, various room sets or exteriors, enough space to build and paint sets, storage for props, areas for wardrobe, makeup, and production offices. Or, your project may require only a simple set on an inexpensive site. And increasingly, virtual sets are important components in television production as well as feature films; these virtual sets are designed and created on computers and then projected behind the action.

Control is the main advantage of shooting on a sound stage. Here, for example, there's a light grid and the lighting can be regulated without interference from clouds or reflections, and electric power isn't an issue. Outside sounds are nonexistent, and no longer an issue. And, there is enough space for talent, meals, equipment, production administration, and other production needs.

A studio or sound stage may come empty, or be fully equipped with cameras, audio equipment, light grids, and/or crew. Studios have different policies and rate structures. Some may be rented by the half-day, whole day, weekly, or for the duration of the project. In most cases, rates can be negotiated.

Because renting a sound stage can be expensive, try to anticipate all related costs. Build in extra time for changes or mistakes, as well as time for the lighting and electric crews to review the sets before the actual shoot. Most budgets factor in rental time *before* the shoot—called load in time—and rental time *after* the shoot, to break down the sets and equipment and clear everything out of the studio.

Locations

Location shooting can add a specific authenticity and mood to the production. And it's generally less expensive than on a sound stage, especially if the location comes with furnishings, props, colors, and/or production space. For example, if you have a certain look you want for a kitchen set, it might be cheaper and easier to find an already-existing kitchen than it is to build one on a sound stage.

But locations can have their downsides, too: space limitations for shooting, production equipment, and areas for the cast and crew. There might be no parking space available, or there is loud construction nearby in the neighborhood. Locations also involve legal agreements, permits, insurance, and fees. You can find an example of a standard location agreement form on this book's web site.

The goal of the production manager and/or producer is to group together all the shots needed in one location before moving the cast, crew, and equipment to the next location. This consolidation is called *shooting out* your location, and is a primary saver of time, money, and everyone's energy.

The producer considers what time is needed to break down the equipment in one location, move it all to the next location, and set up in the new location. That location might be:

- **A static location,** which can be inside someone's home, an office space, a classroom, store, or an outside shot of a building, garage, baseball field, etc.
- **A moving location,** which can include a character on a busy street, shooting a day-in-the-life sequence, or B-roll (extra montage and background footage).

Location Scout

A location scout can be a valuable component in finding just the right location. He's familiar with a range of locations: from a suburban home to an urban loft, from exteriors that match with a set on a sound stage to the right interior that suits the production's requirements. Some locations are free; others charge a fee. It is the job of the location scout or manager to find locations, negotiate the best price, and draw up location agreements. The location manager checks that:

- The locations are right for the project and reflect a look and texture that's compatible with the production. The location scout takes stills or video of the location for the producer.
- A signed location agreement with the owner (or legal representative) of the property is obtained. Some locations charge a fee, but others are free. Verify that the production carries adequate liability insurance to cover any damages in the course of the production. At the completion of the shoot, the property owner signs a release agreement.
- Whenever possible, the locations are close to one another.
- The location can supply adequate electrical power; if not, a generator must be brought in.
- There is enough space to accommodate crew, talent, catering, and equipment.
- The necessary production equipment can fit into the location, and that there are elevators, ramps, and/or loading docks.
- The location can be lit adequately, either with natural light or supplied light.
- The audio in the location has minimal noise interference from traffic, neighbors, animals, conversations, machinery, air conditioning, schoolyards, or construction.

Foreign Locations

Shooting in a foreign location can lend additional depth or mood to the project. Or, it might be part of the show's plotline or theme. Foreign locations can be less expensive if they offer professional local crews with lower pay scales, regional tax incentives, or a strong currency exchange rate. Locations such as Canada, South America, Eastern Europe, Australia, Iceland, and New Zealand can help the producer stretch the budget as well as provide viable locations. In some countries, the weather patterns can also extend a shooting season.

Exterior and Interior Shots

Most producers prefer to shoot their *exteriors*, or outside shots, before they shoot anything else. An exterior may be a master shot of an apartment building, a park, or a crowd shot on a busy street. When these exteriors are shot, the production can move on to the *interior*, or inside shots, with more security. The exteriors are necessary to establish where an interior shot is taking place. For example, when the outside of an apartment building is shown, we know that the next scene we see inside an apartment takes place in that building.

IN THE TRENCHES...

Any number of factors can get in the way of shooting your exterior shots. There's a snowstorm or an earthquake, or a freak fire burns down the vacant building you planned to use, or there's a power blackout. It's happened, so I always have a backup plan—how can I use the cast and crew I'm paying while I figure out my next move? My Plan B is almost always a *cover set*, an alternative *interior* location that has been prepped and dressed for shooting a back-up scene. This Plan B has saved the project, the budget, and my reputation.

~C. Kellison

Day and Night Shoots

A night shoot can be integral to the storyline—it creates dramatic textures and nuance. It can also increase your budget and overall workload. Night shoots require specific lighting and equipment, permits and traffic routing, and put an overall burden on scheduling crews who often have to shoot at night as well as in the daytime. Following is a list of ways for the producer to ease this burden.

- The look of nighttime can be achieved by shooting during the day, by blacking out or relighting the windows to give the appearance of night behind the action.
- The producer can schedule all the night shoots consecutively, building in a break for the crew and talent before switching back to a daytime shooting schedule.
- A producer also might divide the day and night shooting into *splits,* a half-day and half-night schedule.

Actors and Talent

Depending on the contract you've negotiated with the actors' unions, actors must be paid overtime after they've worked for a specified number of hours, usually eight or ten. So, the crew sets up the equipment before the shooting starts, and then breaks it all down after the actors have finished their work. Crews are usually booked for longer shifts to accommodate the talent, so scheduling talent and crew requires a review of the big picture—what needs to be shot and when, what union rules might govern certain decisions, and then balance that with the crew and their needs. This approach also pertains to most non-union shoots.

Other talent-related factors you want to take into consideration when you're scheduling include:

- ***Child actors.*** Union rules require that children have a shorter working schedule, and must have a tutor, parent, or social worker with them at all times, especially if the talent is missing regularly scheduled school time.
- ***Animals.*** Using an animal in a shoot requires a special trainer who can prompt it to do tricks and stunts, and who supervises the animal between takes. Whenever any animal is on set, the American Humane Association (AHA) must be notified. This mandate even extends to cockroaches.
- ***Extras and crowds.*** The producer in charge of the extras will often audition them or find them through other means. Then, she'll schedule their call time on set, arrange a comfortable waiting area, give them the proper release forms to fill out, and decide who needs wardrobe, hair, and/or makeup. While they wait for their scene, extras are provided with food, water, and bathroom facilities; they are usually rehearsed before the shoot.
- ***Stunts.*** The stunt category can include tripping on the stairs, a car chase, explosions, gunshots, falls from buildings, and fist fights. An effective stunt

requires careful design, test runs, and rehearsals, and is generally performed by professional stunt men and women. Stunt work requires rehearsal time as well as fees and additional insurance.

■ **Convenience vehicles.** Some productions require mobile dressing rooms, portable bathrooms, and craft service trucks. The transportation captain is in charge of locating the vehicles, negotiating fees, and arranging for their call times on the production. If extra insurance is necessary, that information is given to the producer, line producer, or UPM.

■ **Meals and craft services.** Provide healthy snacks, coffee, tea, and water, and make them available at all times, close to the set or location. Give everyone a complete, healthy meal at least once a day, ideally every six hours.

■ **Security/crowd control.** If local police are not available, hire a private security company or assign a strong-willed and muscle-bound production assistant (PA) to keep the crowd at a reasonable distance. If any of the people milling around might be shot on camera, the person in charge posts a notice, stating that people may be on camera and they have a choice to stay and be photographed, or to leave. You can find an example of a crowd release notice on the book's web site.

The Timing of the Shoot

To watch the cameramen moving from Position A to Position B during the course of a commercial break—particularly during the live shows because we have a very finite period of time, just two minutes for them to move— it's always incredible.

Laurie Rich, excerpt from interview in Chapter 11

All the production elements just listed need to be choreographed into a seamless set of movements for each shooting day. For this to happen, the producer coordinates them, taking into consideration the extra time that's needed for the:

■ **Art department.** Building, painting, and delivering sets, furnishings, and props.
■ **Transportation department.** Vans or trucks for loading and transporting equipment, sets and set dressings, the crew, and the talent.
■ **Setup.** Prelighting and camera blocking, loading in sets, equipment, and furnishings.
■ **Break down.** Disassembling equipment and sets after the shoot is completed, and either taking much of it to the next location, disposing of it, or returning it.
■ **Hair/makeup.** Some actors or shots need additional prep time, for example, in aging a young actress, applying wounds makeup, or dressing in elaborate sixteenth century costume.

As the producer, your objective is to accomplish what you have planned out for each day's shoot—known as *making the day*. You want to keep the production on schedule, so when you're scheduling, always try to pad your schedule with extra time and add money to the budget. This contingency safeguards the production if you should go over budget or need more time than you originally planned.

Some dramatic and episodic TV productions shoot only a few script pages each day; others might cover 10 to 15 pages, even more with some shows. Other platforms have varying schedules—a commercial could be shot in a day or a week; the same with online or mobile content. Compare this to a feature film that might cover only two to five pages a day.

You want to shoot as many scenes or takes as possible in a short time, and still maintain quality. But you don't want to sacrifice the people who are working with you to make this work. Unless you have a limited budget or time constraint, try to limit your production days to 12 hours, maximum. Have at least one day off a week, and hopefully two—ideally, two in a row. You don't want to burn out the talent or crew, so whenever possible, give everyone an occasional day off or another perk. And when you can't, make sure you feed them well and thank everyone, often.

Call Sheet

A call sheet is a list of what shots are planned for the following day. The call sheet is distributed at the end of each day for the next day, and may be prepared by the producer, the line producer, the UPM, or the 2nd AD, as decided by the producer in charge.

The call sheet lists what will be shot and who needs to be on the shoot, as well as call times for cast and crew, the location(s) for the shoot, equipment needed, and scene numbers. It's typically distributed to the producer(s), director, UPM, production coordinator, clients, department heads, and whomever else the producer puts on the distribution list. An example of a call sheet can be found on this book's web site.

Production Report

At the end of each day's shoot, a summary of what was shot that day is compiled in the production report (PR). It includes call times, scene numbers, deleted shots, setups, video and audio reel numbers, along with the crew members involved and the hours they worked, the locations, meals served, equipment and vehicles, and any delays or accidents on the shoot.

The production report is often (but not always) prepared by the same person who is responsible for the call sheet. Occasionally, the script is changed at the last minute, an actor is replaced, or the dailies show that a mistake was made and needs a reshoot. A producer budgets these realities into the schedule to cover any additional shoot days. For every plan A that you schedule, have a plan B, and even a plan C as a backup.

Preproduction Check List

As you plan your shoot, double-check what you'll need for your specific project. Start by referring to the Preproduction Check List on this book's web site. Look at each item. It may or may not be needed, depending on the genre of your project, the size of your crew, the budget, and needs of each department. You as the producer won't necessarily do every single thing; on larger productions, many of these areas are handled by the head of each department.

> You have to be flexible. Not all producers are flexible, but the good ones are. You have to be creative. Take initiative. Be willing to see the gray when you're telling a story; not everything is always black and white. Find a mentor, someone who has been in the business for a good amount of time, and whose opinion you value. And work on your writing skills; a good writer will have a huge advantage in the job market.
> **Ann Kolbell, excerpt from interview in Chapter 11**

ON A HUMAN LEVEL . . .

Even the most experienced producers forget important details in the midst of the preproduction stage—they're only human, and so are you. You're making decisions all the time, and as the producer, you are being asked a hundred questions a day. You can't know all the answers. Yet each day you do learn something new, and learning as much as possible is what a producer does to be successful.

SUMMARY

Your project can only be as good as the people on your team. They are essential to your project and integral to the actualization of your vision. You want to work with people who believe in your vision, share your work ethic, and are compatible with you as well as with other members of the technical and creative crew. This team can bring your project to life when the production stage begins, as you will see in Chapter 8.

REVIEW QUESTIONS

1. What are the primary elements included in a breakdown sheet?

2. How does a producer benefit by keeping a production book for each project?

3. What is the difference between a storyboard and a floor plan? How do they each augment a project?

4. What steps would you take to cast your project?

5. Who are the key production heads in most productions?

6. What does the location manager contribute to a production?

7. Name five support crew members who you might use in your production.

8. Discuss the pros and cons of shooting on location or on a sound stage.

9. What is the difference between working with child actors and adult actors?

10. Name 10 areas of preproduction that are important to double-check.

The Shoot: Production 8

Hell, there are no rules here—we're trying to
accomplish something!

Thomas Edison

THIS CHAPTER'S TALKING POINTS

I. The Producer's Role

II. On Set and On Location

III. The Camera

IV. Lighting

V. Audio

VI. The Actual Shoot

I. THE PRODUCER'S ROLE

Experience is the name everyone gives to their mistakes.

Oscar Wilde

As the producer, you've carefully developed each stage of your project. Now, you're ready for the actual shoot. Your vision is about to become tangible and visible. Your production schedule might be ambitious, stretching over a few weeks. Or maybe it's a simple, small, and compact two-day shoot. No matter its size, there are always details involved.

When the components are in place, the writer, director, crew, and talent are prepared to collaborate in making this project come alive. The actual shooting, also called *principal photography*, can begin when everything is ready to go: the script has been finalized; the actors rehearsed, made up, and costumed; releases have been signed; the sets built; the crew hired; the equipment is up to speed; all locations are secured; and any other details are all in place.

The Producer's Team

The producer depends on, and is a part of, a team of professionals who are also individuals, each with his or her own style and personality. You want to respect their talents, skills, and moments of real genius, and to be graceful about their human mistakes and mishaps. Successful creative teams often have a history of working together; some producers formed their team early on, as students or interns on a job.

A team can be many people, or just a few; each project's size and budget determines how many people can be part of your team. Your team might be just a camera person and an audio engineer with whom you've worked for years, and who give their best every time you shoot together. Or your team may include your client who believes in your vision, or the actors or on-camera talent who always come through for you. Your team often includes other producers, the production manager, designers, editors, whomever is needed for each specific project.

The producer's team succeeds through mutual trust, respect, humor, and a shared vision. The difference between the "creative" and the "technical" teams is a nonissue. You want the people with whom you work to fit both descriptions, translating your ideas with their skills and the tools of their trade into a true synthesis of art and science.

As the producer, you'll usually have the final word in decision-making, factoring in suggestions from the production team, the client's notes and requirements, and your own goals. Only after all these parts of the equation have been factored together do you make final decisions about production.

Production Protocol and Politics

In almost all television and new media projects, the producer takes an active part in the actual production. The producer keeps everyone focused on their job, knows who is doing what job, stays on top of what needs to get done, and clearly communicates everyone's area of responsibility.

If a director has been hired, the producer makes sure that all the elements are in place so the director can move ahead. As a producer, you can work closely with your team by:

- Explaining your ideas and the vision of the project
- Agreeing on the vision and the creative directions it's taking
- Communicating frequently and openly with your team
- Listening to ideas and suggestions from your team
- Nourishing your team with praise, food, and enthusiasm
- Providing a model of collaboration and mutual respect

II. ON SET AND ON LOCATION

Action springs not from thought, but from a readiness for responsibility.
Dietrich Bonhoeffer

In the previous chapter, you explored the pros and cons of shooting on a set/sound stage and on location. Each of these options can serve you well, depending on the nature of your specific project and its budget. Now, more producers are looking at another increasingly popular alternative to shooting on sound stages and on location – "building" a virtual location.

Virtual Locations

Shooting on location or on a sound stage each has its advantages and limitations, as we saw in Chapter 7. Maybe neither can be negotiated to fit the budget, or isn't available, or can't be duplicated on a sound stage. You can visualize this location, but you can't find its real-world equivalent. An alternative is to use a virtual location, designed and created through *computer-generated imagery* (CGI) capable of contributing a range of creative images—a futuristic building, a vast country landscape dotted with sheep, or an ancient battleground with thousands of charging warriors. It all looks real but it's virtual.

Virtual locations and CGI wizardry can be seen in a variety of looks and uses in most television programs, feature films, high-end commercials, news broadcasts, sports events, and video games, and is continually branching out to all platforms and content.

Building these virtual locations starts with a *blue screen* or a *green screen* background (also called a *chroma key* backdrop), or more recently, a *silver screen* with millions of tiny glass beads that reflect a light ring placed around the camera's lens. These screens can be hundreds of feet long, or simply 8′ × 8′ mobile traveling screens that can easily be folded up and transported. Whichever screen you decide on is then placed behind the action you're shooting. That action is edited later onto another image that replaces the blue, green, or silver screen.

> **Let's say…** that the script calls for an actor to topple over a high iron railing and plunge into Niagara Falls. First, the railing and surrounding set is built on a sound stage. Then, in a medium shot, the actor plays out the scene and falls over the railing, onto a heavy pad that's not in the shot. This action is all shot in front of a special blue, green, or silver screen that fills up the frame. Meanwhile, a camera crew goes to Niagara Falls and shoots the actual waterfalls at an angle that will match up with the action of the actor in the studio. Then, the two scenes are layered together in the editing room. The result is a seamless edit that looks as though the actor really tumbled over Niagara Falls. It's realistic, cheaper expensive than shooting the whole scene on location, and nobody gets hurt.

Other locations can be built entirely on the computer, and don't require the shooting of any footage. Designed and created by a graphic designer, this kind of virtual location can be an elaborate rendition of a futuristic city skyline, a landscape from prehistory, an unknown galaxy. Even an actual photograph, say, of an historical time period, can act as a backdrop for live action or for CGI figures.

III. THE CAMERA

Where observation is concerned, chance favors only the prepared mind.

Louis Pasteur

The camera is the primary tool that producers use to tell a story. And although the use of 16- and 35-mm film is still a presence in television programming, digital video technology is growing at such a rapid rate that the merger of film and video in television has essentially arrived. So, for the purposes of this text, digital video is the format of choice. You can consult additional sources and reference material for shooting and/or editing your production in film, and to update information on digital cameras, lenses, and accessories.

The camera operator (also called the *shooter*) forms a close bond with the camera to compose an image that tells a story, and shoots footage that not only looks good but is of high technical quality and can be easily cut together with other footage shot.

Today's video cameras are sophisticated, comparatively inexpensive, and more and more flexible. Most cameras offer creative options such as choices of formats on which to store the footage and audio, lenses, in-camera settings, varying shutter and shooting speeds, and built-in optical illusions.

Shooting with Digital Video

Think back to the Technicolor films from the 1950s. In Technicolor, negatives were processed into three separate red, green, and blue negatives. Ordinary film processing used only one negative with no color separation in the negatives, but the Technicolor prints made from the three-strip process had vivid, memorable color and resonance.

Now, in much the same way, a mid- to high-range video camera separates the light that hits the lens into three components of color: red, green, and blue (RGB). These three-chip cameras have three separate *charge-coupled devices* (CCDs) that produce a sharper, higher quality color picture, essentially three times better picture quality than from single-chip, lower-end cameras. Most popular digital cameras capture images using these CCD sensors. However, an increasing number of high-end television and film projects are being shot with cameras that relay on CMOS (complementary metal oxide semiconductor) sensors, a more sophisticated version of CCD sensors.

Digital Storage

Each image with its audio is processed as an electrical signal that can be recorded onto a storage medium like digital videotape, P2 memory cards, a hard drive device (HHD), and flash memory. Often, the videotape is fed via a system like FireWire or USB 2.0 directly onto the computer's hard drive.

All these recording formats work. Each has its own creative, technical, and budgetary advantages, and each has its limitations. Superior systems are being developed at a furious pace, and undergoing beta and field tests as you read these words. The hot item on today's top-ten list could be a big yawn tomorrow.

How you get the video into your editing system is as important as how you shoot it. If your editing system can accommodate a digital signal, or has a FireWire input (and most do), then you're best shooting with a DV camera. Your final decisions about what cameras to use, and in what shooting format, are best made with your DP or cameraman/woman. The bottom line is that you want your project to be shot professionally, in broadcast-quality video, with the highest quality and for the best cost that you can manage from your budget.

Shooting High-Definition Video

The increasingly advanced digital technology of high-definition television (HDTV) has created an extraordinary leap in how we view and produce content and programming. HD has been heralded as a revolution because it can "see" better than the human eye with its depth of field, brilliance of color, and its image clarity. Often, HD can see *too* much—every petal on a red rose may be crystal clear, but so is every wrinkle on an actor's face and each badly painted set that might have gone unnoticed in film or standard definition video.

HDTV has arrived in full force. In America, the majority of prime time programming is regularly broadcast in HD, as are many local and national sports specials and events, such as the Academy Awards. Compared to the traditional U.S. analog system that broadcasts NTSC programming in 525 horizontal lines, an HD image has either 720 or 1080 lines, depending on the specific HD format. This difference results in a higher resolution and a clearer picture. And, increasingly, many cameras are equipped to shoot in HD as well as standard definition, 24p, and other formats like 2K, 4K, and 6K scans.

HDTV Systems

Currently, at least 18 versions of HDTV are used in various parts of the world. Two, however, have emerged as the most popular: 720p and 1080i. There are arguments for each system, though HD sets display both equally well in a widescreen 16:9 format. This shape is rectangular, with more picture space on the sides. Compare the size of this screen to the traditional 4:3 TV set, which is nearly square. The 16:9 format TV set is sold almost exclusively now, and the majority of television-bound programming is shot in 16:9, not 4:3.

- ■ ***720p.*** (1280 pixels per line and 720 progressively-scanned lines) Works well for broadcast, though it's usually not recommended for a project that may be transferred later to film, or projected on a large screen.
- ■ ***1080i.*** (1920 pixels per line and 1080 actively-interlaced lines of resolution) Best used when the final product calls for a "reality" aspect, which looks as if the viewer is seeing it live, in vivid sharp detail.

TV RESOLUTION

DESIGNATION	USAGE EXAMPLES	DEFINITION
Low	LDTV, VCD	240; 288
Standard	SDTV, SVCD, DVD, DV	480
Enhanced	EDTV	576
High	HDTV, HD DVD, BD, HDV	720; 1080

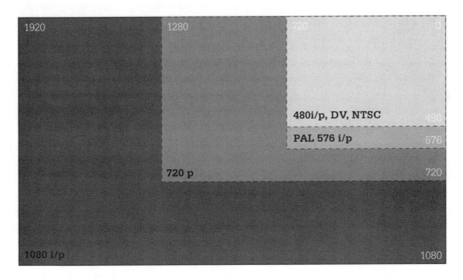

Shooting in 24p Video

When you shoot in 24p (24 frames per second, progressive scan), the process involves video that runs at 24 fps, the same rate as film, with an intermittent flash of black in every frame cycle. Put simply, 24p has a look that is similar to film. It's softer, it has a film "flicker," the colors appear richer than in video, and because it can be shot in both standard and high definition, it's a popular format for shooting, especially for producers who might want the option of transferring their project to 35-mm film for projection purposes.

Before shooting in 24p, talk with your editor and DP. Many cheaper DV cameras have a 24-frame mode but the camera is actually shooting 30 frames; the shutter is only mimicking 24 frames. If you shoot some of your footage in 24 frames per second, and other footage for the same project in 30 frames, you could find yourself in real trouble when you get into the edit room. Because of certain technical limitations, few NLE systems currently can accommodate both formats at the same time.

The majority of producers, editors, and technical experts agree that most projects should be finished in HD with a 24p 16:9 master. It is the best format for broadcasting, progressive streaming on the web, creating PAL versions for broadcast in Europe and other PAL-friendly countries, and for release on DVD. Yet, considering the rapid growth in digital technology, check with your DP or cameraman/woman for their opinion on your specific project.

Choosing Your Camera

Unless you're shooting in film, video cameras today are almost always digital—even the inexpensive home movie cameras. A professional-quality camera is within anyone's budget to purchase, or at least cheap enough to rent, for your shoot. Anything less cheapens the quality of your footage and ultimately does a disservice to your vision.

Budget-Conscious Cameras

The rapid evolution of digital technology is quite evident in the proliferation of excellent professional-quality, or *prosumer,* cameras and a range of peripheral equipment. These cameras tend to be reasonably priced (anywhere from $1,000 to $9,000), and work perfectly fine for most productions—from documentaries and news gathering, to shorts, commercials, music videos, content for online and cellular delivery systems, and even features. Add to this the computerization of the editing process, and shooting your project can be manageable, and inexpensive.

As of the writing of this second edition, certain cameras stand out because of their distinct technological advances. Camera operators want a camera with functions such as manual focus, manual aperture and shutter speed control, a LCD monitor that folds out, control over the white balance function, the capacity to accommodate an external mic, and can output video to the computer.

Digital cameras can now digitally record both the image and the audio onto a variety of formats. The most popular formats include hard-disk drive, flash memory card, mini-DV tape, and DVD disk; some cameras are hybrid and can record video onto either a DVD or a second medium (such as flash memory or hard-disk drive).

Some cameras are more suited to the professional shooter, whereas others work just fine for the producer/editor (also called a *preditor*) who researches, shoots, and edits her own news segment or documentary. All are digital broadcast-quality, work within most budgets, and reflect the most popular cameras currently being used by professionals. As always, check with your DP or camera operator about the best one for your project.

High-End Cameras for Digital Cinematography

This is a category of more expensive and complex cameras, generally focused on independent films and specific television programs with an accommodating budget and other needs beyond the parameters of usual television and new media programming.

These cameras tend to have a single-chip CMOS sensor, a successor to the CCD image sensors in most digital cameras. This allows the camera to duplicate the shallow depth of field and overall look of 35 mm, and with some cameras, shoot in 65 mm. The majority of these cameras can also accommodate professional film camera mounts and lenses. Most capture image and audio onto tape, hard disks, and flash memory; some can capture onto 2K, 4K, and 6K files.

At the moment, the cameras most prominent in this growing area of digital cinematography are:

- Arri's Arriflex D-20
- Dalsa Origin
- GS Vitec noX
- Panavision's Genesis and Varicam
- Silicon Imaging's SI-2K
- Sony's F23 CineAlta
- Red's Red One and Scarlet
- Thomson Viper FilmStream
- Vision Research Phantom 65 and Phantom HD

Studio Cameras

It's like a mini *Saturday Night Live* to see them with the cable pullers, everyone getting from Point A, which could be home base, all the way over to [Point B]…it doesn't sound like a lot, but during the commercial break, that's a fascinating thing to watch.

Laurie Rich, excerpt from interview in Chapter 11

When shooting a talk show or news broadcast, for example, larger DigiBeta cameras are the traditional camera of choice. Most are mounted on moving balanced pedestals that keep the camera stationary; these pedestals can glide smoothly around a limited set, with a feature that can tilt the camera up or down. Most studio-based productions require three to six pedestal cameras, as well as one or two cameras mounted on a swooping jib, or crane, that can fly over the audience and onto the set. Some productions might augment the DigiBeta cameras with a hand-held camera that moves freely; all the cameras are directed by the director from within the control room. Microphones are suspended at regular distances over the audience for their reactions, like laughter and applause.

In a typical multicamera studio shoot, the footage from each camera, as well as the audio from the talent and audience microphones, are all fed into a central control room that is close to the set (or fed to a mobile truck with its own control room). In the central control room the director, producers, technical director, audio mixer, and graphics person all watch each incoming camera feed on its designated monitor. As the crew in the control room records the footage, it is generally edited live. This process is called *live to tape*, and it's how most studio shows are produced. Any additional editing changes can be made later. Or, it's all recorded to tape and edited at another time.

Time Code

When you're shooting video professionally, the camera "burns" a *time code* (TC) signal onto the videotape (or whatever format you're recording onto) and assigns each frame a specific number. You can draw a direct analogy between video and time code in video, and sprocket holes and frame numbers in film. The time code is broken into four sections. If, for example, the time code number is 07:02:45:17, then:

- 07 is the hour
- 02 is the minutes
- 45 is the seconds
- 17 is the exact frame number (there are 30 frames per second); these last two numbers aren't necessary when taking most notes, only in editing when frame-accuracy is necessary

Working with time code is an integral tool for the editor as part of the editing process. It makes the editing frame-accurate and exact. TC is also a valuable tool for producers when screening and logging footage prior to the edit session. As seen in Chapter 9, you can use TC numbers to create a storyboard, or *paper cut*, that the editor uses as a "script" for the edit.

Taking Notes with Time Code

To screen your footage, it must first be dubbed to DVD with the TC displayed visually on the top or bottom of the screen; this is called *visible time code*, or *vizcode*. The TC is exactly the same as on your original footage, and known as *matching time code*. As you screen the dubs, you'll make notes using TC as your reference points.

> **Let's say…** you're screening footage that you've shot for a 10-minute short, and you're putting together a paper cut to give to your editor. On Tape #1, the teenage boy opens the door at 00:03:04:15, and it's a medium shot. Then, you find the close-up of his hand on the doorknob, which is on Tape #4 at 00:06:13:15. These two scenes were shot at different times, and each comes from a different tape but both need to be edited together later. Time code helps you and your editor match them together, perfectly.

As you screen each tape, you'll want to take good notes of what you see and hear; this is called *logging*. As you watch each tape from start to finish, log the TC that describes specific parts of the footage, such as a great cutaway shot, a move from one location to another, the best take of one scene, and so on. Everyone has a personalized system—some people write the shot descriptions, like CU for close-up, WS for wide shot, and so on. Often people also mark the direction in which the action is going; for example, a bird flying to the right could be marked with >, a pair of eyes looking up is ^, and a camera pan from right to left could be marked as <<<.

From these notes, you can create a paper cut (storyboard) for editing. It shows the TC numbers, scene descriptions, length of scene, and which tape each scene is on. This paper cut is a major time-saver. As you refine your own system, you can read your log at a glance and find your shots. You'll find logging and storyboard forms on this book's web site.

Setting Camera Time Code

On a shoot, there are two ways to set and record TC in the camera:

1. *A studio multicamera shoot.* All the cameras are linked into the "house" TC generator. This sends out *time-of-day time code* (TC that records the actual time of day) to all cameras and tape machines, simultaneously, and is located in the control room on the engineering console. This way, the tapes from each camera can be "*synced up*" (synchronized) in the edit room. This system is helpful in organizing notes based on the chronology of events that occurred during the

shoot. It also simplifies the editing, making it easier for the editor to match up each camera's footage simultaneously.

Without this synchronization, the editor wastes time and money going back and forth to each tape and trying to keep video and audio in sync. Not all cameras can take in outside time code, especially low-budget DV cams, so one way to achieve some form of sync, once you've turned all your cameras on, is to keep them all running together. Turn them on and off together on the count of three.

IN THE TRENCHES...

I can virtually guarantee you that attempting a multicam shoot without matching time code will make your editor extremely cranky. Trying to edit different camera feeds together without the same time code using only his blood-shot eye ball? It can be done, but it's pure hell. What's a viable Plan B? Bring an LCD time code reader to the set— it displays the hour, minutes, seconds, and frames per second (00:00:00:00). Before and after each time the cameras roll, each camera shoots the TC reader. This may not make your editor any less grumpy but at least you've given him a reference point. He can use the multisync function in his edit programs to keep all the cameras in sync.

~C. Kellison

---

2. *A single-camera shoot.* An internal TC generator can be set inside the camera itself. Producers usually start Tape 1 at Hour #1 (01:00:00:00), Tape 2 at Hour #2 (02:00:00:00), and so on. Because there are only 24 hours in a video day, TC numbers beyond 23:59:59:29 don't exist. However, Tape 24 can be set at 00:00:00:00 and Tape 25 at 01:00:00:00, and so on. This system helps in logging and screening footage for the edit session later.

Capturing the Image

Prior to shooting, the producer, director, and/or the DP discuss the creative and technical options for shooting each scene. Their decisions work with the narrative flow, affect the style and pace of the program, and ultimately will guide how a viewer sees a story line or character. The perspective of a shot, for example, can convey dramatic tension or character motivation when the viewer knows from whose perspective the story is being told. This perspective is either objective or subjective.

- *Objective perspective.* Captures the viewpoint of an unseen narrator or storyteller who is an onlooker, and views the characters from a third-person viewpoint. The shot is often a wider, more distant shot or a two-shot.
- *Subjective perspective.* Tells a story from a character's first-person point of view. The shot is closer or tighter, such as a close-up or an over-the-shoulder shot.

When planning a shot, the primary factors that play into capturing the image in the shoot include:

- Framing and composition
- Camera angles
- Camera moves
- Camera lenses
- Camera shot list

Framing and Composition

The primary concept of *framing* a shot involves shooting an image—a person or an object—as well as everything that surrounds or affects the image. An extreme close-up of a face gives one kind of narrative message, and an extreme long shot of the same person tells a different story altogether. Each option frames the image and composes the frame around it.

Composition is the relationship of objects to each other in the frame, or to the shape of the subject being shot. Colors, lighting, scenery, props, and camera blocking all contribute to a scene's composition. This total effect is known as *mise-en-scene*, or the setting up of a scene.

Another important aspect of framing concerns whether your project will be shot and/or viewed on either a 4:3 format or 16:9. Because both are feasible, consider shooting your primary action in the middle of the frame, with less important details on both sides in case they get cut off.

Camera Angles

Each time the camera moves, and every angle at which the camera is placed relative to what it's shooting, creates a different effect, both visually and thematically. A sitcom can be shot in a fixed frame, using a stationary or *locked down* camera on a tripod, and the actors move only within that framing. A gritty detective drama might use a *hand-held* approach, moving fluidly in and out of the characters' faces and actions. Both the genre of your show and its content help determine how you'll shoot it. As you decide on camera angles and movement, keep two things in mind:

- *Viewpoint.* The height of the camera's position determines the viewpoint of the character, and gives the viewer a sense of theme and direction. When shot from below, for example, a character has the illusion of superiority, whereas a character shot from above may seem inferior or small. When an actor speaks directly into the camera, the dialogue is directed to the viewer; when the actor looks off to the right or the left of the camera's lens, it appears that he is focusing on something else.
- *Eye-line.* The position of the camera needs to correspond to the character's eye-line, usually in the top third of the frame. The viewer should be able to follow what the actor sees to the actor's eyes. This guarantees that the eye-lines from one character to another match up in editing.

Camera Moves

Your camera can be a flexible tool for capturing the subtleties of an image or the flow of action. The traditional camera moves from which a camera operator can choose include:

- *The tilt.* A camera can maintain the same eye-line, and tilt down (giving the impression of the subject looking toward the ground) or tilt up (suggesting that the subject is looking toward the sky). This tilt can also give an impression of a subject's inferiority or superiority to another character or to the viewer.
- *The Dutch (or canted) angle.* Often used in reality shows and interviews, the camera is rotated so that the image itself appears at an angle, and creates a sense of intimacy or tension.
- *The pan.* The camera swivels on the tripod or on its axis to form an arc from right to left or left to right. A pan is smooth and even-paced. A swish pan moves faster and can be effective in action sequences or as transitions in editing.

- **The tracking shot.** Also known as a *traveling* shot, it pulls the viewer into the action by using a camera mounted on a dolly that moves either on tracks or on special shock-resistant wheels alongside a moving subject. The same effect can be accomplished by mounting a camera on a crane or a jib that swoops above, into, or away from the action in a scene. Another effective approach is a camera rig (such as Steadicam, Glidecam, and the DvRigPro) that's worn by the camera operator for shooting smoothly in any direction.
- **The zoom.** The camera lens—in a *zoom-in*—moves smoothly into a close-up of a person or object. A *zoom-out* starts close and moves back.
- **Extending the frame.** The camera is locked down and stationary, and holds on an object or scenery for a few beats, possibly with off-screen sound effects like a ringing phone, or a closing door before or after the character enters the frame from right or left.

Camera Lenses

Another area of discussion with your DP is about what lenses can be used in the shoot. In some cases, a *wide-angle* lens can add a more spacious feeling to a shot, whereas a *fish-eye* lens creates a subtle distortion that can be interesting when shooting buildings or interiors that are otherwise mediocre. A *close-up* lens can give a clear focus on a small object. Other lenses can add diffusion or hues of color.

Camera Shot List

Prior to the shoot itself, a *shot list* is created and distributed. This is an inventory of each shot needed to be shot for a specific sequence or scene, and uses specific terms for each camera angle, such as ECU for extreme close up, and so forth. The elements that go into a shot list are discussed and illustrated in Chapter 7; a shot list template can be found on this book's web site.

Today's technology is advancing camera design so rapidly that cameras and their formats can upgrade, or become obsolete, in a matter of months; some formats will survive as others disappear. Ultimately, you'll talk with the DP and director, and often the editor, about which camera options are best suited to your particular project.

IV. THE LIGHTING

A picture must possess a real power to generate light…for a long time now, I've been conscious of expressing myself through light or rather in light.
Henri Matisse

Lighting is an essential tool for painting and enhancing the video image. The subtle use of light creates atmosphere and mood, dimension, and texture. It can help to convey a plot line, enhance key elements such as set color or skin tone, and signals the difference between comedy and drama, reality and fantasy.

Hard versus Soft

All lighting falls into either "hard" with sharp and distinct shadows, or "soft" with less defined, softer shadows and fewer background images. The intensity and clarity of the bulb, or its diffusion, combines with placement to design a shooting environment.

- **Hard light.** Aimed directly on its subject, with a brighter single-source illumination. The sun is one example. Other hard light is incandescent, ellipsoidal, and quartz.
- **Soft light.** Diffused, created with less intense lamps that reflect or bounce light off a reflector, a ceiling, or another part of the set. Soft lighting effects are enhanced with scrims, strips, scoops, and banks.

Three-Point

Production lighting involves three major lights and their positions in relation to each other (three-point lighting):

- *Key light.* Powerful, bright light that best defines a primary, or *key*, person or object, creating a deep shadow. It is positioned at roughly a 45 degree angle to the subject being shot.
- *Fill light(s).* Softer light placed at an angle to "fill" any unwanted shadows created by the key light, at about half the key's intensity. It is usually placed opposite the key light at about a 30 degree angle
- *Back light(s).* Throwing light on the subject from behind, it's positioned behind at around a 90 degree angle; it can also be adjusted higher or lower to create other lighting moods. This helps to create an illusion of depth behind the main subject and brings it forward from the background.

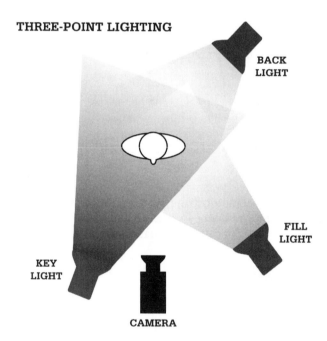

THREE-POINT LIGHTING

BACK LIGHT

FILL LIGHT

KEY LIGHT

CAMERA

High-Key versus Low-Key Lighting

Most TV talk shows, sitcoms, variety shows, musicals, and family entertainment use *high-key* lighting: a high ratio of key light to fill light. *Low-key* lighting creates a more dramatic, moody, and textured effect for dramas, documentaries, music videos, and others.

Hot and Cold Lighting

All lights have a color temperature that influences what the camera records:

- *Daylight (outdoor).* The most powerful and brightest light. Daylight is hot and produces a blue tone on video.
- *Artificial (indoor).* Considered cold. On video, it creates a reddish yellow cast.

Interior and Exterior Lighting

Everything you shoot is either indoors or outdoors. Each light has its advantages and limitations.

- *Exterior lighting.* As you shoot an exterior (outdoor) scene, you may want the spectacular intensity of the sun at high noon. Or, the scene calls for the moody waning light immediately after sunset, known as the magic hour. Each option has its own effect on an exterior scene. However, outdoor shooting can pose real challenges. Along with the sun's continual movement, its degrees of brightness can fluctuate dramatically through the shooting day. When the sun is your key light, it might need to be partially blocked out or augmented by fill lights or back lights. An exterior set can be shot at night but lit to look like daylight, or vice versa.
- *Interior lighting.* Shooting interior (indoor) scenes poses fewer challenges as video cameras and shooting formats become more advanced and light-sensitive. A camera's iris, for example, can play with light and color and go from automatic to manual. This avoids the camera's normal tendency to focus on the best-lit object in the scene.

Both interior and exterior lighting can be adjusted by using *reflectors* (also called *bounce cards*). These are glossy, white lightweight cards in various sizes that reflect light onto an object or actor. Large *silks* (squares of translucent material) can be strategically hung and positioned to filter the sunlight and maintain lighting consistency. In some cases, a light-filtering paper gel called *neutral density* (ND) is placed onto windows to keep outside light from being too harsh; in other situations, thick dark velvet curtain material blocks out sunlight entirely.

When shooting in video, certain colors or patterns can result in unwanted visuals; they require either careful lighting, or avoiding entirely:

- *Stripes.* A striped shirt, for example, can create a wavy effect on the video, known as a moiré pattern.
- *Red.* Certain bright shades of red can "bleed" and morph into other objects nearby.
- *White.* Too much white can overpower a scene and "blow it out."
- *Blues and greens.* Some shades can blend together and become invisible. Don't dress your on-camera talent in blue, green, or silver if you're using blue, green, or silver screens in the background for any special effects you may be considering.

V. THE AUDIO

The power of sound has always been greater than the power of sense.

Joseph Conrad

Sound design is a highly creative art, and the nuance of sound has a profound, if often unconscious, effect on an audience. The careful recording of audio during production, as well as clever mixing in postproduction, can make a visceral impact on the project. What a viewer *hears* has a definitive influence on what he or she *sees*. Sound design is a genuine collaboration between the audio recorded on a location and the extra layers of sound that are added and enhanced in postproduction.

We shot a scene in which a young couple was directed to have a romantic intimate conversation while slow-dancing in a crowded night club. There were another 20 couples on the floor, and a five-piece band on the stage behind them all. This was a highly controlled set—we wanted to record only the couple's dialogue. We asked everyone else to be totally silent, only mouthing a conversation. The band made the motions but didn't play a note. The other sounds— the other dancers' conversations, shuffling feet and body movements, the tone of the room, the music the band was playing— would be recorded separately and added in later, during postproduction. We recorded the couple's dialogue by using a boom and two wireless lavs. But if even these were too muffled or unclear, we had the option of rerecording their conversation later. Then, in the audio studio, we mixed all these layers of sound together. The final result was a seamless integration of dialogue, ambience, music, effects, and acoustics. Voila!

~C. Kellison

Sound Design

An overall choreography of recorded sounds is known as sound design and usually includes:

- **Dialogue.** Conversation between the main characters in a scene
- **Background or ambience.** Muted conversations of extras in the background, barking dogs, sirens, playing children
- **Sound effects.** Narrative information, like a ringing phone or an angry shout
- **Added audio.** More thematic information, like a musical theme or a "sting"

If you could draw an audio storyboard, you would "see" audio everywhere: the dialogue, conversations in the room, the clatter of plates, and the tip tap of walking shoes, as well as outside noises like background traffic, singing birds, children playing, sirens, a parade, and planes flying overhead. These all combine to form an essential layer of ambience that complements the visual images. However, these extraneous noises can also be a major interference if they're not what you want to hear.

In most cases, bad audio is a sure sign of amateurism or sheer negligence. For example, a camera microphone, or *mic*, is limited, seldom sensitive enough to accurately capture the sound or to cover all sound emergencies. You'll want your camera to accommodate an external mic, one that the audio engineer attaches. And before each shoot, test the sound from all mics. When you're shooting sync sound—which is most of the time—consult with your audio engineer about the benefits of using a mixer board.

The Four Major Elements in Audio

In recording the audio, the audio engineer takes four major elements into consideration:

- The microphone (or *mic*)
- Acoustics of the location
- Audio recording formats
- The perspective of the audio

Microphones

Mics fall into these primary categories:

- *Directional mic.* Aimed directly at its subject. Captures only the subject's audio with as little other background sounds as possible. This mic is often a cardioid microphone (so named because of its heart shape) and records dialogue clearly.
- *Shotgun mic.* Mounted either directly on the camera, at the end of a *boom* (a long rigid pole that can extend as long as 18 feet), or mounted in a pistol-grip rig. It has a selective pick-up pattern that primarily records the sound in front of the mic. It can be as far as five feet away from the source of the sound and still get clean audio. A valuable add-on is a fuzzy *windscreen* around the mic that reduces most wind or breeze interferences.
- *Lavalier (lav).* Clips onto a collar or tie, and picks up dialogue close to the speaker's mouth, isolating it from other audio. A lav also solves the problem of seeing a boom or its shadow in the frame. It can either be *hard-wired* and connected by cable to the camera or sound recording device, or it can be *wireless* and powered by a bodypack transmitter worn under clothing.
- *Omnidirectional mic.* Sensitive to sound from any direction and source. It records dialogue and also captures all background sounds. This mic works best for recording man-on-the-street interviews and for dialogue where any ambient sound is required.
- *Handheld mic.* In interview situations, it's the most dependable mic because it requires sound pressure only from the person who's speaking into it. A hand-held mic can be either directional or omni, and can be hard-wired or wireless.
- *Prop mic.* When it isn't feasible to use a boom or lav, the audio crew conceals a microphone in a prop or on set furniture to hide it from the camera. A mic can disappear inside a plant or a book that's close to the dialogue, be taped under a table, or draped inside a curtain.

If there is any audio problem during a take, (i.e. barking dog, honking horn, or low flying plane), the soundman will wait until the take is finished and alert the producer as to the location and severity of the problem. The producer can then decide whether a retake is necessary.

Richard Henning, excerpt from interview in Chapter 11

The Acoustics of the Location

Audio engineers describe what they hear in very visual terms. One sound can be warm, bright, and round; another is hard or soft, fat or thin. The quality of the recorded sound is controlled to a great extent by the microphones used to capture them. Another important factor of recording sound is the acoustical setup of the location.

Sound waves are like fluid impressions. They can be muffled by surfaces that are soft and spongy such as rugs, furniture, clothing, curtains, and even human bodies. Sound bouncing and deflecting off surfaces that are hard and reflective, like glass, tile or vinyl floors, mirrors, and low ceilings, creates echoes or distortion.

Some locations can pose a real challenge to an audio engineer. A location might look just great, but it's got challenging audio problems—humming air conditioners, the buzz of fluorescent ceiling lights, ticking clocks, outside traffic sounds. As the producer, you may choose the controlled environment of a sound stage or studio, avoiding unwanted noises. Or, you may want a buzzing, busy background ambience.

Audio Recording Formats

In shooting most video formats, the audio goes through a *single system*. Here, sound is recorded directly onto the videotape, memory card, hard drive, or other storage mechanism. In the case of a multicamera shoot, the audio from each camera usually is fed directly to a videotape recorder (VTR). The audio engineer monitors the levels and sound from each microphone onto separate channels for mixing later in postproduction.

> In a sit-down interview situation, when only the talent is being recorded, the best and safest sound comes from using two separate mics—a clip-on lavalier, and a directional mic mounted on a boom pole and stand— pointing from above towards the talent. If both the interviewer and interviewee are to be recorded, then a lavalier is clipped onto each of them and the sound, unmixed, is sent to two different channels. Once an audio level is set, and the camera rolls, a slight level adjustment might be made, but abrupt or constant adjusting is not only unnecessary, it's an editor's nightmare. The soundman then stays attentive and focused on what's coming through the headset.
>
> **Richard Henning, excerpt from Chapter 11**

Because you want professional, broadcast-quality sound, most videotape formats come with four separate audio tracks or *channels*. It is possible to assign microphones to each channel. Now you've got the capacity for stereo recording, with two channels on the left and two on the right. These channels can be expanded later in the audio mix. HDTV broadcasting features the additional capability for 5.1 surround sound, a standard feature on DVDs and digital television sets. HD camcorder systems can record audio directly onto HD videotape with at least two tracks of audio.

The Audio Perspective

In the same way that an image is shot from a visual perspective, dialogue and ambient sound is recorded with an audio perspective in mind. For example, dialogue spoken by an actor in a close-up shot sounds clear, intimate, and appears to be coming from the immediate foreground. Dialogue yelled from across a busy street in a wide shot has a different perspective, coming from the background of the shot, as the distance blends in with the ambient sounds from traffic and other street noise.

It's not always possible to record sound that has the same perspective as the footage. A visual might be a very long shot, say, of two mountain climbers as they reach the summit. The only way to record their dialogue is by using a concealed wireless mic, but doing this could result in audio that sounds perfect for a close-up, though not for a long shot. It can be enhanced during postproduction with added sounds like blowing wind and crunching snow.

Recording Production Sound

Audio that is recorded during production on a sound stage or at a location is known as *production sound* and refers to all scripted dialogue, ambient sound, and background noise. If an unwanted sound creeps in, or the dialogue changes after the footage has been shot, most production sound can be rerecorded later in the postproduction stage. This is explored in greater detail in Chapter 9.

Portable Recording

Sometimes in addition to recording audio onto videotape with sync sound, you may also need to record audio independently—a voice-over, ambient sound like traffic or conversation, music from a performance—and mix it with other audio elements in post-production. Professional digital formats for portably recording isolated audio continue to be improved, though currently, each must be researched carefully to make sure it's compatible with both the video equipment and the editing system you're using.

Digital Recording

Today's most popular digital audio recording formats are MP3 24-bit recorders that record onto Secure Digital (SD) cards, and can import and export via USB ports into the computer. The device has both a built-in mic and can accommodate an external mic as well. It's able to monitor the audio levels, and has a time code reference.

In shooting digitally, the audio engineer cautiously monitors any digital distortion caused by audio that may be recorded too hot on the meter, because it's generally unfixable and useless. Loud sounds or high-pitched dialogue can peak the meter in the camera or in the digital recording device, so whenever possible she tests the audio before the shoot and won't allow the meter setting to go over zero. She usually sets the audio at −12 dB and even −20 dB, and is careful never to let the audio levels hit the top of the meter. She also listens to the camera's audio over the headsets before the actual shoot starts, and wears them throughout the shoot.

The Challenges of Recording Sound

Whether you're recording audio on a soundproof set or outside on location, there are situations to be aware of, and that you should try either to prevent or avoid altogether:

- **Obstructions.** Jewelry or clothing can rub or click against a clip-on lav.
- **Boom pole.** Boom poles vary in length (from a few feet to 18′) and in structure. They need to reach long but be lightweight so the boom operator doesn't tire out. Often the actual *handling noise* of the pole itself can create audio interference.
- **Lights.** Neon or fluorescent lights that are barely audible to the ear can cause a noticeable buzz on the audio track.
- **Appliances.** Certain set pieces or existing appliances on location create their own sounds like a refrigerator, radiators, or an air conditioner.
- **Motors.** Your location might be near a busy street or under an air traffic pattern.
- **Weather.** Thunder, the rustling of wind, even a faint breeze can be a detriment in recording clean dialogue.
- **Neighbors.** A school playground, a lumber yard, an auto repair shop, or a house with a lawnmower can create interfering noises.
- **Construction.** Incessant reverberations from jack hammers or saws can travel into a location or a studio, even from a distance.
- **Nature.** Barking dogs, crickets, cicadas, blue jays and robins—each can be nuisance, or exactly what you need to create an added dimension of reality.
- **Batteries.** If the battery power on a mic's body pack goes out, you've lost your sound. Plan ahead with an adequate supply of charged batteries.

Most of these problems can be avoided with foresight, thoughtful use of microphones, and sound mufflers like moving blankets and microphone windscreens. You don't want to depend on the postproduction audio mix to fix your audio problems, but that's where you can often resolve unavoidable audio dilemmas.

Some Sound Advice

Your ultimate objective is to record and mix your audio elements so seamlessly that when you listen to it with your eyes closed, you hear no audio cuts or changes in levels. Any audio transitions from one scene to another should be equally smooth.

Most every challenge in recording production sound has a solution, such as:

- ***Record sound effects and ambience separately.*** If two characters are walking and talking as they pass an outdoor café, sound is around them, everywhere: the clinking of glasses, passing conversations, church bells, and fluttering pigeons. Whenever possible, record each of these sounds separately. In the audio mix, each is blended with the dialogue to create an overall audio impression.

- **Record room tone.** *Room tone* refers to the subtle, nearly inaudible sounds that are unique to each and every set or location. At either the beginning or end of each camera setup or at the completion of a scene, while the entire cast and crew and equipment is still on set, the audio crew asks for complete silence and records 60 seconds of the sound in the room. In the audio mix, this room tone can fill in gaps in the dialogue or effects.

- **Keep continuity.** Just as a script supervisor maintains visual continuity in a shoot, there is a definite continuity in recording audio, too. The audio levels between actors in a scene, for example, need to be constant and unvarying in volume. Any background or ambient sound is measured for consistency of levels so they don't interfere with the dialogue. When a camera angle changes, its accompanying audio might also be different.

- **Rehearse and rerehearse.** There is a real difference between setting up audio for one shot in which both actors are walking and talking on the street, and a shot on a set where they're sitting quietly on a couch. Carefully consider how you can record the audio that fits with the visual camera angles and perspectives for each scene.

- **Keep an audio log.** One person on the audio production crew has the job of keeping track of what is recorded on a set or location, including dialogue, ambient sounds, and special effects. This audio log, or *sound report*, lists details that are pertinent to the audio mix in postproduction such as the tape number with time code numbers (in and out points), the scene number, and the take number with a short description of what's been recorded.

- **Keep your cool.** A lot of details are involved in recording good clean sound. The best place to learn is on the job, so get familiar with the tools of the audio trade, and keep your focus. Troubleshooting comes with the territory, and so does keeping your cool, all the time.

VI. THE ACTUAL SHOOT

A long-playing full shot is what always separates the men from the boys. Anybody can make movies with a pair of scissors and a two-inch lens.

Orson Welles

Before starting principal photography, the producer checks and double-checks all the legal documents. You'll have copies of signed deal memos with the crew, contracts with the talent, release forms from the extras, and final location agreements—everything's been negotiated and signed.

Following are the key elements in most all shoots.

Arrival of Cast and Crew

Based on their call times, crew members arrive on the set or location. Usually the production department arranges for the transportation department to gather equipment, vehicles, set pieces, and other production materials to be delivered and unloaded early in the shooting day. The actors and talent arrive for wardrobe, hair and makeup, and any time-consuming special effects. Everyone's call time is given to them the night before in the call sheet, or by a phone call, email, or text message from the production department, by either the production manager or the AD.

Wardrobe, Hair, and Makeup

Actors and talent (including minor parts, extras, background people, children, and animals) usually need hair, makeup, and/or wardrobe before they're ready to appear in their scene. They may require only a simple hair comb, minimal makeup, and little or no wardrobe. Or, makeup could involve complex blood or scar makeup, facial hair or wigs, or a complicated period wardrobe such as an historical outfit or costume. The wardrobe, hair, and makeup people stay close to the set for any last-minute extra touch-ups such as a hair combing, powdering a sweaty nose, or adjusting clothing.

Dressing the Set or Location

The art director and his crew *dress*, or prepare, the set or location for the shoot. This can include finishing touches on the set pieces, adding furnishings, props, or greenery, and moving pieces around to accommodate the action or movements of the characters.

Craft Services

The craft services crew have set up and are serving food at least a half hour before the overall call time, and assembled set up a table for coffee, tea, water, meals, and/or snacks for the cast and crew that is close to the shoot. They also serve at least one healthy meal a day or every six hours, depending on contractual agreements and the budget. When you pay special attention to craft services, everyone is happier, more productive, energized, and usually grateful.

Blocking for the Camera

The producer, director, DP, and/or gaffer survey the set or location, review their storyboards, and map out the day's shoot. They plan the placement of the cameras, lights, and audio equipment in a process called *blocking the scene*. Any revisions are determined here—all last-minute changes can slow up production and stress out the crew.

IN THE TRENCHES...

No matter what size my production may be, everyone involved is human, and all humans need food and water on a regular basis. My projects are primarily low-budget but I always budget higher for craft services and catering. Keeping my cast and crew well-fed and hydrated could well be the most important form of thank you that I can give my people—besides a huge lump of cash. Water, good coffee, health teas and bars, fruit, full meals— this epicurean gesture buys you a lot of loyalty when the days get longer than you expected.

~C. Kellison

Blocking the Actors

Once the camera movements are decided, the scene is rehearsed for the cameras and lights. Often a stand-in takes the place of an actor in the blocking. Any places for the actors are marked on the floor with masking tape.

Lighting the Set

Properly and thoughtfully lighting a set or location takes time. Depending on the size of the crew, the DP and the gaffer set the lights, replace bulbs, try different scrims and gels, and find various angles that work best. If a stand-in doubles for an actor, the crew can experiment with the lights while the actual actor is in makeup or rehearsal.

Audio Setup

All microphones and recording devices are set up, tested, and rehearsed. The audio may need muffling with heavy *sound blankets* or acoustical equipment. Any mic cables are kept away from electrical cables or wires to prevent interference. If a separate sound mixer is used, it's kept in an area where the audio engineer can monitor the different levels of audio coming from each microphone and keep them all in balance. Any boom shots can be rehearsed with the camera operator so the boom or mic shadows won't enter the camera's frame.

Rehearsing the Actors

Whenever possible, the director or producer rehearses the actors on the set where they will be shooting. This on-set rehearsal gives the talent a chance to loosen up in the shooting environment, and get familiar with the script. Sometimes the rehearsal takes place in another area away from the set, which allows the actors to concentrate.

Rehearsing and Blocking the Extras

Any people in the background (called *extras* or *atmosphere*) must be rehearsed and blocked, just like the main actors. A member of the crew, usually the AD, works closely with the extras in rehearsing movements such as crossing the set from one side to the other, chatting and laughing at tables, or walking behind the action. The extras are directed not to look into or at the camera, and generally only pretend to talk or laugh; usually they're told to move their lips in complete silence. Their audio is recorded later and added into the final mix.

The Technical Run-Through

This final rehearsal checks for technical details of the action being shot. Camera angles, lights, audio mics, dolly moves, the placement of furniture or props—all these are essential steps in the choreography of production. If you're shooting on a location, cover anything that could be damaged with plastic tarps or moving blankets. Move valuable or breakable items, like plants, furniture, china, glassware, that are part of the location. Someone is assigned to take careful notes and photographs of each object in its original place so everything can be put back exactly where it was, after the shoot. Leave each location in better condition than when you started.

Security

On any location, there are items of major value that can tempt hit-and-run thieves. Even on busy sets with people everywhere, things get stolen all the time. Hire a security company, or assign crew members like PAs and interns, to keep a constant watch on whatever you don't want stolen or damaged. Insurance doesn't cover everything. When someone is assigned to be on "fire watch," for example, they're responsible for intently watching the back of the truck(s), and allowing only authorized personnel to come and go.

Shooting Publicity Stills

Often, a still photographer is hired to take publicity photographs that can be important to a publicity campaign as well as for archiving the production. The photos can be taken during the technical rehearsal, or, if the photographer uses a camera with a silent shutter, during the shoot itself. A professional still photographer knows how to get great shots without being obtrusive.

Lights. Camera. Action!

All the equipment, the crew, and the talent are in place and ready. Now, it's time for the shoot. The director calls for action and the camera operator and the audio engineer both confirm by saying "up to speed," or "speeding." Then the scene or action can begin.

Slates. Some video and film productions use a *slate*, or a *clapboard*, which is held in front of the camera each time it rolls. Like a small chalkboard, relevant details are chalked on it: the project title, the names of the producer and director, what camera(s) is in use, the scene number, take number, and date. Other video productions might use a *smart slate*, which matches the camera's time code with the audio. However, because a professional video camera records the sound directly onto the videotape or digital storage, slates are a matter of personal preference, not necessity.

Takes. With few exceptions, a scene is shot several times before it feels right to the producer or director; each attempt is called *a take*. You might run into technical problems like poor lighting, a boom in the shot, a misread line, or a number of other challenges that might occur as part of the production process. Additional takes can cover these problems up, so often a seasoned producer may call for a final take for *safety*, as a contingency.

Each shot in each scene has been planned out with its own camera and lighting angle and often its own lens. Each shot is assigned a description and a specific number on the shot list and production schedule. For example, the close-up of the small child digging in the sandbox might be the third shot in Scene #3. Every time the scene is shot—from "action" to "cut"—it is given a new take number.

Shot coverage. Every shot requires a new setup, usually with new lighting and different camera angles. Whenever possible, get your most important key shots first. Then, as time permits, work down your shot list for any remaining shots you still need. Depending on the creative direction that you want from your project, the general rule of production suggests that you cover one or more of the following shots:

- **Establishing shot.** Also called a *master shot*, it establishes the scene and what's going on in it. It is a wider shot of the whole scene that shows its action, the actors' movements, and their relationships to each other. The master shot can then be intercut with tighter angles, such as:
- **Close-up.** A tight shot, usually of an actor's face or an object. It is revealing and intimate, and shows more crucial detail.
- **Single.** A shot of one actor, in close-up, medium shot, or wide shot. When editing from one single shot to another, pay attention to continuity of eye-line.
- **Two-shot.** A scene with two actors in the frame. Three- and four-shots have three and four actors in the frame, respectively, and are useful for variation and cutaways.
- **Over-the-shoulder.** The camera is placed just behind the shoulder of one person and focuses on the person she is facing. That person's face is in the frame along with a portion of the listener's shoulder. This shot brings the audience closer to the characters and varies the cutting.
- **Insert.** A shot, usually a close-up, that reveals an important and relevant detail in a scene.

Video monitor. It is vital to have a video monitor on the set. Connected by cable to the camera(s), the monitor shows the DP, director, producer, and other technicians what the camera sees as it's being shot. This can be especially important when shooting HD. The camera operator might not see something on the camera's small viewfinder, but can catch it on the larger monitor. It's also an instant playback of what was just shot. The monitor is the centerpiece of the "video village" where one or more monitors are set up for the producer, director, and DP (and often the client or investor) to view the footage as it's being taped as well as to watch playback between scenes.

Audio. Often the sound engineer may hear a problem on her headphones—an airplane overhead, a humming fridge. She'll nonetheless let the scene finish, and not interrupt the take. After the director calls "cut," she'll tell him about the problem. Some of the take may still be useable, and production protocol states that it's only the director's call to stop shooting.

Continuity. The script supervisor (or a competent production assistant in a lower-budget production) is a constant presence on the set. He checks to make sure that each shot can match up with the shot that comes before it—and after it—in the script and in editing. If, for example, an actor puts his hand in his pocket in one shot, his hand must still be in his pocket in the shot that will follow it in editing. Because most projects are shot out of sequence, the script supervisor's notes are a major time-saver for the editor and audio mixer. Continuity notes generally include:

- The shot number and description
- The camera and lens used
- The length of the shot itself
- Comments on the action in the shot
- Comments or notes from the director, producer, or DP/camera crew and/or sound mixer

Cover shots. Even the most experienced producers and directors will finish their shoot and go into the editing room, only to realize they're missing an important shot. During production, the script supervisor can avoid this problem by suggesting cover shots, or additional footage.

IN THE TRENCHES...

In a recent class project, one of my students wrote, produced, and shot a short scene that she could use as a kind of demo reel. Here's how she shot a dramatic scene in a couple's bedroom. In this scene, a man has discovered a letter from his wife's lover—this is how she covered it.

1. First, we get a wide shot, or master shot, as the two characters act out the whole scene. We see the two actors, and their spatial relationship to the set around them. Then, our following tighter shots can match up with this wide shot in editing.
2. Here, the man sees the letter on the bed, she sees him spot it, and both try to grab it. He snatches it first.
3. A medium close-up of the husband, reading it slowly, out loud.

4. A reaction shot of the wife, listening, in total shock, shamed.
5. In a medium two-shot, he angrily tosses the letter back on the bed and the woman reaches for it.
6. The camera follows him as he kneels on the ground, pulls a suitcase out from under the bed.
7. Close-up of her as her face crumples in tears.
8. Close-up of his face, grim, determined, fighting tears.
9. Medium wide shot as wife slumps onto bed, holding letter, and husband strides across the room, holding the suitcase. The door slams behind him.
10. Medium shot as her tears turn to a sly smile.

~*C. Kellison*

Audio pickups. Often there is additional audio that needs to be rerecorded—a line of dialogue that was muffled, ambient background noise, or other sound effects. It is easier in the long run to record it right away. If you wait, the actor may have left the project, or the ambient sounds like heavy traffic or children at play may no longer exist.

And before a scene wraps and sets up somewhere else, the audio engineer asks everyone to say nothing and hold totally still. Then, she records at least 30 seconds of "room tone," which captures the unique sounds that live in each room or location. That room tone comes in handy during postproduction, filling in occasional holes in mixing dialogue and other sound tracks from that scene.

Always pay your sound person well; the audience will forgive a badly composed or out-of-focus shot, but they'll never forgive bad audio.

Michael Moore

When each shot on your shot list has been captured, all the gear is either moved or reset to shoot the next item on the shot list. The camera, lighting angles, and audio are also repositioned.

The Equipment Breakdown and Location Wrap

Everyone is happy with the footage, and the shoot officially wraps for the day. Now, the crew *breaks down*, or disassembles, all the lights, cameras, audio equipment, and whatever else is not needed for the next day's shoot is packed away. On location shoots, the crew removes all tarps, protective coverings, garbage, equipment, and whatever else remains, and puts items back in their original positions, thoroughly clearing out the location. With all this accomplished, your shooting day is over.

The thing I really need is not more money, or food. It's five more hours in the day.

Valerie Walsh, excerpt from interview in Chapter 11

ON A HUMAN LEVEL . . .

The producer is both the leader of the production team and an integral part of it. You set the model for clear communication, mutual respect, a relaxed mood on set, and for forgiveness of the occasional human error. Mistakes get made, so move right on past them, and avoid making them again. You, as the leader, must stay healthy. During the stress of production, it can be tempting to drink too much coffee, and forget to eat well or sleep enough. But if you go down, so does the production. Find a balance that works for you, and let yourself enjoy the process.

SUMMARY

No matter what your project entails, each shot and each scene is recorded and shot with postproduction in mind. No matter how brilliant the scene is by itself, it must be edited with one shot that precedes it and another that follows. The shots must match visually, and the audio must have continuity. Together, they combine to create a narrative flow or storyline, regardless of the show's genre or the delivery system. In the next chapter, you can explore the postproduction process that brings the footage and audio elements into a tangible and cohesive form.

REVIEW QUESTIONS

1. Name five leadership qualities a producer brings into the production process. Describe how each one impacts the project.

2. Discuss the advantages of using a virtual location over a sound stage or location. Create a brief story idea in which virtual locations and backdrops are a key feature.

3. Describe the concept of matching eye-lines or draw an example.

4. Draw a simple sketch of a scene, demonstrating three-point lighting.

5. Describe the microphone options available for recording production sound. Pose a situation in which each mic is put to its most efficient use.

6. What are the typical problems you might run into in recording useable audio in an exterior location? In a sound stage? How could you solve these problems?

7. What are the strategies you would find valuable to make the audio recording process easier?

8. Describe the role of the script supervisor and the importance of this job during production.

The Final Product: Postproduction

Everything you can imagine is real.

Pablo Picasso

First film, then video, and now, new media—each has a language with its own vocabulary, tools, and sets of rules. Your vocabulary is the picture, and your sentence structure is the edit. You're telling your story with images, and the juxtaposition of these images, fleshed out with underlying aural impressions, and the nuance of graphics design. It's in postproduction that the final story comes together.

I. THE PRODUCER'S ROLE

Postproduction can be the least understood aspect of the producer's domain. Before starting postproduction, you want to study any shortcuts that can make the postproduction process more creative and efficient. The producer's job is to know as much as possible about everyone else's job—what they do, the tools of their trade, their rates, the facilities in which they work, and the subtleties of their art. You want to find the most talented and highly qualified people who can work within the limits of your budget. The more prepared you are when you begin postproduction, the faster the process will go.

The Postproduction Supervisor

In producing for TV and new media, the producer usually supervises the project from beginning to end, including the entire postproduction process. A more complex project might require a postproduction supervisor who acts as the producer of postproduction. She works closely with the producer to maintain the vision of the project, and supervises all phases of postproduction including editing, mixing, graphics design, final composite, and delivery of the final master to the end user, client, or broadcaster.

The postproduction supervisor (or the producer, or assigned PA) keeps track of:

- All the **footage** that has been shot as well as all the numbered and organized tape reels or storage devices, screening logs, dubs, and other log sheets
- Other **visual images**, such as all stock footage, archival footage, animation, graphics, art work, and copies of any related legal release forms
- All **audio elements** such as dialogue, background audio, special effects, original and/or stock music, and cue sheets

So whether you are hiring a postproduction supervisor or you're the one in charge, the following guidelines can help you navigate the postproduction process.

Postproduction Guidelines

1. Triple-Check Your Legal Documents

The need to legally protect your project never stops. It continues way past postproduction, so as you put together all the elements you'll need for your edit and mix, be sure that all your legal ducks are in a row. Do you have clearances for all the music you'll use in the mix? Signed releases for stock footage?

> When I'm drafting a contract, after I'm finished, I will always go back over it, not just for each word, but I have a checklist, too: did I do this and did I do this? I make sure that I haven't left anything out.
>
> **J. Stephen Sheppard, excerpt from interview in Chapter 11**

2. Spend Money to Save Money

You want an editor who has a keen sense of storytelling. You want him to be familiar with the best editing system for your project, someone who has kept up with its technical compatibilities and system nuances. He must be able to deliver a color-corrected, audio-balanced final product that's technically up to specification. You want him, ideally, to have experience in cutting a show that's similar to yours, and you want him to be the kind of guy with whom you can spend long hours or days at a time.

Most editors and editing facilities have demo reels or web sites showing their work. If you like what you see, try to meet with the editor before you start shooting. Take a tour of her editing facility. Ask her what you can do to make her job easier. Compare notes on your shooting formats and their compatibility with her editing equipment.

You can save money and time in postproduction when you:

- Organize your tapes or storage devices and location logs
- Screen and log your footage
- Organize editing elements including footage, audio, and graphics
- Write a paper cut for the edit session

Let's say... that your best friend has an excellent computer and the latest upgrade of a popular editing software program. He's offered to edit your project—for free. This sounds good—great, in fact—since your budget is really low. Yet, you're torn. You know this project could be good enough to be your calling card, but you're just not sure if your friend shares your vision, or has the right skills to showcase that vision. Sure, the editing is free, but if it's not cut right the first time, you'll have to edit it again, wasting time and money. In the long run, you can save the project by editing with a seasoned editor on a professional-quality system. And because editing software is cheap enough to buy, or at least, to rent, you (or your friend) can do a rough cut, then hand it over to a pro who can really make it come alive.

3. Organize the Components for the Edit

It isn't unusual for a producer to shoot 20 hours of footage, or 50, or 100, for just a one-hour program, especially for reality shows or documentaries. This requires an organizational system during the actual shoot that keeps track of where that footage is stored. It helps when you label each tape cassette (or disk, memory card, etc.), including:

- The tape number (Tape 1, Tape 2, etc.)
- The location where it was shot (Studio B, in Central Park, etc.)
- The date of the shoot
- The audio tracks (Track 1 is the lav, Track 2 the boom, etc.)
- The camera it was shot with (Camera 1, Camera 2, etc.) in multicamera shoots

When labeling your tapes or memory cards, design an easy system for naming each one. For instance, if you shot in Central Park and used nine tapes, you might label them CP01, CP02, and so on, to CP09. In a studio setting with several cameras, match the camera number with a tape number

Say you're shooting *The Jane Smith Show*. You use two cameras and change the tapes three times. Your first two tapes can be labeled JS0101 (Jane Smith-Tape 1, Camera 1), JS0102 (Jane Smith-Tape 1, Camera 2), and JS0201 (Jane Smith-Tape 2, Camera 1), and so on, through the subsequent tapes.

This may seem unnecessarily obsessive or too time-consuming. But ask any editor and she'll tell you that she's impressed with your organization, and relieved that she's not spending the extra time looking for shots. Whatever your system, organization like this will pay off a hundred-fold over your producing career.

Tape Log

The producer keeps track of the footage that's been shot in a *tape log*. Whether the footage has been shot on tape, on P2 cards, in 2K/4K files, or another storage format, you want to know where everything you've shot is located. During the edit and mix, for example, you may find that you're missing a cutaway shot or need to replace a shot you thought would work but didn't. The tape log provides a fast way to find your footage. You'll find an example of a tape log on this book's web site.

Film-to-Tape

Any footage shot on film (Super 8, Super 16, 16 mm, or 35 mm) must first be transferred to digital video before it can be edited in a *nonlinear editing (NLE)* system. Film-to-tape transfer is a complicated and costly procedure in which the film is converted to video via a *telecine* machine, also called a *film chain*, that scans each frame and converts it into a video signal.

During the film-to-tape transfer process, the image and production sound are transferred, and if needed, the film can also be color-corrected. Some producers like to *color-correct* their footage as they transfer it, adjusting for color and contrast; others prefer to wait until the rough cut is approved, correcting just the approved footage in the final edit. Increasingly, producers color correct their footage in the NLE room, using a program like Final Cut Pro to give the project the right look.

Sometimes, complications can arise from the difference in frame rates between film (24 fps) and video (30 fps) as well as in audio syncing. If you plan to shoot in film and transfer it to video, discuss the *film-to-tape* process with the editor, and research the resources available on the subject.

Tape-to-Film

Producers occasionally need a 35-mm film print of their video work. Regardless of what format it was shot on, if it's been edited and mixed in an NLE system, the master can then be transferred to a 35-mm film print. However, this process is expensive, so research it carefully. Some 4,000 cinemas across the United States now feature digital projection, and increasingly, more festivals project both film and digital video.

Alternative Sources: Stock and Archival Footage

Using high-quality stock footage not only saves you money, but also can add real nuance and production value to your vision.

> **Let's say...** that you want an opening establishing shot of Los Angeles, a glittering nighttime L.A. skyline from an airplane. By the time you hire a helicopter and a pilot, a camera operator and equipment, arrange for shooting permits and insurance, and pray for good weather, you've spent a small fortune. Enter stock footage. Stock footage can be a godsend to a producer's budget.

For considerably less money, you can buy the exact shot you want. Stock footage facilities license a wide range of high-quality footage that's been shot all over the globe by professionals who sell the clearance rights to producers. This footage is high-quality and is often shot on 35-mm film and transferred to video, or shot on high definition, or onto 2K or 4K digital files.

The choice of shots is limitless, covering almost any scene description, ranging from field workers in Vietnam to time-lapse footage of Tokyo at night. You can get exotic flamingoes in flight, migrating Monarch butterflies, vintage cars, sleeping babies, couples in love, beaches at sundown. Stock footage can save you considerable time and money, as well as lend real quality to your final product.

Stock Footage Search

Finding stock footage is relatively simple. Go online, and search "stock footage" facilities. There are dozens, offering a range of footage genres. In most cases, you can see all their footage online—it'll be watermarked in some way so it can't be stolen. After you've made your choices, and picked the footage you want, you'll then negotiate a fee for the rights to use it in your project.

Stock Footage Fees

The fee for using stock footage depends on several factors. If, for example, you wanted to open your show with a shot of the British Museum, the fee for buying that shot depends on how you plan to use it. If your show is airing on a major network or cable channel, the fee is much higher than if the museum shot is in an educational piece with limited distribution. If it is part of a one-time, nonbroadcast project like a training film for an organization, or being used in an industrial film, the fee is more negotiable and usually lower. If you are buying the exclusive rights to use the shot, the cost is even higher.

Other factors that influence the license fee are:

- The amount of time for which you want the rights (usually from two years to perpetuity)
- The territories (just your country, or a few other counties as well, or worldwide)
- Any special advertising or promotional uses

- The total number of runs (broadcasts)
- Use in new media formats (webcasts, mobisodes, etc.)

You also want to double-check the clearances on any copyrights and trademarks. In some cases, stock footage may also require you to obtain releases from any talent or people on screen. Music or narration that is mixed into footage also needs to be cleared. You'll find more information on legal clearances in Chapter 5.

Archival Footage

There are hundreds of sources for footage that has an historical context. The archivists will research, gather, and/or clear the rights for historical footage. They may also transfer it from film to video in whatever format you'll need. As with the stock footage, fees vary and are dependent on their use. Often, the footage may be negotiable, but the underlying music isn't cleared. You want clearances for both images and the music.

> **Let's say...** that you're making a documentary on the history of the Manhattan skyline. You want to contrast the current skyline—you've already got the perfect shot—with the skyline of the city as it looked a hundred years ago. You've found an archival researcher who shows you old photographs, etchings, and a range of skyline images shot in 35- or 16-mm film. She's also found still photographs, magazine covers, old newsreels, and a range of in-depth material that brings an extra texture to your project. She's an expert in finding and clearing the rights, and looks for any good material that's in the public domain and free. Although her fees aren't cheap, she's brought a dimension and credibility to your project that's priceless.

Public Domain Footage

When the copyright has elapsed on footage (or a book or picture or painting or music), it is no longer owned by anyone and its rights are in the *public domain* (PD). You can use it freely, without paying for clearances or royalty fees. Many private companies find and resell PD footage, and will charge you fees for their research and duplication.

In the United States, you can access any footage that has been shot by almost any agency of the U.S. government using taxpayers' money, with no clearances or royalty payments. The National Archives, the Library of Congress, the Smithsonian, and NASA, for example, all offer vast footage collections that are available to the public; the only costs to you are for duplication. You can also consult with an independent archival footage expert who can help you locate options from within these vast collections. Other countries have similar sources for footage that is either inexpensive to clear, or it's free.

4. Screen and Log Your Footage

The use of nonlinear editing systems has revolutionized the postproduction process. This is good news for producers who want to be creative while staying within their budget. Because of the ease of NLE, it can be tempting for producers to bring all their tapes into the editing room and screen them as they download, rather than screening them prior to the edit session. This turns the creative process into an expensive administrative swamp that can be time-consuming as well as frustrating for the editor.

The cost of storage drives is going down, and the storage drives are getting bigger, holding more data. But it's still a waste of time to load all your footage when you know you're using only a small portion for your edit. You may have shot 30 hours of footage for a one-hour piece, and your selections, or *selects,* may boil down to less than three hours.

A cost-effective method of preparing for editing is to screen and log your footage before the edit session. From these log notes, you can construct a *paper cut*, or an editing storyboard. It's like a shooting script for your editor and the sound designer; it gives them a clear outline of what scenes appear in what order, and where each shot can be found. The paper cut lists time code (TC) locations and descriptions of selected edits, as well as notes about graphics and audio, and the order in which footage appears in the script. You'll find a storyboard template on this book's web site.

Ideally, you want to transfer your footage for screening to DVD (or an FTP site) with *matching time code*. This means that the TC on your original footage is exactly the same on your screening cassette. It's called visible time code, also *vizcode*, or *VTC*, and it is displayed in a small box on the bottom or top of the screen.

IN THE TRENCHES...

It's so much better—for me—to screen and log my footage ahead of the actual edit session. I want to look at it objectively and play around with it in my head, then log it and eventually create a script from all the many shots coming together in my head. To make this script work for the editor, I need to know that my screening dubs have exactly the same time code as the masters from which they were copied—otherwise, my notes won't match. Making sure I've got something as basic as matching time code saves time, a lot of money, and my editor's blood pressure.

~*C. Kellison*

Screening Log

As you saw in Chapter 8, TC has eight numbers. For example, 01:03:16:22 is the same as one hour, three minutes, 16 seconds, and 22 frames per second (also the exact number of that frame).

As you screen your footage, *log* it by taking notes of each pertinent shot and its TC number. Let's say that you're screening Tape 1. You like a specific shot where the actor picks up a cup of coffee, sees a letter on the bed, reads it, then angrily throws his cup against a wall. The action starts at 00:01:03:16 (one hour, three minutes, 16 seconds) and ends 10 seconds later (at 00:01:03:26). Your log notes on this scene might look something like this:

Tape #	TC in	Scene description	TC out
# 1	00:01:03:16	(MS) Tom picks up cup, reads letter, throws cup	00:01:03:26

Your tape log details the tape number, the TC numbers for the in-point and the out-point of the scene, the shot's angle (MS, etc.), and a brief description of the scene. If you're logging dialogue, either scripted or unscripted, you might type each word verbatim for an exact transcription. Or, type just the key words and mark irrelevant sections with an ellipsis (...). Often, the tapes are transcribed by a professional transcriber who makes a note of the TC at regular intervals, usually every 30 to 60 seconds.

A number of logging software programs are available, such as The Executive Producer and MediaFiler, along with free programs from Final Cut Pro and Avid. These programs can cut down your screening time and provide notes for the editor during the digitizing process. This saves you download time, which must be done in real time, by more easily transferring your logging notes to the NLE along with the footage. Another choice is to screen and log by hand, using the simple forms found on this book's web site, such as the screening log or the storyboard.

The Scope of the Log

Footage is just one of several elements in your project. Other elements include the audio, animation, music, and graphics. As you did with your footage, you'll keep a log for every element on a tape log, and distribute copies to anyone involved in postproduction such as the postproduction supervisor, production assistants, the editor, graphics designer, and/or the sound designer.

Your log sheet might include any of these elements:

- Studio or location footage (tape or drive numbers, dates, locations, etc.)
- Stock footage (footage that's been professionally shot for resale, like helicopter shots or time lapse photography)
- Archival footage (historical footage or photographs)
- Graphics (opening titles, closing credits, lower thirds)
- Animation (animated insert segments)
- Audio tracks (anything recorded on the footage audio tracks),
- Additional audio components (music, stings, needle drops, special effects, ADR)

5. *Write a Paper Cut*

Not every producer has the ability to "visualize" what shots cut well with other shots. But you know what the primary scenes are, and their sequence in the script. Because you've most likely shot your footage out of order from what appears in the script, you'll include all the reel numbers and TCs onto your paper cut, in the order in which they'll appear in the final edited product.

IN THE TRENCHES...

In my experience of working with editors, the ideal editing paper cut could arguably be called an *80/20 paper cut*. This means that I've screened the footage and come into the edit room with a paper cut that provides details for roughly 80 percent of my key scenes, cutaways, and the sequence in which they'll appear in the final edited product. The paper cut also includes tape numbers, TC, and scene descriptions. The extra 20 percent? That represents extra leeway that the editor can take, making creative and technical choices beyond the written paper cut that enhance the piece and give the editor a chance to add his or her unique signature.

~C. Kellison

After you've transferred your footage for screening, then screened and logged it, and written a paper cut, you're ready to edit and mix your project.

Remember the earlier scene in which Tom picks up his coffee cup, sees the letter, reads it, and angrily hurls the cup against a wall? Although the footage was shot at different times, on different tapes, and maybe at different locations, they all cut together as one smooth sequence. The finished paper cut format might look like this:

Tape #	TC in	Scene description	TC out
Tape 1	01 03 16	WS >>MS Tom picks up cup, reads note	01 03 20
Tape 3	03 10 04	CU the note	03 10 08
Tape 2	02 20 25	CU Tom's reaction to note	02 20 30
Tape 1	01 03 21	MS Tom throws coffee cup	01 03 26

In writing your paper cut, you'll find these terms helpful:

> **Shot.** A single uninterrupted videotaped segment that is the primary element of a scene.
>
> **Scene.** A dramatic or comedic piece consisting of one or more shots. Generally, a scene takes place in one time period, involves the same characters, and is in the same setting.
>
> **Sequence.** A progression of one or more scenes that share the narrative momentum and energy connected by an emotional and narrative energy.

II. THE EDITOR'S ROLE

When you are editing, the final master is Aristotle and his *Poetics*. You might have a terrific episode, but if people are falling out because there are just too many elements in it, you have to begin to get rid of things.

Ken Burns

An editor can be a creative magician, a technical consultant, and an effective arbiter of what works and what doesn't. Each editor has her own strengths and styles of cutting. One editor has an ideal style for MTV, and another editor knowledgeably cuts documentaries for the BBC. An editor might specialize in sports or news, sitcoms, movies-of-the-week, online content, commercials, music videos. And then there are those few editors who can cut almost anything.

An experienced editor can take disparate shots and elements and weave them together, creating a seamless flow. As a creative artist, he can "paint" a mood with pacing, place a perspective on the action, and signal conflict or comedy. A technically adept editor can design special effects or transitions between scenes, color-correct the footage, and make sure your project conforms to broadcast standards. Often, he can "fix it in post," covering up mistakes or finding solutions to seemingly impossible problems that inevitably pop up in everyone's project.

Working with an Editor

I first ask producers for notes and scripts. If I'm lucky, they'll have those, but more and more producers seem to think that editors wave a magic wand over hours worth of footage, and only the good stuff comes up. I remind them that if we first need to screen, log, and digest the material, and then make an insightful and coherent movie, it's going to take time. For every one hour of footage, it takes at least two or three hours to view, log, and highlight it. You then need to knock this down into a script with some kind of theme, and only then can you start to edit.

Jeffrey McLaughlin, excerpt from interview in Chapter 11

Producers come into an editing room with varying levels of experience in postproduction. One producer may have spent hundreds of hours editing and mixing; another has only limited exposure or expertise. Some producers don't have the luxury of extra time, or the foresight to screen their footage, before the edit session. They'll hand over hours of their unscreened footage to the editor, and expect her to work miracles without any script or direction.

The producer's role with the editor is highly collaborative. You want to give the editor specific targets for the project, and you also want to create an environment in which the work can get done. When you're in the edit room, the editor needs to concentrate, so keep phone calls and distracting conversations to a minimum. Discourage people from crowding into his space. When possible, encourage creative leeway with different shots or new ideas. Make sure he gets a genuine "thank you" along with plenty of food, water, and coffee during the edit sessions. The editor is one of your most valuable team members.

With the user-friendly, inexpensive, creative, and evolving NLE systems, like Final Cut Pro, Avid, or iMovie, an entire project can be edited on a laptop. You can now build a functional edit room in your bedroom, or do a rough cut on an airplane. Many producers do their own rough cut first, working out some of the more obvious problems, then bring that rough cut for the editor to fine tune and take to the next level.

But, not every producer has the technical savvy or creative eye to be a good editor. You want your project to reflect your vision, and to adhere to all broadcast standards so it can be aired or connected into other platforms, and also have the technical capacity to be dubbed with no loss of *generations*, or quality. So, how do you find an editor who can satisfy these objectives?

There are dozens of web sites, phone listings, and television industry directories that list professional editors and editing facilities in various countries, regions, and cities. Visit their web sites and when possible, check out their facility. Meet them, screen the editor's reels, and discuss what you need for editing your project. You can also:

- Talk to other producers, directors, and writers about editors they've worked with.
- Call regional or local television stations who may "hire out" their editors and facilities for outside work. If not, ask if they can recommend local freelance editors and/or facilities.
- Check with local high schools and colleges that have editing equipment for their students. Often, their student editors can be hired for low-budget projects, or can work for academic credit.

Working with Editing Technology

One of an editor's golden assets in an edit room is that he was never part of the production process. He wasn't shooting the film for four weeks and feeling the "magic" of that process. The war stories the crew told about shooting in the midst of a hurricane, or when half the staff came down with food poisoning—they mean nothing to the editor. He only sees the dailies, and the only "magic" he feels is what comes out of those dailies. If a shot works, he will use it, but if it doesn't, he can easily let it go. The pain, the love, or the cost of any one element means nothing if it doesn't work in the edit. No one shot is more important than the whole of the film.

Jeffrey McLaughlin, excerpt from interview in Chapter 11

The rapid evolution of postproduction technology has brought editing, sound mixing, and graphics into the digital domain. These advances have expanded the producer's horizons. From prime time broadcast to art gallery installations, from educational teaching tools to high-end commercials, from user-generated content to slick online sites, the creative possibilities of today's digital tools seem limitless.

Yet the learning curve can be steep. The choices seem endless. The terminology is confusing, and everyone has an opinion. Every six months, new equipment and software floods the marketplace; a system that is state-of-the-art this year is either upgraded or replaced next year.

Nonlinear Editing

Fortunately, there are consistencies between these systems. As you research the right editor for your project, also look at the range of digital *nonlinear edit* (NLE) systems that conform to professional, broadcast-quality standards. These systems work on the same basic principle as editing on film with an NLE system, pieces of footage can be digitally "spliced" together out of order, just like film editing.

Film editing has always been nonlinear, done with tape and scissors, and its pieces cut and taped together by hand. Before nonlinear editing, video editing was linear—electronically edited in an "always moving forward" direction. An editor could start only at the beginning and work toward the end because of the nature of electronic recording. The traditional way of editing video has been to edit in the chronological or *lineal order* that shots appeared in the piece.

Now, editing with digital equipment is done in a cut-and-paste mode, just as with film, except it's edited electronically rather than manually. The popular NLE systems Final Cut Pro, Avid Xpress, Premier Pro, Media Composer, and iMovie all work on similar principles. When you can learn one system, it's only a matter of nuance to find the right buttons in the right place on another system. Final Cut Pro and Avid are the systems currently used by most professionals. They offer high-quality options for finishing, are updated consistently, and support more plug-ins . Because these systems are now the pervasive editing modes, we'll be concentrating only on this method of editing and its technology.

If there is one downside to editing on NLE systems, it is the tendency to shoot more footage than is really needed, and to make decisions about your footage in the edit room. This one factor can result in spending valuable time deciding between Take 3 and Take 14 in the editing room, rather than prescreening it. This often translates to spending more money than you budgeted.

> Let's say... you shot your one-hour talk show with six cameras in a multicamera setup. The show ended up being just 23 seconds too long. But you don't want to download and digitize six hours of footage or the line cut that was live-switched at the time. That would mean you're downloading—in real time—seven hours of footage, just to cut out 23 seconds. In a linear room, often called an online room, you're working directly with the tapes themselves, and the job will take about an hour. There aren't as many linear rooms as there used to be, but they will always have their functions as an alternative to NLE. Nonlinear editing isn't always the best editing choice.

Digital versus Analog

Once a subject for lively debate, the topic of digital vs. analog is now essentially a non-issue. Outside of BetaCam SP and Hi8, all professional-quality cameras now shoot a digital signal. Some producers in news or unscripted programming still shoot in Beta—it's a tried-and-true standard. It can be downloaded into an NLE via a component signal, or through a Digibeta with an analog board that can process the analog signal to a component digital path.

On the other end of the technological spectrum are newer cameras like the Red One. It doesn't use tape or a disk, but records image and audio onto a digital file, and this case, files up to 4K. Talk with your DP and editor about your shooting options and how they translate into the editing process. And always back up your digital files. Always.

Compression

Compression relates to digital video, and simply means that the video signal is compressed to reduce the need for extra storage, as well as transmission space and costs. Compression techniques involve removing redundant data, or data that is less critical to the viewer's eye. The more the digital signal is compressed, the more distorted the image's details. You can see this effect in pirated copies of DVDs when the picture dissolves or fades to black—the sharpness of the image disintegrates and the pixels become larger. You can see this same effect on your NLE at a low resolution, also called *low rez*.

At what compression rate should you load your video into the NLE? Making this decision depends on the number of hours you have shot, and the disk space you have available. You can start at the lowest rate of 1-1, which results in the highest resolution (best quality picture). You can also load in at a low resolution, up to 40-1 (the poorest quality picture). This decision is based on how much storage you have and how much material you're working with. Downloading at 40-1 gets you 40 times more dailies and footage you can access, but the quality suffers. If you download at 1-1 or 2-1, your footage is high resolution (high rez), and doesn't need to be conformed later.

Drop Frame versus Nondrop Frame

During the shoot, the DP or camera operator might ask if the footage needs to be shot with a TC setting that's either *drop frame* (DF) or *nondrop frame* (NDF). Because video runs at 29.97 fps and not 30 fps, *nondrop frame* footage has a:03 frame discrepancy. By the end of a one-hour show, there are 3.6 extra seconds to account for. Broadcasters demand an exact program length, so a 60-minute program is usually delivered in DF, because it's exactly 60 minutes long and the show's timings are in real time.

Why work in NDF? If your show doesn't have to be frame-accurate or an exact length, it's easier for the editor to work with graphics and match edits in NDF because every frame has a sequential number. Some edit systems encounter problems in dealing with both DF and NDF simultaneously, though with the advent of HD and its different frame rates, most NLE systems can now easily make the necessary adjustments.

The Steps in Editing

There are several steps you'll follow if you're editing with a nonlinear system, as described next.

1. Download and Store Footage

Before you begin editing, your footage must first be transferred, or *downloaded*, into the NLE. There it is *digitized*. The downloaded tapes are digitized in *real time*—it takes eight hours to digitize eight hours of footage, so build digitizing time and costs into your budget. When it's downloaded, it's converted into a digital file that can be read by editing software, such as Final Cut Pro or Avid.

More on Downloading and Digitizing

The editor of your project is not always the person who does the digitizing; often, it's done overnight at a lower rate by a dubber on the night staff. As it is being digitized, perhaps you and/or the editor can categorize the footage with recognizable information like tape numbers, time codes, and scene descriptions, and store everything in computer folders or *bins*. Producers often designate only certain segments or portions of tapes to digitize, called *selects*, so they don't take up storage space for footage they won't use. This is an area in which a good logging program is an invaluable tool.

The amount of storage available to the NLE is a real consideration if you've got excessive footage, complicated audio components, animation, or graphics. But for most projects, storage isn't a problem with the drives currently available. Only a few years ago, the biggest drives available were one gigabyte drives that sold for $10,000. Today, a 500-gig portable hard drive costs under a tiny fraction of that, and a 4-terabyte drive has been promised by a major manufacturer for a price that's easy for most production budgets.

This luxury of digital storage no longer limits the producer to loading footage and editing in low resolution. You can now cut in high rez, which looks much better than low rez, get client comments, and do any revisions in high rez as well.

FireWire

Initiated by Apple Computer, FireWire is also called known as IEEE-1394 and is a standard communications protocol for high-speed, short-distance data transfer. Sony's version is iLink, Avid uses this protocol in its Adrenaline series, and Panavision calls it DV. Think of it as a transfer pipe that receives and stores data in its native compression/decompression scheme, or *codec*.

FireWire theoretically presents itself as the only "lossless" way to digitize footage directly into an NLE. It's currently considered the most efficient way to load editing components into an NLE. Though FireWire initially worked only with DV, it is now capable of working with uncompressed standard definition video, and with data transfer as high as 65 mps. FireWire allows you to transfer video to and from your hard drive without paying the higher costs of JPEG compression, or buying NLE software or banks of RAID-striped hard drives. It also deals well with artifacts.

2. *Make the First Rough Cut*

After all the footage, audio, and graphic elements have been loaded into the NLE, the editor cuts together her first rough cut—a basic edit. It forms the core of your finished piece, and reflects all the basic editing decisions. Over time, and as part of the creative editing process, this rough cut changes and evolves, but it's this first cut that shapes the project.

Some editors refer to the rough cut as a *radio edit* or an *A-roll edit*. This describes the process of first laying down all the sound bites, with video, and listening to it as much as watching it. This helps make sense of the project's narrative viewpoint and its pace.

The next step is to make it visually interesting by editing in all the video footage. But each project is unique, and it dictates its own approach to the rough cut. In a music video, the editor first lays the music down and then cuts the footage to synchronize with the musical beats.

In some programs, the narration is laid down first. Then, the footage is edited to fit the narration. If the narration, or the voice-over, hasn't been finalized, you can record the script by using a *scratch track* as your cue. This preliminary scratch track of narration, read by you or someone else, helps set the timings and beats for your rough cut. It is replaced later by a professional narrator. Regardless of what your particular project calls for, your rough cut clearly shows what works and what doesn't, what shots cut well with other shots, and the total running time (TRT) of this first pass.

3. Mix the Rough Audio

Throughout the editing process, the editor works closely with the audio tracks: she's separating them, balancing out levels, and keeping track of where everything is in the computer. She may do all the rough audio mixes as well as the final mix. Or, she'll do just a rough mix and then give all the tracks to an audio mixer or sound designer in an audio facility who'll do the final audio mix.

Most editors lay out their audio tracks like this:

Track 1:	Narration
Track 2:	Sound on tape
Tracks 3 & 4:	Stereo music
Track 5:	Sound effects
Tracks 6, etc.:	Overlapping audio, music, or dialogue

4. Agree on the Final Cut

Most projects take time to edit. The editing process usually goes through several rough versions before there's a final product that makes everyone happy. Then, the editor makes a frame-accurate *edit decision list (EDL)* that provides exact notes of all the reel numbers, time codes, cuts, and transitions in the rough cut. Finally, the editor re-edits or *conforms* the rough cut by matching the original footage in high rez, using the EDL. The final cut is the result of all these decisions that come from fine-tuning, tweaking, shortening, or lengthening the piece in editing.

This online finishing stage, also called the *conform*, concentrates on adding any high-end graphics, color corrections, and audio leveling that your project needs. The entire process is known as going from *off-line to online*, and is a system that many seasoned producers follow to save money and maintain their vision.

Editors go into their NLE at 1-1 compression and output the project, saving them hours of redigitizing and conforming. They can also digitize at 2-1, getting twice as much storage space. This works fine in the standard definition world, but with the advent of high definition, editors can use several terabytes (one trillion bytes) of storage to work in a high-rez quality. So for now, the offline to online process has become the norm in HD editing. However, as disk space gets cheaper and computers speed up, this final conform stage may eventually be phased out.

Editing High Definition TV—In Five Steps

NLE technology is making real inroads in editing high definition footage. Although it's still going through changes, and is a kind of work-in-progress, HD is clearly the direction the market is going. So, the producer needs to plan ahead.

Step One

The first step is to know what downconversion format you want to use. This means that the HD footage is converted to an NTSC (standard definition) tape that can be downloaded into your NLE system. (For example, when your 24p project is downconverted, the video changes from 23.98 fps to 59.94, and the TC changes from 24 to 30 frames.)

Shooting 24 frames in HD can occasionally complicate the editing process. Some producers downconvert the 24 frames to 30-frame DVCam, and then rely on a conversion program to reconvert the 30 frames back to 24 frames for the conform session. Other producers stay in 24 frames, feeding the 24 frames directly into the NLE. Both systems work, yet each has its pros and cons, so talk the process over with your editor before you start the edit process.

Because a mistake can be costly down the line, professionals recommend that projects that are shot in 1080i or 24p be edited in the NTSC video format; it's easier and cheaper at the moment. The standard downconversion formats are DVCAM, DVCPRO, and Digital Betacam. They all share similar high-quality images, digital audio, and TC capabilities. Other formats like MiniDV and DV aren't recommended because of the problems with embedding TC that exactly matches those of the field tapes.

Step Two

Next, the downconverted footage is digitized into the NLE system. Before you download, clearly mark each reel with a name or number that can be easily read by the computer. Ideally, limit it to four to six characters so the computer can easily read and distinguish each name. For example, Tape 1 shot in Griffith Park could be named GP01. Also make sure that the TC from your original field tapes is downconverted properly with an exact match.

Step Three

Although it's easy to import animation, graphics, and computer generated imagery (CGI) into an NLE system, taking these elements into an online session can be tricky. You can either have them created in the final HD resolution, or you can bring them into the online session, render them out to frames, and transfer these to an HD tape. These are then downconverted and treated like all the other elements in your edit.

Step Four

After you've completed your NLE edit, the editor can export an *EDL (edit decision list)* with all the information needed to conform in the online session, if needed. After you've made your final cut of your project, send its EDL and the digital cut to the online editing facility in advance of your actual session. Come prepared to the online session with all your original camera reels, graphics files, CGI and effects reels, and any titling or credits information that may be added to your cut.

Step Five

The online editor then assembles the show, using the EDL information. Your presence in this phase of editing is critical—the editor isn't familiar with your project, and the EDL is only an impersonal list of numbers that may not include transitions, wipes, dissolves, and other important creative details.

You don't have to be an expert in postproduction. That's why you're working with an editor you can trust, who'll answer your questions, and let you observe. If you're unsure of how to edit your project, talk to an experienced editor who has worked on a range of projects from start to finish.

Styles of Editing

Looking at a first assembly is kind of like looking at an overgrown garden. You can't just wade in with a weed whacker; you don't yet know where the stems of the flowers are.

Walter Murch, editor

What *is* editing? Essentially, certain shots take on specific meanings when they are juxtaposed with other shots. This juxtaposition is editing. It can manipulate time and create drama, tension, action, and comedy. Without editing, you'd only have disconnected pieces of an idea floating in isolation, looking for a connection.

Whether it's for TV, the Internet, podcasts, mobisodes, or a 50-monitor video wall, editing in today's media world still follows classic editing guidelines. These were established by American director D. W. Griffith, and Russian directors V. I. Pudovkin and Sergei Eisenstein, early in the last century. These pioneer filmmakers realized a century ago that film possessed its own language, with rules for "speaking" that language. They set the standards for editing that are used today by virtually all editors, no matter what the format.

During the production phase, the producer and director shoot their footage with carefully chosen camera angles and movements that tell a story from a certain narrative vantage point. The editor then takes this footage and—consulting with the producer, editor, and/or the postproduction supervisor—makes artistic decisions about how to cut the footage together. Some styles of editing include the following.

> *Parallel editing.* Two separate yet related events appear to be happening at the same time, as the editor intercuts sequences in which the camera shifts back and forth between one event and another.

Let's say... that the main tension and conflict of the story focuses on a man on death row who is being taken down the prison hallway to the execution chamber. The audience knows he's innocent. At the same time, the state governor is trying frantically to maneuver through rush-hour traffic to save the condemned man; the innocent man trips on his shoelace and hits his head while the guards laugh; the governor is on his cell phone but no one will believe he's the governor and they hang up on him. The innocent man asks the guard to give his wife a note. And so on. This use of parallel editing heightens the tension between both situations.

> *Montage editing.* Short shots or sequences are cut together to represent action, ideas, or to condense a series of events. The montage usually relies on close-ups, dissolves, frequent cuts, and even jump cuts to suggest a specific theme. For example, a single mother on the run from a hired killer moves to a small town with her child. A montage might show them happily moving into their new home, shopping for groceries, unpacking boxes, hanging clothes in the closet, and snuggling in bed on their first night together—all this in about a minute, and with underlying music usually fraught with some kind of emotional guidance. This montage effect gives the viewer a lot of information in minimal screen time.
>
> *Seamless editing.* This style of editing is used in many dramatic series, some sitcoms, and in feature films. The viewer is unaware of the editing because it is unobtrusive except for special dramatic shots. It supports the narrative and doesn't distract with effects. The characters are the focus, and the cuts are motivated by the story's events. Seamless editing motivates the realism of the story, and traditionally uses longer takes, match cuts rather than jump cuts, and selective audio that can act as a bridge between scenes.
>
> *Quick cut editing.* This style of editing is highly effective in action and youth-targeted programming, originated primarily by MTV in its infancy. It's used in music videos, promos, commercials, children's TV, UGC, and in programs on fashion, lifestyle, and youth culture. It combines fast cuts, jump cuts, montages, and special graphics effects.

Techniques in Editing

An editor looks at the footage with the producer, then edits the shots together to get from one shot to the next, telling the story. These editing techniques might include:

Cut. A quick change from one shot with one viewpoint or location to another. It's almost always better to use a cut rather than a slower transition like a dissolve or wipe. On most TV shows there is a cut every five to nine seconds, and much faster in some shows. A cut can compress time, change the scene or point of view, or emphasize an image or an idea. Most cuts are usually made on an action, like a door slamming or a slap to the face.

Match cut. A cut between two different camera angles of the same movement or action in which the change appears to be one smooth action.

Jump cut. Two similar angles of the same picture cut together, such as two close-up shots of the same actor. This style of editing can occasionally be edgy, or make a dramatic point, but it can also signal poor editing and continuity.

Cutaway. A shot that is edited to act as a bridge between two other shots of the same action. For example, an actor may look off to the distance; a cutaway shows what the actor sees. A cutaway also helps to avoid awkward jumps in time, place, or viewpoint, and can shorten the passing of time.

Reaction shot. A shot in which an actor responds to something that has just occurred.

Insert shot. A close-up shot that is edited into the larger context and provides an important detail of the scene. When an actor, for example, reads a sign on the door, a shot of the sign itself then is inserted into the edit.

Editing Pace and Rhythm

The genre of your program, and the footage you have shot, can both dictate the editing pace and rhythm. For example, an editor can start with longer cuts, then make more frequent cuts that surprise the viewer or build suspense. This rhythm can create excitement, romance, and even comedy.

Editing to Manipulate Time

Few shows on television, online, or on other platforms are viewed or seen in real time. What the viewer sees is known as *screen time*, a period of time in which events are happening on screen: an hour, a day, or a much longer time span. There are several devices that an editor can use to give the viewer an impression of compressed time or time that has passed or is passing.

Compressed time. The condensing of long periods of time is traditionally achieved by using long dissolves or fades, as well as cuts to close-ups, reaction shots, cutaways, montages, and parallel situations. Our experiences as a viewer can then fill in gaps of time.

Simultaneous time. Parallel editing, or cross-cutting, shifts the viewer's attention to two or more events that are happening at the same time. The editor can build split screens with several images on the screen at once, or can simply cut back and forth from one event to another. When the stories eventually converge, the passage of time stops. A show like *24* is an example.

Long take. This one uninterrupted shot lasts for a longer period of time than usual. There is no editing interruption, which gives the feeling of time passing more slowly.

Slow motion (slo-mo). A shot that is moving at a normal speed, and then slowed down. This can emphasize a dramatic moment, make an action easier to see at slower speed, or create an effect that is strange or eerie.

Fast motion. A shot that is taking place at a normal speed that the editor speeds up. This effect can add a layer of humor to familiar action, or can create the thrill of speed.

Reverse motion. By taking the action and running it backward, the editor creates a sense of comedy or magic. Reverse motion can also help to explain action in a scene or act as a flashback in time or action.

Instant replay. Most commonly used in sports or news, a specific play from the game or news event is repeated and replayed, usually in slo-mo.

Freeze-frame. The editor finds a specific frame from the video and holds on it or freezes it. This effect abruptly halts the action for specific narrative effects. A freeze frame can also create the look of a still photo.

Flashback. A break in the story in which the viewer is taken back in time. The flashback is usually indicated by a dissolve or when the camera intentionally loses focus.

Editing Transitions

A simple cut is a transition from one shot to the next—it's abrupt and quick. Some storylines require another kind of transition from one shot or scene to another that signals going from one idea to another, moving from one location to the next, or one action that changes to another. These transitions can be achieved in the editing by selectively using any of the following transition devices:

Dissolve. When one image begins to disappear gradually and another image appears and overlaps it. Dissolves can be quick (5 frames, or 1/6 of a second), or they can be slow and deliberate (20 to 60 frames). Both signal a change in mood or action.

Fade outs and fade ins. There are two kinds of fades. A fade out is when an image fades slowly out into a blank black frame signaling either a gradual transition or an ending. A fade in is when an image fades in from a black frame introducing a scene. A fade out or fade in can also be effective from a white blank frame rather than a black one; like a dissolve, this editing transition also works to show time passing or to create a special "look."

Wipe. An effect in which one shot essentially "wipes off" another shot. There are dozens of wipes available in editing systems, though a professional editor uses them sparingly. Examples are page and circle wipes, sliding an image from right to left or vice versa, and breaking an image into thousands of particles. A wipe can be effective, or it can be a distraction; overuse of wipes can be the mark of an amateur.

Split screen. The screen is divided into boxes or parts. Each has its own shot and action that connect the story. The boxes might also show different angles of the same image, or can contrast one action with another. It works as a kind of montage, telling a story more quickly. The split-screen device can be done cleverly, though too many moving images can also strain the viewer's attention span.

Overlays. Two or more images superimposed over one another, creating a variety of effects that can work as a transition from one idea to the next.

Graphics, Animation, and Plug-Ins

Most programs or content include graphic elements of some kind. These graphics can be a simple show title and closing credits, or they can be complicated animation sequences and special effects within the program itself. Graphics can be generated in the edit session with programs such as After Effects and Photoshop, or might be created by artistic designers in a graphics design facility. Graphics, however, can be expensive, and usually require extra consideration in your budget. Following are a few examples of graphics you might use in your project:

Text. Almost every show has opening titles (including the name of the show) and a limited list of the top creative people (such as the producer, writer, director, actors, etc.); these are called *opening credits*. Titles that appear at the end of the show are called *closing credits*, and they list the actors' names and roles, or positions on the production, as well as other detailed production information. Words that slide under someone on screen and spell out a name, location, or profession are called *lower thirds* because they're generally inserted in the lower-third portion of the screen.

The electronic text is known generically as chyron (pronounced *ky-ron*, originally the name of a company that for years was the only professional system that could output high-resolution graphics). Now, chyron can be generated by most editing software programs. The overall impression that the text conveys is determined by its size, color, font, and general style. The text can be digitally imported onto the picture with various speed, rhythms, and movement and from any angle—say, from one side of the screen to another. The graphics give the viewer an impression of the tone and pace of the show, and when combined with music, text can create a unique style for your piece.

Opening and closing credits might be superimposed over a scene from the show, or on top of stills, background animation, or simple black. Some projects require subtitles for foreign languages or close captioning for the hearing-impaired. As the producer, you're responsible for double-checking all names, spellings, and legal or contractual information for the lower-thirds and final end credits.

Animation. Simple animation can be created easily and cheaply by using software like Flash and After Effects. More complex animation is created by an animation designer who uses storyboards and narration, and manages an impressive crew of people who draw, color, and edit animated sequences.

Motion control camera. Special computer-controlled cameras that shoot a variety of flat art such as old newspapers, artwork, and photos, sometimes called title cameras. They are designed to pinpoint detail and to create a sense of motion for otherwise static material with zooms, pans, and other camera moves.

Design elements. Some project genres—documentaries, news shows, commercials, educational, and corporate industrials—depend on the use of various design elements to add depth and information to the content. These elements include logos, maps, diagrams, charts, and graphs, as well as historical photographs, still shots, and illustrations.

The look of film. Falling loosely into the graphics realm, there are several postproduction processes that give video the appearance of film by closely mirroring the color levels, contrasts, saturation, and grain patterns of film at a fraction of the cost and time of film.

Color-correction. The process of reducing or boosting color, contrast, or brightness levels can be done by using color-correcting tools such as Flame or After Effects.

Retouching. This plug-in process offers a gamut of tricks that can enhance an image, like "erasing" a boom dangling into the shot, or a wire holding up a prop. However, the time involved can be costly.

Compositing. Two or more images are combined, layered, or superimposed in the composite plug-in process.

Rotoscoping. Frame-by-frame manipulation of an image, either adding or removing a graphic component. Human action can be rotoscoped as can the blemish erased from a celebrity's face with this plug-in process.

The editing process is vital to the ultimate success of your project. It is aesthetic, intuitive, and often technically challenging. Yet the visuals are only one half of the picture. The second half is the enhancement of audio with its many layers of nuance and possibilities.

> But the most important thing is that you really have to have a feel for the music and the artist, and what's going on, and creatively pull all this stuff together. The creative part is really why I'm hired and what you need from the head person pulling this all together, though as a producer, you also have to be aware of all this technical stuff.
>
> **Stephen Reed, excerpt from interview in Chapter 11**

III. THE SOUND DESIGNER'S ROLE

> Tones sound, and roar and storm about me until I have set them down in notes.
>
> **Ludwig van Beethoven**

The sound designer, like the editor, can perform small miracles by manipulating audio to create an emotional impact on the viewer. The sound designer adds another dimension to your vision by raising or lowering levels of dialogue or ambient sounds, removing distracting background hums, adding sound effects and Foley and adding the right musical elements. His expertise lends a higher production quality to your finished project.

In a less complex project, the video editor can mix all the audio requirements and components in the edit session. However, some projects have more complicated audio elements that require an audio facility for additional work and refining. Here, the *audio mixer*, sometimes called the *sound editor* or *sound designer*, takes over. An audio facility might be a simple, room-sized studio with one or two sound editors who work on audio equipment that synchronizes TC and computers and, depending on the facility, can charge $50 to $200 an hour. It could also be an elaborate, theater-sized studio with several audio mixers and assistants, extensive equipment, and a setup that could be quite costly. Before you book time in an audio facility, discuss your project's audio needs and their possible costs.

The sound designer works with two contrasting "qualities" of sound (direct and studio), and approaches them differently, both aesthetically and technically:

- ■ ***Direct sound.*** Live sound. This is recorded on location, and sounds real, spontaneous, and authentic, though it may not be acoustically ideal.
- ■ ***Studio sound.*** Sound recorded in the studio. This method improves the sound quality, and eliminates unwanted background noise, and can then be mixed with live sound.

Working with the Sound Designer

> There are no passengers on spaceship earth. We are all crew.
>
> **Marshall McLuhan**

As the producer, you want to work closely with the sound designer: supply the necessary audio elements and logs, then discuss the final cut of your piece; offer your ideas and ask for suggestions. In the first stages of an audio mix session, you and the audio crew sit in a *spotting* session during which you review each area of your project that needs music and effects for dramatic or comedic tension. In this session you're listening for variations in sound levels, for hums and hisses, and anything else that wasn't caught in the rough mix. The sound designer can mix tracks, smooth out dialogue, equalize levels and intensity of sound, and add and layer other elements like music and effects that all contribute depth to the project.

The spotting process takes time. So does the mixing, or *sweetening*. You're paying for each minute, so based on what you decided to do in the spotting session, discuss with the audio facility how much time you will need to book. Often, an audio facility is willing to negotiate a flat fee for the whole job. You may have booked only six hours but the actual mix ran 10, or vice versa; it not only cost you more money but it placed a real strain on the facility—they may have booked the studio for another job after your estimated six hours was scheduled to end.

Working with the sound editor is much more effective if you can:

1. *Be prepared.* When possible, send a rough cut of the project to the sound editor before the mix session. Come to the mix with a show run-down that lists important audio-related details like transitions and music. Provide a music cue sheet that lists all the music selection titles, the composers and their performing rights society affiliation, the recording artists, the length and timing of each cue, the name and address of the copyright owner(s) for each sound recording and musical composition, and the name and address of the publisher and company controlling the recording. You'll find an example of this music cue sheet on this book's web site.

2. *Be patient.* At the beginning of the mix, the sound editor needs to do several things before the actual mix can begin, including separating the audio elements, patching them into the console, adjusting the gear, and finally, carefully listening to everything. Be patient during this stage and don't put pressure on the process.

3. *Be quiet.* Although you may have worked with these audio tracks for days in the editing room, it is the first time the sound editor has heard them. Keep your conversations, phone calls, and interruptions to a minimum.

4. *Be realistic.* Your mix may sound excellent in the audio mixing room because the speakers are professional quality, balanced, and the acoustics are ideal. But most TV shows and online projects are played on TV sets or computer monitors with mediocre speakers. Many of the subtler sound effects you could spend hours mixing may never be heard, so listen to the mix on small speakers that simulate the sound that the end user will hear.

The Technology of Audio Mixing

The digital revolution has provided a wealth of creative and technical opportunities for the producer. Images and sound can interact in dynamic new ways that were previously difficult to achieve if not impossible. Digital sound offers an unparalleled clarity of sound. There is no loss of quality when dubbed, and because digital requires less storage space than video, it doesn't need compression.

By editing sound in the NLE domain, the audio mixer can work freely with sound in the same way an editor can play with visuals: sound elements can be cut, copied, pasted, looped, or altered. Digital audio is easily labeled and stored, making it more efficient to keep audio in sync and to slide it around when needed. Most sound tracks are now prepared on a multitrack digital storage system. The popular professional options include:

- DAW (digital audio workstation): Programs such as Pro Tools
- Digital multitracks: Programs include DASH 3324 or 3348
- Analog multitracks: 24-track Dolby SR or A

Often the editor can handle the entire audio mix in the NLE system. In other situations where the mix is more complex, the picture is first *locked*, or finalized, and then the audio tracks are exported, usually to a DAW. The tracks are either married to the video or are separate. In the DAW, for example, the sound designer uses software such as Pro Tools and digital storage techniques to focus on specific tracks; clean up audio problems; and record and add narration, music and special effects (*M&E*), and dialogue.

This process gives the sound editor an impressive range of options: moving the tracks forward and backward, looping music, and extending dialogue and effects. Finally, when everyone's satisfied with the audio, the track is ready for a *lay-back* where the final audio mix track is married to the picture using TC. The piece can be delivered in stereo, mono, 5.1, or in all versions.

In high-definition or DVD projects, the audio can work well for a 5.1 audio system sound mix. This gives you five full channels (left, center, right, right rear, and left rear) plus one low frequency effects channel. The result is an impressive clarity and fullness of sound that 5.1 audio lends to a final product.

The Creative Components in Sound Design

Just as visual components are edited together, so audio elements are mixed together to create new layers of sound. In larger, more complicated audio mixes, each of the following components might be supervised by an expert who specializes in that specific area. The sound designer works with any or all of these components:

- Dialogue
- Sound effects (SFX)
- Automatic dialogue replacement (ADR)
- Voice-over (VO) or narration
- Foley
- Music

Dialogue

Dialogue is the primary audio element. Words spoken between two (or more) actors or people onscreen is called dialogue. Sometimes it's recorded with background ambient sound, although usually it is recorded in isolation from other audio.

Sound Effects

On a set or on location, any background sounds that surround the dialogue are ideally recorded separately. These sounds include blowing wind, singing birds, insects or tree frogs, water lapping on shore, traffic, children playing, glasses clinking, and so on. These existing effects are known as *wild sounds*, or recorded sounds that will later be synchronized to the footage. If the sounds don't exist on that location, the sound editor can search through prerecorded sound effects available from a sound effects library. These options can range from a door slam to the howl of a monkey. Producers often buy libraries of sound effects and stock music that offer thousands of audio options and their royalty fees covered in the initial cost.

Automatic Dialogue Replacement (ADR) or Dubbed Dialogue

After all their scenes have been shot, actors may need to rerecord lines of dialogue, or add a line written after the shoot was over. In the recording studio, actors read their lines, keeping them in sync with their on-screen lip movements. Another option is to record new lines that will be mixed into the program later, either over a cutaway or in a long shot if their lips don't match the new lines. Actors might also read a script in a different language that is later dubbed over the original track. Often, a *loop group* of people is brought into an ADR session to create crowd sounds like background conversations, laughter, mumblings, or yelling that will be mixed into the dialogue. This area of ADR is called *wallah*, which is intentionally unintelligible so audible words won't intrude on the dialogue.

Voice-Over (Narration)

The narrator who reads a script or commentary adds another layer to the audio. Narration can introduce a theme or link elements of a story together. It adds extra information with an air of authority, and helps interpret ideas or images for the viewer. Often, an on-camera character speaks over the picture in the first person as though she is directly speaking to the viewer. A minor character can tell the story in the third person, or an unidentified narrator who is not on camera can distance the viewer from the image by adding an objective voice to the story. Narration is generally recorded in a separate audio session and mixed in later over the picture. Voice-over can be dialogue that is shot originally on-camera and later played over another picture. For instance, we see a two-shot of a mother who is reading aloud to her child. That shot cuts to a CU of the child's face while the mother's audio continues over the picture. Her audio is the voice-over; on a script, it is written as VO.

Foley

Foley are the sounds of an actor's movements, hands clapping, rustling clothing, a kiss, quiet footsteps, or a fistfight. If these sounds can't be found in a sound effects library, they can be created by the Foley artist who uses audio props, tools, hands and feet—objects and devices that create the right sound effect. They're recorded separately in an audio facility, often in sync with the action, and then mixed with other sound elements.

Music Options

- *Original.* This is music that's been composed specifically for a project. It may include themes for the opening and closing, and/or for the body of the show; its emotional direction can highlight the action, characters, and their relationships. The composer is familiar with the creative and technical process, and either hires the musicians or creates the music alone or with a partner. A composer can use computer language known as musical instrument digital interface (MIDI). It is capable of simulating a range of music from a single guitar to an entire orchestra. The final score can go straight from the computer into the mix.
- *Stock.* This is music that has been specifically composed and recorded to be available for multiple uses. The composers use audio sampling and composition software and sophisticated equipment to create vast libraries of engaging and effective music that is both versatile and inexpensive. Stock music is a creative alternative used in every genre from corporate videos, documentaries, news, and commercials, to talk shows, sitcoms, online and UGC, even drama. It's less expensive than hiring a composer, and the negotiated rights can be either exclusive or shared, depending on your budget and the end use. Stock music houses can be researched and located by an online search, and most offer samplings that can be downloaded from the Internet.
- *Prerecorded.* The source of this music could range from a popular song to an obscure CD, but a strong soundtrack adds an extra appeal to your project. Regardless of the source, you'll first need to clear all music rights, a time-consuming process that is reviewed in Chapter 5.

- **Music cue sheet.** Regardless of where your music comes from, you'll make a *music cue sheet* that lists every piece of music, its source, its length, and who holds the rights. An example of a cue sheet is on this book's web site.

Stylistic Uses of Sound

In addition to creating a clear audio track for your project, manipulation of sound can create stylistic impressions for the viewer. Here are a few classic examples.

- **Diegetic.** Music that the characters in the scene hear. They're playing a guitar, or in a club with a jazz band playing behind the action.
- **Non-diegetic.** Music not heard by the characters that is added later, such as a soundtrack.
- **Sound bridge.** Audio elements, dialogue, sound effects, music and narration can act as a transition between one shot (or scene) to the next.
- **Selective sound.** Lowering some sounds in a scene, and raising others, can focus the viewer on an aspect of the story, such as heavy breathing or quiet footsteps.
- **Overlapping dialogue.** In natural speech patterns, people tend to speak over one another and interrupt. Yet dialogue is usually recorded on separate tracks without this overlap. The sound editor can recreate this authentic-sounding effect in the mix, and can also separate dialogue tracks that are too close together. Conversations between several people, like those in two different groups, are often recorded on separate tracks so they can be woven together in the mix for a natural sound.

The Steps in Mixing Audio

Steps in audio mixing vary from project to project. During your video edit session, the editor separates the dialogue, music, effects, and other audio elements onto various tracks or channels. Depending on the complexity of your project, the editor can mix the elements in the edit room, or will do a preliminary mix that needs to be completed in an audio facility. During the mix, all the separate audio elements are blended together into a final mix track that is then "married" to the picture and locked in.

The Final Cut and Locked-in Audio

Before the final audio mix begins, make sure that all the video and audio edits have been agreed upon by the clients and other creative team members, and won't require any further changes. Any revisions involving audio after the picture is locked can mean costly remixes.

Sound editors take varying routes in mixing, and each has a unique style of approaching the process. Depending on the complexity of the project, any or all of the following components are part of an audio mix.

- **Dialogue.** All dialogue is cleaned up and extra sound effects or extraneous noise are either deleted or moved to separate effects tracks. Any ADR, narration, or voice-overs are also laid onto their own tracks.
- **Special effects.** Any special effects tracks—wild sound, ambience, prerecorded effects, and Foley—are separated, cleaned up, and each put onto its own channel. Ideally, there is ample room tone from each location that can fill in any gaps in the audio.
- **Music tracks.** The music is generally the last element that is mixed into the audio. All the musical tracks are separated and divided into two categories: *diegetic* or *source music* (music the characters or actors hear on screen, like a car radio) or *underscore music* (music that only the audience hears, such as an opening theme).

- **5.1 Audio.** 5.1 refers to the positions in a five-speaker setup in which speakers are placed to the right, center, left, right rear, and left rear of the TV set. This kind of mixing is also called AC3 and Dolby Digital, and is prominent in DVDs, theatrically released films using SDDS and DTS systems, and in some TV broadcasts. 5.1 audio requires a specially equipped television set to hear it at home.
- To achieve a full 5.1 sound mix, the audio is synchronized and laid off onto the field tapes that have been downconverted to 29.97, taken into editing, and then transferred as open media format (OMF) files into the audio mix. Here, the elements are synced up, mixed, and sweetened to a downconvert of the assembled HD master that can be used for HD distribution or converted to standard definition. However, because each of the five channels delivers sound to a specific spatial position, extra time is needed in the audio sessions to deliver a multi-channel mix that works in this medium.

IV. DELIVERING THE FINAL PRODUCT

As the producer, you want to deliver a project that's the highest possible quality. It may be broadcast on a network, sold to a distributor, seen online, or used for training and education purposes. All these venues require broadcast-quality work that adheres to certain technical standards, which make it possible to dub, copy, and transfer to DVD or other formats without losing quality.

The Client Deliverables

Most clients are very specific about what they expect as a *deliverable* or final product. Deliverables are generally part of your overall contract with a client, so you want to find out exactly what their expectations and specifications are. Ask for these deliverables in writing so there are no mistakes. The most common requirements for deliverables include:

- **Video format.** If your project is being broadcast, it is usually evaluated by a station engineer to make sure it meets broadcast standards. If it's being dubbed, the dub house has technical specifications, too. You may be asked to provide a clean copy of the show that has no text superimposed on it.
- **Audio format.** This might include separate mono mixes and stereo mixes, or a 5.1 mix, an M&E mix, special tracking, levels that are constant or undipped, and often one mix in English and another in a different language.
- **Length.** The required program length can be quite specific. For example, some American public television stations set a standard half-hour length at 26:46 minutes, and a one-hour show at 56:46 minutes. In most cases, PBS show lengths are 6 seconds less to accommodate a PBS logo. Commercial stations may require a half-hour show to be 22 minutes, while premium and cable channels are less demanding. Most nonbroadcast projects are more flexible.
- **Dubbing.** Depending on the client's requirements, you may be responsible for making protection copies, which are exact copies of your final master. These serve as backups in case of damages or loss in shipping. You might also need to provide DVD copies of the project to the client. The amount of copies and their format should be spelled out in your contract, as should any special labeling or packaging and related shipping costs.
- **Abridged versions.** You may need to provide an edited version of your project in which any nudity, violence, or offensive language has been removed or "bleeped out." This version can be required by airlines, certain broadcasters, and foreign distributors.

- *Subtitling.* Written text under a picture that translates only those words being spoken on screen from one language into another; for example, the French translation of an American production. However, song lyrics or sounds are seldom subtitled.
- *Closed captioning.* Also called close captions, this method of supplying visible text under a broadcast picture is mandated by law to be built into all American TV sets sold after 1993. These sets are designed with a special decoding chip that translates all the audio on the screen into text, such as spoken dialogue, and describes unseen sounds like a dog bark or a knock at the door. Especially designed for the hearing impaired, closed captioning is also useful in loud public places, when learning a language, and when the dialogue isn't clear. The text usually appears in white letters in a black box at the bottom or top of the screen. It is decoded in the TV set or with a special decoder box attached to the set.

All these deliverables are those most commonly required in television and new media projects. They should be clearly stated in all contract negotiations and included in your postproduction budget.

> Be in control, but allow for creativity and open up your budget for that extra time. As a producer, your golden rule is to always be prepared. You are in a creative business, so sometimes even the best preparation is not enough. At that point, look to the future and learn from your mistakes.
> **Jeffrey McLaughlin, excerpt from interview in Chapter 11**

ON A HUMAN LEVEL . . .

Finishing the postproduction process is a kind of triumph in its own right. It signals your project's completion, and it's the result of the teamwork and collaboration of everyone involved. Allow yourself time to celebrate that teamwork. And resign yourself to the fact that every single time you watch it, you'll see something you'd like to change, or wish you'd done differently. Congratulations—you're a producer.

SUMMARY

At this stage, you may have a tangible product you can see on the screen. You have delivered all the final dubs to the client, and said goodbye to the editor and audio mixer. But your project itself isn't really finished. As you'll see in Chapter 10, there are more details to wrap up, as well as guidelines for getting exposure for your project and, for yourself.

REVIEW QUESTIONS

1. What is the producer's role in postproduction? How is it different from that of the postproduction supervisor?

2. Name four important legal documents that are essential to check prior to the postproduction process.

3. Why is time code so important in the editing and mixing of a project?

4. Describe the uses and the differences between stock footage, archival footage, and footage that is public domain.

5. What can you do as a producer to prepare for the edit session? For the audio mix?

6. What would you look for in hiring an editor? How could you find one in your area?

7. Compare an NLE system with linear film editing.

8. What audio elements are needed in mixing most projects?

9. Briefly describe the audio mixing process.

10. Name three deliverables that are required in most contracts.

It's a Wrap! Now, the Next Steps

Life shrinks or expands in proportion to one's courage.

Anaïs Nin

THIS CHAPTER'S TALKING POINTS

I. It's a Wrap!

II. Professional Next Steps

III. Festivals

IV. Grants

V. Publicity

VI. Starting Your Own Production Company

I. IT'S A WRAP!

After you've completed all the stages of postproduction, your next step is to *wrap* the project and tie up all the loose ends. There are dozens of details to clear up. Some can be fun, many are tedious, but they all add up to a list of finalized elements that help your project succeed as well as mark you as a producer who gets things done. These steps can include any or all of the following:

- *The wrap party.* Your entire team has dedicated considerable time and energy to your project. You can say thank you by throwing them a great wrap party. Usually it's informal, and only the cast and crew are invited. It can be held at a restaurant, a bar, or on set; you can have it elegantly catered, or just serve beer and pizza. It's money well spent when you can show your team how valuable they are to you.
- *Final budget and billings.* When all the final bills have come in, you want to review each one for accuracy. Clients can make mistakes, and when they do, it's usually in their favor. Check your bills against your purchase orders. Compare your original estimated budget with what you actually have spent on the project. As discussed in Chapter 4, the estimates can be different from the actuals.

- *Petty cash and receipts.* This area often is underestimated, throwing your budget off target. If, for example, you've doled out $1,000 of petty cash, you want to have $1,000 worth of matching receipts.
- *Complimentary copies.* A surprising number of professionals seldom see their finished work or their name in the credits. It shows your respect when you send copies of the final product to the cast and crew. If dubs are a drain on your budget, make sure that at least the key department heads and primary talent each receives a personal copy.
- *A screening party.* Unlike a wrap party, this event is more formal and carefully planned, essentially a premiere of your project for the press, clients, top talent, and potential investors, buyers, or distributors. Generally, you rent a screening room or theater and distribute a press kit (see Section II) to attendees. The project may be introduced by you or another project representative and then screened. Usually wine and cheese is served before or after. A screening party can be a great opportunity to mingle with the press and potential buyers.
- *Thank-you notes.* Other than cold cash, nothing goes farther than a personal thank you. Send notes or emails to the cast and crew, and the client or investors, as well as editing and audio facilities, locations, and others who helped you in the project.
- *Dubs.* In addition to making complimentary copies, make additional DVD dubs made of your project to send to clients, or to potential buyers, distributors, or investors. Dubs can be expensive because they require copying, labeling, packing, and shipping. Your editing facility can make dubs for you, or you can burn DVD copies in your computer. Keep a log of who has been sent a dub and the date it was shipped so that you can follow up later.
- *Tape or data storage.* After the project has wrapped, all the elements need to be stored. Your original footage and masters, the graphics, music elements, dubs, and other material is organized and delivered to a storage area that is safe and dry. Your editing facility may have library space to rent, or check into local storage warehouses.
- *Update your production book.* The binder in which you've kept all your notes is a valuable tool for future projects. As you are wrapping the project, go through your production book (refer back to Chapter 4) and update any notes, contact information, contracts, and budgets while they are fresh in your mind.

II. PROFESSIONAL NEXT STEPS

Seasoned and experienced producers are no different than a motivated first-timer—they'll take advantage of a few simple tricks of the trade to build and expand their careers. They also realize that no matter what project they are working on now, they'll soon be looking for their next job. As a producer of any kind of TV or new media project, you want people to know about you and the quality of your work. Following are just a few directions you can take to reach these objectives.

Create a Resume

There are dozens of resume formats and templates that you can use for your own resume. Whatever style you choose, your resume ultimately reflects you both professionally and personally. In the television and new media industries, "real-world" experiences are a plus, so include any internships, jobs, and production work you've done, no matter how insignificant they seem to you. Mention skills such as fluency in a foreign language, your talents in computer graphics, skateboarding, or working in a summer camp—these are aspects of your uniqueness that make you stand out and can be valuable to a potential employer.

You want your resume to look professional. Use a simple 10- or 12-point font, allow for white space so the information isn't crowded, print it with a good printer, and use quality, noncolored 8½ × 11 paper. Be brief and use action verbs for impact. Limit any personal information, don't include your salary history or requirements, and mention that you have references available if needed. Most software word processing programs feature templates for resumes, and the Internet has hundreds of sites that offer examples and constructive advice.

Build a Demo Reel

The purpose of a demo reel is to reflect your professional abilities, your creativity, and your technical know-how. Each producer's demo reel is unique, because it reflects his or her specific vision and talent. The demo reel contains short clips and excerpts of one's best work. They can be edited to a music track with quick cuts, or are clips strung together with special effects and wipes. Because most people won't view more than three or four minutes, put your best work at the beginning and at the end. Be objective about your choices. A demo reel should open and close with graphics that include your name and contact information. It can be on DVD or on your web site.

Make a Short

Your long-range goal may be to produce a dramatic series or a two-hour documentary special, but in the meantime, start by producing a short. Usually five to 30 minutes long, a short is easier than a full-length project to conceptualize and produce, to raise funds for, and to enlist people's help for production and postproduction. A good short is an excellent calling card that can be put onto YouTube and your web site, entered in festivals, shown to potential clients, or broadcast on channels that showcase shorts in their programming. Some of the cable and premium channels often air short pieces called *interstitials* in between their regularly scheduled programs to fill the time gaps. Other channels specialize in shorts.

Top Ten Helpful Hints for Creating a Short Film in Both Narrative and Unscripted Formats

1. Avoid the overuse of voice-over narration to carry your vision. Think about narration as a means to introduce your story, or express salient points, but do not allow the focus of your project to be the voice-over.
2. The first few minutes of your project are integral in creating the tone. Think about your opening very carefully, and stay away from traditional and oversaturated openings, such as "alarm-goes-off-character-wakes-up" or "pan-across-a-mantle-of-photographs," for example.
3. Consider the running time of your project while it is still in the concept stage and have a clear idea of content vs. running time. The longer your project, the stronger your story should be. Remember, it's all about the story, regardless of whether it is narrative or documentary.

(Continued)

Top Ten Helpful Hints for Creating a Short Film in Both Narrative and Unscripted Formats—Cont'd

4. Particularly with documentary projects, think about your story progression. You still should have an idea where the film is "going." Twenty minutes of talking heads interspersed with archive footage does not a documentary make. What is your viewer going to learn/experience by the end of the film and how do we get there?
5. Montage sequences serve a very specific purpose to move the story ahead in an expedient manner. Regurgitating previously viewed shots simply for the sake of putting them to music is not in your best interest, and detracts from the overall impact of the film.
6. Speaking of music, the use of songs should not undermine the visuals, but enhance them. Too many filmmakers who grew up as part of the MTV generation cavalierly use song lyrics to express their vision. This is not a music video.
7. Your main credit sequence should not imitate a feature film. A 10-minute short with a two-minute main credit sequence is unnecessary. Give "credit where credit is due" in the end credits! If you produce a lavish opening credit sequence, make sure it matches the style of the film, and does not jar the viewer when it goes from credits to first shot.
8. The one-character documentary has its own set of challenges. A producer may think someone's life is unique by the hurdles he or she has overcome or something in his or her life that warrants capturing the experience, but others should as well. Before you produce a film about a friend or relative, keep your audience (and objectivity) in mind. Is this person interesting enough on-camera to sustain a viewer's attention for 10, 20, or 30 minutes?
9. One of the most exhilarating aspects of short-form filmmaking is that "there are no rules." Don't feel confined by the structure imposed by features. Programmers are looking for creativity, new voices, and a captivating story supported by visual imagery.
10. Finally, be aware that you're not going to get rich from a short film. Your goal should be to produce a project that accurately reflects your talent and the ability to create and complete a vision. A common and accurate descriptive is that a short film is your "calling card."

Sharon Badal, excerpt from interview in Chapter 11

Network and Make Contacts

Agents and managers can certainly be helpful, especially if you're already successful. But, if you're still on your way up the ladder, most producers find work opportunities from the people they know—colleagues, fellow producers, members of professional organizations. You want to meet people at the top of the ladder, or who are on their way up. You can find them in TV and new media industry organizations, on web sites, blogs, in classes, internships, and at festivals.

If there are no festivals in your area, start one: create a festival theme and focus, find a local movie theater or screening facility, get a couple of like-minded people to help you, study models of successful festivals, and throw a fundraising event to get you started. Or, start one online.

Find a Mentor

A mentor or advisor is a valuable asset for a beginning producer, someone who has worked hard to achieve success, and understands the importance of giving back to people who are on their way up. Mentors can be found in the workplace, in television, new media, and film-oriented organizations, and in the classroom.

You may also know *about* a person whose work impresses you and who models success in ways you admire. Take a chance, request a meeting. Because you've already carefully thought about how she can be of benefit to you, you can explain your position and how you would like to be mentored. Do you want to work alongside her? Can she give you valuable advice, internships, or contacts? Be respectful of her time and keep the meetings brief. If she agrees to work further with you, always let her call the shots about scheduling time, place, and duration of your meetings.

Take on Internships

A good internship can give you invaluable learning experience, and great contacts. Most producers in television started their careers as an intern or production assistant. Whether you're doing an internship for school credit or simply for the experience, keep in mind that an intern who regularly shows up on set or in the production offices becomes a steady, dependable presence. Producers and directors start to depend on the intern, and over time, they give him more work and more responsibility. Often a valued intern is offered employment after a few months or when an entry-level job opens up. At the end of the internship, he can ask for a letter of recommendation or a referral to another internship.

As an intern, you're an asset to the project. You're giving them your energy, education, and unique skills. If you've done other internships, you're also sharing your experiences. You want to be punctual, keep your word, and anticipate what needs to be done before you're told. Your behavior in the workplace is appropriate, and you're respectful of everyone in the workplace. You may only be photocopying dozens of full-length scripts, but do it with a smile. In return for your time, you're exposed to professionals who model both positive and negative learning experiences, as well as having on-set duties or sitting in on meetings.

And, unlike a full-time job, you can leave an internship guilt-free if it isn't a good match. In some cases, the internships aren't well organized, and you can feel as though your time isn't being fully utilized. Ask for more work. Look for areas in which you can be helpful; often, taking that initiative is really appreciated.

> Internships fill the void between the dream of the industry and the reality of it. They are a safe space between the educational environment and the professional one. They give an important educational experience, one that represents a transitional reality not available in school, one that you can sample, and one that you can easily retreat from at the end of the semester. A trial run if you will, without penalty. More important, internships can allow you to learn what you really *don't* want to do.
>
> **Sheril Antonio, excerpt from interview in Chapter 11**

Get Experience

You may not want to commit to a formal internship, but you do want real-world experience. Most cities and towns have local production companies and TV stations where you can volunteer your services in exchange for a chance to be part of the action and learn in the process. Often colleges and universities with TV, new media, and film departments have bulletin boards on which students can post notices about their upcoming projects that you might be able to work on for more experience. You can also post your own notice, offering your services. Meanwhile, buy or rent a prosumer camera and make your own projects.

Take a Course

Depending on your location, you can find courses, seminars, or programs that can expand your knowledge in the area of producing. You may not be interested in directing or editing, for example, but the more you know about how these jobs are performed, the better producer you can be. The course instructor may be actively involved in the profession that she is teaching, and can hook you up with internships, jobs, and/or networking opportunities. Your classmates, too, could be valuable members of your future production team. Look into classes in universities with continuing professional studies for producing, business writing, public speaking, marketing and sales, computer science, graphic design, editing, and even foreign languages. Each of these areas improves your overall skills set, and increases your marketability as a producer.

Stay Current

By subscribing to online news letters and publications that report on both new media and television, you can familiarize yourself with the latest trends, as well as with financial, legal, technological, and creative directions. Although the sheer amount of information and names can be overwhelming at first, you'll eventually connect the dots. This book's web site features more information in the Publications and Trade Journals and Web Site sections.

Get a Job

Producers often started off as interns, production assistants, personal assistants, or secretaries. Other producers came from careers as lawyers, writers, accountants, and even actors. If you're starting out in the business, look for an entry-level job in a network, production company, online start-up, entertainment law firm, or other areas of the media industry that can help you build up your producing skills and contacts.

If you've got strong office skills, you can often find temporary jobs in entertainment and communications companies. In larger cities, temp agencies specialize in providing staff for short-term jobs such as receptionist, secretary, assistant, and so on. If you like the people at the company and they like you, they'll keep you in mind when a job opens up. If it isn't promising, you can simply go back to the temp agency and ask for a different job.

Ten Ways to Be a Great PA and Keep Moving Up

1. Be prepared to work for little if any money at first. You'll make it eventually.
2. Be willing to work long, long hours.
3. Always keep a smile on your face, as hard as it may be.
4. Work hard! Go above and beyond your duties.
5. Know everyone's name and their position on the production.
6. Never complain. No task is too small, even if it is.
7. Remember that everyone has been where you are, even if they act like they haven't.
8. Ask questions and show a genuine interest in the business. Most people like to talk about what they do for a living.
9. Listen carefully, and know that observing is a learning experience.
10. When you have a choice, work for the right people. Your gut instinct usually lets you know if they're a good fit or not.

Becky Teitel & Jonna McLaughlin, *former PAs*

III. FESTIVALS

Maybe your Big Picture goal is to produce a prime time series for a major network. Or, you've got your eye on an online series, or a 15-minute short. These are perfectly reasonable goals, and ones you could well achieve one day.

But in the meantime, the best way to refine and expand your producing skills is by producing—raise funds, produce small-but-meaningful projects, and make sure that people see your work. You also want to promote yourself as an effective producer who can tackle other people's projects, too. Understanding the festival circuit, researching grant sources, and knowing more about publicity can help you take these steps with more confidence.

The number of television and new media festivals, both domestically and internationally, has tripled in the last few years. There are currently about 6,000 festivals worldwide. Festivals are a valuable venue in which to screen your project and get visceral reactions from a real audience. At festivals you'll meet other producers and filmmakers, network with potential clients, and maybe sell your project to a broadcaster or distributor who has seen it during a screening. In addition to the following information, refer to the Internet for information on Television and Film Festivals.

Package Your Project: Press Kits

> There's not much you can do about what other people are creating, but there's almost always something you can do about what *you* are doing.
>
> **Michael Bonfiglio, excerpt from interview in Chapter 11**

Press kits may vary in content and graphic approach, and a good press kit reflects the unique tone of your project. You can inquire at specific festivals or go online for additional information, but essentially, a compelling press kit is a primary piece of the festival circuit and includes these elements:

- A project with a good title (short, sweet and/or memorable—easy to market)
- A story synopsis that's compelling, brief, and hooks the reader
- Copies of any positive newspaper, online, or magazine reviews or articles
- Bios on key personnel and the cast and crew
- If pertinent, background on the genesis of your project
- Relevant production notes
- Still photographs that are high-quality representations of the project's images
- Graphics and artwork, such as posters and handouts
- A DVD of selected scenes, promos, and/or trailer
- Contact information including your name (or your representative), address, phone, fax, and email
- A screener of the project itself that might be sent only to specific people

Submissions to Festivals

In the United States, a one-hour slot on commercial television is actually just 42 to 48 minutes of programming; internationally, the TV hour varies, and may be 50 to 60 minutes long. Because representatives from networks, cable channels, and distribution companies come to festivals to shop for programming, your project has a better chance of appealing to them if it fits comfortably within their programming framework; keep these parameters in mind when you submit material to festivals. Most festivals are also quite clear about programming lengths—the short film category tends to run no longer than 40 minutes, for example.

As the producer, you want to research which festivals are best suited for your specific project. There are literally thousands of festivals around the world, and most are "branded"— they focus on specific genres like narrative features, documentaries, gay and lesbian, human rights, African-American, Jewish, animated, music-oriented, and experimental.

Although most festivals feature programming that could be bought for television broadcast, there are specific festivals, like Banff, RealScreen Summit, and Independent Film Week that are geared to the television market. They tend to attract professionals and generally don't have audience participation. Research the range of festivals, then target those that feel right for your specific project and its genre. Enter at least 10 festivals, more if you can afford the submission fees and the time. Start with the top-tier festivals, then work your way down to the lesser known festivals. Keep a careful log of where you've sent your piece.

There are web sites such as www.withoutabox.com that provide excellent information about television festivals. These sites are navigated easily and are inexpensive to join. Details about these festivals can be accessed online, and many accept online submissions. Regardless of the festivals you enter, your log line, compelling synopsis, good reviews, and the information in the festival's catalogue page can help jurors consider your project for their festival.

For every project that is submitted to a festival, there is at least one festival juror who screens it and makes the decision to either reject your project or recommends it for further consideration. Jurors screen each and every festival submission, usually on DVD; few watch each one from start to finish. If they're not engaged within the first four or five minutes, they will either fast-forward through it or hit the eject button.

Acceptance to a Festival

Even if your dream is to be accepted in a major festival, be careful what you wish for. After the initial thrill fades away, the work starts. You want to consider some of the following areas.

Publicists

If your project has been accepted by a major festival such as Cannes, Berlin, Sundance, Tribeca, or Toronto, it's going to generate a significant buzz. You're wise to hire an experienced publicist who can help you navigate the media frenzy that comes with the territory, and can keep the buzz going.

Publicists charge a fee for their work. You also pay for various publicity materials and expenses. If you can't afford a publicist, you can contact the press office of the festival that has accepted your piece and talk to their publicists about promotional ideas. And, as you'll see in Section V, you have quite a few options for creating your own publicity campaign.

A Producer's Representative

Festivals attract buyers and distributors; they attend lots of screenings, chosen primarily on advanced word of mouth. A producer's "rep" is experienced in convincing these potential buyers to screen your project. He designs a strategy for the initial introduction of a program into the marketplace, creates a buzz, and knows how to talk directly to buyers in their own language. Generally, the producer's rep works on a percentage basis, which you want to discuss at the beginning of any negotiations.

Festival Premieres

The competition is fierce in the festival world, and most require that your project be deemed a "premiere," or first-time festival screening. This term can be somewhat ambiguous, however. A premiere in Boston can be considered to be the Massachusetts premiere by one festival, or as the American premiere in another. Carefully read each festival's guidelines. Many festivals won't accept your piece if it has been screened or broadcast somewhere else first. Others don't care.

Attending the Festival

Not many festivals can afford to pay finalists' expenses to come to the festival, so covering most of the costs is up to the producer. But it could be worth the money to experience sitting in the midst of a real audience and watching their reactions to your project. Your festival acceptance speaks to your skills as a producer for future projects; if you're in the lobby after the screening, the audience and interested buyers can meet you while their reactions to your work is still fresh.

Networking in the Festival Circuit

Festivals are a fertile ground for networking. You'll meet other producers, filmmakers, writers, directors, attorneys, agents, any of whom are potential collaborators in future projects. Fellow producers can be your allies and can spread valuable word-of-mouth about your work, so attend their screenings and get to know them. Go to panels, attend the social mixers and events, and introduce yourself. Be sure to bring plenty of your business cards or hand outs, and generously pass them out.

At a festival you can use creative tricks to grab people's attention. For example, you can hand out promotional mini-posters, about the size of a post card, with the name of your piece and the location, date, and time of the screening. Other attention-getters include a DVD of your project or behind-the-scenes extras not included as well as classic items like mugs, T-shirts, key chains, notepads, pens, hats, or other useful or fun items that advertise your project. You can throw a party with a theme, or host a unique event. Ask other producers how they have generated interest for their films or video projects.

If your project features a well-known actor, writer, and/or director, consider bringing them to the festival. Their presence on panels or at a question and answer (Q&A) session after the screening can add extra credibility and weight to your work. If your project is nonnarrative, bring the subjects of the piece for the Q&A.

Making a Deal

You might find yourself chatting with a buyer or broadcaster at a festival event, and they'll ask if you have other finished projects or story ideas to pitch, in addition to the project being screened at the festival. Be mentally prepared to pitch new ideas whenever an opportunity arises.

Deals for distribution or foreign sales are occasionally negotiated and secured on the spot in the festival lobby, but not always. Unless your project has triumphed at Toronto, Sundance, or another high-profile festival, potential buyers may hold back and won't make immediate decisions. They know that a project can elicit a great response at the festival, but might not find a broader audience in the real world. You might get a call weeks after the festival from an interested buyer or it may never come; don't expect instant results.

Regardless of the festivals that accepted your project, you still may not be offered a network deal for your comedy, or secure distribution for your documentary or educational project. Still, as you learned in Chapters 3 and 6, you do have other options, like the Internet, straight-to-cable, direct-to-video, or a broadcast by a lesser-known cable channel, just to name a few.

IV. GRANTS

Why do you need grant money? You might be looking for money to edit and mix the footage you have already shot but can't afford to finish. You could want an entire project to be funded, or you simply need the donation of services, like tape stock or legal advice.

Most private funding is awarded to nonprofit organizations with a 501(c)(3) status, so you as an individual grant-seeker can usually apply for grants through an umbrella organization that has the required nonprofit status. If you qualify, you might be able to establish your own company with 501(c)(3) status. The Internet offers a range of sites that can give you more information on this process.

Guidelines from Funders and Grant-Makers

Funders and grant-makers can be an important resource for you as a producer. They have gone to considerable lengths to set up their foundations, define their goals, and make money or services available to the public. Most foundations insist that you stick closely to their required proposal format; their guidelines outline all the requirements, so study them closely. Each granting foundation establishes very specific goals, with their objectives and a set of guidelines that include these elements:

- **General purposes.** The history and background of the foundation, and the primary purposes of establishing the grant.
- **Current program interests.** The themes, subject matter, and shared assumptions of the projects that the foundation seeks to promote and encourage through its funding, as well as specific eligibility components.
- **Grant-making policies.** Specific restrictions, limitations, and parameters regarding the conditions for which funds, services, and endowments are awarded.
- **Application process.** Components required by the foundation, such as a letter of inquiry, a detailed proposal, the grant-seeker's qualifications, a project budget and the amount being requested, proof of nonprofit status, and other aspects of future accountability.

Grant writing is a highly valuable skill, but one that almost anyone can acquire with time and practice. You want to focus your energies on targeting the right funding sources, and on writing the grant itself. You can explore the process through foundation centers, web sites, and specialized directories and publications. Refer to the web site in the Grants and Funding Sources and Web Site sections for more information.

Preparing and Writing a Grant in Five Steps

The grant-writing process can truly challenge the patience of a first-time grant writer. It can be time-consuming, it requires you to maintain an uncomfortable objectivity to your own work, and it involves copious paperwork. Each grant has its own specific guidelines and objectives that require intensive research. But when you can feel the rhythm of the process and explore the many grants for which you qualify, your efforts could well pay off.

After you have researched and targeted the specific grant-makers who might be responsive to your proposal, you'll follow these basic steps to write and apply for a grant.

1. Describe Your Project
- Write a brief mission or vision statement that clarifies the goals of the project.
- Assign the project a specific genre, discipline, and/or geographic area.
- Clarify the project's goals and how the funding can promote those goals.
- Draw up a grant-writing schedule that includes the planning, proposal writing, submissions, and anticipated start date for the project.

2. *Find and Contact the Funders*

- Consider applying to many funders, not limiting the search to just one or two.
- Carefully review the objectives and priorities of each funder.
- Determine what amounts the funder awards, and what funds they have previously issued and to whom.
- Ask the funding organization for their proposal guidelines and application specifics.
- Locate a project officer at the granting organization who can answer questions, such as how the proposal review process is conducted, and if there might be any budgetary limitations or requirements that aren't outlined in the guidelines.

3. *Review the Guidelines for the Proposal*

- Look carefully at the guidelines for details that include eligibility qualifications, timetables, deadlines, budget information, and the specifics for formatting the proposal.
- If not outlined in the guidelines, inquire about the goals of the funder, the various award levels, and any contact names and addresses for submission. Ask about the notification process and the date of the notice.

4. *Write the Proposal*

Structure the format for the proposal by following the guidelines provided by each funder; often a deviation can disqualify a proposal. Traditionally it includes a narrative, an estimated budget, an appendix of supporting material, and an authorized signature of the grant-seeker.

- ***The narrative***. This opens the proposal and states what is needed and how it can be approached. Provide your goals and objectives, and reasons why the funder should support your proposal. Delineate your approach for setting and meeting these goals, an outline of the process, and the personnel needed to accomplish the goal. The narrative also provides a schedule of activities, workflow, and projected results, as well as pertinent information about the grant-seeker that assures the funder that you can assume all responsibilities.

As with any professional project, you want to make sure that the narrative is well written and reflects the tone of the project as well as your own ability to carry it through. Any grammatical mistakes or spelling errors can cast doubt on your professionalism. Give it a subtle personality.

- ***The project budget***. A carefully planned budget reflects the goals and sensibilities of the grant-seeker, and gives the funder an indication of how well a project might be managed. The budget needs to be detailed and consistent with realistic prices and rates. It should request a specific amount needed to get the job done. Often, funders supply a budget form that you must fill out in order to meet their specifications.
- ***Supporting materials***. A funder often requests a compilation of supporting materials that is then organized into an appendix. This could include sponsoring agencies or institutions, advisory committees, charts and tables, biographies on key personnel, letters of recommendation, any pertinent newspaper articles and positive reviews, endorsements, and validating certification that can lend credibility to the grant-seeker. Most foundations also require proof of your tax-exempt status or that of your umbrella organization.
- ***Authorized signature***. Funders require the signature of the grant-seeker who may be awarded the grant and who is responsible for the funds.

5. *Follow through*

- Keep a log of the funders that you have contacted, when they were contacted, and their deadlines for your submission of grant applications.
- Keep track of their notification dates; know when to expect a letter of either rejection or acceptance from each funder.
- If possible, ask for feedback on the proposal and ways in which it could be improved for a follow-up submission if it's not accepted the first time around.
- Ask if they can recommend other funding sources that might be better suited to your project.

These are the five most fundamental steps that explore grant writing—yet each grant has its own unique guidelines and expectations. Take advantage of courses and seminars on grant writing, and read examples of grant proposals that have been awarded with funding. You can also consult the Grants and Funding section on the web site for this book.

V. PUBLICITY

> Today's wind is one of spectacle. It may not be of our making. Its origins may not be the pure lands of the Enlightenment but instead the commercial barrens of advertising and entertainment. But use it we must, for without the wind, we are becalmed, stuck, going nowhere.
>
> **Andrew Boyd and Stephen Duncombe, The Manufacture of Dissent:**
> **What the Left Can Learn from Las Vegas**

Unless you create projects solely for your own enjoyment, you want people to see your work. You want it to reach out and communicate your ideas to a viewer. You want to win festival awards, secure distribution, be seen via broadcast or narrow cast, and to attract the attention of potential buyers. You want to earn your living, and even enjoy some profit along the way.

As the producer, you are the liaison between your project and the end buyer. It's important to make people aware of your work. This is where publicity comes into the picture. Hiring a publicist can be an excellent way to get the word out on you, but it's also expensive. Often, you can do just as good a job as a professional, and for free. Following are a couple of tips for getting the word out about you and your project.

- ***Define your audience.*** It's easier to focus your publicity when you know your audience. If, for example, you're promoting a children's television program, you want children and their parents and teachers to know about it. So target your publicity to parenting magazines, PTAs, online sites, teachers' publications, school fairs, libraries, family-focused festivals and events, and other child-oriented possibilities. Every genre of programming has an audience—find them and involve them in your project.
- ***Write a press release.*** A good press release can make your project newsworthy. A press release provides information that is interesting enough to be repurposed for news sources like local or national newspapers, local TV news stations, magazines, web sites, or other audiences. A press release is simple, direct, and brief—a few well-written lines are more effective than a long-winded description. And a well-written press release makes a newspaper editor's job a lot easier.

A Sample Press Release

You might want to issue a press release about your project, your new production company, or even your latest festival nomination. A finished press release is folded in thirds so that it can be opened and read more easily. Whether mailing or emailing a press release, give the recipient time to respond before you follow up.

Here's a brief checklist of the elements included in a press release.

> **Your letterhead**
> - **FOR IMMEDIATE RELEASE.** This is standard wording, in all caps, that appears in the upper left-hand margin under your letterhead.
> - **Contact information.** Skip two lines, then list the name(s) and title(s), email, and telephone and fax numbers of the primary contact person.
> - **Headline.** Skip two more lines, use a boldface type, and briefly describe your news in a headline language that grabs the reader's attention.
> - **Dateline.** This gives the release date, and often the city/state from where you've issued the release.
> - **Lead paragraph (introduction).** The first one or two sentences of your opening paragraph are crucial. They keep the reader interested—or not. Like any compelling narrative, use clear language, action verbs, and few adjectives. Present highlights.
> - **Supporting text (body).** Ideally, try to fit all the information into one paragraph, and focus on the areas of what, who, where, when, and why.
> - **Boilerplate.** Additional information on the person, company, or organization issuing the release.
> - **Recap.** You can restate your news in the lower left-hand corner of the last page. For example, you might include the date a program is airing, the festival screening, a release date for your DVD, or the location of your new production company.
> - **End of release.** Three number symbols (# # #) follow the last paragraph of the release itself, centered, and indicate that the press release has ended.
> - **Media contact information.** The name, address, email address, phone number, and any other pertinent information for the media relations representative or other contact person.

Press Release Formatting

A press release generally includes these formatting components:

- *Paper.* Use 8 ½ × 11 high-quality, white or cream, printed on only one side.
- *Typeface.* Use 12-point Times New Roman or Courier, in upper- and lowercase font, except in the IMMEDIATE RELEASE line (always written in all uppercase letters).
- *Margins.* All sides of each page have 1½-inch margins.
- *Headlines.* Use a bold typeface to draw attention.
- *Continuation.* Finish the paragraph on one page, rather than carrying it over to the next page. When the word "more" is placed between two dashes (–more–) and centered at the bottom of the page, it lets the reader know that another page follows. But try to keep it to one page.

Some Other Thoughts on Generating Buzz

Contact your local newspapers. Your project may have a human-interest story behind it—how you originated the idea, the use of local talent, interesting locations, unraveling an unsolved mystery. Most local newspapers, magazines, online sites, and business publications gravitate toward a good story that is compelling to their readers. Research these publications and look for a newsworthy aspect about your project that could be of interest. Find out, by calling first or through your research, just who's the right person to receive your letter of inquiry that briefly outlines your idea.

Get someone important attached. If your project has garnered praise in a newspaper review or won a festival award, you might consider taking it to a well-known actor, producer, or director who would be willing to sign on as an executive producer. This lends it extra credibility for publicity and investors.

Ignore your own hype. It can be tempting to believe that you actually are as cool as your own PR says you are. Keep an objective frame of mind as you do your job, and maintain your own emotional anchor

Know when to move on. You may have to face the candid truth that a reasonable amount of time has passed, but your project still hasn't sold, or the deal you were offered wasn't nearly what you had hoped for. Chalk it up to experience, and give yourself validation for having learned so much. You are a creative and motivated person, and you've got new projects ahead of you, so take a deep breath and move on.

You have to be flexible. Not all producers are flexible, but *good* producers are.

Ann Kolbell, excerpt from interview in Chapter 11

VI. STARTING YOUR OWN PRODUCTION COMPANY

Some producers prefer working within the structure of an existing network or production company, and others are more comfortable working for themselves. Maybe you've considered starting your own production company, giving you the creative and financial freedom of being your own boss. Or, you've found the perfect partner with whom you can coproduce your ideas. Possibly, you'll form a company solely to produce one specific project, or you may want your company to develop and produce several ideas.

The Realistic Components of Being Your Own Boss

By starting up a production company, you're automatically adding another large chunk of work to your already overbooked life. The many details of running a production company can fall between the cracks during production, so before you rush into what can be a demanding challenge, focus for a moment on these questions.

- *Do you have the right personality?* Some people are happiest when they can work within the comfortable structure of an existing company, with regular co-workers, realistic hours and working conditions. Others like to set their own deadlines and goals, as well as take the risks that could go along with that freedom. Examine your own personality traits, and ask yourself if you've honestly got the motivation and energy to be self-employed. Can you devote way more than 40 hours a week, and possibly a six- or seven-day work week? Consider taking on a partner whose strengths and character work well with yours, or who is adept in areas you're not, like administration or pitching or budgeting. Sometimes a partner can come in with funds and specific abilities, but if there isn't a positive chemistry between the two of you, it's not worth the trade-off.
- *Can you support the business for a period of time?* A start-up company needs money to cover initial costs such as office space and furniture, phones, computers, high-speed Internet, faxes, utility bills and deposits, and printing stationery and business cards. If you're hiring other people, they need to be paid while you look for clients and jobs. You have your own personal rent and expenses to cover, too. Explore these realities by creating a spreadsheet that lists your realistic income potential and weigh them against your planned expenses. Come into a business with enough money to cover your expenses for at least six months to a year.

■ *What investors could you bring into the business?* You may not have a large cache of personal funds with which to start your business, so look for friends, family, colleagues, and private investors who might invest in your business. You can consult with an attorney and/or accountant to prepare an *investment offering* that details your cash flow projections and notes, how the funds will be used, tax consequences, and a projection of returns on the investment. This document also includes information about the producer's team, the manager of the project, and other details. You can grow your business from these investments without giving up ownership and personal control. If you have a good credit rating, business integrity and expertise, and have compiled a strong business plan, you may qualify for funds from a lending institution. In order to receive these funds, you may be asked to offer up security, like a home, a boat, or land.

■ *What do you bring to the business?* Take an objective look at yourself: have you got the skills, personality, experience, and endurance to run a business? And, to be a creative producer at the same time? Just like a good story needs a hook to capture our imagination, you want to identify your own company's hook or "brand" and then build on it. Maybe you are an excellent administrator who can spot good talent, or you are a creative and inventive hyphenate—a producer–director or writer–producer. These are attributes that you can use to market yourself or your business.

■ *Who is your competition?* As clever and energetic as you may be, there are other companies out there competing for the same clients. You want to be genuinely confident that you can maintain an advantage over other businesses by delivering better services, reasonable rates, and star treatment.

■ *Can you create a demand for your services?* Promoting your business is a huge part of success, so get the word out about your new company. This requires advertising, press releases, making a lot of cold sales calls, talking to all your friends and business acquaintances, and thinking of clever approaches to connect with potential clients.

An Independent Production Company Checklist

If you've answered these last few questions honestly, and still want to forge ahead, you're clearly prepared and on your way to making it happen. This mini-checklist details the main components that are part of creating and forming your production company:

■ A **company name**. Sometimes it's used just for a specific project, or it covers all the work you do.
■ A dependable and reputable **entertainment attorney.**
■ An **accounting service** or a good accounting spreadsheet program for doing your own payroll, taxes, and production expenses.
■ An **insurance policy** that covers liability and other production-related coverage.
■ A **legal structuring of your company,** such as general partnership, incorporation, sole-proprietorship, or limited liability company (LLC).
■ An **office location** ideally includes parking, proximity to a roadway or public transportation, adequate utilities, and a welcoming neighborhood; also look into zoning requirements, local taxes, rents, and lease options. You can *invest* in your office space and buy it outright. Or, you *rent* space to cover the production only, or for an ongoing business. It needs furniture and equipment like phones, computers, faxes, printers, kitchen appliances, and a cleaning service.
■ A company **web site** that's easy to navigate, competitive in design, reflects your company's attitude and product, and is consistently updated.

Study the winners. Look closely at companies similar to yours, or to what you hope yours will grow into, that are successful. Read their promotional material, research their client list, see how they solve their clients' problems and what has helped them succeed. This applies to success in general—read biographies and research elements of success that appeal to your personal goals and what you think you can adapt to your own style.

Keep It All Legal

You don't want to ignore the legal issues involved in starting a business. Meet with an accountant and/or attorney before you officially open your doors for business. Depending on where and how you plan to set up a business, there are several elements to carefully research first:

- *Business license.* Most towns and cities, counties, states/provinces, and/or countries require a license to operate a business within their boundaries.
- *Business organization.* Options include general partnership, limited partnership, sole proprietorship, limited liability company (LLC), or incorporation, and each choice affects issues like taxes and liability. Each country has its own options but most fall in these general areas.
- *Certificate of Occupancy (C of O).* Some U.S. city or county zoning departments require this document if you plan on moving your business into a new or used building.
- *Business name.* When an American company's name is different than the name of the owner, this fictitious name needs to be registered with the county. It doesn't apply to a corporation doing business under its corporate name.
- *Taxes.* Depending on the country, state or province, as well as a company's legal structure, its owner could be responsible for withholding money from an employee's wages for taxes. In the United States, the owner pays state and federal (and sometimes city) income taxes and Social Security insurance, known as FICA. If you're self-employed, you pay your own FICA. Businesses are required by the state to pay unemployment insurance in some cases, as well as state and federal income taxes and in some cases, city income taxes on their company's earnings. If a business employs three or more people, it must provide workers' compensation insurance to cover accidents incurred on the job.
- *Business insurance.* Coverage for a business is essential. Insurance coverage might include protection against fire, flood, earthquake, and hurricane, as well as additional insurance that covers theft or damage of property, equipment, and automobile, or interruption of business. In some cases, insurance is needed to cover an officer or director of a corporation—or you—who could be held personally liable on behalf of the company.
- *Federal Employer Identification Number (EIN).* A one-of-a-kind number in the United States that the IRS assigns to a business by which it is identified and accessed, somewhat like a social security number for a business. More information can be found at the IRS web site, www.irs.org.

Dealing with Clients

The word "client" casts a wide net. A client can be a major network, a producer you're working for, a nonprofit funding group, a government department, or your rich brother-in-law. A client pays the bills, gives you creative direction, and has demands that must be met in order for you to be paid. No matter how independent a producer you might hope to be, there is always a client. And the client is always right.

Keep Your Clients Happy

Getting clients is hard enough, and keeping them can be even harder. The television and new media industries make, and spend, billions of dollars, pounds, and Euros to get ahead, and this competition can be either chilling or exhilarating. But the harsh truth is that few of us are truly irreplaceable, and most clients can usually find a better deal somewhere else. You want to make yourself valuable to them. Create a plan that can make your clients feel valued. Take a genuine interest in their goals and ideas, be collaborative, and earn (and keep) their trust. Thank them for their business by treating them well.

IN THE TRENCHES...

You don't have to make your client your best friend. You don't even have to like them. But they don't have to know that, and you do want to treat them with respect. No matter what you think of them, don't gossip about them behind their backs. It could come back to haunt you when you least expect it.

~C. Kellison

Negotiate

If you've got a client who can provide you with steady business, consider bringing your rates down and negotiating a long-term deal. However, if a client tries to consistently nickel-and-dime you, the price of your sanity may not be enough of a trade-off. There is a subtle difference between the two. Your intuition is usually right when you listen to it.

Ask Questions

Often a client has great ideas and directives, but they aren't clearly stated. Don't hold back: ask for clarification. Take notes and then write a memo to the client after the meeting, detailing what you think was said. This way, if there is still confusion, changes can be made by both you and the client.

Keep a Paper Trail

In the midst of virtually every project, there's chaos no matter how well-planned. Things are promised, and somehow forgotten, or one budget number turns into another. Save all your emails, as well as interoffice memos, deal memos, contracts, and agreements. In each meeting and for every phone call, take notes and date them. In your daily calendar, keep track of times and dates of meetings, and who attended. This kind of attention to detail and backup documentation usually prevents disagreements or future litigation.

Simplicity Is the Key

It could benefit you to subcontract your work rather than hire full-time employees, and to hire employees and crew on an as-needed basis. Technology has made it feasible for a producer to run a successful business by just using cellular technology and a laptop, and to work from a home office until your projects and budgets allow for expansion.

For a larger project, or if you're consistently getting work and need the space, consider working out of a turnkey office space that you can rent on a monthly basis. And, on each project, hire a team of the most experienced freelancers you can find. This includes writers, other producers, graphic designers, sales people, production coordinators, PAs, interns; all work on a per-project, freelance basis. In most cases, you agree only on a salary and pay them that amount. They're responsible for paying their own taxes and insurance. You work out reasonable rates with them, give them credit whenever possible, and have a collaborative, fun time in the process.

And, when the project is over, everyone moves on to their next job.

> You try to get across that "We've got certain things we have to accomplish, we understand that you have certain things you have to accomplish, let's work together to see how we can do as much of that as possible" and find ways where we can compromise as necessary. It's as much about personal relationships and schmoozing as it is about, technically, how you're going to achieve whatever it is that you need to do.
>
> **Stephen Reed, excerpt from interview in Chapter 11**

ON A HUMAN LEVEL . . .

The changing dimensions and details that are involved in producing for TV and new media never end. These learning experiences continue getting better, and you bring them with you into the next production. For those of you who savor the never-ending possibilities that are inherent in producing, and in life, each new phase is a journey. You may well have found a profession that is rich in potential and tailor-made for your unique skills and personality.

SUMMARY

Over the last 10 chapters, you have explored the myriad elements that play integral roles in taking a project from its beginnings to its very end. Each chapter offered ideas and details pertinent to the producer—each is part of the process called "producing."

The final chapter of this book is designed to give you yet another perspective. In Chapter 11, you'll meet people with diverse ideas, advice, and experiences. These experienced TV and new media producers and industry professionals actively produce in television and new media. Each contributor talks about his or her area of expertise, and each conversation provides its own unique lens into this job call producing. After all, a good producer learns from the best.

REVIEW QUESTIONS

1. Name three key aspects of wrapping a project. Why are they important?

2. Create your own resume. Ask two people to critique it for you.

3. What steps could you take to promote your project? To promote yourself as a producer?

4. What are the benefits of entering a project in a festival? What are the drawbacks?

5. Discuss the components of an effective press kit.

6. Research the foundations that award funds and services. Pick one and write a brief report on the organization's requirements.

7. What three areas of publicizing your project are you most comfortable doing? Why?

8. Write a sample press release announcing an imaginary news item you want to promote.

9. List the pros and cons of starting your own production company.

10. Outline your own professional next steps.

Conversations with the Pros:
Producing in the Real World

When you follow your bliss...doors will open where
you would not have thought there would be doors;
and where there wouldn't be a door for anyone else.

Joseph Campbell

In this chapter, an impressive array of producers and industry professionals share their professional practices and their personal odysseys; each chronicles that search for bliss that Joseph Campbell speaks about. Through sit-down interviews, emails, faxes, and transcontinental phone calls, each person shared his or her unique story; each injected moments of rich dimension into the preceding chapters. Their collective interviews form a body of work that is so interesting, it had to become a chapter all of its own.

The contributing producers, academics, and industry professionals are:

- Sheril Antonio: New York University, Associate Dean
- Sharon Badal: Tribeca Film Festival, Programmer for Shorts Program
- Michael Bonfiglio: Executive Producer/Producer, nonfiction and documentary
- Sheila Possner Emery: Producer, *The Dog Whisperer*
- Barbara Gaines: Executive Producer, *The Late Show with David Letterman*
- Richard Henning: Audio Engineer
- Ann Kolbell and Matthew Lombardi: Producers, NBC and CBS
- Jeffrey McLaughlin: Senior Editor and Director of Postproduction
- Brett Morgen: Producer/Director, documentaries for theatrical release and television
- Stephen Reed: Executive Producer/Producer, live events
- John Rosas: Producer, promotional and added value content
- Tom Sellitti: Supervising Producer, *Rescue Me*
- J. Stephen Sheppard: Entertainment Lawyer
- Valerie Walsh: Executive Producer, Cocreator, *Dora the Explorer* and *Go, Diego! Go!*
- Justin Wilkes: Executive Producer/Producer, TV series, features, and documentaries
- Scott A. Williams: Co-Executive Producer, *Bones*
- Bernie Young and Laurie Rich: Executive Producer and Executive in Charge of Production, *The Martha Stewart Show*

SHERIL ANTONIO
Associate Dean for Film, Television, and New Media at
New York University's Tisch School of the Arts

CK: Let's address the classic argument: is television an art form or merely a craft? What is it about television that creates such controversy?

SA: My ideas about this question have changed somewhat as I've had new experiences, some of which have been quite profound. Today, television is many different things to many different people at once: art, craft, silly-putty, company, a device that provides worldwide information and education on myriad subjects, and that's how I think television should be. That is in fact what makes it important and so popular.

I think of the difference between my childhood television experiences versus today. In the 1960s and 1970s there was one TV in our home, no remote, and only 13 channels. Television was not on during the day and when we watched, it was as a family, in particular the news, *The Carol Burnett Show*, or *The Flip Wilson Show*. There were shows I watched alone before the news if I finished my homework, shows like *The Addams Family* or *Batman*. Today, each of our homes has two TV sets and everyone watches what they want.

The controversy about whether it is art or craft stems from the fact that television is seen as a piece of technology, and in terms of content, is not "one" fixed aesthetic or practical thing, not definable by one pedagogy, genre, age group or format. Thus, those who think of it as caviar—maybe your BBC, Public Television folks—speak about viewing selectivity, and those who feel it is just crap complain about it. Most of us fall in between and watch the range of things from art to commerce. Television is both art and craft.

Before, I spoke about the fact that it had the characteristic of an appliance, something that everyone has and controls, thus it had become mundane, innocuous even, more like a piece of furniture which would encourage people to think of it as craft. However, as it turns out, I've never seen folks gather around an appliance laughing, crying, getting information, hooting or rooting for something or someone, or using it as a means to combat loneliness. I'm also more aware of the fact that television goes to places where other mediums don't—like hospitals, the dentist's office, and schools. There they take on new meaning for those offering its services and for those watching it.

It has the ability to give personal meaning to your individual needs or to allow large groups of people to share the same event or images, particularly in a crisis or disaster. I recall Princess Diana's funeral, the Challenger explosion, and of course 9/11; you knew most of the nation and maybe the world was watching the same thing you were. That's an intense and meaningful thing. Yes, it has a very different relationship with each of us, but its great power still lies in that fact that it has a way of connecting us individually to something important, or bringing us together around a particular subject.

CK: There was a time, not all that long ago, when film and radio and television each had its specific and separate domain. Now they're merging, not only technologically, but also creatively.

SA: This merger has continued since we last spoke [in the first edition]. Satellite radio, music videos, podcasts or movies on iPods, news on cell phones, and you can find almost anything from either medium on the Internet. These are some of the ways I've experienced this blurring of the lines when it comes to audiences and these various domains.

I actually have a hard time keeping up with some of the advances. Think of how far the technology has come to be able to offer TV, phone, and Internet service from the same provider. Wow! I remember some time ago being so surprised that you could get "radio" on the Internet, it's amazing when you take the time to think about it.

I teach a class that culminates in student presentations that require some form of media clip. This semester, for the first time since I've been teaching, some of my students used clips from films and other forms of media that were on the Internet. So instead of using the VCR or DVD player, they needed an Internet cable for their computer. This is one of the reasons I'm so glad I teach. Not only am I kept up to date on what's happening in all media, students let me know how they are using them individually or in concert.

CK: As you've mentioned, TV is like a family member. You can argue with it, you can disagree with it, you can even turn it off, but it's still part of our daily life.
SA: Indeed, television *is* important to us, and there is one easy way to find out what it means to you. Spend some time in a place without a TV or try not turning it on for a week. I had the opportunity to do that recently and it was eye opening. I knew how much TV meant to me and what an essential part it played in my day and life, but I was amazed at how much I relied on it for a variety of things. The most intense realization was that in a significant way I felt quite cut off from several things; news, weather, and entertainment, or distraction. And in the quiet moments I realized it also provided some strange form of companionship. TV, as it turns out, provides us with the security that other folks are out there, often telling us things we want to know. Sometimes it gives quick information we don't have time to pursue. That for me used to be the weather; I remember having to "wait" for it to come on the radio or network stations; now NY1 has it at the bottom of the screen, and there is the Weather Channel.

And there are other conveniences. I, for example, don't have time to read the paper, and love listening to NY1's "In the Papers" where they share the headlining stories from the major papers. As it turns out, it is a great family member, very informative, entertaining, and willing to change regularly to meet our needs.

CK: In your position at NYU, what do you suggest that a student of producing look for in getting an education?
SA: Education has to be about excellent education, no matter what the geographical location, tuition cost, or pedagogy of the institution. It is our moral imperative as educators to provide the highest level of education to students, no matter what the school. The most important element, though, is that producing students need to be where other students are making films, videos, radio, music, animation, television, web-media, as well as studying the business and the history of each medium.

He or she has to look for a place where they can be engaged, where the whole of the process is taking place so they can be plugged in to a variety of experiences and exercises. I've watched this play out at NYU over the last few years. We had business students from the Stern School of Business wanting to be producers so they were paired with filmmakers from Tisch to create projects together. This was so successful that the leadership of both schools got together and created a dual-degree program to facilitate this pairing, this vital experience while at school so that they are more than ready when they enter the business.

A producer is making something that is for a "market" or a particular group, without a doubt. That product can be informative, shocking, comfortable, funny, or challenging. Producers need to get involved in whatever they find value in doing. In television producing, it is important not to be in a vacuum, given the variety of channels and individual tastes that exist in the population. The educational institution must provide ways for producers to see how different people interpret the same assignment, understand that there are different ways of seeing, different ways of mixing the stew to get the desired results, and provide different working groups to shake things up a bit.

They also have to be in the room when this production is viewed by an audience of other students in their class, their faculty, or strangers at festivals to see how it reads out in the world. That is vital. Getting feedback is an essential part of this kind of laboratory setting. You can't take these kinds of risks in the real world. Educational institutions are sites for rapid and compressed learning in certain fields such as television.

CK: How valuable are internships?
SA: Critical! Vital! Essential! Internships fill the void between the dream of the industry and the reality of it. They are a safe space between the educational environment and the professional one. They give an important educational experience, one that represents a transitional reality not available in school, one that you can sample, and one that you can easily retreat from at the end of the semester. A trial run without a penalty.

More important, internships can allow you to learn what you really *don't* want to do.

CK: In your experience in working with students who are on a producing track, do you notice any shared traits or commonalities?
SA: While the personalities of producers vary, they have several things in common: they don't just tolerate chaos, they love it! They can work with almost anyone and have a great deal of patience. They love doing lots of things at once and engaging with and organizing people. They each operate at a different pace and engage different stylistic methods but they are problem-solvers, it has to be second nature to them.

Producers also have the ability to see where things can go wrong and plan for it. They are facilitators and therapists and have the creative meter to see the project through from the widest perspective and the finest of details. In television, the producer is king while film is the director's domain. Television has a different way of reading audiences, advertisers, networks, cable stations, time slots, etc. It's not a job you can be engaged in if you don't have the passion, energy or interest.

CK: How important is it for a television producer to have a backdrop of television history?
SA: Critical! As far as I'm concerned, you can't say you love a field and not have any interest in its history, its evolution, its mistakes, and its accomplishments. You can't be cutting edge or do anything new if you don't know what came before. You have to be curious about how things worked years ago, how they work in other countries, what traditions and formats were used and why. Being informed is being serious about what you are doing. One of the things NYU does is to require that students not only participate in a production-heavy curriculum but in history and critical studies as well.

There is an intellectual aspect to all forms of art and media. This is a vital matter when it comes to television. One has to know where it is placed in the larger world, especially in times of crises, such as 9/11 or a war. One has to observe trends and ask who television is representing, all the time. For me, the most critical aspect of television is the flow of information. You have to do some work, to sort out history in the making and see how things are being reported. I still believe that television is probably better with the past than it is with the present or the future. Sometimes I think reporting has turned into "convincing," "predicting," or "wishing." We all remember a certain network predicting a presidential winner who did not in fact win the election.

I'm always interested in the today of television, the really strong work as well as the trendy programs. It all has value. Television producers have to know it all, past and present, to know how to do what they want to do best.

CK: Here's the classic question: does television reflect our culture or is our culture shaped by television, or do we need to care?
SA: This is a really important question. We most certainly should care whether television reflects or shapes our culture. We have to care! Last time we spoke about how D.W. Griffith's film, *The Birth of a Nation* caused an increase in lynchings and clan membership in the early 1900s. Right now we are at war and heading towards another election. So the question is most important, and we should be thinking about this all the time with regard to the vital issues facing our nation—like the war, the election, the economy, healthcare, and global politics.

What still worries me is when television is shaping without consciousness. Whether the producers are not conscious or the viewers are not conscious, does not matter. It's the same problem. Let's take a look at hurricane Katrina and the devastation in New Orleans. Some of the network and cable channels did their best to "reflect" the horrible aftermath of the hurricane and the systematic failures that led to the devastation. I'm not sure we are getting the same quality of reporting when it comes to Iraq. Sometimes, just reflecting something can turn it into shaping.

CK: How important is the choice of schools for a producing student?
SA: You will end up where you are meant to be, no matter what school you go to. Having said that, it is clear that some schools have geographical advantages, some schools are better connected, and curriculum and faculty are at the center of the educational experience. Given that the success of any student comes from that student's innate skills and talents, the selection of a school is important. We don't teach talent, we teach craft that unleashes talent.

When schools do well getting alumni into the business, I think it has a lot to do with their admissions policy and financial aid. Both can allow them to "attract" good students, the best students. So the simple answer is, any good school with a full curriculum that engages the student completely in all aspects of creative projects will forge a good producer. We all know the so-called "top" schools and everyone tries to say this one or that one is good at this or that. The truth is we are all in the same business and we all want the same thing and do our best to achieve it. I think where we do compete is for good students since that's what makes or breaks us, that's where our long-term reputation comes from. Students need to look for a place where they can find the best experiences all around, inside and outside the classrooms.

CK: What are the essential points that you would emphasize to your students about producing for television?
SA: I would emphasize being as conscious a creator as you are a spectator; be informed about your subject, no matter what it is, and be passionate about whatever you decide to do. You see, if you are passionate and really invested in what you are doing, and say it fails, then you know you did the best job. Also, for any artist/creator, the spectator is someone that you should keep in mind all the time: whom am I making this for and why? Just as directors study the work of other directors, so should producers. Look at a variety of producing styles, the cutting edge ones, the standards, and the old timers.

There is no one way of doing things any more, and most successful folks these days are doing a variety of things, changing all the time and not getting stagnant. And, pick a school that has many industry guests coming to events and classes so you can talk to some of these folks. Their story won't be your path but you will undoubtedly learn some vital bit of information from this "insider" that would never occur to you.

CK: What do you feel the role of ethics plays in a producer's job description?
SA: Ethics are crucial in any and all job descriptions. I think of it as having integrity, a sense of responsibility, and a conscious desire to connect in a meaningful way to a portion of the viewing audience. Given our discussion about television reflecting versus shaping, I think we can see immediately that ethical decisions pop up all the time. Notions of ethics have several levels of importance. One is that you have to know the ethical and political landscape of the different networks and various cable stations, the ethics of the various time slots. Obviously, the "after-school" programs will have different limitations from "late-night" shows.

Two, you need to study the differences between them and where they each have boundaries. I remember one issue that stood out to me, was when Whoopi Goldberg's show was cancelled because she was too "political" and as a result lost Slim Fast as a sponsor. These are real decisions that are connected to real money.

And, finally, knowing all this will help you either conform, or know just how far you can go. I'm not sure if there is a document for television but I always show my students the one for film, *The Production Code of Ethics–1934*. It is a telling document if you want to know the "ethics" or politics as the case may be, of the time. As a viewer it is important to me, very important, especially when watching news, election coverage, to know the "ethics" of the network or the reporter.

CK: What's important to you about this vast subject of producing for television and new media ?
SA: I remember something my mother always told me: never give anyone anything you would not want for yourself or your family. That's what I have to say about producing for television. That's not to say you can't challenge or shock folks, let them know things that are going on that we all deny or ignore. Television is a formidable cultural, political, social, economical, tool. I actually think it should be studied in all schools and colleges. It is the single most important vehicle for the dissemination of the so-called American Dream. Now, with the cable stations, we have very different versions of the dream, in many different languages, age groups, etc. We even have shows mocking the dream, shows like *The Office, The Simpsons,* and *The Riches*. Television producing is an important job, I don't think people know how important it is.

CK: What is your sense of the explosive advances of digital technology?
SA: Amazing! The whole interactive nature of television now is part of why I think it's so important. Its status, power, and reach have to be discussed. We can now vote on issues with our cable remote, go online and communicate with a program's personnel while the program is in progress, and feel very much that we have a voice that is immediately reflected in real time. The only thing lacking as far as I'm concerned is a national notification system like they used to have in the old days. You know, that piercing beep followed by " this is not an emergency, if it were a real emergency…" It should have been put in place by now since 9/11 and Katrina. It is the best tool to get to people in an emergency and I am surprised we are not there yet. Fortunately, any local news station will break in with needed information in such cases but it can reach the level of a national tool for communication.

So here we are, talking about a very portable television, no more the stationary screen at home, in the office, etc. Last time we spoke [in edition one], I said: "I can imagine it becoming more like a cell phone." Now, it is as portable as a cell phone or an iPod. I can't wait to see what's next!

SHARON BADAL
Tribeca Film Festival/Short Films Programmer; NYU Professor/Producing for Film; and author of *Swimming Upstream: A Lifesaving Guide to Short Film Distribution*

Navigating the film festival labyrinth…for most new producers, entering their project into the film festival circuit represents their first foray into the "real world" of the entertainment industry. Most of these initial projects involve the short film format, that is less than 40 minutes. As one of the Programmers for the Tribeca Film Festival, I have watched literally thousands of short film submissions over the past several years, in addition to the shorts I watch from my students at New York University, where I am a full-time faculty member of the Tisch School of the Arts Undergraduate Department of Film and Television.

With my eyesight still intact, I offer the following Top Ten Helpful Hints for creating a short film in both narrative and unscripted formats:

1. Avoid the overuse of voiceover narration to carry your vision. Think about narration as a means to introduce your story, or express salient points, but do not allow the focus of your project to be the voiceover.
2. The first few minutes of your project are integral in creating the tone. Think about your opening very carefully, and stay away from traditional and oversaturated openings, such as "alarm-goes-off-character-wakes-up" or "pan-across-a-mantle-of-photographs," for example.
3. Consider the running time of your project while it is still in the concept stage and have a clear idea of content vs. running time. The longer your project, the stronger your story should be. Remember, it's all about the story, regardless of whether it is narrative or documentary.
4. Particularly with documentary projects, think about your story progression. You still should have an idea where the film is "going." Twenty minutes of talking heads interspersed with archive footage does not a documentary make. What is your viewer going to learn/experience by the end of the film and how do we get there?
5. Montage sequences serve a very specific purpose—to move the story ahead in an expedient manner. Regurgitating previously viewed shots simply for the sake of putting them to music is not in your best interest, and detracts from the overall impact of the film.
6. Speaking of music, the use of songs should not undermine the visuals, but enhance them. Too many filmmakers who grew up as part of the MTV generation cavalierly use song lyrics to express their vision. This is not a music video.
7. Your main credit sequence should not imitate a feature film. A 10-minute short with a two-minute main credit sequences is unnecessary. Give "credit where credit is due" in the end credits! If you produce a lavish opening credit sequence, make sure it matches the style of the film, and does not jar the viewer when it goes from credits to first shot.
8. The one-character documentary has its own set of challenges. A producer may think someone's life is unique by the hurdles he/she has overcome or something in his/her life that warrants capturing the experience, but others should as

well. Before you produce a film about a friend or relative, keep your audience (and objectivity) in mind. Is this person interesting enough on-camera to sustain a viewer's attention for 10, 20, or 30 minutes?

9. One of the most exhilarating aspects of short-form filmmaking is that "there are no rules." Don't feel confined by the structure imposed by features. Programmers are looking for creativity, new voices, and a captivating story supported by visual imagery.

10. Finally, be aware that you're not going to get rich from a short film. Your goal should be to produce a project that accurately reflects your talent and the ability to create and complete a vision. A common and accurate descriptive is that a short film is your "calling card."

As a producer, you are the ultimate creator and decision-maker on the project. Make certain that the decisions you make result in the best film that you can create.

MICHAEL BONFIGLIO
Producer (including *Metallica: Some Kind of Monster; Iconoclast; Addiction*)

CK: The projects you've worked on cover quite a spectrum. What's your role?
MB: I work as a documentary producer, primarily in cinéma-vérité films. I work for @radical.media, a multifaceted international production company that specializes in television commercials, but includes divisions that create a variety of other forms of media. I've been working in documentaries for more than a decade, having worked my way up as an intern for directors Joe Berlinger and Bruce Sinofsky (*Metallica: Some Kind of Monster, Paradise Lost, Brother's Keeper*), whom I now produce for. Working with Joe and Bruce is my main job within the larger umbrella of @radical.media.

As Joe and Bruce's producer, I am responsible for a wide and varying set of tasks, which really run the gamut between coordinating and line producing to generating ideas for new projects, getting projects financed, and helping shape the films creatively. I've also been involved in PR and distribution for our projects.

We usually operate with a skeleton crew, so I wear a lot of hats. Every project with us is different, so I am very fortunate in that my role is constantly changing and evolving, and I have a level of freedom that I enjoy. The flipside is that since our projects are not terribly heavily financed, on any given day I also find myself doing work that would probably be considered the duties of a PA. That said, working with filmmakers of Joe and Bruce's caliber ensures that I very rarely find myself working on things that bore me or that I am not happy to be involved in.

CK: The demands of your job, of any producer's job, are extensive. How do you juggle your work pressures and still keep a perspective on your personal life?
MB: This is a fantastic question, and one that really should be part of the larger cultural debate, not just in regards to producing for television. I'm a working guy in the relatively low-paying documentary field, not some big Hollywood producer who buys properties and gets them set up, so work for me literally means making the money to pay my rent and hopefully start chipping away at my debt—it's not some glamorous situation.

The "entertainment business" (which is such a regrettable term for the unfortunate reality) is however, a pretty cutthroat field. It's also somewhat capricious and you're constantly at the whim of networks, studios, or whomever it is you have convinced that your project is the best, or, in the case of an assignment, that you're going to do the job better than anyone else.

A guy I know says, "You're only as good as your last project," which is also a reality that creates a great deal of pressure, though this is often self-imposed, too. I do think this is a good thing in many ways, because it forces you to always push yourself to make everything you do better than the last thing you did. That said, you make choices. I often find myself neglecting my personal life and my personal projects in order to do the best that I can at my job. My girlfriend is always saying, "When you're on your deathbed, are you *really* going to regret not going in to the office/making that phone call/writing that email, etc.?" And she's right. I don't usually listen, though, largely due to the tenuous nature of my work, but also because of a personal need to do my best work.

Back to my initial point, though, I don't think that this quality is specific to producing. Cell phones, email, and other technological advantages have made it nearly impossible to get away from work, and corporate downsizing and our out-of-control consumer culture (and in New York City, skyrocketing rents that are pricing regular people out of town) have made it almost a necessity to work harder and more often than ever before (well, maybe not *harder*—I wouldn't make that argument to a dairy farmer, say, or the immigrants who built the railroads).

Technology has also blurred the line between when you are working and when you are not. Even in the short time that I have been in this field, I have experienced a tremendous difference in this regard. But this is really true in most fields—my father works for the phone company and was never home when I was growing up because he was always working. There are tons of people like him who probably regret those decisions who I could learn from, but the need to keep one's career together is really a necessity, not completely a choice. It certainly is true in producing, but it's far from exclusive to it. It hasn't always been that way, and it's not like that everywhere in the world, which is why I wish it were part of our larger social discourse.

CK: Who might be your historical counterparts, in your area of producing?
MB: The clearest historical counterparts to the kinds of work that I do are the cinéma-vérité films of the 1960s by people like Pennebaker, Leacock, Robert Drew, Albert and David Maysles, Chris Marker, and Frederick Wiseman. On any given project, though, I've taken inspiration from all kinds of places, though it may not be obvious to anyone but me—feature films, television shows, paintings, photographs, books, and life experiences.

CK: You often work with other producers. Do you see a predominant "producer's personality"?
MB: I don't really think there is a "producer's personality," but I do think there are many qualities that a good producer should have, if he or she wants to do the job well and also be able to sleep at night. Despite the clichés of what a producer acts like (sharp-dressed, fast-talking megalomaniacs), I think that honesty is very important. Anything else will eventually come out anyway, so aside from basic ethics, there's really no point in making crap up to cover your bases, or to convince someone of something that isn't true, just so you can get out of them what you want.

Being adaptable is also very important. Nothing ever works out exactly the way you expect it to, so you have to be able to adapt to situations that are in flux. I think that a lot of good producers are also very anal and a bit obsessive—I'm not really this way, but I sometimes wish I were (in my work). Working well with people is also very important. The people you are working with are so important in a field that is so collaborative, so if you get the opportunity to work with great people (as I've been lucky enough to do), you'd better get along well with them so they'll want to work with you again.

CK: What are your speculations on this intriguing world of new media?

MB: I have positive and negative feelings about the future of television. With every step forward, there seems to be a step backward. As media consolidation puts control into the hands of fewer and fewer corporations, there have been some alarming trends. The bottom line is all that matters at the networks, to the detriment of the viewing public.

The perceived power of right-wing groups who try to censor voices on television is also pretty terrifying. The prospect of "branded entertainment" is awfully unseemly, as well. For someone whose livelihood hinges upon working in the field, the decreases in production budgets for documentaries is also a bummer. However, these decreases are largely due to the greater number of programming outlets that are fighting for the same number of viewers, which is a good thing. There are now more places where you can make things, and that has opened up the field to some truly original voices.

Before the rise of cable, shows like *South Park*, *The Daily Show with Jon Stewart*, *The Sopranos*, and pretty much anything on the Cartoon Network's *Adult Swim* never would have made it to the air. The increased need for content has also allowed for an expansion in the industry that has allowed more people to actually have jobs in it, and advances in technology have made it easier and cheaper to create things of good production value, so the type of person who can get his or her voice heard is no longer an archetype. So I guess I am cautiously optimistic about the future.

CK: What do you wish someone had told you early in your career?

MB: That there's no secret formula. I didn't actually set out to do this, and it's far from the career goals I am still hoping and working to achieve, but here I am doing it. It's not rocket science—you just have to learn from your mistakes, rise to the challenges in front of you, and be willing to ask someone who knows better than you when you need to. And there's *always* someone who knows better than you.

CK: And your Top Ten list? What would that look like?

MB: My own Top Ten list of things a producer of documentaries should know are:

1. There's no substitute for a good story.
2. Working with great people is better than working with a lot of money.
3. How to write.
4. How to use as much of your production gear as possible (just in case).
5. How to budget (and stay within it).
6. If you're traveling with equipment, show up really early at the airport.
7. If you're going on location somewhere, it's best to have someone local on the crew.
8. It's never going to be the way you expect it to be.
9. It's okay to ask for advice.
10. Everything takes longer than you think it will.

CK: If you were to be a guest lecturer in a producing-for-television class, what would you tell the students?

MB: Don't do this work if you want to get rich and/or famous, or you think it's a glamorous, cool-sounding job. Chances are, it won't work out that way anyway, but if that's the reason you want to do this work, please don't. As corny as it sounds, it really is a privilege to create and help create mass media, and there is a responsibility inherent in that, not only to the people who are seeing your work, but to your own soul.

There's not much you can do about what other people are creating, but there's almost always something you can do about what *you* are doing.

SHEILA POSSNER EMERY
Producer, *The Dog Whisperer*

CK: You're the producer of a highly popular series called The Dog Whisperer. *This show was born from an article you read in 2002?*

SE: I had just partnered up with my producing partner, Kay Sumner, and a few days after we decided we wanted to make a show about animals, she read an article in the *L.A. Times* about Cesar Millan. She called me up and she said, "Why don't you try to get a meeting with him?" So, I called the Dog Psychology Center—and at that time Cesar had a lot more time than he does now—and he talked with me for about 45 minutes. He told me his entire philosophy and I was madly writing down notes about what he said. I kept thinking, this is fascinating. This is incredible. This guy is really something.

I made an appointment, we went down and we talked with him about how much we wanted to do a show on him. We found out later that a lot of producers, after reading the same article in the *L.A. Times,* had also contacted him about producing a show. But I overheard him later telling someone that he liked the way the dogs reacted to us. So we got the A-OK first from the dogs!

CK: How many dogs gave you the OK?

SE: That was when Cesar's center was really full. There were at least 30 or 40 dogs.

CK: You had already decided to do a show with Kay about animals, before meeting Cesar. Why this interest in animals?

SE: Well, I had only met Kay a few days before. Her dog had just had puppies, and I'm a big animal person and I love horses—and we both like animals—so, why don't we do something about animals? It was just like that, and then a very few days later—maybe three days—after we had that discussion and we didn't have anything in mind, this article came out. It really changed our life.

CK: So Cesar and his dogs, not necessarily in that order, gave you the OK. How did it proceed from there?

SE: We made a promo that was about five minutes long. It basically was what the show is now—showing him knocking on the door, going in, talking to the dog's owner, what was the problem—that was called the consultation—and then he would take the dog and do whatever was necessary to rehabilitate it and tell the owner what to do.

We followed him around for a day—just shot a typical day of Cesar Millan—and we made a promo. We only went to three companies to pitch it. We wanted to make sure that we both liked whoever it was, and we eliminated about everybody. Then the company, MPH, where we both knew Jim Milio—he's the "M" in MPH, from a group at the Television Academy—from working on the show *Rescue 911*. We said we'll take the promo there. They really liked it, then we had another meeting and Cesar came in with one of his canine clients, which is always very impressive, and we all made a deal. Kay had had prior meetings with National Geographic, so MPH made another promo, a little bit longer than ours, and we had more meetings with National Geographic. Normally, a network will do a special, or they make a pilot. But Nat Geo said we'll do 26 half-hours—right off the bat. Not even 13—we did 26! And that's how we started. It's amazing.

CK: The show airs on Nat Geo, sells on DVDs, plus you've got pet products, books. Talk about the business model you've all built.
SE: That evolved very slowly. Our partners, MPH, had a lot of the business experience so they very carefully and slowly developed the business. We knew that he was going to "be" somebody, and that there was an incredible market for anything to do with cats and dogs. There's 69 million dogs in America. The dog industry is bigger than the entertainment industry in revenue.

Our first product was the DVD *People Training for Dogs*, and we've only sold it on the Internet, yet we have sold over 100,000 copies. So, as we progressed through the seasons, by the end of our fourth season, it became evident that there was a need for dog-related products. We're in the process now of branding Cesar. He has his own brand of dog food, dog beds, dog toys, and dog vitamins—and dog water.

CK: Every producer wants a piece of the pie, somewhere along the line. Have you worked out a deal in order to do that?
SE: Yes, we're all partners. In our producing, it's a team effort, so that the building of a good team is paramount for success. If you have somebody who's really good at business, or on the creative end, or is good at relating, that's a good mix of talent.

CK: There are five of you. What is each person's job?
SE: Kay and I teamed up with MPH—that is the production company, with the editing facilities and the office. They have the infrastructure. MPH is Jim Milio, Melissa Peltier, and Mark Hufnail. Jim is one of the writers on the show and he sometimes directs. Melissa also writes; she was the writer of the two best-selling books, and Mark Hufnail is the business contract brain of the outfit.

CK: As for you and your partner, Kay. Who does what?
SE: We ask people to send in videos showing their dog's behavior, and showing them. We all screen the videos…there will usually be a couple of us screening. There's a coordinating producer and an associate producer, so one day somebody's out with the field, segment producing—and if we're in the office and there's a bunch of tapes for screening, two people usually go through them and pick out the best ones. So once we have a pile of the best possibilities, then Sue Ann Fincke—she's the supervising producer and the director who directs 95 percent of the stories—she'll come in and we'll all discuss the choices.

We analyze the story—how many pit bulls have we already done? Or poodles. Maybe we just did a poodle story, so even though there might be a good tape on a poodle, we might not shoot that story because we've already done something similar. When we're looking at the tapes, we're looking at the dog, what breed is it, have we ever done this breed before. And we're also looking at the problem. Is it another aggressive pit bull? We've already done that one. Unless there's something about the people: is the problem really about the dog, or about the people?

And it's a mix of all those elements. Let's say someone's got a great personality and we think that they'd be a great interview, and is interesting to watch. It's a mix of the dog, the problem and the people—and also the location in the country because in the last two seasons, we've traveled to New York, Florida, Seattle, San Diego, Nebraska, Atlanta, the Chicago area—so, if we've already been to Chicago and we get a tape from Chicago, then that's not going to work this time around.

CK: Does the same crew travel with you to all these locations, or do you pick up local crews?
SE: We have an incredible crew. It's very small and everybody is superb at what they do.

Bryan Duggan is our main camera; he has the camera on Cesar. Chris Komives, he's the second camera and he'll be out getting footage of the dog. And then in the interview, the consultation, Bryan's camera will be on Cesar and Chris's camera will be on the subjects—the dog owners. What's really neat about them is that since this is a reality show, they have to be ready and they have to know that when he opens the door, they have to intuit what's going to happen and they have to be technically great, and just have to be ready for whatever happens. And then there's the sound person, Myles Ghormley, and he's been working with Bryan for over 20 years, so they're all in sync.

So one of the most important things is that the crew has to be very calm/assertive because they can't add any energy into the mix. One of the things that's different about our show than just about any reality show, is that what Cesar is focusing on is energy: the dog's energy, and the owner's energy. What he is doing is creating balance between the dog and the owner, so the crew has to be very neutral. They can't get afraid or have any kind of an emotion that the dog can pick up on and that would affect how it's behaving.

Everyone is very respectful and kind to the dog owners. They are just regular people, and we're going into their house. It's very emotional a lot of times—they're usually at their wit's end, they're desperate, and here we are. There's two cameras in their home, so we want to put them at ease. In the end, usually people will say it's the most fun they've had in their entire life, spending the day with Cesar Millan. Because they do love their dogs, and they see miracles happen before their eyes—and that's what he does.

It's really amazing. I have to say, for four seasons I still haven't gotten used to, "Oh, there's just another miracle." I keep trying to come up with stories that will stump him but he's just a genius with dogs—and people.

CK: Do you ever go back and revisit any of the animals and their owners?
SE: Oh yes. If the owner needs us to come back or the dog is so "red zone," then we will. We've had dogs this season where Cesar's taken the dog for two months. Sometimes he's gone back three or four times.

CK: Let's talk about a basic belief that a producer has a certain kind of a personality. What are your own personality traits that help you as a producer?
SE: I think enthusiasm and passion and persistence. For me, persistence has been number one. You just have to keep going, no matter what. And, being a creative problem solver, resourceful.

CK: What do you think the role of ethics plays in being a producer?
SE: I've worked in production on and off for over 25 years—on feature films and television and documentaries—and I've been disappointed many times in terms of ethics. Our success on *Dog Whisperer*, and our initial success in getting Cesar to sign with us, was that we went to see what he needed to feel comfortable. And we gave it to him. I told him, "If you give us this free option and tomorrow Stephen Spielberg comes and says, 'I want to make a movie about you,' we're not going to say no—I'm not going to stand in the way of your success. We want to get your message out—what we believe in about you. We think what you do is incredible but we're not going to stand in the way."

We aren't big producers ourselves. My partner, Kay, was a producer in Canada and she had her own shows—a lot of other shows—and this is really my first show as a producer. I think the reason that Cesar eventually signed with us was because we made it comfortable for him. We wanted him to be himself. We didn't want him to have to be somebody else, we weren't going to mold him into somebody. So I don't know if that's ethics, but I think it's a sensitivity to whoever it is, and to your talent. It may sound a little hokey but I think being honest is a good way to be in life. It works.

There are a lot of unethical people out there. They're dealing with large sums of money, and that kind of money has a tendency to not bring out the best in people (laughs). The dogs—they know. They don't care if you're a big TV producer or if you sell doughnuts—they know if you've got weird energy or not.

CK: What was your start in producing, prior to Cesar and his dogs?
SE: I'll give you the fast version of a long story. I was at UCLA studying Interpersonal and Mass Media Communications, and I saw how the media influences our lives—what we think and buy and eat. I was very idealistic, and wanted to produce socially significant films. I just woke up one morning and said that—like that's what I want to do! So I got on the phone and started calling production companies. Plus, in my film class at UCLA, a talent manager came and spoke and I asked him afterwards to give me a name of a director that directs like a European. You know, like I'm a sophomore in college. That's what I wanted…a European director—not like some crummy old American (laughs). And he gave me a name and I just kept calling this movie director's manager, until finally one of them said I should get in the Screen Extra's Guild because then I can be on the set, and get insurance, and meet people and ask questions.

So I was an extra. I got into the Screen Extra's Guild and every show that I was on, I would talk with the producer and the director, and tell them what I wanted to do, and see if they had a job, and I just kept talking and talking and calling. I called Ray Stark, I called him every single day for I think three months. Finally he said, "Who is Sheila Possner and what does she want??" (laughs). Somebody had told me that he made *Funny Girl* and I liked that movie so I just kept calling and calling and calling him, till he gave me a job on a feature as a production assistant. Finally.

And when I got one job, then I just kind of bounced around between different jobs and I was always starving. Then, you get on a show and they pay you $200 a week, and it would be over and then do it over and over again. And I said, OK, I've had it. My career has been in and out of TV and film. I got to the point where I just couldn't take it anymore. I'd try to be normal and do something else and then I'd just come back to it again. I moved to New York and worked on a couple more films and then I came back to L.A. to do the Peter Stark Producing Program.

Actually, (laughs) I gave Ray Stark the idea for that program. One day, I was talking to him and I said, "You know, wouldn't it be great to go to school and learn how to do all this?" I was so frustrated, you know, trying to make something happen, and to learn. It was so hard as a production assistant to get up the ladder. This was back in the '70s, when there weren't a lot of women in the business. When I was working on one of Ray's films, I would write him letters and I'd say, "This is what I learned today." It was so emotional for me, I'd call him and I'd give him my progress report, this is what I learned today. When I came back off the film, I told him, "Ray, there needs to be some kind of a program that you can go to, and learn producing."

And that was it. He never said anything to me. Then I moved to New York and was working as a temp when I looked at *Variety* and I saw this tiny one-inch ad—it was complete serendipity that I happened to pick this up—and there it was, the Peter Stark Producing Program at USC. Of course I applied, and I was in the second class that they had there.

CK: Where did you go from there?
SE: From there, I moved to Spain. I worked on a lot of different films, like *Paris, Texas*— that was my art film. I worked for Hal Ashby, and then I got into television because film was just so slow. I saw the show on TV, *Heroes, Made in the USA*, and this is my quality of persistence. I just saw the show, saw who produced it in the end credits, called him up and said, "I love your show—I'll work on it for free." And that was how I got started in TV. I worked for free, and then the next season they hired me.

That's how I got into reality TV. *Heroes, Made in the USA* was all about heroes and it's so positive—it was just my thing. It's the best job I ever had in my life. It was just wonderful. From there, I worked on all the junky reality shows that you can work on. And then I got on *Rescue 911*, which was a really good show. After that, I couldn't think of any more ideas, so I left America and lived in Barcelona, Spain for eight years.

CK: And what made you come back?
SE: In Barcelona, I helped start the Barcelona Film Commission, and I got into international TV sales, and going to the markets—MIP and MipCom. They needed people who knew television, and who could speak English. That was really great. I came home because I saw into my future in Spain. There were a lot of women in their forties who were foreigners, who were single and broke. We all had fun but OK, I've had enough fun. I'm done here. Eight years…that's a long time.

CK: Speaking of the international market, what sort of global presence does The Dog Whisperer *have?*
SE: Oh, there's an incredible international presence. It's everywhere. It's all over the world, and it just gets better and better with every season.

CK: Do you have to make any modifications for foreign sales, other than the language? Do you ever have to edit it differently, or think about it differently?
SE: No. It's the same show. And there are certain countries, Spain being one of them, and Japan, who we're talking to about shooting some segments in those countries.

CK: Are you finding that some of your material is now going into the new media world?
SE: Oh yes. The international phone rights are taken, and they're working on that. There are so many different avenues for the webisodes. Cesar did some "webinars" where people would pay a fee for what would be like a live seminar. I know there are all different kind of plans of what to do with Cesar in the new media. We're entertaining the idea of him going, well, everywhere.

CK: All of a sudden, it's possible to do anything with one basic idea.
SE: Right. Because of the technology. These digital cameras now? People can make a show—make a movie. That's what I like. The industry is just so hard to get into, you know, unless you have a lot of money. Now, people that have an idea of some kind of media that they want to share can put things on YouTube—the sky's the limit now. It's wide open for people to be as creative as they can possibly be.

CK: All this is truly wonderful, but when you're through work, you go home to a second life with a very small person…
SE: Oh my God. That's my two-year old.

CK: How do you find your balance in all of this?
SE: Well, it's really great that you asked. I have to say that's where my attention is right now. It's balancing, because working in television is very tiring, and I have *two* jobs. Plus, we have Millan, Inc., which is the company and I'm in meetings for that, and then the show itself. There are no excuses, I have to be on top of it because this is a team effort, and everybody has to do their part, and nobody really cares if you were up half the night.

That's the thing about TV: if we're lucky enough to have a show, you have to go with it—because as an independent producer, it's like now, the money is here now, but when we're done, then what? So there's that, and then I have a two-year old who keeps going every day and I don't want to look back in 10 years, and go, what happened? I wasn't there, so fortunately we go to music class once a week and we go to Mommy and Me, and I'm going to work it out in the fifth season to maybe have a four-day work week, and work some from home.

I'm definitely committed to having it work out. I'll be a much nicer wife, and I'll be there for my son if I'm not working so much. You know, we've been shooting for nine months straight, and we're all stressed. We're tired; everybody's tired and I'm tired-er than they are (laughs). But I'm committed to making it work—and reading books on how to do it. Believe me.

CK: The more you have to do, the more you can get done?
SE: I think that's true, but then if you go over the line, you just can't do anything. Sometimes I come home and I just think—I can't believe what I did today. The multi-tasking, the number of people that I spoke to on the phone, and the energy that it takes to get new projects going. You can't take your eye off of anything!

CK: Knowing what you know—as a producer and a person—what advice would you share?
SE: I would encourage people to follow their dreams. See, I'm a big believer in personal growth. I did Landmark Education for over 25 years, but I think do anything that causes one to be more effective as a person.

And, to be a good producer—I mean a *good* producer—you're going to be as evolved as possible. I would encourage people to do some form of personal growth—whatever kind—and be available to themselves to make something happen. To be really "in" the possibility of what's possible and to really make a difference. Because I look at media, and I look at movies that are beautiful and the acting is incredible. But the story? It's not inspiring….

No, I would encourage people to make media that makes a difference. To not be dependent, to be independent. Buy a little camera and go make something. Take a class on how to write a good screenplay. Stay true to their vision of what they want to do and hopefully, I would say, how to be worth the energy and effort that it takes to get something done. But I really think that's the most important thing, because you study and be up on all the different ways that people can see a project, looking at all this new media. It's tremendous, now, the possibilities that are available to people.

CK: You started out in this business wanting to make films that have something to say, something socially relevant. Clearly, you still believe that's possible.
SE: When we first started, our first season, we would shoot two stories in one day. We didn't have a motor home, so Cesar would change clothes on the street. I did his makeup, and I remember putting all the powder and stuff on the hood of somebody's car parked on the street. Now, here we are—four seasons later—we have a motor home now, and a lot more. It really changes if you can hang in there, it gets better.

I really believe that. If you have a good idea, go and shoot it. You don't need all the equipment and everything that was needed so many years ago. Now you can make it happen. You know, hook up with good people that you admire and that you can learn from. That's challenging, it takes some effort. You want to create an environment that makes it as fun and wonderful as possible.

CK: How much do people skills enter into producing?
SE: I think it's really important—one of the most important qualities in a producer is the ability to get along with people. You have to get along because you need to work with people of all different kinds of temperament, and must get along with everyone. Everyone!

BARBARA GAINES
Executive Producer, *The Late Show with David Letterman*

CK: As an Executive Producer, what is it that you do?
BG: This is a question my mother went to her grave asking. "What exactly do you do? Did you talk to any celebrities? What can I tell my friends?" There are actually nine "Emmy eligible" producers, and four of us are Executive Producers.

CK: How do you divide producing responsibilities among you?
BG: Rob Burnett is the CEO/President of Worldwide Pants, Dave Letterman's production company. The company's shows include our namesake program, *The Late Show with David Letterman*, *Everybody Loves Raymond*, and *The Late Late Show with Craig Ferguson*. Maria Pope is in charge of the talent department, Jude Brennan is our liaison with the network (CBS), the press, the world. And me, Barbara Gaines.

What is it I do? Let's see. I routine the show (order and times), I oversee all of production. I'm really what we used to call a Floor Producer. Beginning in July of 2002, now I man the podium. I think Dave would probably say out of the five people who have had this job I'm not the best, and I'm not the worst.

CK: And your day-to-day job? What does that look like?
BG: First thing in the morning, I send an intern for coffee. I have a Starbucks and cereal for breakfast. Then I participate in a production meeting where the staff discusses the bones of the show and I make determinations about how much time things will take. I ask for a certain number of segment questions/acts of comedy accordingly. Back in my office, I discuss or write notes to Dave about the bones of the show and make adjustments according to his desires. I go over the jokes for the Act One comedy segments and pitch/cut jokes accordingly, and discuss with the head writers how to change the comedy to suit Dave's needs.

Throughout that process I answer budget questions, personnel questions, scheduling questions, and listen to people complain about their coworkers. Around 12:30, I revise the official rundown for the day's rehearsal, with all of the elements to be rehearsed or pretaped filled in. Then I meet with people from the talent department about future bookings and have a nice lunch.

Around 2:00 I go down to the stage for rehearsal where I watch the tapes the writers have cut, see the graphics married to the jokes for the first time, or listen to the stage manager stand in for Dave. While I'm in rehearsal, I try to get more answers from Dave about how he feels about the show.

Then I come up to my office. I read and answer even more email about booking, budget, and personnel problems. I make a revised rundown as a guide for the pitches in Dave's dressing room. I may have a light snack. Around 4:20 I go to Dave's dressing room and continue to discuss the elements of that night's show, including guest segment notes/questions. Around 4:45 I participate with the Head Writers/Producers in pitching the comedy to Dave. Then I make a list of suggestions from those pitches and choose a running order for the comedy in Act One. Dave looks at it, asks for changes, and I make adjustments.

Then I go down to the show and set the desk and stand at the podium onstage so that I can produce the show. I talk to the control room about segment orders and running times and make decisions on the spot about what to do in the next segment. I tell Dave what I think we should do during the commercial breaks and try to take care of problems that arise during the taping. Then I come upstairs and start to choose edits for the show. I give the edit room ins and outs and show the edits to Dave and discuss with him their merits and make changes according to his desires. I eat a nice dinner at my desk. I may also listen to staffers complain again, read and answer yet more email with questions and concerns about bookings, budgets, and staff issues. And also get the information from the writers about what they plan to do the next day and make a rundown for the production meeting.

Then I put the show to bed and remain vaguely nauseous at the thought that someone may (and half the time will) call me between 11:35 and the end of the show's broadcast (12:37) to tell me about things that were wrong (which I'll then fix for West Coast feeds).

CK: People think of the show as a late-night talk show, but you think of it as a variety show. What's the difference?
BG: I would most certainly call the show a variety show (not a talk show). A talk show is one that is built around talk—we always felt our show was built around comedy. I would call *SCTV* and *Saturday Night Live* sketch shows. And for that matter, I would not call Dave Letterman a talk-show host, I would call him a broadcaster. *Donahue, Oprah, The View*—they are talk shows.

And while there are a hundred syndicated and local talk shows, the variety show is not as easy. Just ask Joey Bishop, Jerry Lewis, Chevy Chase, and Arsenio Hall—the legends. I think the idea of a "talk show" came in the early '60s when shows began to drop the sketches and the jugglers and just talk to people. In some way I suppose after the years went by, the talk shows started to add back music, comics, and then with us, the sketch as well. Carson, the greatest of them all, did comedy bits but not to our extent.

CK: In 2002, the show won an Emmy and you went on stage to accept it on behalf of the producers' team. Can you remember what you said?
BG: It went like this…"I started as the receptionist on Dave's morning show over 25 years ago. We've all worked for Dave forever *(turned to other producers)* which I think

shows what kind of man Dave is, that he inspires that kind of loyalty. Dave always says, 'All credit to the team.' We're just a very small part of that team. And we, of course, say all credit to Dave. This *(held up the Emmy Award)* is all Dave. We want to thank our very wonderful staff and crew; they are the hardest working group of men and women in the world. They're up there *(pointed to the balcony)*. And we'd like to thank the Academy for thinking that after 20 years on the air; we still put on a quality show. On behalf of *The Late Show*, thank you very much."

CK: So what's next? What do you see happening in the future of television?
BG: In the future, people are going to spend more time on the Internet. They will use their televisions simply as monitors for their computer. I think the Internet/monitor will make things more interactive. No longer will you just sit on the couch and watch.

CK: This interview wouldn't be complete without asking the obvious: What are the Top Ten Things that an Executive Producer needs to know?
BG: The Top Ten Things you need to be a good Executive Producer:

1. Loyalty to the host and show that borders on insanity.
2. A long fuse.
3. A small ego.
4. Attention to detail.
5. Organizational ability.
6. Ability to make a split-second decision.
7. Learn to take a joke.
8. Pick your battles.
9. Good listening skills.
10. Snappy dresser.

RICHARD HENNING
Audio Engineer

The Top Ten Things a Producer Should Understand about Working with a Small Crew:

1. While working on a large production can be fun and exciting, like the circus coming to town, with everyone busy, busy with their areas of expertise, a scaled down crew of producer, cameraman, and soundman has its own set of challenges and rewards. A smaller production team has the ability to stealthily slip in and out of locations with a minimal amount of disruption and clamor, which is especially valuable in documentary, news, and "behind the scenes" shooting.
2. Many of the specialized jobs in the larger productions are absorbed by the three key players on a smaller job:
   - The producer might double as the art director and craft services department.
   - The cameraman is also the lighting department.
   - The soundman may be the gaffer and transportation department.
     On a smaller shoot everyone crosses over to assist the others when needed, something which is taboo on larger union shoots, where a soundman wouldn't even think of touching a light, and a producer wouldn't powder a guest's shiny nose, and could be penalized for doing so.

3. The relationships between a successful team of producer, cameraman, and soundman are more intimate, with a knowledge of each other's needs, limitations, and working styles, for they usually have less time and fewer hands to get the job done.

4. When a producer hires a cameraman (or "DP", director of photography), the DP will hire the soundman, usually someone he has worked with before so they are an experienced team. The DP can also find any additionally needed personnel such as a lighting designer or teleprompter operator.

5. It's key that the producer choose a DP who is not only skilled in his job, but is someone who is easy to communicate with and is flexible under sometimes tense or hurried working conditions. A simpatico working relationship goes a long, long way in making the shoot run smoothly and efficiently.

6. When a producer first starts working with a new cameraman, a monitor is essential to check the footage to see if you're both on the same page. Once a good working relationship has been established between the producer and camera team, and the producer has been satisfied that the cameraman has understood, executed, and, hopefully, enhanced her vision, she can lose her dependence on the monitor, and develop the trust and shorthand necessary to expedite the shoot.

7. The camera and the sound mixer are tethered together by a cable that is commonly referred to as the "umbilical cord." When they're working with hand-held cameras, the cameraman and soundman have to be acutely aware of each others' position and anticipate each others' movements in order to coordinate the camera shot and the boom placement, and the myriad cables that have to be reined in or let out. In a volatile news-gathering situation, where other crews are present and fighting for the best shot, it's easy to see why these two have to be a well-oiled machine.

8. On a smaller, portable production, the soundman is usually working with a mixer that has three or four inputs, but only two outputs—right and left—that feed the camera's VTR:
   - If employing two inputs, the outputs are kept separate, unmixed.
   - If using more than two inputs, there is usually a discussion between producer and soundman as to which inputs are mixed, and the dials are set before the camera starts to roll.

   There is usually very little mixing while the sound is being recorded, as the editor appreciates receiving as clean and separate sound as possible.

9. In a sit-down interview situation, when only the talent is being recorded, the best and safest sound comes from using two separate mics—a clip-on lavalier and a directional mic mounted on a boom pole and stand—pointing from above towards the talent. If both the interviewer and interviewee are to be recorded, then a lavalier is clipped onto each of them and the sound, unmixed, is sent to two different channels. Once an audio level is set, and the camera rolls, a slight level adjustment might be made, but abrupt or constant adjusting is not only unnecessary, but an editor's nightmare. The soundman then stays attentive and focused on what's coming through the headset.

10. If there is any audio problem during a take, like a barking dog, honking horn, or low-flying plane, the soundman will wait until the take is finished and alert the producer as to the location and severity of the problem. The producer can then decide whether a retake is necessary.

ANN KOLBELL
Supervising Producer (Peacock Productions, NBC News)
MATT LOMBARDI
Producer *(CBS Evening News with Katie Couric)*

CK: You've both kindly agreed to be interviewed together because your career paths have intersected for years. Let's go back to before you met.

AK: My career in television began, interestingly enough, through radio, when I interviewed Jane Pauley, then anchor for *The Today Show,* for a public radio program I was hosting in Ann Arbor, Michigan. I created the opportunity to meet her because I was looking to move to a television producing job.

CK: And you knew what producing was, as an actual job description?

AK: Yes. I developed a series called *Women in Broadcasting*, which gave me an opportunity to talk to women broadcasters. Jane Pauley was one of the women I interviewed, and it was a really good one because I was well prepared. By the end of the interview we had established a good rapport, and I grabbed the chance to pitch myself as a prospective producing colleague. I outlined a job proposal that I thought might appeal to Jane. I had identified what I thought might be a need, and then speculated on how I might be helpful. I had read an article about Barbara Walters and her assistant producer who was described as Barbara's right hand with responsibilities of a substantive editorial nature. I figured that Jane, having been on the job for only two years at that point, probably hadn't yet formed a relationship like that with anyone yet. Plus, I had already been working seven years and had a resume and experience of my own to offer. As it turned out, I was right. Jane and I hit it off, kept in touch, and I started working with her six months later. We worked together for the next 24 years until the end of her NBC News career.

CK: What were you hoping you would be doing with Jane then? What did you propose?

AK: I was interested in content, specifically, news content. I knew how to organize things, I was reasonably smart, and I knew how to research. I think those were some of the skills I offered up.

CK: Did you start off as a producer?

AK: Because of personnel considerations, I was initially hired as a researcher, but eventually I became a producer.

CK: Your turn, Matt. How did you start as a producer?

ML: I carried my tape recorder with me everywhere as a kid. I had this odd fascination with recording things and playing them back. I taped everything. I even brought my video camera to school. By the time I was old enough to try and figure out what I was supposed to do for a living, all I really knew was I wanted to continue this process of recording something and making it into something else. Film school was sort of a logical step in my mind because I was working in a movie theater at the time. I thought, "This is how you go to Hollywood, you work in a movie theater and go to film school." I enrolled at The School of Visual Arts in New York City. While I was there, my parents were sort of kicking me in the butt saying "You really ought to have some plan after school" and I had none. They suggested I get an internship somewhere. So, ironically, at the same time I'm excelling in my career at the movie theater (I'm now the manager hiring box-office cashiers), one of the applicants said, "I can't work on Fridays because I have an internship at NBC." I said, "That's interesting. I'm actually looking for an internship, how do you get one?" She said, "It's easy, they'll hire anyone for free."

So I got an internship at NBC, but I was late getting to the party because it was the end of August, when the internships for the fall are already taken. So they said, "We've got one left and it's at *The Today Show,* have you ever watched it?" I said no. And they said, "It's yours if you want it. Take it or leave it." So I took it. Around my first week, I met someone named Ann Kolbell—who is my partner in this interview—who was working for Jane Pauley. But within a week of my starting, Jane announced she was leaving *The Today Show* after 13 years.

CK: How did you and Ann begin working together?
ML: This was in October of 1989. Talk about identifying a need! Ann identified a need for someone to answer the phones, which were going crazy because Jane had just made this announcement and the mail is pouring in, literally by the buckets full, everyday. It was impossible for anybody to keep up. So I was the intern, I met Ann, and she basically brought me into Jane's office and gave me five buckets full of mail and said, "Please sort these. If the phone rings, answer it." The real breakthrough was three months later when Jane was actually going to leave the show. Ann hurt her back, and couldn't be in the office for Jane's last week. And Ann said, "I'm going to need help. I know you have school and two jobs, but if you can be 'me' for the next month and extend your internship into the next semester, you will have a job when you graduate from school." She guaranteed it. So there you go. I graduated on a Friday and started on the payroll at NBC on the following Monday.

CK: So now fast-forward to the present. Can you describe your jobs?
ML: When I was a *Dateline* producer, I sort of likened my job to making movies because your role is very much like that of the director. Producing for TV and producing for film are very different. A lot of people say they're the same; I think they're very different, especially in news. What's unique about producing for news is you really have the entire finished product from the time it's budgeted, researched, to the time it's shot, to the time it's written and, ultimately, to the time it's edited and aired; it's your baby. From conception to the broadcast, you're really responsible, in some way, for every bit of it.

From the moment a story is assigned you are responsible for conceptualizing it, trying to figure out what it's ultimately supposed to be, and hopefully being open to it changing if that's editorially what's supposed to happen, budgeting for it responsibly, then getting it on the air. Currently, I am a producer for the *CBS Evening News with Katie Couric*, and although the mission of the show is obviously different than that of a news magazine, the process of producing is not very dissimilar.

CK: Ann, you've worked for NBC for most of your professional life. What are you doing these days?
AK: I am the Supervising Producer for Peacock Productions, the long-form production unit for NBC News. We produce programs that air in many venues—the network, cable (MSNBC, A&E, Discovery, The History Channel, among others), the Internet, in schools—we are content providers for pretty much any delivery system. We also do a good amount of international business. Basically, we're for hire. Our mission is to deliver quality content, and make money in the process. We have a very eclectic portfolio.

As Supervising Producer, it's my job to keep track of everything that's going on. I deal with personnel, assign producers to projects, and coordinate the flow of information within our unit. I deal with management, producers, finance people, lawyers, marketing, and so on. I am also the Supervising Producer of a weekly syndicated program, *Your Total Health*, where I have a substantive editorial role. It gives me a chance for more hands-on producing which I continue to enjoy.

CK: Matt, how similar is the TV producer's job to the film producer's?
ML: Between film and TV? Well, I've never been fortunate enough to follow my dream of producing for film, but from what I understand, producers for film have limited control over the film in that, at a certain point, the director is the person who really controls the editorial content of the film. He controls the editing and the shooting; specifically "the look" of each shot is the director's.

A list of duties for a film producer can be anywhere from the budget, to scouting the locations, to hiring the crew and casting the film. But ultimately, at some point, the producer is going, "Well okay, Mr. Director, we brought you all this wonderful stuff, now go make a film out of it." With producing for TV, the final product is, ultimately, your whole responsibility. The producer's cap is a big one because you have responsibility for the entire thing, which is more fun, I think. For me, particularly at *Dateline*, I was half living my dream because I could sort of control all these little movies I made. It was fun, in that every segment is different so you never really had a chance to get bored, at least I didn't for that reason.

CK: You are both producers. You've worked with one another for years, and you work with dozens of other producers from all areas of film and television. What traits or personalities do they share, if any?
AK: In terms of personality traits, a producer is likely a person who is probably pretty organized because that's important to the job. Not everybody's methods are the same, but most producers have a system that somehow works for them. They are probably detail oriented. And many are good collaborators.

ML: To produce anything, I think you need to have some communication skills because you end up turning over a lot of work to other people. When you go out on location, you're trusting a cameraman and a soundman. You are not operating the equipment; you're turning it over to them, and hoping that what you have asked this crew to capture is what will ultimately wind up on the tape. You're putting your faith in those people. It happens to be unique to news where the producers have to turn over the editing of the piece to another person, in this case, an editor. Graphics—once again—you're not physically designing the graphics. Someone else is designing the graphics. So you need to be able to communicate an idea to a series of individuals who, hopefully, will be able to interpret your vision and translate it onto tape.

Even in the research stage, it's almost impossible to do all the research yourself so at some point, you have other individuals who are pulling research for you. You have to be able to trust that those people are finding the information that you want. I think all producers are control freaks and the irony of that is that you really don't have control over any of it. The entire thing at some point is turned over to different people and you're hoping and praying that it comes back to you in the way you envisioned it.

And even when it goes on the air, you've turned it over to someone in a control room somewhere. You have to pray that the settings are right, that the vector scope is the way it's supposed to be, and that the luminescence level is where it's supposed to be. You go home and watch it on the air and you cringe sometimes because you realize that something was way off. It's weird stuff like that you really have no control over.

AK: Keep in mind what Matt's talking about is taking place in a network environment. Obviously, at a local station, you are doing a lot of these things yourself so you're not turning it over. I think that's important to remember. And nowadays at the networks, there's less of a reliance on full crews; we're seeing more and more of the digital journalist—the one-person band who produces, shoots, and edits her own work [also called a 'preditor']. The digital journalist is likely the network model for the future.

ML: If you look at *60 Minutes* now, the style of the way they tell stories is almost identical to the way it was 30 years ago. The biggest change is they went to shooting it on film to video, which I think was a big leap for them. I mean this technically. Visually, the show looks exactly the same. As one example, if I did a profile of Bob Dylan, which they did awhile back, I'd probably have about 40 edits in a two-minute period. Because I would be cutting to music I would probably have a shot change on almost on every downbeat, every drum roll. Because I grew up on MTV, that's how I'm used to seeing things. In contrast, *60 Minutes* would probably have 40 edits in a 10-minute profile.

CK: You've both talked to hundreds of students in producing for television classes. What insights and advice have you shared with these students?
AK: You have to be flexible. Not all producers are flexible, but the good ones are. You have to be creative. Take initiative. Be willing to see the gray when you're telling a story; not everything is always black and white. Find a mentor, someone who has been in the business for a good amount of time, and whose opinion you value. And work on your writing skills; a good writer will have a huge advantage in the job market.

ML: You have to have the willingness to collaborate, and definitely the ability to tell a story. At the end of the day, you're telling stories. You have to be able to structure a story so that someone knows what you're talking about. In the news field, the challenge for a news producer is that nine times out of 10, you are writing a story for someone else's voice. One of the functions of a news producer is to write a story and collaborate with the on-air talent. If you don't have the writing skills to write a story and collaborate with someone who may have a different vision for that story, you're not going to be very happy.

JEFFREY MCLAUGHLIN
Senior Editor, Director of Postproduction, All Mobile Video in New York City

CK: As an editor, you have been a great resource in the writing of this book's chapter on postproduction. You give the art and process of editing a lot of thought, don't you?
JM: You know, if I were to write a book on editing, I would start with George Bush's quote on the Battleship USS Abraham Lincoln in May of 2003. It was at that point that he proclaimed to the American public, "Mission accomplished," in response to the war on Iraq—which of course is still very active, years later, and is in no way done.

I say this because I have been editing for 30 years, and I've worked with producers who think that after they write the story, raise the money, and shoot the project, they've won the war. Little do they know that the real mission has just begun.

Editing is part of the process, and in my estimation, the most important part of the process. Don't celebrate too much at the "wrap party" on the last day of shooting, because there is still much work to be done.

CK: What are the main qualities that a producer should look for in an editor?
JM: Each editor is different. In terms of "a style," most editors fall into one of these three categories. Then off those categories, there are numerous combinations and degrees.

Category 1 is the storyteller. This is a classic editor who is able to take footage and script and tell a story. He or she is "an author of images." If you need someone who can sit through hours of footage and come up with a cohesive story with a good pace, this is your candidate.

Category 2 is the graphic artist. This category did not exist a few years ago. An editor always edited, and a graphic artist always designed. Now, that line between these two is fading. An editor's style has as much to do with their look as their pacing. Editing is not always storytelling as much as it's the layering of images and graphics. This editor doesn't see story as much they see energy and image. I was critical of this nonnarrative style for years, but have grown to appreciate it when it is done well.

Category 3 is the technical editor. This is an editor who isn't always the go-to person for creativity, yet is often the one every producer should worship. They are important in the preproduction stage as well as the postproduction stage. No matter how creative you may be, the final look of your project better be technically solid.

Recently, a fourth group of editors has begun to take shape. They are producer/editors or "preditors"—one person who writes, produces, shoots, and edits a project. Traditionally, roles between producer, writer, cameraman, director, and editor were more defined. Within the last few years with the influx of inexpensive cameras and edit systems that are also very easy to master, many people are becoming one-man bands.

This is both good and bad. In the past, the edit room was a place where magic could happen (if you were lucky) because the editor had a fresh eye that wasn't emotionally attached to the footage or the shoot. Though one person alone can also be a creative process, in our industry it's beneficial to have the input of others' creative visions, too.

CK: So in knowing this, how does a producer find the right editor?
JM: Look at the project first, then look at your own skills. How creative are you in making editing decisions? Are you organized? Do you have the time or the budget to experiment? What "type" of editing style will benefit your vision? The obvious choice would be an editor who possesses all skills equally, but that's not always possible. Plus, each project is different and each project needs a different style. Look at your project and your skills and keep these categories in mind when interviewing editors.

Another factor in choosing your editor is based on organization. If you and your project are totally unorganized, make your first priority an editor who is obsessive-compulsive. If you do have an organized work style, look for someone who is looser and less predictable, and probably more creative.

Communication skills between the producer and the editor are a must. After your marriage, your relationship with your editor is going to be the most stressful relationship of your life. Think about it: you and this editor will be sitting in a room together for 10 to 12 hours a day, six or seven days a week, till the project has been completed. You are going to be sharing your dreams with this editor, and he or she is going to disagree with almost everything you want to do.

It can get rough in an edit room, but like a marriage, it's all about trust. Make sure your editor trusts your vision, and vice versa. The final result always looks better when there's peace in the house. The TV and new media business is a collaborative world. Listen to your vision and follow that vision, but look to the editor for outside help. You can get so engrossed in your idea that you may need a new more objective voice.

CK: What has been your career path in editing?
JM: I have been editing since 1976—I started editing in film, on a flatbed. Now, I edit in video, on whatever tools come my way that can make editing better, easier, and cheaper. I became an editor because I felt that it was the single most important step of the whole film-making process. It was also a job where my OCD tendencies actually worked in my favor.

I don't prefer one software program or one product over another. I found out through the years that the process is always getting better. To adopt one edit system over another works for individual projects, but not for career decisions. Editing is always changing and there is always a newer software out there that could benefit a project.

CK: What do producers need to know when they come into the postproduction facility?
JM: Walking into the final stage of your project—editing—without any preparation is a mistake many producers make. Planning the budget, the script, and the shoot are obvious to every producer, but planning, or at least being aware of, some issues you will face in postproduction are just as important. No matter how good your budget is going along, or how good the script is, or how magical the shooting may have felt—you eventually have to put all the pieces together and make it work. You can blow a good film in the edit room, or you can save a bad one.

One of editors' golden assets in an edit process is that they were never part of the production process. They weren't shooting the film for four weeks and feeling the "magic" of that process. The war stories the crew told about shooting in the midst of a hurricane or when half the staff came down with food poisoning—they mean nothing to the editor. Editors only see the dailies, and the only "magic" they feel is what comes out of those dailies. If a shot works, they will use it, but if it doesn't, they can easily let it go. The pain, the love, or the cost of any one element means nothing if it doesn't work in the edit. No one thing is more important than the whole of the film.

CK: When you were a student studying filmmaking and editing, what were some of the lessons then that have stuck with you?
JM: It's really important to understand the unique vocabulary of television and film, and now, new media. As you develop your skills as a producer, be aware of the medium that you are working in and the visual and audio vocabulary that is part of the process.

The history of editing has always fascinated me. In 1918, I think, a Russian filmmaker, Lev Kuleshov, realized that film possessed its own language and its own grammatical rules for that language. He conducted an experiment in the use of montage that's come to be called the Kuleshov Effect. This was a short film sequence that began with a neutral expression close-up of a man, an actor from the day. Kuleshov then intercut this same neutral shot back and forth between shots of a bowl of soup, an old woman lying in a coffin, and a little girl playing. The filmmakers showed these sequences to audiences and asked them to comment on the actor's performance.

The responses of the audiences were that the actor's face showed hunger, sorrow, and joy. The varied reactions were caused by the juxtaposition of the neutral expression with other shots—the soup, the coffin, the girl. The conclusion of this experiment was that film has its own language. The juxtaposition of images creates a meaning. Editing creates the meaning. The audience feels the emotions through the relationship between shots. I read about this experiment at age 21 and it changed my life. I saw the power of editing and realized what it could do. It's a communications tool with endless potential if you understand how to use it.

CK: How important is telling the truth in editing?
JM: Whether you're a producer of documentaries, a narrative filmmaker, or a TV commercial producer, you have the power to tell the truth, or make it up. For example, most Americans think of the Civil War as it was portrayed in *Gone with the Wind*. The facts of John F. Kennedy's assassination are now deeply rooted in Oliver Stone's film, *JFK*. Fox TV and Bill O'Reilly show the "truth" every day and they inform a large audience, while Michael Moore shows another "truth" that is equally convincing.

What are your responsibilities to the truth? If you are searching for truth you have to tell the truth. It is easy to slant your side. If you are interpreting the truth you are making propaganda. History paints this picture of the German filmmaker, Leni Riefenstahl, as the master of evil propaganda. Her films portrayed Hitler and the Nazis as heroes. She was able to do this because she understood editing. She only showed what she wanted you to see. A "well-edited" documentary can make any war seem justified or evil. TV commercials can make beer and high-fat hamburgers seem like something we have to eat. As a producer, you can take a stand, and be aware of your power and the different rules that TV images and their juxtaposition can follow.

CK: When you start a project with a producer, what is involved in that process?
JM: Often I try to meet with producers prior to the edit, but often I come into the project after it has been completely shot. I usually meet the producers on the first day of editing when they show up with a suitcase of tapes. They tell me how much time they have booked to edit the piece, yet usually don't realize how much footage they have shot. Sometimes they have roughly a hundred hours worth of film that they want to cut in the next two weeks.

I first ask them for notes and scripts. If I'm lucky, they'll have those, but more and more producers seem to think that editors wave a magic wand over hours worth of footage, and only the good stuff comes up. I remind them that if we first need to screen, log, and digest the material, and then make an insightful and coherent movie, it's going to take time. For every one hour of footage, it takes at least two or three hours to view, log, and highlight clips. You then need to knock this down into a script with some kind of theme, and only then can you start to edit.

Many producers don't get this, especially if they're new at the job, or when there's a time deadline. Editing doesn't start until you have control of the script and the images. Screening and taking notes of the footage is a major part of this process, and it has to be dealt with before you structure the project. Editing is not an abstract art where you throw paint on a canvas until it looks good. Editing works best when it's planned out.

CK: The budgeting process for postproduction can be an area that the producer gets nervous about—even the most experienced producer can get bogged down here.
JM: Budgets can be real, but they fall apart when producers lose control of the project. They have to find a fine line, for example, between allowing some experimentation but not too much. A producer wants to give both the client and the editor the control they demand, while maintaining the overall vision of the project.

How do you play the middle? Know your clients, know your postproduction people. Be in control, but allow creativity and open up your budget for that extra time. As a producer, your golden rule is to always be prepared. You are in a creative business, so sometimes even the best preparation is not enough. At that point look to the future and learn from your mistakes.

The biggest mistake producers make in budgeting is the fact they don't budget enough for post and tend to hope that things will work out at the end. One example is a producer who spent $5,000 on a helicopter shoot for 10 seconds of footage, yet didn't have even $5,000 in her budget for the entire postproduction budget. I don't get it. How could a 10-second shot equal the entire editing process?

CK: Conventional wisdom assures us that a good story is always at the core of editing a project. How do you tell that story as an editor?
JM: I'll give you an example. One of my favorite films of all times was made by Steven Spielberg when he was 25. It was called *Duel*. It's a story of a man driving his car who is being followed by a giant black tractor trailer—period. The entire plot is this one sentence, yet it is a great 90 minutes of nonstop tension and action. The guy in his car, played by Dennis Weaver, has one goal: to escape from this truck on his tail. That's it. But the editing created conflict, tension, split-second timing, and so on, and made this a classic.

CK: You work with producers each day. What advice would you give a producer who is starting out in the business?
JM: The easiest way to become a great producer is to work harder than any other producer. Try some writing, try directing, and definitely, try to learn more about editing. A good producer will try to walk in everyone's shoes. Sit behind an edit console and edit for 20-hour days for a couple of weeks and you will learn as much about how to produce your next project as you will about editing. Know the process—you don't have to necessarily master it. In the end it gives you more freedom and control over your project. And as with any job in TV, don't look at producing as a job. Look at it as part of your life.

CK: What do you most appreciate and hope for in a producer?
JM: I like anyone who respects me, laughs at my jokes, and asks me how my kids are doing—simple people skills.

There are many producers out there who lack creative talent. That's not necessarily a problem. It only becomes a problem when this lack of creativity turns into giving me attitude. An example is the producer who has no idea of what he wants, or how to take his footage and make it into a coherent idea. Sometimes, these producers try to mask the fact that they are essentially creatively clueless, or don't understand much about editing. So they'll give the editor no guidance and no real concept, and I've got to start from scratch and make something out of it all. You learn to accept this, it's part of the job.

If, as a producer, for whatever reason—like a time crunch or limited budget—you have to walk into an edit room totally unprepared, just admit it up front. Seek advice from the creatives around you and give them a semi-solution, or some direction. But don't give them attitude.

CK: Can you share your favorite examples of editing—film or television?
JM: My favorite examples…I've got a few that I really like. Films like *Duel* and of course, *Jaws*—especially the scene where everyone is told it is safe to go back in the water. There's also the Odessa Steps sequence in *Battleship Potemkin* that is a great example of early constructive editing. *Hearts and Minds* is a classic example of a good documentary—but like most documentaries, it is able to slant the viewer to the filmmaker's view. Leni Riefenstahl's films fall into the same category with her brilliant films that promoted the Nazi agenda.

A terrifying example of parallel editing is at the end of *Silence of the Lambs*, where Jodie Foster's character is meeting the killer who both she and the audience think is being arrested at another location. After a series of cuts between the bogus arrest and the look in Jodie Foster's eye, we find out that she is alone with the killer. This parallel editing was used when the damsel in distress was saved at the very last moment by the hero in countless early films.

Another important use of editing in film was D.W. Griffith's *The Birth of a Nation*. The film was made in 1915, and was so powerful in its depiction of the director's deluded racist vision of the south after the Civil War, that the KKK was able to come out of hiding for the next 50 years.

But it's important to look at the editing in anything you're watching—TV, films, content on the Internet. They're all examples of editing. Good editing, not-so-good editing, and editing that is really bad. When you can consciously study editing as the art form it is, you can learn to prepare for editing, and you can learn what and how to shoot in ways that work for editing later.

My final thought about editing—think of it as a Zen experience. It's a process that continues to ask questions and come up with solutions. It can be the ultimate journey.

BRETT MORGEN
Executive Producer, Producer, and Director (including *The Kid Stays in the Picture, Chicago 10, Nimrod Nation*)

CK: Brett, how do you decide if a project is better suited for television or for theatrical distribution?
BM: Sometimes you don't know when you start a show if it's going to end up on television or go theatrical. Often, people set out to do it for television, and the story takes on a sort of life of its own and you finish the piece and say, "Hey, this has theatrical potential." Most of the time, though, you know if it's intended for television or for theater when you start a production, and you need to be aware because the transition from TV to theater is so expensive. For example, if you're doing a television production, for an hour-long show, you'll do a one-day or two-day sound mix, tops! And a five-day sound mix is almost unheard of. I'll spend six weeks to three months doing a sound edit or a sound mix on a theatrical. In television, the bandwidth is so small that very few sounds cut through so it's a waste of time to even try a complex mix.

On television, your work is being seen by more people. I remember when *The Kid Stays in the Picture* went into theatrical release, we did 1.5 million dollars which at the time was, I think, the fifteenth highest earning theatrical documentary. But when it premiered on HBO, we had 1.6 million people watching it that first night, which was five times the amount of people who actually saw it in theaters. Then in subsequent viewings, we added it all up and it's probably now 30, 40 times the number of people who saw it in the theaters.

When you have a message you're trying to get across, you're much better off being on television than being in a movie theater, especially with a smaller type movie, say, about Romanian street children. You know people aren't going to pay to see it in a movie theater. Ultimately, however, if you're trying to get your message across, you're better off doing it as a fiction film anyway. Take a movie like *Hotel Rwanda*. Far more people will see *Hotel Rwanda* than will ever see a documentary about Rwanda.

I do think there are a lot of creative advantages to television—the immediacy, the amount of financing, funding—making it vastly superior to film, particularly now in cable television.

CK: When you develop a television project, do you want it on HBO or a major network?
BM: I think more people still watch the networks than anywhere else. In terms of sheer eyeballs, networks are the best, but getting a project on the networks is very challenging if not impossible. In terms of documentary—cable, premium, or PBS—I think it's a toss-up between HBO and PBS. I think HBO appeals more to our egos as filmmakers. It's sexier. However, PBS is available in every household in America. They're getting three million people watching per night, whereas HBO may get a million, a million plus. Their viewers are different in terms of social activism. On PBS you'll reach the grassroots; you'll reach your core audience a lot easier than on HBO. But then again, HBO is an easier exercise. If they're into your project, they'll finance it and there you go. I think a lot of filmmakers have qualms about PBS in terms of their national distribution and promotion. I did a series for PBS that ran at a different time on a different day in every city, and it was a nightmare to promote.

I think the most important thing for young producers, for television producers, is to understand that you can take the same pitch to about nine different places, but you need to alter that pitch for each place. So I think a lot of times when people come up with ideas, it's really helpful to know to whom you're pitching. Know which networks serve what audience, and is there a way to change certain aspects of your pitch so it appeals to different networks.

CK: OK...here's a hypothetical: let's say you've developed a show called Public Defenders. *You want to pitch it to a range of places. Talk us through that pitch process.*
BM: On Lifetime, it features all women public defenders, defenders with more feel-good stories, no rape, no sex abuse, no incest. Now, for truTV, they might say, "All right, we need more men in the show, because our demographics lean toward men, so the women need to be good-looking. Make it a little sexier and a little more hard-hitting." Take it to HBO, and either it becomes a family of public defenders or it's dealing with some of the most hard-core crimes around. And you take that same show to VH1 and it's former celebrities who are now lawyers.

Then, you take that to NBC and it's a reality show for a search for the world's greatest lawyer. The winner gets a contract working with Alan Dershowitz and they're going to compete against each other in an eight-week survival challenge. Guess what? It doesn't stop there. You can do a cartoon series for the Cartoon Network about a bunch of public defenders.

Up until the late '90s, television documentary was all about PBS. When you asked someone who they were working for everyone would say, "PBS." Then I started realizing that PBS only has *P.O.V.*, *The American Experience*, and *American Masters*. So, people were producing work thinking "Oh, it's for PBS," but if it doesn't go on PBS, where is it going?

You've really got to know your audience. A lot of us are elitists. A lot of people in our industry don't watch television. A lot of academics and intellectuals, particularly on the documentary side, would rather read a book than watch television. I watch a LOT of television and I'm not embarrassed to admit it. I watch probably three hours of television a night. I think it makes me a better producer. My wife will sometimes walk into the room and she'll turn to the television and say, "What are you doing?" and I'll say, "I'm working," and she'll say, "You're watching *The Apprentice*." But the show has great production values.

I remember the first time I saw *Survivor*—everyone in America might have been screaming and talking about how amazing these personality conflicts were, but I was obsessed with the way they were doing sound and their coverage of these scenes. This is the slickest, prettiest, nonfiction work I have ever seen. And so you can learn that way, but more importantly, you need to learn and understand the networks. You need to know what those networks are developing, and how they're growing. For example, TLC is a different network today than it was four or five years ago.

You can't just watch television for three months every 10 years. Spike TV has changed dramatically. Bravo has changed dramatically. Every cable station with the exception of MTV has completely shifted their programming in the last five years. And even MTV has shifted more to celebrity rather than reality series with younger icons. VH1, which was all about *Behind the Music*, is now all about celebrities in reality shows. They ALL are constantly evolving and we need to evolve with them.

CK: Do you think of yourself more as a producer or a director or both?
BM: Well, in television I'm more of a producer because as a member of the Director's Guild, it's very difficult for me to work in nonfiction on television and basic cable. It's almost impossible. Economically, what I'll do now is come up with ideas for shows and hire them out for people to do. I'm not even a showrunner anymore. I basically am a creator at this point.

CK: Expand on that job description, please.
BM: I would hire what is called the "showrunner," someone who is essentially going to take the project over. At the end of the day, the show would probably say, "Created by Brett Morgen," and then I would be one of a number of executive producers. My job is to find the right people to run that show who can implement and protect my vision for the program. My job then becomes to put that in motion—make sure the script is tight, oversee the casting, and oversee the editing. The showrunner is technically the director and I'm the executive producer.

CK: Where do you make your money in this structure?
BM: You can't start a series and then bail out after the first season and think you're going to get rich by taking some sort of royalty—unless it's *The Osbournes* or some mind-blowing exception to the rule. Cable budgets are between $75,000 and $200,000 for a half-hour reality show. You can't take $50,000 off the top just because you came up with an idea. If I didn't direct commercials, then I would be the showrunner. I'd come up with an idea and I'd be the showrunner and I would make my living that way. At the end of the day, I'm just a guy who likes to watch television. I feel that there are certain programs that aren't on the air that I'd like to see so I try to push those through.

CK: As a producer, how involved are you in the budget—not only creating it but the day-to-day supervision of it?
BM: I'm very involved in creating the budget. I work with the line producer in shaping the original budget. Once the budget is approved, I want to know that we're on budget, and if we're not on budget, why are we not on budget and how can we get back on track. But the line producer is dealing with all financial issues. I like to keep my role, at that point, more administrative and creative, dealing with the network, answering questions that the line-producer might have. But I don't want to know about the day-to-day.

CK: Do you tend to hire the same people from one production to the next? Do you have a team?

BM: You know, if they're good, if they're talented, often they don't want to be hired to do the same job. I find that anyone I work with, whether they're associate producers, line producers, editors—unless they're directors or executive producers—everyone wants to be in the cat-bird seat, everybody wants to be in the position of power. If it's a theatrical movie, it's the director or producer and if it's a television show, it's the executive producer. So everyone else, for the most part, is working to get to those places, so if you have someone that's really talented—if it's the line producer on one project—chances are that on the next project, they're not going to want to take a line producer credit, they're going to want full producer credit, and you've got to decide if you want to go there or not. So I find it really hard to maintain. I just lost my editor who I've been working with for years because he's now becoming a director, and my old line producers are now producers. But it's incredibly helpful to have a team around that you trust and respect.

CK: Do you think there is a producer's personality?

BM: There are so many different types of producers. In television, there are people who are really brash and confident and charismatic. Then there's soft-spoken but talented producers. The key is to exude confidence. When you ask someone to give you more than one million dollars, they need to share your confidence, understand that you're professional and trustworthy. Most producers who work in television tend to be very authoritative, very strong personalities who are generals with their team.

CK: How much do you think that "people skills" connect with producing?

BM: I think a really good producer is someone who knows how to sweet-talk people to get what they want. And I think, you know, just as in life, if you treat people with respect, they give it back. Some people work better under threat and intimidation, and some people do their best work feeling valued all along, so it's tough to say. I know one television producer, this guy could sell anyone anything. He's a showman. And then there are people who are just very quiet and soft-spoken who happen to do really good work.

CK: You're a former NYU film student. What's your advice for students starting off in television producing?

BM: Something I already said: know your audience. When you come up with an idea, know the answer to "Who is this for?" You have to have a certain sense of responsibility with money. TV is a business and therefore you don't want to pitch a show that's going to cost $300,000 and sell it for $300,000. There's no profit in it. Try to keep costs down.

The most important thing is to know your audience, and also know that probably any idea you have, there are a hundred other people with that same idea and you'd better have something unique and special about your particular take on it. There is not an original idea—there hasn't been since I've been around. There are just reinterpretations of things, and particularly nonfiction, where you can't copyright an idea.

I did a film about the Chicago Seven, from the 1960s. I can't prevent anyone else from doing a film about the Chicago Seven. What's going to make my film different from the next person is my take on the events from back then, and my package that I put together. I have a very unique spin to my movie and so therefore if somebody else happens to do a film on the Chicago Seven, I'm not really going to be too bothered by it. When you go to pitch, chances are they've already heard it—unless you've got something very specific about a very specific person, they've heard the pitch. So why are they going to hire you? You have to make sure to give them a reason.

CK: What is your sense of the direction television is taking?

BM: Two words: branded entertainment. When TV first started, each program was sponsored, like General Electric Theater. I think we're going back to that now as a result of TiVo and DVR, which is going to open a lot of doors for producers. So, in my show about high school basketball in Michigan, [*Nimrod Nation*], I'm going to start thinking about that in terms of what products exist in that world. Are they basketball players? They play with a Wilson basketball. Can I go to Wilson and get a sponsorship from them? They need shoes, so I might think Nike. Can I go to Nike and get a sponsorship from them?

CK: If you have to think about showing a sponsor's product or logo, along with all the other details of a shot, won't that get in your way?

BM: It may. But I think commercials are far more intrusive. You cut away from the action for three minutes and it's totally intrusive. Often times you can deal with some of these companies. It's not product shots they're asking for as much as lifestyles and attitude that they want to embrace and endorse.

CK: What if the viewers feel they're being preached to?

BM: Someone has to pay for it, so unless the audience is willing to shell out $5.00 every time they turn on the television, which no one wants to do, we're going to live with it. Does it compromise the integrity of the program? It depends on the project. It depends on how it's incorporated.

CK: What's ahead for us in the field of technology?

BM: We all know we're heading toward an HD world. If I want to sell a program five years from now, it's going to be a whole lot easier if I shoot it in high-def now, rather than standard def. Everything goes in cycles, though. I don't know what the next one is going to be.

STEPHEN REED
Executive Producer, Producer, and Producer/Director (including The Newport Jazz Festival)

CK: Because you produce in so many different genres, what kind of producer do you usually think of yourself as being?

SR: I overlap between executive producer and producer these days. In the past, I've been a line producer, and an executive in charge of production. One is often a more glorified term for the other.

CK: What area of producing, what genre, are you most comfortable working in?

SR: The things I like doing best are these big music productions of live events. Sometimes we do them as live broadcasts, and sometimes we do them live-to-tape for a quick delivery. Sometimes they're heavily edited. At The Newport Jazz Festival one year, we shot about 10 hours of music and 20 hours, maybe, of B-roll, and interviews. And all this gets condensed. The 10 hours of music is actually five or six cameras, for each hour. So you're dealing with a huge amount of material to cull down to a one-hour program.

There are two challenges in this: capturing everything right in the first place, and then an enormous postproduction editing process to bring it down to a one-hour finished program.

I've also produced a few commercials, I've done music videos, and I've done some documentaries, as well as live satellite feeds, award shows. We even did boxing. We did Golden Gloves boxing over several days, many hours of live broadcast boxing. And then we cut that down to four to six hours, as another program for an HD channel.

CK: Do these larger, live events pose certain challenges to you as a producer?
SR: I guess the challenge is understanding what the event is, and who our client is, and, is that client the same person that's putting on the event? Which is sometimes the case. Is the client a broadcast partner in an event that someone else is putting on? And what is the relationship there? Often, I'll produce the event specifically for television, and then I produce the television coverage as well. That's the ideal situation because you plan the whole event in the way it's going to run, in the venue, in the available camera positions, set design, lighting.

The ideal situation is designing the whole event for television, because all of those things are taken into account, right from the beginning. It's clear that television is the priority. The live audience, while you want to accommodate them, is not the priority. The other extreme is when you're brought in to cover an event that's already planned and is going to be happening anyway, and we have to cover it for television. Sometimes we have a really cooperative relationship with the producer or promoter of a live event. And sometimes we don't. So you've got to be sensitive to that relationship and that audience.

CK: This is all live, with no chance to do another take. How do you avoid feeling pinned against the wall?
SR: You try not to come up against the wall. You try to avoid that part right from the beginning by going in and meeting with the people who are running the event—understanding what their priorities are and what their necessities are, letting them know that you understand what those are, and trying to debunk their preconceptions about what it means to have a television crew come in and disrupt everything to cover their event.

I've found that many times the perception going in is that *these television guys* are a "pain in the butt" and they think they're going to control everything and run everything, and that it's all about them and they run roughshod, and they're not very nice about it. Maybe it's just my personality, or maybe because I do a lot of music and have done a lot of music, but I'm aware of that preconception and I do my best to go in the opposite direction so that people feel comfortable. You try to get across that "we've got certain things we have to accomplish, we understand that you have certain things you have to accomplish, let's work together to see how we can do as much of that as possible" and find ways where we can compromise as necessary. It's as much about personal relationships and schmoozing as it is about, technically, how you're going to achieve whatever it is that you need to do.

CK: Let's take the Newport Jazz Festival as a working example. How do you set up an event that is so massive? Are you essentially the director as well as the producer?
SR: Yeah, I'm essentially the director. I don't do the multicamera live directing in the truck. But I have all the other responsibilities of the director. I do all the interview stuff. I direct, generally, all the B-roll shots, knowing where that's going. I do the host stuff, I write the voice-over as needed. So, I usually have a concept of how we're going to pull the show together a little bit and try do it differently each year, although I never know what kind of music I'm going to get.

So you want to have a loose plan in mind. We usually know how many artists we're going to shoot, but we don't know how well their sets are going to turn out and how we're going to juggle that whole balance. All of the direction of that show from the start to the finish, with the exception of calling the cameras live, is what I do. Even to the point of once we've selected a song, we go back and take out all of the isolated shots, and recut the entire show anyway. So we don't even use the line cut.

A couple of examples: If you want to put a jib in the audience to get some nice big sweeping shots, that's uniformly rejected because the jib could, conceivably, interfere with someone in the audience's view of the stage. So they won't allow that. We had a heck of a time trying to clean up the stage a little bit at the festival. There are a lot of hangers-on around the stage area. Which leads to a lot of clutter in the background of the shots, which detracts from what you're trying to do in focusing on the artist. So we tried to clean up the stage with design elements, keeping more people off the stage... things like that.

There are only 20 minutes between sets. An entire band is taken off stage, a new band is put on stage, people are scurrying around putting microphones in place, and so on. We also have only 20 minutes to get set up between each artist. We don't have any influence on how microphones are positioned, for example. Sometimes we can position a mike so that it's still just as effective to capture the music from an instrument or a singer, but it's not in the way of the camera angles that you're able to get.

The more cameras you have, the more positions you have, and the more flexibility with moving the cameras around, the more you can compensate for those things. But then again, we're getting into, "Are we interfering with the audience's appreciation of the show by distracting their eye or their focus, or actually being in front of them?" Those kinds of issues we juggle back and forth, and we compromise and try to still come out with as good a show as we possibly can.

The essential point is that you have to try to gain the trust and the confidence of the client, and all the other parties—from all the audio people, from the staging people, the artists, all the parties involved in this event. You have to gain their trust, showing that you understand what their issues are and bringing them on board to be on the same team for the overall good of the project.

CK: On a live music event, capturing the audio must be a huge challenge.
SR: Here's how it works. There are a lot of different audio requirements for putting on a concert. First of all, the musicians on the stage have their own monitors that allow them to hear their own music being played back to them. Every single person on the stage has to have a mix so that they can hear themselves, know if they're in tune, and hear the rest of the musicians clearly and plainly, despite where they may be located on the stage. The microphones all go to a central place, then are divided into different purposes.

But our primary objective is to do an adequate mix for the musicians on the stage. That's the stage mix. Then there's a split of that audio that goes out to the center of the house where somebody else is mixing the sound for the audience. There you want a much more full, balanced mix than you would for the individual musicians on the stage. The singer primarily wants to hear himself or herself louder than they would in a normal mix, but that's not an appropriate mix for the house. So you've got five or six different mixes, depending on how many musicians you have on stage. Each one wants their own kind of mix featuring themselves. The house gets a different kind of mix.

The third split goes to the television truck, where we mix. Here, we do two things: The number one priority in the Newport show, which is a heavily posted show, is to get the multitrack recording done properly. It's usually 24 or 32, sometimes as much as 48 individual tracks that we're recording. That's the number one priority there. The number two priority of our TV truck mix is to get a rough mix, for reference purposes, that goes on the videotapes that we use for postproduction to decide what goes into the show and to cut the whole show together. Only at the very end do we go back to those multitracks, and mix the music that ends up being the show. That's how the ultimate audio ends up getting done. But right now, with the way I've described it to you, you have three splits.

My audio guy says every year, "Hey, don't use anybody's first song if you can possibly avoid it," because he's always trying to figure out where everything is and get his tracking down. We have no opportunity to do a sound check ahead of time, so the first song is always the sound check. The trouble is that the artist usually wants to start with a bang and capture everyone's attention. Frequently, the coolest song is the first one, and you want to use it.

It's all so second nature to me that I kind of forget that not everyone knows all these things. But it also relates to your point that a producer is a producer is a producer. Which is true in many ways. But there are so many nuances for different kinds of things, like getting the crew there, getting the facilities, thinking to the punt. That's transferable. But things like this, if you haven't done this kind of show multiple times, you're not even going to be aware of what the issues are, let alone, how to handle them. So in some ways, that producer, producer thing is accurate. But there are a lot of exceptions.

CK: What are the pros and cons of shooting in a hi-def situation?
SR: It's more expensive, of course. It's easier, in that there are more trucks, more facilities, people are more experienced with it, cameras are smaller and lighter for the handheld people, and you have more lensing opportunity, variability, and options. From all those points of view, it's gotten a lot better. From an editing point of view, you have to shoot all this stuff in HD, then convert it to an NTSC format for editing. So there's a time-consuming and extensive transfer process that takes place—that's the biggest hassle. Then you have to marry everything back together later.

CK: What's involved in the postproduction part of shooting in hi-def?
SR: We do an offline nonlinear edit using this NTSC stuff. When it's all done, we send the edit decision list and a tape of the finished offline to the audio house for their mixing purposes, then they marry it back, according to the edit decision list. And then the EDL also goes to the online facility and there we start to, in theory, auto-conform the show based on the EDL. Then we fly in the audio track, which is now all done, and then throw in the graphics. All of that stuff has to really be designed ahead of time. The coordination of how it flows together and how it's going to look, and the sweetening, and smoothly going from artist to artist and artist to interview, and all that kind of stuff has to be planned pretty carefully between a number of different parties to make it work well.

That's all the technical stuff. But the most important thing is that you really have to have a feel for the music and the artist, and what's going on, and creatively pull all this stuff together. The creative part is really why I'm hired and what you need from the head person pulling this all together. That's why I'm the producer-director I am, but as a producer, you also have to be aware of all this technical stuff.

JOHN ROSAS
Producer, promotional and added value/behind-the-scenes material on DVDs

CK: What area of producing do you specialize in, John?
JR: I'm a DVD Producer. At one time I did promotional marketing, producing press kits, electronic press kits, corporate image, stuff like that, but for the past 10 years, it's been strictly "added value" for DVDs.

CK: What is "added value"?
JR: Different studios call it different things, like special features, behind the scenes, added value, but it's all the special things that go on a DVD beside, or along with, the movie. For the first couple of years, all that went on the DVD was the movie. Now, every studio has their own DVD division with their own department that deals only with these added features. And then you have the menu content, and the people who do the marketing, and the graphics people who decide what the menus look like.

CK: That's more of a graphics area, isn't it?
JR: Yeah, but it all has to interlace. You know, it's all about the look. You want to produce something that matches the overall look of the project. What we do is specialized. We're shooting the behind-the-scenes, we're doing the featurettes, editing the deleted scenes, taking 30 hours of footage previously shot on a set, maybe all the deleted comedic scenes, and either making it into an edited piece that makes some sense, or is in some cases, simply eye candy.

CK: Who makes those decisions about what else goes on the DVD besides the film?
JR: It depends on the studio. They may say, "This is what we have." We're maybe told that, "We have 37 reels of MiniDVs that someone shot on the set. And apparently they got some good stuff so we'd like to do something with this. We'd like to get a featurette out of it." Then we come in and say, "We'll tell you what you have." You may have someone who walked around just shooting people's feet—you just don't know. What we normally do is tell them, "Send us everything you have, be it trailers, deleted scenes, whatever. Let us go through all the footage and we'll come back to you with a proposal for what we can do."

For *Party of Five*, for example, 10 years after the series, they wanted to put out Season I, Season II, and Season III. So we said, "Let us go interview whoever wants to be interviewed, and let's see what we get." We interviewed the creators of the series, and came away with enough footage that we could have easily cut a two-hour piece from. Well, that's a bit of overkill for the subject matter. What we did was just about an hour, a cohesive hour, going between the different people and footage behind the scenes and then we cut it into segments. We cut it into a 20-minute piece and a 10-minute piece because it all made sense. It could all be played together.

I like to keep going back to something like the movie *Wilde,* which was the Oscar Wilde film. It was wonderful. It was a really well-done film about someone bigger than life. We produced a one-hour documentary, going back and revisiting the subject with the creators, the writers, the directors, the producers, and Stephen Fry who was the star. So when the movie comes out, it's released with a brand new documentary about what makes the film and its subject relevant today.

CK: So you write, as well as produce?
JR: Well, we don't write in the traditional way. It's not a narrative or voice-over thing. Most everything we produce tells its own story.

CK: But you still have to be able to tell the story. How do you do that?
JR: From your interviews. What's interesting is that if you know what you're going after before you start, you can talk to people and say, "Look, truthfully we need some strong sound bites. So I'm not going to sit down with you for an hour and interview you about things that I know aren't going to be on the DVD or aren't going to be part of this."

Often, I'll do much more extensive interviews. For example, I interviewed Paul Mazursky about everything—his style of shooting, his style of writing, about making movies in the 1960s, his approach to comedy, how he works, because he has a 40-year track record of making films. My feeling is that I have Paul Mazursky here. I better sit down while he's here and talk to him about all of this—about the 1950s and John Cassavetes, and *Blackboard Jungle,* and working on *Harry and Tonto.* Luckily he wrote a book that helps me talk to him for hours and focus on the film, and then interlace his opinions on this, his styles, knowing Fellini and directing him in a film. I can talk to him about working with Woody Allen, about writing for Woody Allen and Peter Sellers. Later, you screen it and map out what you have, then go to the editor and say, "I've got three hours of Paul Mazursky talking, let's see how we can cut this up."

CK: So research is important?
JR: Oh yeah. You've got to be familiar with the films, you want to know the person, and I think you've got to be excited. You go into something like that the way you would go in if someone said, "Hey, you've got an opportunity to interview Spielberg, what are you going to do with it?" How much time do I have? If I only have an hour, I'm not going to just talk about his latest film, I'm going to try to get inside his head a little bit. And you let them know ahead of time you're going to touch on different topics.

CK: Ultimately, you're still dictated to by your client. What happens when you want to approach a project one way but the client has other ideas?
JR: It's how you position it. Usually they don't dictate because they don't know what we're going to get in the way of footage or interviews. So I say, "It will be great." You have to understand that the people who fund these are going to look at the packaging and say, "Wow, there's a half-hour interview Paul Mazursky." They're buying the film because it's a Paul Mazursky film so to get Paul Mazursky talking about his craft, that's an added value that is a very special feature.

CK: How does the budget determine your creative directions?
JR: You have to know what things cost because you have to know when you can say yes and when you can say no. We've got $30 K to do this, and $30 K seems like a lot but then you realize that $30 K covers your travel, your crew, three days of shooting, your transfers, the editing. You have to know what is in the budget. What is allocated for what portion, and realistically, can it be done?

When you're young, you want the work, so when someone says "Can you do this?" you say "sure" and then you get there and find out that your crew costs X. Now all of a sudden, a third of the budget is gone, and then soon it's another third, and then you're screwed. You can't ask people who work for $3,000 a day to work for $500 a day. You can crew it with the person that makes $500 a day, but you're not going to get the skill.

You're as good as your shooter, you're as good as your sound person. You can have the best footage in the world but if the audio is crap, well, you know what happens then. So you get what you pay for. After a certain amount of time, you've established those relationships so when you need to pull in a favor, you can get what you need for less.

CK: How do you find the right people to work with?
JR: That takes time. That's why when you're starting out, it's important to, again, surround yourself with the best people. Listen to what they say, watch them. Try to learn not only what they do, but how they do it. If you don't like the way they do it, remember that, too.

CK: What resources do you rely on when you're researching costs?
JR: Make phone calls. You can call a production company and say, "I'm thinking about putting together a shoot for So and So. I've got an opportunity to do this project but I have to know my budget. Can you take a few minutes and sketch one out for me?" Cold calls. I've called PR firms and other production companies earlier in my years because I didn't know what something would cost. Talk to people. Go into that production company on West 48th Street, or in Santa Monica, and talk to them.

You don't want to lie, but it's okay to call and say I'm working for this company and they've asked me to get some prices, or I'm thinking about doing a mini-doc and I'm trying to figure out what I can do. Can you tell me what a three-man HD crew will cost for this project? Call transfer houses to find what tape transfers will cost. Call duplication houses. These people are legitimate business people and they don't know if you're calling for a production house or you have an uncle who is a billionaire and wants to shoot his life story.

CK: You work with and interview high-profile talent. How do you maneuver yourself around their wall of protective PR people?
JR: You let them know that you have their client's best interest in mind. We are here to make their client look good. It's kind of loaded in my favor because I usually know the talent wants to do the project. After all, it is promoting them and their project. It depends on the situation, but you let the PR people know that it is *their* client who told the studio they wanted to do something. *Their* client asked us to call him or her to arrange it.

Recently we were getting responses from a PR person, saying "Well, she's so busy promoting this new movie that she can't possibly do the interview until blah, blah, blah." And I say, "Okay, by that date, I'll have missed my deadline and it won't get on the DVD. That's really weird because she was talking to the creator of the show, saying she wanted to do this. It's weird she would actually say she didn't want to do it. I guess it'll all wash out." The next thing you know, the PR person is calling you back and saying, "Oh, she can do the interview next Tuesday." It's about occasionally playing some games to get what you need.

CK: Do you deal with celebrities' agents or lawyers?
JR: Often. It doesn't hurt to find out who the manager is and go through them to get what you need. You always have to be aware that you need to put something in writing. You have to be able to present it in a few paragraphs very succinctly; what you want, what's expected, how long, what you'll do, where it's going to be used, how it's going to be used, and so on. It's in their best interest. Plus, remember that everyone on camera has to sign a release. Very important.

TOM SELLITTI
Supervising Producer, *Rescue Me* (FX)

CK: On your series, Rescue Me, you are part of a tight producing team. As the Supervising Producer, how do you and the other producers divide the work among you?
TS: Jim (Serpico, EP), Kerry Orent (Co-EP), and myself work very closely together. We weigh in with writers Peter (Tolan) and Denis (Leary) on a lot of things, but they leave the physical producing to us. When the scripts are written, we read the scripts and give notes back to Denis and Peter. We participate in phone calls with FX—the network—and the studio, Sony.

CK: How much involvement do FX and Sony have in the show, on a day-to-day basis?
TS: They read the scripts, watch the cuts and tell us what concerns them and what things they would like to change. They are both very supportive. We take their notes into account and talk amongst ourselves afterwards, creatively, to figure out what we want to do. Is this a note from network that we should listen to and go ahead with it? FX is great to work for, the notes they give are helpful. They are not giving notes for the sake of giving notes. They have a good eye for story and production, so for us, it is usually a note that we try to accommodate as it only makes the show better.

But sometimes there is a creative difference and we may feel that even though they feel we should do something, they usually give us the creative license to agree or to disagree. We would then go back to them afterward and say, "Here are the 15 notes that you gave us, and these are the ones we are going to make changes with, and these are the ones we want to keep the way they are. They are usually able to accept that and we move on.

CK: How is working with the studio different than with the network?
TS: The studio is watching the budget more, but in terms of the final product everyone has the same common goal, which is to make a great show.

CK: How involved are you with the budgets?
TS: Kerry (Orent) our Co-EP oversees it and he is in charge of budget day-to-day. Jim and I try to make sure that the creative ideas will fit in with those guidelines. If there is something that works creatively with our storylines but will take us over budget then one of us will make a call to the studio to talk about getting an overage for it.

CK: What are you involved with as supervising producer on the show?
TS: It's just really across the board, creatively and production-wise. I'm involved in casting, locations, script issues, editing, etc. There aren't really any aspects that I'm not made aware of.

CK: Locations are an integral part of the show. How do you find them?
TS: We have a location department that breaks down the scripts so they have a list of locations that are needed. Usually the scene description will tell you what we are looking for, and then they will go out and do the scout and bring back photo choices, not only to us but to the director as well. The director has a lot of input on that. A lot of times, we will defer to him unless it is completely wrong. Then, we'll set up a time to visit the locations and check them out. That scout will include the producers, the director, the locations people, the production designer, and the DP (cinematographer) and the 1st AD. And that's not the big scouts. Those are the scouts when we are trying to figure out what locations we can select.

CK: What are you looking for in a location?
TS: There are a lot of logistics that go into it. We want to make sure that the location will work for the scene, creatively as well as practically. The look of it needs to fit into our show organically. We want to make sure that we can get good looks and camera angles. We also want to make sure it's available for our schedule and that it is going to work for our production. It should be easily accessible with room for our trucks in the surrounding area. You have to be aware of the neighborhood as well. Some are more friendly than others and we need to take that into account also.

CK: On Rescue Me*, what is the percentage of locations compared to built sets?*
TS: We probably shoot about 60 percent on location.

CK: How many people are usually on your crew?
TS: About 150.

CK: You're shooting the show in 24p. How is that working for you?
TS: Very good. It looks like film. It's easy to shoot, because it's tape. It's less expensive than film. The cameras are a little bit bigger, if you use the cameras that we use, but the operators who handle the cameras have gotten used to working with them and do a really good job. For us, it is a very efficient way to shoot the show.

CK: You use an approach called cross-boarding *when you shoot. Can you explain it?*
TS: What we do is take two scripts together and we shoot it like a film. It's just a more efficient way to shoot, especially when you are on location as much as we are. We'll take two scripts—and one director directs two episodes—so that one director will do both of them. We will schedule them so that when we have a scene that takes place in a particular location, then we'll shoot everything that takes place in that location for both scripts. Consecutively. So if we have a day's worth of shots in the two scripts at one location, we'll do it all in one day. We'll have the actors' change clothes from whatever particular scenes are for whatever episodes. When we did *The Job*, we used to cross-board four episodes at a time and that would get a little confusing. But this isn't so bad. It's just a matter of keeping continuity correct. A lot of that falls on the script supervisor, at least production wise, but the actors' seem to handle it, no problem.

CK: How involved do you get in postproduction?
TS: I'm involved in a large portion. I'll watch dailies, give notes on rough cuts, speak to the studio and network about notes. I'm involved in the music that we will put into an episode.

CK: How do you and your team set up your shoots?
TS: We shoot our rehearsals. But we try to keep our takes limited. Denis [Leary] likes to work in his own way, doing as few takes as possible. And we usually will work with the directors, making sure they know about that ahead of time. We have to be efficient to make our days.

CK: What's your relationship with your directors?
TS: We give them the freedom to do their thing. You try to hire people that are adding something, so you never want to hold anyone back. We will watch to make sure their choices fit in with our show and for the most part, support them as much as possible. If something seems out of place we will step in at that point.

CK: Speaking of personalities, is there a producer personality? Do you have one?
TS: I don't think that I have the typical producer's personality. Every producer I meet is different. Some of them are crazy Type A personalities, some are very laid back, some are jerks. It has a lot to do with the way a person handles pressure and stress. Me, myself? I am pretty laid back. I guess the common denominator is that a producer makes things happen so in that sense I do have the producer personality.

CK: You don't seem to mind the pressures.
TS: To us, it's something we want to do and we are of the mind set that we can do whatever needs to be done, at least creatively, and we find a way to do it. Whatever it takes… there is always a way to compromise, and get what you need. We hire good people to work on our shows because they like to work on our shows. We treat them well and that plays a big part in it, too.

CK: You have also created and co-executive-produced shows for Comedy Central?
TS: For Comedy Central, we have done a lot of things. We had an animated show called *Shorties Watchin' Shorties*. We've done their *Comedy Central Roast*. And we had a series called *Contest Searchlight* that's a parody of the show *Project Greenlight*.

CK: You're obviously involved in creating new programming ideas on an ongoing basis.
TS: Yes, we have several other shows in different stages of development with just about every network at this point, including a Fox show called *Canterbury's Law*, which launched in the spring of 2008 with Julianna Margulies playing a criminal defense attorney.

CK: Who is the "we" in this case?
TS: Apostle. This is Denis' production company with myself and Jim Serpico. Creatively, we produce the project but we pretty much work as producers the same way all the time.

CK: You've been doing this for a while now. Looking back, what do you wish someone had told you way back then?
TS: I wish someone told me it's not as easy as it sounds. There are some things that you need to know—things that are helpful. That you have to be flexible. You have to be willing to roll with the punches, you have to believe in what you are doing and believe you can do it. If someone is telling you something is impossible, it is usually not. Anything is possible. There are some things that are impossible for budgetary reasons, but there are always compromises and ways to make your vision come to life. I think you need to treat the people around you right.

The way that we work, most people don't think of us as difficult producers (when I say us, I mean Jim and Dennis and Apostle). For one of the other shows that we are doing, I was going to a sound mix and when I got there, the production supervisor was laughing. She was talking to the sound mixer and she said one of the producers was coming over to listen to the mix and he said, "Oh, the suits," and she said, "No, these guys are not the suits, it's the last thing they would be." We are pretty down to earth and just normal—we like to have fun while we are doing it. We pretty much see ourselves as just like everyone else on the crew.

CK: Can you find some balance in your life with the kind of schedule you have?
TS: I try. My wife says I don't… but I do. I do a lot of stuff. I have a wife, I have two boys, ages 3 and 1. I box. I play hockey. When we are not in production, we come to work at

10 o'clock and stay until 7 or 8. And the rest of the time, we try to do normal things like go out on the weekends. But when we're shooting, it is harder. On the other hand, some of our projects are easier. We have an animated show, and it's not like you have to stand on the set for that. With *Rescue Me* or *Canterbury's* you're on the set for 12 hours a day. So you do lose a little bit of your life during the week. But we shoot five days and we don't shoot on the weekends, so you get your time on the weekend.

CK: So you have created some semblance of balance.
TS: We try. Sometimes it feels like it is not balanced, but we know the work that has to go into it to be successful, and how to put out a good product and make things run properly and we try to be responsible. It would be easy to say I want to do this, and I am not going to go to work. But you wouldn't get anything done.

CK: How important is the original vision? How do you keep that vision intact?
TS: The vision of the show is Peter and Denis. Really, we just try and facilitate what their vision is. With Denis, he is the one who really always has it in his mind—what he puts on the page, what he tells us in our conversations about what he's thinking or what he wants to do. We just help to bring it to life as much as we can. And we will tell him if we think something is not working, or if we feel there is some inconsistency in something. We will bring it up and say, "Hey, you want to do this but is it supposed to be this way?" and we bring it up for discussion.

CK: As someone who's producing for TV, where do you think it's going, and where do you think you'll fit into the equation?
TS: Not sure. Every year brings something different. The Internet is a new frontier for programming. I think television is either going to become a great place for programming that rivals feature films or it's going to crash and burn with bad reality TV. Only time will tell.

J. STEPHEN SHEPPARD
Entertainment Lawyer, Partner, Cowan DeBaets Abrahams and Sheppard

CK: How did you become an entertainment lawyer, Steve?
JSS: I always wanted to be in the entertainment business and I didn't have any talent to do anything else. Seriously, I'm not a writer, I'm not a director, and I'm certainly not an actor. Publishing, television, movies, and theater always interested me. Law was the thing that I could do well to be in that world.

I've been lots of things. I finished law school and I worked as a lawyer, then I left that and was an agent for five or six years. Then, I was in the producing business, the feature motion picture business, for three or four years, and went back into the agency business. Finally, I migrated back to this desk.

CK: Does your producing experience help you as an entertainment attorney?
JSS: I think it works for me, I think it works for the clients. I'd like to think that the whole is greater than the sum of the parts. I've seen this business from various perspectives, from the agent's perspective, from the producer's perspective. I think it all helps. When I come into a project on behalf of the producer, I'm seeing it as a lawyer, in terms of the issues that need to be attended to, where the problems may be, or how to solve this problem, or write a contract for that. But I also look at it from the producer's perspective who is much less interested in the piece of paper I write and much more interested in getting it on film. So, I think I bring a pragmatic view.

CK: The majority of your clients fall into what category?
JSS: The nice thing about my practice is that it's really varied—I represent a lot of producers, I represent a cable television network for its original movies of the week, but I also represent literary estates, in the protection and exploitation of deceased authors' works, and I represent an advertising agency.

CK: What does an entertainment lawyer do?
JSS: I can tell you what *I* do. Different entertainment lawyers do things differently. One of my partners is an entertainment lawyer, for instance, and functions in a mixed bag of semi-agenting, and semi-producing, and semi-deal-making business affairs, and what I call opportunity creating—introducing one party to another party. A lot of entertainment lawyers function that way, and I do a certain amount of that.

My practice tends to be a little more traditional lawyering. I negotiate and draft contracts, which is itself kind of unusual. Many senior lawyers have other people do the drafting and then they fix it. I don't like to do that. The value lies in getting it said right, and I believe that I need to do most of that myself, and I am good at it. I negotiate, I draft, I review materials for libel and privacy issues, mainly for documentaries. I work with insurance brokers to get insurance for films. I also negotiate contracts between producers and distributors, networks or distribution companies.

If I have a relationship that is useful, I can make an introduction. I'll call a network and say, "You should take a look at this project," or "I've got this client who is making this great movie," so that is sort of a little agenting. I never like to hold myself out as that; it's not my principal job as I see it. I also do some business counseling—what is the smartest, best way to come at this project? I'm often regarded by my clients as their "smart friend." It is business counseling, it's strategizing.

CK: Do you simply make the introduction, or do you follow a project through distribution?
JSS: It really depends on the client and the project. I had a new client in yesterday with a new project, really interesting project, at square one. It's beyond the idea stage, they've already made good progress in terms of creating access to the subject, but that is as far as we've gotten. We talked about what steps were necessary, and what kind of documents were necessary to get the project started, and what their ideas were for what the project should be. They saw it as a documentary series. I suggested this project should go to such and such a network. I pointed out that they should be prepared to think about this as a one-off single special because, though we may be very intrigued about the subject, I wasn't sure that it could support a series.

When other clients come to me, this advice is not what they are looking for. Or the deal is already done and it's just doing a contract or production legal work, and doing every release for network nonfiction. Production legal work can involve making distribution contracts, acquiring rights and life rights—it really is driven by what the client needs and what the project needs.

CK: At what point in the development of a project do people usually go to a lawyer?
JSS: Certainly, at some point in the course of the life of a project, when you have to start dealing with third parties, with other people. If a book, for example, is going to be the basis of a movie, or if there is somebody's story, somebody's life rights, or if you need to get particular access to a building—these are all obvious triggers for a conversation with a lawyer. When you start dealing with third parties, you have to make arrangements with them, and you have to get certain rights or permissions or clearances from them.

That's when it probably makes sense to start talking to a lawyer and make sure that you are getting what you need—and that you are not getting more than you need, and not overpaying for what you need.

CK: Are there situations in which a producer wouldn't want to involve a lawyer?
JSS: That is an interesting point, I hear it all the time and it pains me to hear it—this notion that bringing in a lawyer is a hostile, aggressive, negative thing to do. It is not, it doesn't have to be, and it certainly shouldn't be. Anyone starting off as a producer really needs to get over that. A lawyer who knows what he or she is doing, and is good at it, is there to effect a simple agreement that is really fair to both people.

I always tell clients that the best deals are deals where both sides are just a little unhappy. As long as both sides are just a little unhappy, then neither one got every single thing they wanted, which means there was compromise and that it is probably a fair deal. That's the way a good lawyer should come at this. You are here to get it done. You as a producer, and whomever you are dealing with, are going to be better off in the long run if you have done it right in the beginning.

I'm asked the question, "Can any contract can be undone?" And the answer is "Probably," if someone is inventive or hostile enough to do it. Let's say that you make an oral hand-shake deal with Jane Doe to do a movie about her. You don't want to bring in a lawyer, because that feels like a hostile thing to do, so you both agree that that is just fine and you make the movie and you've spent time, money, and energy and you've made the movie. Then, Jane Doe says, "I've changed my mind, I don't want you to do this, and I don't like it." You are stuck. Whereas if you have a simple agreement up front, it is harder for the other person to do that. Is it impossible? No, it's just harder because then, you are both relying on this agreement.

CK: How does a producer find a good lawyer?
JSS: It's not black magic. You meet with somebody and you get a sense of what kind of person they are, if they understand you and they get what you're talking about, and see how you want to come at this. I have people who haven't retained me, because they want some kind of red meat killer who grabs the other guy by the throat. That is not the way I function, but if that is what the client wants, then he is in the wrong place and he knows that. I am not offended when somebody says, "You're not mean enough for me."

For a young/new producer, there is an organization here in New York, and I think it exists in many cities, called Volunteer Lawyers for the Arts (VLA). That is exactly what they do. They make legal services available to people in the arts who can't afford to pay for them; whether they are young producers, or authors, or dancers, or whatever. They are all volunteers, they're very good young lawyers who work in big law firms and make their services available on a *pro bono* basis. Law schools very often have programs. It's great experience for the students, and it creates some kind of access to lawyering.

CK: What are the most important legal areas that producers should know about?
JSS: In any business or project, there are a certain number of hot-button issues that need to be paid attention to. An obvious example is rights. If you are dealing with existing material, you have to get the rights. If you are dealing with a person, you have to have a release and get permission to tell his or her story.

Another hot-button issue is collaboration; if you have a partner, look at the terms on which that partnership is supposed to operate—who is in charge, how are the decisions made, how does the money get split up, who get what kinds of credit? What happens if it doesn't work out? At what point do you walk away, and who gets to walk away with what? At that point there will have been time, money, and talent invested in coming up with a treatment, a demo, a something.

Insurance is a big item. Sometimes it's as simple as calling your neighborhood broker, someone who knows what they are doing. It may be as simple as calling and saying, "I need an insurance package for this project," and you'll get one. There are other instances where it may be more complicated than that but insurance is a big area. There is a bundle of insurance coverage that a picture needs. It needs liability insurance, it needs property insurance, general liability if you smash your camera through someone's plate glass window, or if someone trips over a cable, or if you've rented a car and have an accident during production. Then, there is producers' liability, or Errors and Omissions, that protects against claims arising out of the content and copyright trademark, and libel and privacy claims.

If you are doing a larger picture, there are union issues and guild issues. It's not so much a function of the size of the project, it is more about the people involved. I am involved now with a project of relatively modest budget, a television project, but it needs to be done with guilds, so there are WGA issues, and DGA issues, and SAG and AFTRA issues, which then throw off another bundle of residuals and pension and welfare issues.

CK: What does a producer need to know about financial markets and financing?
JSS: A producer needs to know a good lawyer or a good financial advisor, in all areas of financing an independent film. It is a very highly specialized area. I've done a fair amount of work on a network that is producing pictures in Canada. This is its own whole universe; there are very specific rules and requirements that you have to comply with in Canada for the benefits, which are all sorts of really good subsidies and tax credits. For a general-purpose discussion like this, that is almost too complicated. It really depends on the project, the producer, and the producer's access to money and ability to raise money.

CK: What is a producer's rep and what do they do?
JSS: They serve a variety of functions. They can help securing financing, and they can help find distributors. They sell the film to distributors; they will get it into festivals. They can function earlier in the process to find coproduction financing and pre-sales, obviously before it has been shot.

CK: From your viewpoint as a producer's lawyer, what skills should a producer have?
JSS: I'll tell you what I respond to in a client: someone who asks the right questions. Having some common sense about the questions to ask is enormously valuable because if there's a problem, and nobody thought to ask the question and I never had the kind of information that I would need in order to think about the question myself, then you find yourself trying to solve the problem after it happens—and that can be really difficult.

My job isn't to say, "No, you can't." It is to say, "Here is how," or "Let's solve this problem." But very often, all I can do is say, "Here are the risks and you have to make the decision. This is a business decision, it's not a legal decision." In that situation, having a client, a producer, who listens and is thoughtful and makes a decision is pretty good for both of us.

CK: What is the function of a copyright?
JSS: When someone writes a book or writes a play or makes a movie, or paints a painting, the law creates a certain right that it calls "copyright," for this purpose. This says

that the creator of the material is the only person that can do anything with it. He/she/ it (if it is a company) is the only person who can sell it, can make copies of it, can do anything with it, so anybody else who wants to do anything with that thing needs the permission of the author/the creator to make copies of it, to make different versions of it, to translate it, to do anything.

And that right, that control, is called "intellectual property," and it applies to the proceeds of somebody's work that gets manifested into some content. And that intellectual property is an intangible. You can own that book, that is tangible, but you have no right to do anything with the contents of it. You can't make a xeroxed copy of it, you can't make a movie of it, you can't do anything with the content of the book unless you buy it from my client.

CK: How can producers protect their work?
JSS: You secure copyright. Securing copyright is very easy. You put a copyright notice on it, a little c in the circle and the year, date, and your name, and you put it on the film or script or whatever. That tells the world that somebody owns it. So, if anybody else wants to do anything with it, they have to get the permission of the guy whose name is on the copyright. You take a couple copies of it and you fill out a form that has about eight questions on it. You send it to the Library of Congress with whatever the filing fee is, and it gets registered. Then, anyone who looks at the copyright registry knows it's yours.

CK: Can you protect your work by mailing it to yourself?
JSS: Before 1976, that was a useful device because of the way that the copyright law was structured, but now it is not at all meaningful. The only reason it has any meaning is if it is important to identify a specific date in which something was created. That is a very simple method—mail it to yourself and get a mail receipt.

You're never protecting ideas; you can only protect the *expression* of an idea. So, the business of mailing something to yourself is of limited use. The Writers Guild Registration has certain value within the Writers Guild, but mostly it's from the perspective of identifying a date. If you are sending a treatment or script to the WGA, you are going to put a copyright notice on it anyway. It's the copyright notice that really gets you what you want. As soon as it is in some sort of tangible form, you're entitled to copyright and you get it by putting a notice on it, and it doesn't matter if it's published or not.

CK: Can you explain the meaning of fair use?
JSS: Fair use was a concept that the courts developed under the pre-1976 law. The way I think and talk about it is as a concept of a "permitted infringement." You are using somebody's copyrighted material without his or her permission. Under certain circumstances, the court said that they were going to allow that, that fair use is a defense to what would otherwise be a copyright infringement. The things that the courts look at to see if something qualifies for this fair use defense are: How much footage or material did you take? What was the purpose for which it was taken? Was it scholarship and review, or educational, or was it commercial? Does the use in any way supplant or interfere with the sale of the original?

In 1976 when Congress passed the law, they built fair use into the statute, into the copyright law. So there is a provision in the copyright law that lays out four or five tests for fair use. They made it clear from the language that these tests were not the only tests; there may be other factors that one might look to determine if something is fair use. It looks at the quantity of the use, relative to the whole, and the purpose of the use.

If you are writing a book review, you can quote big chunks of the book, which might look like you are taking a lot of the book except that relative to the whole, it is not so much, and that it is a review. Parody is another element of fair use. Parody is a whole world unto itself. The parody defense is sort of like fair use except that usually if there is a parody, you are taking the whole thing. If it is a song parody, you are going to use the whole song, it's not like you are taking just eight bars. That is a whole different set of tests.

CK: Are copyright laws the same in all countries?
JSS: There are differences, but there are international conventions that help to smooth out these differences. When the copyright law changed here in America in 1976, one of the big reasons for the change was that we were the only country, among those that paid attention to copyright, that measured the term of copyright by years from that mysterious moment of publication. Everywhere else in the copyright world, they measured the term of copyright by the life of the author plus 50 years. When we changed the copyright law, we got rid of the whole term of years with renewals, and we went to the life of the authors—plus, the number of years keeps changing.

CK: What does Right of Publicity mean?
JSS: Right of Publicity exists in some states, but not all states. Some states recognize what is called the Right of Privacy. It is variously defined in various places, but basically it means the right to be left alone. You have the right not to have your name and face and your stories told without your permission, to a certain extent. It depends on who you are, on the circumstances, if it's a public event. In New York, for example, the Right of Privacy is fairly limited. It implies almost exclusively to somebody's name and likeness in advertising. The Right of Privacy is what is called a personal right—once you die, it's gone. There is no such thing as the invasion of privacy or libel of a dead person; when somebody dies, they are fair game.

The Right of Publicity is a relatively new extension of the Right of Privacy that doesn't exist in New York. It exists in a number of states, most notably in California. It is a property right as opposed to a personal right. It has to do with using a person's identity for commercial purposes to sell goods, so that it was created in California largely to protect celebrities. And because it's a property right, it carries over after the death of the person and, in that way, protects dead celebrities. The key is that the name has to have value and has to have been exploited commercially during the person's life.

CK: What is the ultimate goal of a contract?
JSS: The ultimate goal of a contract is to articulate to the parties what the understanding is between them in such a way that you never have to look at it again. It's to describe the understanding between the parties. It's a very valuable process. What happens in drafting contracts is that I will write something down and send it to the client, or to the other side, and very often they say, "I can't agree to that," so it's a very good thing that we wrote it down that way. So then we change it to what you can agree to or what you think you are agreeing to.

CK: Is an oral agreement legally binding?

JSS: Sometimes. Samuel Goldwyn once said an oral agreement isn't worth the paper it's written on. Yes, oral agreements can be binding, they can be enforceable, but they are harder to enforce because if there is any dispute as to what the understanding was, there is no piece of paper. With an oral agreement, one person says, "I agreed to this," and the other guy said, "well, I only agreed to that." There is something called the statute of frauds, which requires that certain kinds of contracts must be in writing. Copyright licenses must be in writing; any license of intellectual property must also be in writing.

CK: Do student producers need a lawyer for their projects?
JSS: If you are making a $15,000 movie as a thesis project, then maybe not. But if you have any notion of ever doing anything with it beyond showing it to the department, then you probably will need to get a lawyer involved at some point because nobody will distribute it unless they know that you have all the rights and clearances that you need, and that there won't be a bunch of claims flying in as soon as this thing ends up on television somewhere.

CK: When would a producer involve a lawyer if she wanted to shop it around to festivals?
JSS: Earlier rather than later. I recognize the financial implications of that bit of advice, but that is the truth—that's when you should do it.

CK: How are lawyers paid for their services?
JSS: Variously. Some lawyers charge by the hour. Sometimes with a production, with a producer, the lawyer will be a budget item; there will be a line item in the budget that covers legal services. Lawyers may get a percentage, almost like a commission on some of the afterlife uses, so when you are finished with the production, the line item will cover the production legal services. But it very well might be that once the picture is shot, and there is a distributor and the lawyer is making a distribution deal, he may get some sort of percentage of what the producer gets.

CK: What good legal resources would you recommend to producers?
JSS: We have an office in California and one of the partners, Michael Donaldson, has just put out the second edition of a book called *Copyright and Clearance.* It's good. It's broken down by subject matter with text and forms. There is another book that I use, called *This Business of Music* that's a useful handy guide to music issues.

CK: How do you handle the pressure that must surely come with the territory?
JSS: When you have been doing this for a while, you know what you are looking for and what you need to pay attention to. When I look at contracts, I actually read them, and I pay a lot of attention to them, but I know what I am looking for. I know with respect to any given project where the problems might be, what won't be a problem, or what I know may be a problem but nobody is going to be able to do anything about it anyway.

I have been doing this for longer than 20 minutes, so I bring a body of judgment to it that is mostly pretty good, most of the time. Do I worry about missing stuff? Sometimes. When I'm drafting contracts, after I'm finished, I will always go back over it, not just for each word, but I have a checklist: Did I do this and did I do this? I make sure that I haven't left anything out. Do I ever make mistakes? I'm sure that I do. Not bad ones, but I do. I'm not always calm, sometimes I yell, but I know that I'm good at it because I've been doing this a long time and I have pretty decent judgment, and not just about the specific words in a contract but about people and their relationships to people and the business they do. You just sort of develop a feel for it.

JUSTIN WILKES
Executive Producer, @radical.media (including *Iconoclasts; Jay-Z in Fade To Black; The Exonerated*)

CK: How do you define your job?
JW: I love this question because my mom still asks me this every day: "So. You direct the actors?" "No, Mom." "You work the camera?" "No, Mom." "You do the editing?"

"No, Mom." There's no simple answer, at least not one that I've ever heard. The best description is (which I can't even take credit for, but since the person who said it is a good friend of mine, I can rip him off): The producer is like the air traffic controller. Your job is to land the plane.

Getting into producing is a funny thing, and you'll find it's the only profession where you don't really have to do anything to get the title. If you look at a list of every producer on the planet, you'll find that only the smallest percentage of them actually do what I'd consider producing. This is bizarre to me because you can't just wake up one day and say, "I'm a cobbler." First, you have to become an apprentice and work for many years studying the craft. Then finally, after many pairs of shoes, you finally earn the right to call yourself a cobbler. Not so with producing. Anyone can be a producer. You can have money and call yourself a producer. You can have an idea and become a producer. It's truly the easiest title in the world to assume. But I don't suppose you'd be reading this book if the title was all you were interested in. My personal story is that I worked my butt off and did any job I could get my hands on. I got my current job by sitting on the couch in reception until they hired me.

CK: One premise of this book is that "a producer is a producer is a producer," that most producing skills can be applied to most areas of TV and new media. What's your take on this?
JW: Absolutely. It can even be applied to other mediums. The art of producing is a specific skill set with a different set of tools for each job. Every project is a challenge in its own specific way, but ultimately it's the same. It's like dating.

CK: Is there a producer's personality?
JW: Incredibly handsome. Deliciously charming.

CK: Totally true, at least in your case. What else are you good at?
JW: As an executive producer in @radical.media's entertainment division, I develop and oversee an assortment of projects ranging from episodic television, one-offs, and feature film projects. It's not as glamorous as it sounds. On any given project, it involves everything from writing, developing, being a liaison to the client/agency/network, scheduling, budgeting, line producing, and overseeing the editorial.

Some of @radical.media's recent credits are the feature films *Jay-Z in Fade To Black, Metallica: Some Kind of Monster,* the Academy Award-winning documentary *Fog of War,* and the Grammy Award-winning *Concert for George.* Our television credits include *Iconoclasts* on the Sundance Channel, *The Exonerated* for truTV; *Nike Battlegrounds: King of the World* for MTV, and *The Life* for ESPN.

CK: The pitching process is an integral part of the producer's job. What's your approach?
JW: I believe there are two main parts to a good pitch. Getting in the door, and then delivering once you get in the door. Both are critical, and both require some thought and strategy. Fortunately, we're at the point as a company where we have a reputation for our past work and we've developed relationships with many people at most of the major networks and studios. However, there are still plenty of times where we'll cold-call an assistant to set up a meeting with a development or programming person at a network. Whether there's a relationship or not, it usually takes multiple calls and persistence to actually schedule a meeting (not to mention the constant *rescheduling* that often occurs after an initial time is set).

Now for the pitch itself. We're big fans of not sending our pitch materials ahead of time and instead, showing up with a simple, but well art-directed pitch book that takes the reader through the concept. We'll usually talk through the pitch and refer to the book as we go. Occasionally, we'll use a piece of video or still photos to capture the essence of what we're presenting.

The power of a pitch book shouldn't be underestimated. Basically, until your show is produced, the pitch book *is* the show. Everything from the overall look and feel, to the writing, to the design should be reflected in the book. It becomes a great presentational tool and a great way to solidify your own vision of the project.

CK: What is it about producing that's so attractive to you?
JW: I love bringing talented people together. There's no greater feeling than standing on a shoot, sitting in an edit session, or watching the final product on TV, knowing that you as the producer pulled together an incredible, hard-working group of people to create it.

CK: What is it about producing that you don't love?
JW: I hate how slow development takes. I hate raising money. I hate people who say they're going to do something and then don't.

CK: What does the future of television look like from your perspective?
JW: There will be a continual increase in channels and other methods of delivery. You'll receive so much content through your cable, satellite dish, Internet, cell phone, car, washing machine, and toaster that you'll finally turn the damn thing off and read a good book. In the world of advertising, we're seeing a return to one of the earliest forms whereby a brand goes beyond sponsorship of a program and actually owns the content embedded within it.

CK: The producer's job is a hard and demanding one. How do you keep a balance between your job and your other life?
JW: What's the other life? Have you actually seen it? Oh, please tell me what's it like!

CK: What would be on your Top Ten list of what a producer should know?
JW: OK. Here goes…

Top Ten List of What a Producer Should Know

1. You're always going to come in over budget, so budget accordingly.
2. The network/client will always ask you to make an impossible change at the last minute and you have to make it possible.
3. Put your day-to-day problems into a larger project context when making decisions.
4. Lawyers and agents are not producers. Many would like to be. Many others think they are. But they're not.
5. Your lawyer works for you (not the other way around). Best advice I ever got from another producer.
6. You set the vibe for the entire production. If you yell, others will yell. Lead by example.
7. Great ideas are easy to come by. Actually *making* great ideas is the challenge.
8. Learn every job. A good producer knows how to shoot, edit, gaff, grip, and hold a boom. Not only do people in those positions respect you for knowing

something about their craft, but also it is invaluable when you're figuring out production logistics and budgeting.

9. Craft services is the key to success.
10. Don't date the PA. I know you want to. But don't do it.

SCOTT A. WILLIAMS
Co-Executive Producer, *Bones* (Fox Television)

CK: So, Scott…you are the co-executive producer of the Fox show Bones. *What's your particular job on the show?*

SW: As the ranks of being a television writer go, from staff writer on up, by the time you reach co-executive producer, it's where you have the most responsibility, short of being the actual showrunner or executive producer. One of the luxuries of being the co-EP is that you are not the one under the hot spotlight. You're just to the left of the spotlight. Which is a double-edged sword, really. While the showrunner has final say over all decisions, he or she also has the most pressure. A good co-EP wants most to serve the showrunner, and by extension the show, but the pressure's dialed down considerably. I have the showrunner to deal with, but the showrunner has EVERYONE ELSE to deal with, like network, studio, actors, etc. Hopefully, I'm taking some of that burden off. A good Co-EP is the showrunner's right-hand. You learn to be a good lieutenant, not the general. You learn to carry out the show's vision, while lending your own creativity to it.

CK: What is the difference between an executive producer and a showrunner?

SW: On my current show *Bones*, Hart Hanson is the creator/showrunner. He wrote the pilot and he's got a ton of experience—he's worked on *Judging Amy*, prior to that, *Joan of Arcadia*, and *Traders* in Canada. So his is the actual voice of the show. Our other executive producer, Stephen Nathan, is also a brilliant writer, and he handles all our postproduction, but he acquiesces final say on the running of the show to Hart, to the creator.

Every show's a bit different. *Third Watch* was a John Wells' show, and ultimately John is the master of all of his shows, but he delegates superbly. Ed Bernero, who co-created the show, was the actual showrunner and ultimately, the only person who had the power to overrule Ed was John, and that's an unusual position.

With Hart, because he's the showrunner of *Bones*, the only person with jurisdiction to override him would be the network or the studio. And even then he has a fighting voice in all that. They respect his voice.

CK: As the right-hand person to Hart—as his lieutenant—what are your day-to-day duties?

SW: Like I said, it varies from show to show. What Hart asks from me on a day-to-day basis at *Bones* is primarily to keep the writers' room constantly running and creating new story lines. So basically I'm the conduit between the writing staff and Hart. While Hart is busy writing, rewriting, fielding phone calls from the cast, the network, the studio, above-the-line people, below-the-line people and lots of people I can't even think of at the moment, I'm the person who keeps shoveling coal into the furnace, if you will—making sure that we have three or four scripts in the pipeline.

In television there's a saying: You've got to feed the monster every eight days. Every eight days, you've got to have another great script ready to be shot. So I'm constantly conferring with Hart and Stephen: "What do you think about this or that story?" If they like it, we'll pursue it with their personal spin or wants. I'm in there always making sure that we as a staff are ahead of the curve on stories and scripts. We have a staff of nine. That's a lot of people up there to be in one room, breaking one story, breaking one episode. So we'll break it up into two rooms, even three, so that we're constantly ahead of schedule. When we've got episode 10 about to shoot, we've got to be coming up with episodes 11, 12, and 13. We've got to be talking about all those things at once. The focus for me is to just always keep the writers' room going and make sure that new stories are constantly being generated. That's the responsibility that Hart gives to me.

CK: Does Hart provide some sort of an overall story arc for the series, with the characters' relationships and plotlines, that the writers can use for guidelines?
SW: Absolutely. Hart or Stephen will come in and say "OK, over the next few episodes, I would like to see if you can get this character to find a girlfriend, a love interest, a boyfriend, or, this person's mother is going to come to town, or this person is in an auto accident, we've got to work that into a story. On a show like *Bones*, or any of these crime shows that I've worked on in the last few years, we're going to solve the crime in the episode, but we've also got this three- or four-episode arc, this journey that one of our lead characters has taken, and we have to service that. So that gives us a guideline where it's like, OK, what kind of crime can you solve that can dramatically and thematically work with the journey our individual character has taken.

You've got a show like *Bones*, that has our lead character, Brennan, played by Emily Deschanel, whose father is going through some legal troubles. But while she's dealing with that, she also doing her job solving a crime. Ideally, she'll learn something about herself with relation to her father based upon the crime she's solving.

CK: You have a staff of nine writers on Bones. *Does each have a specialty? Say, is one a forensics expert, maybe someone else is good at dialogue, another is sort of a relationships person—how do you allocate writing assignments?*
SW: When you put together a staff, you try to do that. I've heard it described as assembling a really great dinner party. You want people who can inspire one another creatively. And generally, this means a good mix of experiences and backgrounds. For example, every staff I've been on has had at least one lawyer. We have a great lawyer on our staff now. He no longer practices law, but he practiced for years, then went into writing. He's the guy that we're always able to turn to for accurate legalese. I've learned a lot over the years just from experience on television, but if you need a legal question answered, you turn to him. And yes, there's also the medical person. I worked on a staff that had a doctor; if you work on a show like *ER*, you're going to have doctors who are on the staff who know all the medical stuff.

That's not to say we don't have researchers as well. It really helps to have a wide range of strengths and experiences on your staff. If you're writing a *CSI* show, you might have writers that are more technical working with you on a day-to-day basis, but if you're writing a more character-driven show, you obviously want writers great with character. Ideally, you want to be that well-rounded writer who does it all pretty well.

CK: As a Kathy Reichs' fan, I was curious if Bones *could capture the character of Temperance Brennan, who's melancholy yet intense about her work and good at it. And her relationship with Special Agent Seeley Booth walks a thin line. The show works—the writing, the lighting, the music, all paint this picture of Brennan and her relationship to everyone around her. Was this consciously discussed, and how much simply evolved as the show did?*
SW: I think if you were to watch the first few episodes of *Bones*, you might say some of those earlier ones were perhaps the most faithful to the Kathy Reichs' books. But then as

you're working with Hart and with David Boreanaz and Emily Deschanel, you know there are going to be these little changes, because they bring different things to the characters than perhaps what Kathy represents in her books.

But a natural evolution happens with the characters and the stories you tell. Obviously Hart is not writing a Kathy Reichs novel, Hart is writing a Hart Hanson teleplay, so it's Hart's voice. Kathy's a great writer and her books are a huge success, but I think that people who are fans of both can't help but read Kathy Reichs' books now and see Brennan as Emily Deschanel, despite the age difference. You can't help but hear her voice in the voice of that character. So, at some point, they meet in the middle. The show has taken on its own tone, and while all the characters are based on Kathy Reichs' books, the stories we're telling are not her books at all.

We're writing 22 to 24 scripts a season, so we have to keep coming up with a new and original way to tell them. I've been on the phone with Kathy—and she's great, by the way, and scary smart—and she'll say, "This is not necessarily the way I would do it, but I recognize the needs of your show to do it this way." This might be not the way Kathy Reichs would have her Brennan solve the crime but she recognizes that the show has taken on a life of its own. She's very gracious about that. I think she also recognizes that the show definitely is a boost to her books in the same way that her books were initially a boost to the show.

CK: So many scripted shows now are "ripped from the headlines." Where do you go for your stories?
SW: It's pretty hard not to rip from the headlines today. It's pretty competitive in terms of trying not to tell a story you've seen on another show. Every crime show I've been on, for instance, has done their "buried alive" episode, with the ticking clock to save that person who's been buried alive. Any actual crimes having to do with finding lost remains or deteriorated bones, we're all over those, obviously. Often, too, we start off with the real crime that we see as a jumping-off point, but the final episode is not at all reminiscent of the actual crime. I was on the show *Without a Trace* for a season, and that's a terrific show that's generally not about its lead characters. It's about the people who go missing and their lives, so you tend not to have as many personal main character arcs on a show like that as we did on *Third Watch* for one.

CK: A great show, Third Watch. *It was very much about personal relationships, and much less about actual crime, or paramedics, or police car action.*
SW: It's still the show I'm proudest to have been a part of. Having been on it during 9/11, it made it very personal to a lot of us. Here we were, dealing with cops and firemen and paramedics who were most directly affected by 9/11. That show struck the best balance between personal stories and crime stories. There's an audience for both, and we tried to make fans of both genres happy. It was never a huge breakout hit, but it hung on for six years, with a very loyal following. The fans of *Third Watch* tuned in because they liked cop shows, but they were also deeply invested in our characters.

CK: Programmers today are increasingly being pressured to get the advertising message into the body of the show rather than in the commercial breaks. Have you had to deal with anything like that yet, or do you see it looming ahead?
SW: I think product placement is the way it's all going to go eventually. Depending on technology, we're going to go to our computer to buy a sweater that one of the characters on the show is wearing. Absolutely. We have never been asked to product-place on any of the shows that I've worked on, but I do know we get good deals if we use a certain cell phone on a show, or there's a certain gadget that they want promoted. The GE

products at NBC—I can't say they're not featured in a show on occasion, or that GE's friendly and they'll give us X-amount of microwave ovens for this appliance store scene. But I do think the wave of the future is going to go in that direction, especially with the advent of TiVo and DVR. Since we're able to fast-forward through commercials, it's all headed toward new media. Five to 10 years from now, nobody's going to have a TV at home anyway. It's all going to be on computer or cell phones.

CK: Most shows now offer webisode and mobisodes. Does Bones?
SW: Yeah, we were asked to come up with short scenes that were just promotional for the show, and that's a lot of what the Writers Guild strike was about—what they call "promotion" is what we call writing content. They wanted us to do mobisodes that could be downloaded to a phone for a buck, two bucks. And we said, "Hey wait a minute. That's revenue, and why is that not being shared with us?" That's all gotten worked out in negotiation, and at the end of the strike there were the beginnings of reasonably fair compensation for that stuff.

Personally, I can't see anybody wanting to watch an episode of a show on their cell phone...call me crazy. I have a video iPod and I'll occasionally download something to watch on an airplane, but on a cell phone? I'm not that desperate for content. I'd rather be old-fashioned and read a book. But it seems to be the way it's going, and it's what we're preparing for.

CK: Let's talk about your entry into this world of producing and writing for TV.
SW: I was very lucky in that it sort of found me. I had been an actor when I moved out to Los Angeles, where I started a small theatre company, and through that I began writing plays and one-act plays. I really got bit by the bug. The minute I was two pages into my first one-act play, suddenly, the applause came from within for the first time in my life. I was enjoying what I was writing, and so I went ahead and pursued it. The first time you hear something you wrote performed on the stage and you hear all this response—it's a great drug.

I studied and took classes, and wrote like crazy. I managed to get an agent and got some work in feature films. I was really only pursuing feature films, working with some really good people. The first thing I sold was to Ray Liotta, and on the strength of that script, I got a writing assignment for Ron Howard and Imagine, and Kevin Costner. I worked my way up through writing all sorts of screenplays that just weren't getting made.

And then, by a complete stroke of luck, David Milch, who was the creator of *NYPD Blue* and *Deadwood*, had lunch with a producer friend, and he said, "Do you know any writers who I don't know?" The producer gave him my Ray Liotta script. Milch read it, and I got a call to have lunch with him. He said, "Did you ever think about writing television?" And naively, I said, "I'm more of a feature guy," and God bless Milch, he said, "Really? When was the last time you heard 'action'?" I was like, "duh well...never." He said, "OK, come with me and you'll hear 'action' every week."

I owe my career to David Milch reaching out for me. He gave me an *NYPD Blue* script to write. It was sort of an audition piece. On the strength of that, I got my first staff job on *Brooklyn South*, which was a one-season show on CBS. I was a staff writer with Ed Bernero, who then went on to co-create *Third Watch*. After *Brooklyn South* was cancelled, I worked my way up the ladder on various shows that were short-lived, until Ed brought me over to *Third Watch* for season three and I stayed for three years. That was pretty much my ascendancy into producing.

You go from staff writer to story editor, to executive story editor, co-producer, producer, supervising producer, co-EP, and executive producer. John Wells is the guy who really breeds showrunners. He teaches you from the very earliest part of your writing career. You write an episode, it gets shot, you're in the editing room overseeing certain things. He delegates well, he teaches you from the ground up how to complete an episode of television. I owe so much to having worked with people like Wells and Bernero and Tim Kring on *Crossing Jordan* and Hart and Stephen on *Bones*. I learned so much from these guys and it's been great for me ever since. I've been blessed. Like I said, television found me and I was just lucky that it really appealed to me.

CK: As a writer, do you see a distinct difference between television and film?
SW: What's fun about a film is that it's your own little world, and you're getting to create every little aspect of it. But you hand your screenplay into the studio, and the system now is that they just throw more writers at it. The script gets rewritten to the nines. I've rewritten people, people have rewritten me, which is just fine, that's just the movie biz. In television, I find it more rewarding, because you write something and it's being shot in a couple of weeks. It's a great, great feeling to write and rewrite and create with real live actors and directors and technical people on a real live set. And in a few more weeks, it's airing on television—so your rewards are more immediate.

Television's great for that. Obviously, when you see a great movie, you say, "Ah, I gotta do one of those." But I'll go back to full-time feature writing when I retire from television. The rigors of television are so demanding that you rarely have time to write independently. I tried to do it for a few years where I would moonlight with features, but that can burn you out in a hurry.

CK: That brings me to the question of maintaining balance. How do you balance real life with work life?
SW: Balance? Oh, I've heard of that (laughs). It comes and goes. There are times in television when you're completely overwhelmed. You've got to pump it out every eight days, and it's not always great. You get scripts thrown back at you by the networks sometimes. You get a ton of notes at all times. You're having to please a lot of different people, and you have fights, but you have to pick your battles.

Depending on the show you're on, some shows work late into the night. Me, I want to be home for dinner with my family. Life's too short to live it at work. But there's still a job to do and that monster to feed, so I do have dinner with my family, and I kiss my daughter goodnight and then say goodnight to my wife, and I close my office door and I'm back to writing. There's always the next script. It's a rare occasion that you have the weekend where you don't have to spend some time sitting down writing. Weekends? What are those?

There's such demand placed on having to put out a script every eight days. That is, unless you're a savant like David Kelley, who pumps these things out by himself and really quickly. Kelley delegates really well in terms of having people handle a lot of the other responsibilities, so he's free to write. But most showrunners and exec-producers and co-EPs that I know have so many other responsibilities they can never be doing just one thing.

Balance is a hard thing to achieve, but it's a must. You learn to appreciate free time like never before. Sometimes, it's like, I'm sorry, I've got to put this down and clear my head for a weekend, and just go away with the family. Do something that's not work-related or you'll just go crazy otherwise. For me, it's just time with my wife and my daughter.

Plus I like playing sports, running around. People say, "What's your hobby?" and I say, "Writing is my hobby, and I'm lucky they're sort of paying me for it."

CK: For anyone thinking of getting into producing content for television or some future permutation of TV, what would you want them to know?

SW: I've worked with USC Film School grads, and I've worked with people who worked at 7-Eleven in Texas. I myself got out of college and I tended bar in New York and L.A. for a total of about 12 years—that's including college—and I wouldn't necessarily recommend that path for anyone, but I do know that experience is a huge part of why I'm here. David Milch hired me not only because he liked my writing, but because I had lived a life.

So whenever I get a 22-year-old kid fresh out of film school who says, "I'm ready to write television," I tell her or him that yes, there are people who can do it. J.J. Abrams was one young wunderkind who came out of college, but if you look at his earliest work, it's clearly the work of someone who was fairly naive about life. He learned on the job and he'd probably be the first to tell you. *Regarding Henry* was a fine film, but it was still life according to a 24-year-old.

There is no wasted job, no wasted time for a writer. Life experience is everything. Without it, what is there to write about? If you're working at a McDonalds and you're an aspiring writer, you can write the greatest story about the French-fryer that anyone ever wrote. When I was in my twenties, I was in a very big hurry—I wanted to succeed yesterday. But what I know now is "get a life," continue to work out there in the world, continue to write, and know that everything you do is material for your work.

I thank God for those 12 years behind the bar because I have a catalog of Runyonesque types forever in my head. I've seen people at their worst and at their best—under the influence of alcohol and not. Every little experience adds up to the writer I am now. I've worked with people who ascended as professional students, and I find that they're the first people who'll usually say, "Oh, people wouldn't say that," or "Oh, that wouldn't happen." The worst thing I hear is "I don't buy it—I don't buy that that could happen." Are you kidding me? In a world where anything is possible, you can make anything happen on the page. You can make anything believable and real, because all things are possible in this world.

When I deal with people who are professional students, they may certainly know things that I don't but it's still no substitute for living a life, and being out there in the world. Every experience has value and worth in your writing.

BERNIE YOUNG
Executive Producer, *The Martha Stewart Show*
LAURIE RICH
Executive in Charge of Production, *The Martha Stewart Show*

CK: Bernie and Laurie, thanks for taking the time to share what you each do on The Martha Stewart Show. *Let's start with you, Laurie. As the Executive in Charge of Production, what areas of production are you in charge of?*
LR: We need to complete an order of shows every year, and that number has been 180. I think next year we're going to 160. Every show is different—when we did *Rosie* [*The*

Rosie O'Donnell Show], it was 195 shows. We've been producing 180 shows during the course of the season, doing anywhere from five to six shows a week.

Many weeks we shoot six shows and that's not easy. We're live usually three days a week and then we do afternoon shows on those weeks. The days are usually Tuesday to Thursday, we all kind of prefer that. It's good to have a Monday to prep and a Friday to prep, but it's not always the case. A lot of it depends on Martha's schedule. Occasionally we need to put in special shows at times like Halloween. Our schedules fluctuate around the special shows.

It takes a village or an army to produce this kind of show. It's very unusual because it's not a talk show, and it's not a variety show, it sort of falls in the lifestyle category—that's probably the best way to describe it because there's a little bit of everything. There's crafting, there's cooking, we have gardening segments, we have animal segments, and we have some fashion shows. Every single one of those segments is well-produced— each needs to look fabulous.

CK: How many producers work for you at one time? Are they on staff or freelancers?
LR: Most are staff people, though occasionally we'll pick up freelancers in the art department. Or, if a producer is not around or ill for a period of time, we'll need to go with a freelancer. Most are staff—there are even some shows where one segment may have more than one producer.

If we have a celebrity guest, there may be a producer who's working with the celebrity, prepping them—maybe they're doing a gardening segment or they're going to cook with Martha—while other producers are working on the different elements of the gardening or cooking or the crafting they're doing.

I think what goes on behind the scenes is what makes the show very unusual and very special. With the producer comes a lighting designer whose cues and different looks depend on what we're doing that day. There's an art department staff, which is a very large one because they're responsible for dressing not just that segment but the entire look of the set each day, and that can change, depending on the seasonal requirements, depending what's going on that day. And we do special theme shows, so that's also very unusual. Then there's the directing team—our directors have to take the camera shots, make sure it's all perfect, make sure the tapes are rolled perfectly, the graphics look great. You've got the support of the production team in the background, making sure that everything else in the promo looks fabulous, making sure the feeds are leaving the building properly, to the transportation of the guests and the audience members getting to the studio each and every day, so that security knows what's going on. That's what I'm saying, it takes a village here to get each show done.

CK: Bernie, you're the Executive Producer of the show. Just how many staff do you work with to make this show happen?
BY: About 70, I'd say. You know, there is so much coordination that goes into producing this show, and it's Laurie's department—the production department—that is responsible for the coordination of the show on that stage. The stagehands, the directing team, the art department, the set design, the producers, in and out—it is a real ballet. And when it's live, anything can happen. Hopefully we've thought about it, we've anticipated the timing and the changes that could occur, so when Laurie says it takes a village, it truly does. Everybody knows their role, and the coordination of that is really key. So the more successful shows have the best coordination. I think our team is second to none.

LR: And Bernie's the man who heads the whole village up. He's Mayor of the village!

BY: It's always interesting. This is a very unique show. It's unique because the company is unique. The fact that the founder, Martha Stewart, had a vision for what her business could and should be is what we carry out. So, to start as a caterer and build a business based on making your life better, improving things in ways you would never think about makes our lives really interesting and unique.

We look at those areas in which Martha's interested and make them come to life on television. For our show, someone in her corporation has already thought about an idea, somebody's done the research and development, someone else has photographed it, has already written a story in one of the publications. We bring it to light here, on the show.

We're not recreating the wheel. We know what the brand is, so let's sell the brand. We do that every day, and we do that while we're trying to entertain the audience and keep them interested. Hopefully everybody's learning something because after all, Martha is a teacher and she wants to learn, too.

CK: Has Martha established parameters that define what her brand is, or isn't?
BY: You just know it. You can feel the aesthetic. You see it. It's in front of you. If you just let yourself live it, you can bring it to life. So it's not "this is the brand, that isn't." It's working within a system that has already been built. But you don't stop there—how do you make that better on a daily basis? How do you improve on what you think is perfect? Something may be the right answer at that moment, but in the next moment, life has moved on. So you have to continue growing, continue to look at things in a way like, "that was yesterday, this is today." What do we need today to make it different and still keep it interesting?

LR: And make everything look beautiful. That is something that Martha did tell us. I think that is something that a lot of us have taken with us in our personal lives and in the way we look at things. "What can we do to make that look even more attractive?" We all take a sense of pride in the way our offices look, and we've followed through with that in our homes. The art department are masters at this, it's amazing to watch them work each day and do their thing, because they're bringing in Martha's aesthetic and what she envisions, and what she wants to see is so beautiful to look at.

BY: It is aspirational. People look at the show and say, "I want to emulate that. I want to do that, I want to be precise in what I do. I want to make it just as beautiful as that." And it's all possible, you see that every single day. Say there's a segment with a beautiful dish. Somebody made that dish. If it's a particular project with sewing or crafts, somebody actually made that; somebody gave that idea some real thought, looked at it, figured out exactly what would make it just right, and then did that.

Martha said something once that gives an insight into the company. She really believes that it's not just a corporation, it's a company of creative people. In that way, you know what she's thinking and how everyone looks at it. They continue to create, continue to dream, continue to grow in that way. Together, we'll make a great business.

CK: How do you measure who and what your audience and their demographics are?
BY: We've been lucky. We have a very honest audience who tells us what they think. Occasionally we'll ask our viewers questions online and they tell us what they like, what they'd rather not see more of, what they'd like to see more of, how it impacts their life and, quite frankly, they really like the "how-to" segments—they want to learn, they want to see how Martha does all the things she does. They have followed her for 25 years or so in everything she's done.

CK: The show is in its fourth season. Have you been with it since the beginning, Bernie?

BY: No, I've been here a year and a half. But I'm very familiar with the old show. The old show was a How-To, but it was a How-To without an [live] audience—yet it still resonated with her core audience. It had very loyal viewers who wanted to see gardening, even to see how you can raise chickens—so many different avenues.

The thought—coming back to this show now—was to do more entertainment. We have celebrity guests, there's some entertainment there, but the core is still How-To. So you just add those few elements—and with a live audience, you get different energy. Plus, you're in the studio now, you're not out on a field piece. We still do field pieces which Martha does by herself or with experts who we call in for every area that we have a segment on. So it's just about adding a few elements to get the old format to work.

CK: Laurie, you've built what is essentially a core set for the show that you can then add design elements onto. What might change on this set from one show to another?

LR: We have the home base kitchen area, where you see Martha at the beginning of the show and where, when she has celebrity guests, the cooking takes place. We have a real working prep kitchen which everyone loves. Sometimes, we'll have celebrities in that kitchen, or we'll do various segments in there. There's work going on there all through the show, before the show, after the show—it's also where they prepare and test recipes for future shows.

Then we have the craft area which is next to the home base; it's where crafty segments take place. We have a swing area where our beautiful greenhouse was set up by a greenhouse company. And we can do anything in this area—from music performances to fashion shows. Often, the stacking of the show is what determines where the segments get produced during the course of the program.

It's a great studio—it's so large. There are very few like it in New York. We're very lucky that we have that. To watch the cameramen moving from Position A to Position B during the course of a commercial break—particularly during the live shows because we have a very finite period of time, just two minutes for them to move—it's always incredible. It's like a mini Saturday Night Live to see them with the cable pullers, everyone getting from Point A which could be home base, all the way over to the potting shed. It doesn't sound like a lot, but during the commercial break, that's a fascinating thing to watch.

CK: How many cameras do you use?

LR: We have seven cameras. We have a jib camera, a Steadicam, three pedestal cameras, and two handhelds.

CK: How many overhead microphones do you hang above your audience?

LR: I don't know the number, but a lot—they need to catch the ambient audience applause. All of our guests have wireless lavs on them.

CK: Your show has a better sound quality to my ears than most live-audience shows do...

LR: We can totally credit that to our sound engineer who not only does our daily show but also created the sound design on the show. In the past, we've had musical performances, very popular people who have been on shows all over the country who have come on our show and have commented on how wonderful the sound is. Everyone does a fantastic job. We're very proud of that.

CK: Laurie, how did you get into producing as a career?
LR: In my case, this is not what I was going to do. I was going to dance in musical comedy. I ended up at Hunter College here in New York, and they couldn't find me an internship in my interests, so they suggested that I meet this gentleman who was the arts editor for WCBS television in New York. I met with him and he wanted me to work with him every day. I wasn't sure that's what I wanted but when I walked into the news room at WCBS, I fell in love with it. I don't think I left there for about seven months.

And that's how I wound up in the business. I worked at a local station for years, producing. I started out as a production secretary—which they don't have anymore—even though I flunked my first typing test so I didn't get the job. I was brave enough to go to a secretarial school where they put headsets on me; I had to learn how to type with someone talking in my ear. Then they called me back again because they'd given the job to someone else who dropped out. I did every crummy job there was to do back then and worked my way up the ranks.

CK: Would you recommend this route to someone else?
LR: I do, but not everyone has that attitude that, "I'll just come in this door and take this job." Very often I'll speak to somebody for a PA position and they say, "Oh that's not what I want to do, I want to be an assistant talent booker or I want to be on the producer team." I do think that folks who have gone up through the ranks can really appreciate what everyone else around them does. They get a much better picture of the overall picture of how everything gets produced, how the show gets put together.

People have started as interns and receptionists, then moved up to be APs and EPs and other producers, and I think they're terrific. Someone may start out as a PA and then two months later, they're a producer on a show—it happens.

CK: Bernie, what was your path to producing?
BY: I started as a personal manager. I would represent talent. One of the first talent I managed was Ben Vereen. I got very lucky with Ben because he did everything—from television to film. So I got a chance to watch Bob Fosse put together *All That Jazz*. I got the chance to talk with producers all the time, and learned about what they did. I'd ask them a lot of questions and annoy them.

In the comedy business, a number of my clients had series TV, and Rosie O'Donnell was one of my clients for over 22 years. My actual production experience started with her talk show—by then, I'd been around all these shows and certainly understood what it took to put a show like that together and what everybody did. So coming in, although it was my first real production, hands-on production experience, I had seen it from another angle. I was absolutely prepared for it and enjoyed it.

To see it from the outside looking in, it was always exciting to me. Anything in this business that helps you learn, to me, is always interesting. It's never the same, it changes every day. It's not a job where you go, "Okay, I've got to do that for another eight hours." You know what's coming, it's always about being prepared for what could happen. *The Rosie O'Donnell Show* is where I met Laurie, and we worked together for six years.

Then this show came along. My production experience was always about knowing what everybody did on the show. From Day One, I wanted to know everyone—the PA up to the EP—to understand their responsibilities, what do they do on a daily basis. I believe that you're always better off when you know exactly what it is you're responsible for.

I got lucky in this job, to have been able to coordinate a great staff like this and to help to make this show come together, each day.

> To be nobody-but-yourself—in a world which is doing its best, night and day, to make you everybody else—means to fight the hardest battle which any human being can fight; and never stop fighting.
>
> **e. e. cummings**

REVIEW QUESTIONS

1. Choose two producers from this chapter and compare and contrast their views on the qualifications and responsibilities of a producer.

2. Examine the roles and skills sets of various types of producers (e.g., line producer vs. supervising producer).

3. How does a good producer prepare for postproduction?

4. From your perspective, what should a good producer's chief concerns be?

5. Research the concept of "convergence" and discuss its current and future effects on television.

6. What genre most interests you? Research two notable producers and their projects in that genre and briefly discuss what made them stand out.

7. What are five internship opportunities available to you? Get the contact names and addresses for these possibilities.

8. Who do you know? You may know someone, somewhere, who works in media. If so, arrange for an interview. Ask what his or her responsibilities are now, and the steps taken to get to this position. Write a brief report, or tape a short piece, on this process.

9. Design a pitch for a specific project and examine its possible outlets (broadcast network, cable channel, pay-per-view, film festival, direct-to-video release, etc.). Explain how you would tailor your pitch for each outlet.

10. Research the pilots created for your favorite channel in the last season. Look for patterns between the shows that were picked up for air versus those that were not.

GLOSSARY

24p 24 frames per second, progressive scan.

5.1 audio Refers to the positions in a five-speaker set up, with five speakers placed to the right, center, left, right rear, and left rear of the TV set and one ban speaker. This kind of mixing is also called AC3 and Dolby Digital, and is prominent in DVDs, theatrically released films using SDDS and DTS systems, and in some television broadcasts. 5.1 audio requires a specially-equipped television set to hear it at home.

A

Above-the-line People on a project who are paid a fixed amount, such as producers, writers, directors, primary actors, and legal counsel. Each requires a negotiated fee, including union affiliation, time required, special perks, and star power. This group is also known as the "creatives." This category includes acquisitions to script rights.

Account (or Key Budget Category) The accounts on a budget, including all the departments, all costs above and below the line, and all expenses.

Acoustics The quality of sound and noise in an enclosed environment used for recording sound during a shoot, such as a sound stage, or a room.

Actual In a budget, the amount actually spent as opposed to an estimated amount.

ADR (Automatic Dialogue Replacement) Also known as *looping*, this process involves actors recording, or rerecording, dialogue. In the controlled conditions of a recording studio or sound stage, clean dialogue is recorded to replace lines with noise interference, a bad reading, or a new line not in the original performance. The actor matches his or her performance in the scene by synchronizing to lip movements in the picture on a monitor in the studio.

AEA Actors Equity Association, a union for on-stage actors.

AFTRA American Federation of Television and Radio Actors, a union that represents actors in television and radio.

Agent (for talent) A talent agent suggests the actors or performers that he or she represents to casting directors, producers, and/or directors. The agent sets up auditions, negotiates contracts, and is responsible for the actor's schedule, makeup, and wardrobe calls, call times, and so on. The agent is generally franchised by the Screen Actors Guild (SAG) and American Federation of Television and Radio Actors (AFTRA), and commonly receives 10 percent of the actor's earnings.

AGVA American Guild of Variety Artists, a union that represents performers such as fire jugglers, sword acts, etc.

Ambient sound Sound effects or noise in the background that are natural to the location and don't include dialogue or production audio.

Angle The direction at which a camera or microphone is aimed at the subject that it is recording.

Art director Assists the production designer or, when there is no production designer, serves as the production designer.

Assistant director (AD) Depending on the project, the AD might hire and be in charge of background extras, as well as direct any action in the background. In a studio shoot, the AD works with the director in the control room and communicates the director's orders to the crew on the studio floor.

Associate producer (AP) Also called the assistant producer, he or she does specific jobs that the producer assigns, such as creating production schedules, providing budgets to departments, booking talent and/or crew, research, interviewing talent, finding locations, supervising union-related functions, etc.

Attached An actor, director, or other talent who has committed to an involvement in a project, thus adding extra value to a project's viability.

Audio crew The mixer and boom operators on the set/location.

Audio editing Includes editing, positioning, and mixing dialogue, music, sound effects, and other audio components.

Audio log A form kept by the producer and/or postproduction supervisor with details pertinent to the audio mix, such as the tape number with time codes (in and out point numbers), the scene number, and the take number with a short description of what's been recorded.

Audio mixer (or audio editor) The person responsible for mixing all audio sources, such as dialogue, music, and sound effects.

B

B-roll Extra footage that isn't the primary shot, used for montages or cutaways.

Back-end Revenue that comes at the end of the project, such as royalties or fees for participation.

Background People walking in the background, eating at tables around the actors, or as audience members in a talk show. They lend credibility and energy to the project.

Back light One of three main light sources, the back light helps illuminate the background and allows the subject to stand out.

Bars Color bars that are generated by the video camera and help in the edit process.

Below-the-line The costs involved in the actual production process, they are more easily predicted, and cover crew and equipment, resources, special effects, and other standard expenses such as overhead, insurance, and more.

Bible A standard set of guidelines for a television series that includes character outlines, plot progressions, and elements that can and can't go into the show.

Bins Digital storage folders in an NLE system in which sequences, clips, and blocks of footage are named and described to make editing easier.

Blocking Comparable to a sequence of steps and actions, like choreography in dance, the director or producer "blocks the scene" before shooting. Blocking examines the positions between actors that the camera is shooting, as well as the movement that takes place, where the camera is going to be, and what is it shooting. The final placement of the actors is often marked with masking tape on the floor as reminders.

Blue screen (or green screen) A screen or background material that is blue (or green) against which the action is shot. These screens can be hundreds of feet long, or can be 8′ × 8′ mobile traveling screens. In editing, the subject is "lifted" off the background and combined with other visual effects. This process is called a *chroma key effect*.

Boom A microphone at the end of a long pole that is aimed over or under the audio source.

Boom operator Person responsible for operating the microphone boom (a long pole with a microphone at the end and mic cables) that records an actor's dialogue during the filming of a scene. The boom operator follows the action with the microphone as the actors move around the set or location.

Bounce light Indirect light that results from deflected light off special reflectors, white cards, or set pieces.

Branding The specific process of attaching an image, a personal association, and/or a powerful meaning to a product or company. Branding results in higher consumer comfort for buying the product or using the company's services.

Breakdown sheet A form used by the producer, director, and/or key department heads that lists all the elements needed in a scene, such as actors, furnishings, props, etc.

Break down At the end of a shoot, the crew disassembles, or *breaks down*, all the lights, cameras, and audio equipment, and whatever isn't needed for the next shot is packed away. On locations, the crew removes protective coverings, and masking tape, puts items back in their original positions, and cleans up the location.

Business Physical movements and actions performed by an actor that add to the character's nuance, such as smoking a cigarette in anger.

C

C-stand (century stand) A metal pole with a secure base that is strong enough to hold lighting equipment, sound blankets, and other devices during production.

Call back The second or third audition for an actor for the same part.

Call sheet The daily production schedule that tells each person in the cast and crew what time to arrive on set or location and what scenes are scheduled to be shot.

Camera crew Works under the direction of the director of photography to capture action on film/video of the scene, as it will appear on film.

Camera operator The camera man or woman who operates the camera. Also called the *shooter*, he or she either works with the DP or doubles as the DP.

Camera setups Each time the camera and microphone is moved for a new angle.

Casting Finding actors for all the principle roles, as well as supporting actors and extras through the audition process.

Casting director A professional who is familiar with a variety of actors and their performance range. He or she first interests the actor's agent or manager in the role, arranges for auditions, and works with the producer and director in the selection.

Cathode ray tube (CRT) An electronic vacuum tube that transmits a focused stream of electrons onto a phosphorous screen, and results in an image on a television set, computer monitor, and other devices.

CCD (charge coupled device) An electronic chip in most recent video cameras that converts light and images to electrical impulses. For example, a three-chip video camera has three separate CCDs, and produces a sharper, higher-quality color picture than the standard single-chip cameras with only one CCD.

CG (character generator) Often called *chyron*, the CG is used to "write" text electronically on the video picture, in opening and closing credits, show titles, and in the lower third of the picture to identify a speaker or what's happening on the screen.

CGI (computer generated imagery) The creation and manipulation of images through digital computer technology.

Character actor An actor or performer who specializes in playing secondary roles that are more focused on character than star power.

Choreographer The person responsible for the planning and staging of the dance number(s) for a show.

Chroma A video term relating to true color, with no blacks or grays.

Chroma key backdrop See *blue screen*.

Clearance Obtaining legal written permission to use music, a script, footage, or other aspects necessary in a project.

Close-up (CU) A camera frame that shows a close view of a face or an object.

Closing credits Text that details the cast and crew of a program, along with other production information.

Co-executive producer An additional executive producer who may share some of the responsibilities of executive producing, or who may bring funding or other added value to the production.

Color bars The traditional test of a video signal, this series of vertical bars—white, yellow, cyan, green, magenta, red, blue, and black—appears at the beginning of a reel.

Color correction Changing or correcting the color, hues, or tones of footage by using a color corrector or time base corrector.

Completion bond A form of "insurance" that guarantees that the project, usually a film, will be finished on schedule or else the bank and/or investors will get their money back.

Component video A video signal that separates the chrominance (the color) from the luminance (the blacks and whites), resulting in sharper detail and color.

Composer Responsible for the project's musical score, he or she works closely with the producer and director in finding the musical direction of the project, and writes music that matches the picture, as well as opening and closing themes.

Composite video The luminance and chrominance are combined to form one analog signal.

Compression A digital video storage system that reduces, or compresses, the data in the footage, which facilitates storage space.

Conform In the editing process, the editor takes the final cut from the NLE or offline and matches it with the original, high-resolution footage in an online session.

Conglomerates Large corporations that are involved in and control a variety of media, such as television stations, film studios, newspapers, magazines, and more.

Content Another word for a show, program, or project for distribution on cable, network, nonbroadcast, and Internet.

Content provider A media company or independent producer who produces program material, or content for delivery.

Contingency A back-up fund, usually about 10% of the final budget total, that covers mistakes on the shoot, bad-weather days, and other realities in production.

Continuity The seamless movement from one shot or scene to the next that isn't interrupted by mismatched clothing, actions, set pieces, etc.

Co-production A partnership or joint venture formed for the production of a specific project or projects.

Copyright The exclusive legal right of a writer, author, composer, artist, or publisher to control and dispose of his or her work.

Courtesy credit The acknowledgment of contributors, investors, or services by listing their names or businesses in the closing credits of a program.

Coverage The variety of angles at which a scene is shot.

Cover set A fully-dressed interior location that the production can move to in case of sudden problems from an exterior location, such as equipment failure or bad weather.

Craft services Catered food, snacks, and beverages brought on set or on location.

Crane Similar to a dolly, a crane moves the camera using a balanced arm. Unlike a dolly, a crane has more mobility to rise or descend.

Crawl Also known as *end credits* or *closing credits*, the graphic text information moves vertically or horizontally on the screen.

Creatives Above-the-line personnel, writers, actors, directors, or other key union members.

Credits The complete list of all the cast and crew who worked on a project, from its beginning to end, and who are given "credit" for their work.

Cross-boarding Shooting scenes consecutively from two or three different episodes that all take place on the same set or location.

Cross-cutting See *parallel editing*.

Crossfade In an audio mix, one sound is faded out as another sound fades in; similar to a visual dissolve.

Cue sheet A list of any music used on a project that includes the titles of the music selections, the composers and performing rights society affiliation, etc.

Cutaway A shot that is inserted between two other shots. It can prevent a jarring jump cut, enhancing and adding to the edited sequence.

Cyc (cyclorama) A backdrop, like a curtain, that acts as a background for action.

D

Dailies The footage shot by the end of each working day.

DAT (digital audio tape) A high-quality system for recording digital sound with no distortion, used in professional audio recording and for storing computer data.

DAW (digital audio workstation) An electronic system that uses digital audio for mixing sounds, dialogue, music, and effects.

Deal memo An agreement between two parties, usually between the producer and the cast, crew, writer, director, or other people who are part of the production. It defines the time to be worked and the rates to be paid, and other details.

Deferment payment When, or if, a project makes money down the line, all who agreed to defer their payments are paid later, often with interest or bonuses on top of their original salary agreement.

Demographics A precise measurement of a specific population to determine their level of interest, as consumers or viewers.

Demo reel Similar to a portfolio of short clips from a producer's projects that show a potential client examples of the producer's work.

Deregulation Removing government restrictions on media-related industries.

Detailed budget This budget addresses every aspect of the project's production. Each detail in a project translates into a cost that's part of a key budget account.

DGA Directors Guild of America.

Dialogue track An audio track on which an individual actor's dialogue is recorded and stored. There is no other interference of music or sound effect.

Diegetic music Also called source music, music that is heard by the characters in a scene, such as a radio or a live band.

Digitize To download footage into data storage.

Directional microphone A microphone that is pointed at a specific actor or source of sound, and picks up only that dialogue or sound.

Director In some television programs (such as dramatic series, sitcoms, movies of the week, etc.), the director is the primary artistic influence, or is more of a technical director who works from a control room.

Director of photography (DP) The DP works with the producer and/or director to actualize the visual images and textures of the footage. The DP may supervise the camera operator(s), or may double as the shooter, and shots, lighting, and camera setups.

Dissolve The overlap of one shot over another, one fades out and the other fades in.

Distributor A company or individual who owns or licenses the rights to a project for rentals, lease, broadcast, or final sale.

Dolly A small vehicle, like a mobile platform with stabilized wheels, on which a camera is mounted.

Domestic territory Specifically, the United States and Canada, usually referred to as North American territory.

Downconversion The HD footage is converted to an NTSC, or standard definition, tape that can be inputted into your NLE system.

Download The transfer of digital data into a nonlinear editing storage system.

Draft A version, or revision, of a script or program idea.

Dubs Both audio and video are duplicated and copied, onto a variety of video formats.

E

E & O Insurance (Errors and Omissions) An insurance against third-party claims, such as ownership, chain of title, as well as protection from unanticipated problems.

Editor The person responsible for the assembly of the various film, video, and audio elements into a cohesive and creative finished visual representation of the story.

EDL (Edit Decision List) A sequential list compiled by the editor of all reel numbers, time code locations, music cues, and other data in the final cut.

Effects track A track of audio that is assigned to a specific audio effect, such as chirping crickets or background conversations.

Equalizer An audio device that can increase, decrease, or modulate high, medium, or low frequencies when mixing dialogue, music, ambient sound, etc.

Establishing shot (also called a *master shot*) Usually the opening scene, it sets up the scene and what's happening in it. Generally a wide shot establishes the action.

Executive producer (also known as the *showrunner*) The job varies considerably from project to project. Often, the executive producer has the final word on decision-making, and maintains overall control over a TV project, from acquisition and financing, to developing and selling an idea, marketing it, to its final delivery to the network.

Exteriors A location that is outside, rather than inside (interiors).

Extras People who provide a nonspeaking background atmosphere to a production, like passers-by in a street scene or as background people in a crowd scene.

Eyeballs An informal term used as measurement for viewers watching a show.

Eye line The line of attention that begins in an actor's eyes and follows the direction in which the actor is looking.

F

Fade in An image slowly emerges from a black screen.

Fade out An image slowly fades into a black screen.

Favored nations A legal contractual term in which everyone involved in a project is paid the same amount, or in other ways share in equal parity.

Fields A video frame is made of two parts, or *fields*.

Fill light Light that is positioned or reflected to fill in shadows on a face or location that are cast by the key light.

Filmlook A special effects design program used in postproduction that can treat video footage to give it the grain, texture, and scratches usually associated with film.

Film-to-tape A process of transferring film (super 8, super 16, 16mm, or 35mm) to video via a *telecine*, also called a *film chain*.

Final cut The last and final version that reflects all visual and sound edits and creative decision.

First look deal A network or production company that has the right to be the first to negotiate for a project, or to buy the option to purchase certain rights to the project.

Floor plans An overview of a location, drawn to scale and often from an overhead perspective, that guides the crew in positioning the cameras, lights, and actors.

Foley Additional sound effects that are performed and recorded, like footsteps, or doors closing.

Foley mixer Mixes and records the sounds created by the Foley artists (see *Foley*).

Format Includes several genres—a quiz show, reality-adventure, talk show—that have specific script formats, sets, musical themes, or lighting that can be packaged, sold, and adapted by local programmers.

Format The aspect ratio of a television screen or motion picture frame.

FPS Frames per second.

Framing An aspect of composition of an image in the camera's frame, the framing can range from a close-up to an extreme long shot.

Freelancers Independent contractors who are employed on a per-project or an as-needed basis, with no benefits or full-time compensation.

Freeze frame A single frame of video is held on, or *frozen*, on the screen.

Fringes The extra costs for union personnel and talent, it includes pension and welfare (P&W), health benefit, union payments, etc.

G

Gaffer Often the primary lighting technician who works with electricity, and assists the DP, adjusting the "barn doors" on free-standing and suspended lights.

Gels (gelatins) Durable, translucent material that is available in various colors and hues. Gels are positioned in front of lights to create different colored light.

Genny (generator) A supplemental source of power for video equipment.

Genre In television, the format, style, content, and pacing generally marks its genre, such as a sitcom, drama, talk show, etc.

Gobo Durable, opaque material that hangs from an adjustable arm on a stand with a firm base, and directs or deflects light to specific areas.

Graphic artist A person trained in visual artistic representation through illustration, painting, drawing, font design, photography, and/or printing.

Green light Getting the OK from a client or network to start a project.

Green room An area set aside for actors and talent that is comfortable and quiet.

Greens Plants, real and/or fake, that are used in a scene.

Greens person The individual responsible for all plants seen on the screen. This can be as simple as houseplants, or as detailed as a life-size English country garden.

Grid In a studio or sound stage, an overhead system of pipes from which hang lighting equipment and occasionally, microphones.

Grip Works with the camera and camera equipment, and other mechanical aspects of production, like setting up C-stands, maintaining and moving the dolly, and tripods.

H

HDTV (High Definition Television) Video signals with a high resolution (roughly twice the lines of standard TV) and a sharp visual clarity similar to film.

Hand-held camera A camera that is held in the shooter's hand or on the shoulder, rather than on a tripod.

Hard light Lighting that is strong and directed, resulting in sharp-edged, distinct shadows.

Headshots Professional photographs of actors and talent. They are usually close-up vanity shots, with a resume of their experiences on the back.

High-key light Lighting produced by the combination of less key light and more fill light, resulting in almost no shadows.

Honey wagon A vehicle with several portable toilets, sinks, and showers on-location.

Hook An aspect of an idea that is unique enough to grab the reader's attention.

Hyphenate Double tasking, such as a writer-producer, writer-director, etc.

I

Independent production company A small business usually formed by a producer(s) that produces programming for a network, studio, or corporate client, and also handles all the administrative and technical requirements needed to satisfy the client.

Indirect costs The additional money that is factored into a production budget that covers areas such as legal fees, accounting services, insurance, and contingency fees.

In point In the editing process, the starting point of a specific edit.

Insert shot A shot, usually a close-up, that reveals an important detail in a scene.

J

Jib A crane with a camera at the end that can fly over an audience or into a set or location. It can be either manually controlled or by remote.

Jump cut An obvious edit made by putting two very similar images together that share identical angles and framing.

K

Key The head, or most important person, of each department.

Key light The most important light source in the three-point lighting system. Its illumination of a subject is bright and hard, and produces deep shadows.

Kinescope A process developed before the invention of videotape in which a 16mm camera filmed television programs that were broadcast live.

L

Lav (lavalier) An easily concealed small microphone that clips onto clothing; it's generally omnidirectional and picks up dialogue clearly.

Layback In postproduction, the process of joining the final completed audio track to the finished picture.

Letterbox format On a television screen, a black strip above and below the picture frames the image in a film-style aspect ratio.

Lighting board The piece of equipment that controls all the lighting dimmers in a studio or remote location.

Lighting director The person responsible for the lighting design of a television production.

Linear editing A traditional system of editing video in which shots are edited together in a linear fashion, moving forward.

Line item Each entry in a budget that relates to a specific cost.

Line producer Beginning in preproduction and continuing through completion of principal photography or through the completion of postproduction, the line producer is responsible for the day-to-day running of the production.

Lip sync To speak or sing in synchronization with a picture, with the appearance of an exact match.

Load in The transfer of footage and audio into a data storage device, such as a nonlinear editing system.

Location scout The person responsible for finding the necessary locations for a project, as well as securing permits, negotiating location agreements and rentals, and obtaining all other permissions required for filming.

Locked When the editing has been finalized, the project is considered locked.

Locked down camera A camera that is stationary, usually on a tripod or a pedestal, and not hand-held.

Log Taking notes of each pertinent shot, with its description and time code number.

Log line Also called a *one-liner* or *tag line*, a log line is a concise sentence that grabs the reader's attention and sums up a project idea.

Logo A distinctive graphic designed to give a television show a graphic identity.

Long-form contract A substantial, detailed agreement that includes all the provisions of the contract.

Long shot (LS) Camera framing that captures an image from a distance, usually from a substantial distance.

Long take A continual, uninterrupted shot, usually lasting at least 20 seconds.

Low-key lighting A style of lighting produced by the contrast between key light and fill lights, resulting in darker light marked by shadows and occasional high-light.

Lower thirds Electronic text that appears under a person's face on screen, giving his or her name, location, or profession.

Luminance In a video image, the measurement of pure white in the picture.

M

M & E (Music and special effects) Two important areas of audio components in a mix.

Magic hour Twilight, or dusk, that limited time between sunset and dark when the light has a special luminescent quality to it that's ideal for certain effects.

Making the day Accomplishing what's been planned for each day's shoot.

Makeup artist The person who works closely with the producer and director to design the makeup for the cast, including special effects, aging, wounds, etc.

Manager The manager oversees an actor's career, and may hire an agent, lawyer, accountants, etc. The manager works with the actor on career decisions, such as scripts to review, and advises in a range of professional areas.

Marketing Presenting an idea or product to potential viewers or consumers, using methods that sway or convince the target audience.

Markup fee A percentage added to the costs that covers office and personnel overhead, expenses, and any profits.

Master shot (also called an establishing shot) Establishes the scene and the actors' movements and their relationships to each other.

Master In video, the original footage; also, the completed high-quality first-generation version of a project that is used for dubbing.

Matching time code The time code on the original footage is exactly the same on the screening cassette. It's visible time code, also called *vizcode* or *VTC*, that's displayed in a small box on the bottom or top of the screen.

Media buy Purchasing airtime (usually in 30- or 60-second blocks) on a network or channel in which to air a commercial.

Medium shot A camera framing in which the person or object is shown almost in its entirety.

Meme Trends and ideas that are propagated—usually virally—and either mutate and expand, or eventually die off.

Merchandising Adapting the likeness of a popular TV or film character to nonmedia products such as T-shirts, hats, and pencils, and cashing in on that character's branding.

Mic ("mike") A shortened version of *microphone*.

Mix The combining together of various audio tracks—dialogue, music, effects—and merging them into a single track.

Montage A story telling device that can compress time or impose a narrative over images, and is built by editing together a series of quick shots to tell the story.

MOS "Mit out sound," shooting video only, with no audio being recorded.

Most favored nation See Favored nations.

Motion control camera (also called *title camera*) A computer-controlled camera designed to pinpoint details, with zooms, pans, and other camera angles.

Music clearance Written legal permission to use pre-existing music in a project

Music director Works with the pre-existing music (including popular recordings) to craft together a musical score for a production.

Music supervisor The supervisor of the overall creation of a musical score that uses original music and/or existing or prerecorded music, he or she is often responsible for the legal clearances and licensing of any music needed in the project.

N

Narration Also called *voice-over*, narration is provided by an off-camera person who records the script at a recording studio.

Needle drop During audio postproduction, various sound effects and music cues from a sound effects or music library might be added and dropped into the mix.

Network A national broadcasting entity made up of many stations in various locations, usually larger cities.

Neutral-density (ND) filters A grayish filtering material often used in shooting video, placed over windows to filter the natural outdoor light.

Niche marketing A specific smaller television market with precise demographics and interests for which a broadcaster creates programming. Also *narrowcasting*.

NLE (nonlinear editor) Referring to both the editor and the editing system itself, a digital system that edits footage in a random, nonsequential way, like film-style editing.

Noise In video, noise on the video signal is created by distortion, and results in the visual effect of "snow" or a hissing sound in the audio.

NTSC (National Television Standards Committee) A national standard for American color television, consisting of 525 interlaced scan lines per frame, and running at 30 frames per second.

O

Offline edit Versions of an edited project, cut at a low resolution, that require much less storage space and usually conformed in an online session.

Omnidirectional A microphone that can pick up audio from all directions.

Online edit The final cut from the offline session is brought into an online session, during which the original high-resolution footage is assembled. The final audio track along with graphics or other elements are also married to the picture.

On-set dresser A person responsible for dressing a set with appropriate furnishings.

One-off A program that is self-contained, usually one or two hours in length. An example might be a documentary or a news-oriented special.

Opening titles (also known as *opening credits*) The name of the show and a limited list of the creatives, such as the producer, writer, director, principal actor(s), etc., written in text at the beginning of the program.

Option/optioning Obtaining exclusive ownership and/or rights to a script, book, or story for a period of time long enough to develop and hopefully sell as a project.

Out of sequence During a shoot, the scenes are seldom shot in the sequence in which they appear in the script or in the final product.

P

PA (Production Assistant) An entry-level position on a project that involves every aspect of work, from running errands to making copies to getting lunch.

PAL Phase Alternating Line is used in the United Kingdom, Australia, China, and parts of Western Europe. This video format is 625 lines and runs at 25fps.

Pan A camera movement in which the camera moves smoothly, either horizontally (from right to left, or vice versa) or vertically (from top to bottom, or vice versa).

Paper cut (editing storyboard) A paper cut gives the editor the sequence of shots for the final product, including exact in-points of selected shots, their descriptions, time code locations, reel numbers, and the duration of each shot.

Paper edit See *Paper cut*.

Parallel editing Two separate yet somehow related events appear to be happening at the same time, shifting back and forth between one scene and another.

Pay-or-play A contractual agreement stating that if the talent is not used in a project for whatever reason, he or she will still be paid the agreed-upon fees.

Pay Per View (PPV) In television, paying a fee for watching a single program or event on a specific PPV channel.

Petty cash (PC) Cash kept on hand during a production that pays for expenses on set, such as meals, supplies needed for the crew, props, and other costs that arise.

Perma-lancers Permanent freelancers who are employed full-time, but aren't paid employee benefits or given any contractual certainty.

Pistol grip A special mounting device for a hand-held camera.

Pitch Selling an idea for a television show to a network, client, independent producer, or other end-user.

Pixels (picture element) The smallest resolvable rectangular area of an image, made of three close dots of color: red, green, and blue.

Point of view shot (POV shot) A shot taken from roughly the same place that the actor's eyes would be.

Postproduction supervisor In larger or more complex projects, he or she is responsible for the coordination of all aspects of postproduction.

Presale contracts Selling specific rights of a project, such as international sales or for DVD distribution, in order to interest investors or to obtain a loan.

Prime time In television, the hours in the programming schedule that attract the highest number of viewers, usually 7:30 to 11 P.M.

Principal cast The main actors or central characters in a television show.

Principal photography The actual process of shooting that can begin when everything is ready to go.

Producer The producer deals with creative and technical logistics, administrative details, often hires the talent, writers, and director, additional producers, and others. The producer may create or acquire the idea, and obtains funding or sale to a broadcaster, and most or all details, from the beginning to the end of the project.

Product placement The use of a specific product (such as a cereal box, a car, sports gear) in a scene in return for a fee.

Production designer Creates the environment for a project and designs the space in which the action takes place. He or she hires the set builders, scenic artists, set dressers, and prop masters to actualize the design plans, and more.

Prompter An individual who helps actors or talk-show talent when needed by holding up signs, or cue cards, on which their lines are written in large print.

Prop master The person who designs, buys, or rents each prop needed in a production. Generally, he or she is the head of the property department.

Proposal A written prospectus or pitch that details the idea of a project, and is given to a network or potential buyer or investor.

Props An object on a set or on location that will be handled by the actor as part of the action. A prop can be anything from a telephone to a toothbrush.

Protection copies Duplicate exact copies of original footage or the final master that can act as backup protections in case of damage or loss in shipping.

Public domain When the copyright has elapsed on specific footage, it has no owner, and it can be used with no clearances or royalty fees.

R

Rack focus A shot in which the camera changes focus from a person or object in the foreground to the background, or vice versa.

Ratings A measurement of the number of viewers who are watching a television program.

Reaction shot A close-up of an actor's face that registers a reaction to the shot before it or to actions in the storyline.

Reality TV A form of television program that is theoretically unscripted, and relies on "real people" in real-life situations.

Recce ("recky") A shortened version of "reconnaissance" in the preproduction phase that involves scouting for a location and looking all aspects of the location.

Reel A cassette of video tape.

Reflected light During a shot, light that is deflected or bounced off objects.

Release A legal agreement between the producer and an on-camera person, allowing the producer to use his or her likeness in ways stipulated on the release.

Resolution In video, the level of detail and clarity in an image.

RGB In video, the primary colors of red, green, and blue.

Rotoscope An animation process that involves projecting live action by an actor onto a software drawing pad and creating realistic-looking animation.

Room tone Refers to sounds that are a natural part of each and every set or location.

Rough cut The rough cut reflects the overall sequence of shots and audio in editing, with the approximate in and out points of the edits and the order in which they'll appear.

Royalty A fee paid to an actor, author, composer, performer, or other artist, for the use of his or her copyrighted material.

S

Safety In video, the inner area of the television screen that will be seen on a broadcast or standard monitor.

SAG Screen Actors Guild, a union protecting on-camera actors and talent. The SAG contract also protects members of SEG, AFTRA, and AGVA.

Scale The lowest minimum wage allowed under a union contract.

Scene A segment in a program that happens in one space and period of time, and consists of one or more shots. A scene is often known as a *sequence*.

Scenic artist The scenic artist's job includes painting sets, aging walls or floors, creating the look of stone or other materials, and achieving textures or moods on a set.

Scratch track A preliminary track of narration read by the producer or someone else that helps determine final timings and beats in a rough cut.

Screen time A period of time in which events are happening on screen. It might be an hour, a day, or a longer time span, depending on the storyline.

Script supervisor Also called *continuity*, the script supervisor observes each shot for details of continuity from one scene to the next.

SECAM (Sequential Color with Memory) The video standard of 625 lines that runs at 25 fps, used in Russia, eastern Europe, and France.

Second assistant director (2nd AD) The person who helps the director and 1st AD, usually preparing the call sheets for the next day's shoot.

Second unit A smaller production team that independently shoots extra footage, like exteriors, background reactions, etc., to be tied into primary scenes in the editing.

Set decorator Creates the visual look of the project, including the purchase, rental, and placement of furnishings that add to the set environments.

Set designer Takes the production designer's rough drawings and creates working blueprints and construction drawings that guide the building of the sets.

Set dressing The physical and aesthetic placement of furnishings and props in preparation for rehearsals and the actual shooting.

Set mixer The set mixer records the dialogue and any other production sound that is produced on the set, as clearly as possible.

Setup All the elements needed for a specific shot, such as the placement of the camera, the lenses and microphones, and the composition of the frame.

Shooter Another term for a camera operator or cameraman.

Shooting out In production, all the shots needed in one location are grouped together and shot before moving on to the next location.

Shooting ratio The amount of material shot in production in relation to the actual footage used in editing.

Shooting schedule A mapped-out plan for the shoot, generally given to all cast and crew for each day's shoot.

Shorts Projects that are usually less than 30 to 40 minutes in length.

Shot A short, single take that is edited into a longer sequence or scene.

Showrunner Might also be the executive producer of a weekly television show, and is responsible for the creative direction of a series, guiding the writers along with the script, casting the actors, pitching a show idea to a network, and more.

Signatory A person or company that has agreed to comply with the regulations of any union that covers writers, directors, talent, and/or crew members.

Silks Medium to large squares of translucent material that can be strategically hung and positioned to filter the sunlight and maintain lighting consistency.

Single system The audio that is recorded directly onto the videotape.

Slo mo (slow motion) In video, the speed of a shot is slowed down to create a slower action or other desired effect.

SMPTE (Society of Motion Picture and Television Engineers) In addition to being the acronym for this organization, SMPTE time code is the standard 8-digit time code used in video that represents hours, minutes, seconds, and frames per second.

Soft lighting Also called *diffuse lighting,* it is the lighting on a subject that avoids extreme bright and dark areas, a gradual transition between highlights and shadows.

Sound blankets Large moving blankets made of a dense absorbent material that can be hung or placed on a set or location to muffle sound.

Sound effects (SFX) A sound effects track includes natural sounds from the production (such as background ambience) or Foley, or audio effects from a sound effects library.

Sound stage A building specially equipped for shooting a production; generally sound-proof, often furnished with video and audio equipment, lighting grids and equipment, rooms for talent, set construction, and other amenities.

Spec script A script written on speculation. The writer uses it as a sample of his or her work, and does not get paid unless the screenplay is sold.

Special effects makeup Makeup that might include artificial wounds or body parts (prosthetics) used to change an actor's appearance.

SPFX (special effects) Special effects created on the set or location—like fog, rain, snow, an open flame—that are not added later in postproduction.

Split screen The screen is divided into boxes or parts, from two to eight, that are all active at the same time. Each box shows an image of a character or action.

Splits During production, the producer might divide the day and night shooting into splits that are then sectioned into a half-day and half-night shift.

Spotting session Starting audio postproduction, the producer or director reviews the show for areas in which to add music, narration, ADR, Foley, and SFX.

Stand-in A person who bears a strong resemblance to an actor "stands-in" for the actor in technical rehearsals and often in a long shot when the actor isn't available.

Star The lead actor or performer in a production.

Steadicam A counterbalanced rig worn by a camera operator that allows for smoother camera movement, midway between hand-held and tripod camera mounts.

Step deal A contract for writers that indicates a series of incremental payments for each version of a script or story.

Still photographer Takes photographs during rehearsals or actual production that may be used for publicity purposes.

Stills The photographs taken with a still camera that catalog various aspects of the production, like actors in scenes, the director working with the actors and crew, etc.

Stock The unused videotape or audiotape on which images or sound are recorded.

Stock footage Pre-existing, high-quality footage that is sold by a stock footage company for a negotiated fee and licensing agreement that is dependent on its final use.

Stock music Royalty-free prerecorded music that is sold by a stock music company. The fees for its use are dependent on its final use.

Storyboard Simple, cartoon-like sketches of each scene in a script.

Storyboard artist The artist responsible for rendering a sequence of drawings based on a script to aid in planning and coordinating action, drawn by hand or with software.

Striking the set The breaking down of a set, including the removal of furnishings and props after shooting, and disassembling the equipment.

Stunt double A person of about the same size and look of an actor who is capable of substituting for an actor to perform difficult or dangerous action sequences.

Superimpose The layering, or *superimposition*, of one image over another.

Supporting actors Secondary cast members in a production whose characters and roles support those of the primary cast.

Sweeten In audio postproduction, the process of mixing the audio tracks of narration, music, and sound effects with the master audio track.

Swish pan Also called a *whip pan*, a camera movement that pans rapidly from right to left or vice versa, as an editing transition from one scene to another.

Sync Short for synchronization, an exact match between the video and the audio.

Synopsis A brief and compelling distillation of a story idea into a short form, usually in one or two paragraphs.

T

Take Each repetition of a specific scene that is shot.

Talent Anyone who appears on camera, such as an actor, performer, host, guests, etc.

Target audience The specific audience for whom a show is developed or produced.

Technical director The person, generally in the control room of a studio, who takes in the various camera feeds, graphics, and special video effects, and "edits" them, live.

Telecine Also called a *film chain*, this device facilitates the transfer of film to videotape. During this process, film images and audio are converted to a format that is used by a broadcast network, or for nonlinear editing purposes.

Teleprompter A small device that is mounted directly under the camera lens that displays the performer's lines in a roll-down scroll.

Textless copy A "clean" copy of the final project with no text or graphics superimposed on it.

Time code (TC) A signal "burned on" the videotape that gives every frame a specific number in hours, minutes, seconds, and frames per second.

Time-of-day time code TC that can be set in the camera itself that records the actual time of day as opposed to an arbitrary time code numbering system.

Thirteen outline A comprehensive outline of the first thirteen episodes of a series, agreed upon by the producers, prior to the start of production.

Three-point lighting A standard lighting set up that utilizes the three sources of lighting—the key light, fill lights, and back lights.

Top sheet A quick summary of the costs in each department that provides an overview of necessary information at a glance.

Tracking shot Usually accomplished by using a dolly, crane, or a jib, a tracking shot travels forward, backward, or laterally through space in order to capture movement.

Trades Entertainment publications, such as *Variety* and *The Hollywood Reporter*.

Transition In editing, the moving of one shot or scene to the next by using a cut, dissolve, wipe, etc.

TRT The "total running time" of a program or show.

Treatment An abbreviated narrative outline of a script, story, or idea, shorter in length than a script.

Turnaround When a studio or network has abandoned a project and removed its support for further development, a producer is free to take it to another studio who can buy it by reimbursing the original studio or network for any incurred costs.

Turnaround time Actors' unions requirements for a 12-hour break of time between the end of one shooting day and the call time for the next day.

Two-shot A scene with two actors in the frame. Three-shots and four-shots have three and four actors in the frame, respectively.

U

Underlighting Placing lights under the people or objects in a scene.

Up-fronts An annual gathering of the networks and their affiliates, during which new shows and pilots are unveiled and camaraderie is maintained.

UPM (Unit Production Manager) Acts as the right hand of the producer(s), and works with administrative below-the-line issues, technical equipment, and the needs of the crew.

V

VCR A machine that can play and/or record on half-inch VHS tapes.

VTR A videotape recorder.

Video monitor In production, a small video monitor attached by a cable to each camera that shows what the camera sees as it's being shot, and can also provide instant playback of what was just shot.

Visible time code (also called *Vizcode* or *VTC*) Time code that matches the original footage, and is visible on a screen.

Voice-over (VO) A recorded voice of a commentator in a documentary or a narrator of a storyline.

W

Wardrobe designer Does a wardrobe breakdown of all characters and their roles, their time period, the time that wardrobe or costumes are needed, and more.

Wardrobe supervisor Supervises the costume department with the wardrobe designer, keeps track of the budget, maintains the wardrobe, and more.

WGA Writers Guild of America, the union that represents and protects writers of film, television, and radio projects.

White balance In shooting video, a white card or piece of paper is often held in front of the camera lens to adjust its sensitivity to a light source.

Windscreen An absorbent fuzzy material that can be wrapped around a microphone. The windscreen helps deflect or absorb the noise from wind or breezes.

Wipe A special effects transition used in video editing that wipes out one scene and brings in another, such as a page turn or one image that drops down over another.

Wireless microphone Also known as a *radio microphone*, a cordless microphone that operates on a battery-powered pack hidden on the person speaking, under clothing.

Wrangler A specially trained person who manages the activities and work of a specific kind of talent, such as a child, an animal, or a stunt person.

Wrap the project Tying up all the loose ends, after completion of the production.

Writer The writer creates the story, action, and characters for TV narrative programs, like sitcoms, drama series, and mini-series. He or she may have created the original material, or may have been brought in to work with an existing script or story outline.

Z

Zoom A movement by the camera lens that allows it to move quickly either into an object (zoom in) or away from an object (zoom out).

RESOURCES BY CHAPTER

Because today's producer is likely to work in television, new media, and/or film, the following resources generally apply to all three venues. Although they are specific to each chapter, several apply to more than one chapter or area of a producer's responsibilities. You are also encouraged to consult the Internet and search for key words and phrases like The Producers Guild of America, stock footage, legal forms, for more resources and options. Check this book's web site for a wealth of budgets, forms, agreements, web site links, additional books, and industry publications.

CHAPTER 1. WHAT DOES A TV PRODUCER *REALLY* DO?

Cury, Ivan. *Directing & Producing for Television: A Format Approach.* 3rd edition. Focal Press, 2006.

Gardner, Howard. *Multiple Intelligences for the 21st Century.* Basic Books, 2000.

Goleman, Daniel. *Primal Leadership: Learning to Lead with EQ.* Harvard Business School Press, 2004.

Lee, John J. *The Producer's Business Handbook.* 2nd edition. Focal Press, 2005.

Litwak, Mark. *Dealmaking in the Film and Television Industry From Negotiations Through Final Contracts.* 2nd edition. *Expanded and Updated.* Silman-James Press, 2002.

Rea, Peter and Irving, David K. *Producing and Directing the Short Film and Video.* 3rd edition. Focal Press, 2006.

Schreibman, Myrl A. *The Indie Producer's Handbook: Creative Producing from A to Z.* Lone Eagle Publishing Company, 2001.

Tompkins, Al. *Aim for the Heart: Write for the Ear, Shoot for the Eye: A Guide for TV Producers and Reporters.* Bonus Books, 2002.

Vachon, Christine. *A Killer Life: How an Independent Film Producer Survives Deals and Disasters in Hollywood and Beyond.* Hal Leonard Corporation, 2007.

Vachon, Christine. *Shooting to Kill.* Avon Books, 1998.

Wiese, Michael. *Producer to Producer: Insider Tips for Success in Media.* Michael Wiese Productions, 1997.

CHAPTER 2. TV: ITS PAST, PRESENT, AND FUTURE

Barnouw, Erik. *A History of Broadcasting in the United States.* Oxford University Press, New York, 1968.

Barnouw, Erik. *Conglomerates and the Media.* New Press, 1998.

Barnouw, Erik. *Tube of Plenty: The Evolution of American Television.* 2nd edition. Oxford University Press, 1990.

Bianculli, David. *Teleliteracy.* Ungar Pub Co., 1992.

Boyd, Andrew and Duncombe, Stephen. "The Manufacture of Dissent: What the Left Can Learn From Las Vegas." *The Journal of Aesthetics and Protest* Vol. 1, #3, 2004.

Chomsky, Noam and Herman, Edward S. *Manufacturing Consent: The Political Economy of the Mass Media.* Pantheon, 2002.

Lechner, Jack. *Can't Take My Eyes Off of You: 1 Man, 7 Days, 12 Televisions*. Crown, 2000.

McChesney, Robert W. *Corporate Media and the Threat to Democracy (Open Media Pamphlet Series)*. Seven Stories Press, 1997.

McChesney, Robert W. *The Problem of the Media: U.S. Communication Politics in the Twenty-First Century*. Monthly Review Press, March 1, 2004.

Miller, Mark Crispin. *Boxed In: The Culture of TV*. Northwestern University Press, 1988.

Packard, Vance and Miller, Mark Crispin. *The Hidden Persuaders*. IG Publications. Reissued, 2007.

Postman, Neil. *Amusing Ourselves to Death: Public Discourse in the Age of Show Business*. Penguin Books, 2005.

Postman, Neil and Powers, Steve. *How to Watch TV News*. Penguin, 1992.

Schwartz, Evan. *The Last Lone Inventor: A Tale of Genius, Deceit, and the Birth of Television*. HarperCollins, 2003.

Stashower, Daniel. *The Boy Genius and the Mogul: The Untold Story of Television*. Broadway, 2002.

Tinker, Grant and Rukeyser, Bud. *Tinker in Television: From General Sarnoff to General Electric*. Simon and Schuster, 1994.

CHAPTER 3. THE BIG IDEA: SCRIPT AND PROJECT DEVELOPMENT

Blumenthal, Howard J. and Goodenough, Oliver R. *This Business of Television.* 2nd Edition. Watson-Guptill Publ, Inc., 1998.

Branston, Gill and Stafford, Roy. *The Media Student's Book*. 3rd edition. Routledge, 2003.

Cameron, Julia. *The Right to Write: An Invitation and Initiation into the Writing Life*. Tarcher, 1999.

Field, Syd. *Screenplay: The Foundations of Screenwriting*. Delta, 2005.

Brody, Larry. *Television Writing from the Inside Out: Your Channel to Success*. Applause Books, 2003.

Jones, Laurie Beth. *The Path: Creating Your Mission Statement for Work and for Life*. Hyperion, 1996.

Longworth, James L. *TV Creators: Conversations with America's Top Producers of Television Drama (The Television Series)*. Syracuse University Press, 2002.

McKee, Robert. *Story: Substance, Structure, Style, and the Principles of Screenwriting*. Harper Entertainment, 1997.

Pepper, Steven C. *The Basis of Criticism in the Arts*. Harvard University Press, 1970.

Seger, Linda. *Creating Unforgettable Characters*. Holt, 1990.

Seger, Linda. *Making a Good Script Great*. 2nd edition. Samuel French Trade, 1994.

Straczynski, J. Michael. *The Complete Book of Scriptwriting*. Revised. Writer's Digest Books, 2002.

Tierno, Michael. *Aristotle's Poetics for Screenwriters: Storytelling Secrets from the Greatest Mind in Western Civilzation*. Hyperion, 2002.

Trottier, David. *The Screenwriter's Bible*. 4th edition. Silman-James Press, 2007.

Ueland, Brenda and Codrescu, Andrei. *If You Want to Write: A Book about Art, Independence and Spirit*. Greywolf Press, 2007.

Vogler, Christopher. *The Writer's Journey: Mythic Structure for Writers*. 3rd edition. Michael Wiese Productions, 1992.

Additional Resources: Writing and Storytelling

TIP: Keyword search for ideas such as "screenwriting contests" and "TV script writing."

WEBLINK The ABC/Disney Fellowship:
abctalentdevelopment.com/programs_writers.htm
Nickelodeon Fellowship Program:
www.nickwriting.com/
Warner Bros. Writers Workshop:
www2.warnerbros.com/writersworkshop/
Daily Variety:
www.variety.com
Hollywood Reporter:
www.hollywoodreporter.com
Hollywood Creative Directory:
www.hcdonline.com/
New York Screenwriter Monthly:
www.screenwritersutopia.com
Script Writers Network:
www.scriptwritersnetwork.org
Writers Guild of America:
www.wga.org

CHAPTER 4. CONNECTING THE DOTS: BREAKDOWNS, BUDGETS, AND FINANCE

Cleve, Bastian. *Film Production Management*. 3rd edition. Focal Press, 2005.
Donaldson, Michael C. *Fearless Negotiating*. McGraw-Hill, 2007.
Honthaner, Eve Light. *The Complete Film Production Handbook*. 3rd edition. Focal Press, 2001.
Lee, John J. *The Producer's Business Handbook*. 2nd edition. Focal Press, 2005.
Moore, Schuyler M. *The Biz: The Basic Business, Legal, and Financial Aspects of the Film Industry*. 2nd edition. Silman-James Press, 2003.
Newton, Dale and Gaspard, John. *Digital Filmmaking 101: An Essential Guide to Producing Low-Budget Movies*. Michael Wiese Productions, 2001.
Schreibman, Myrl. A. *The Indie Producer's Handbook: Creative Producing from A to Z*. Lone Eagle, 2001.
Simens, Dov S-S. *From Reel to Deal*. Warner Books, 2003.
Wiese, Michael. *Producer to Producer: Inside Tips for Success in Media*. Michael Wiese Productions, 1997.

CHAPTER 5. WELCOME TO REALITY: LEGALITIES AND RIGHTS

Cleve, Bastian. *Film Production Management*. 3rd edition. Focal Press, 2005.
Donaldson, Michael C. *Clearance and Copyright: Everything the Independent Filmmaker Needs to Know*. 2nd revised update. Silman-James Press, 2003.

Erickson, Gunnar, Harris Tulchin and Mark Halloran. *The Independent Film Producer's Survival Guide: A Business and Legal Sourcebook*. 2nd edition. Schirmer Trade Books, 2005.

Honthaner, Eve Light. *The Complete Film Production Handbook*. 3rd edition. Focal Press, 2001.

Garon, Jon M. *The Independent Filmmaker's Law and Business Guide: Financing, Shooting, and Distributing Independent and Digital Film*. Chicago Review Press, 2002.

Krasilovsky, M. William, Shemel, Sidney, Gross, John M. *This Business of Music: The Definitive Guide to the Music Industry*. 10th edition. Billboard Books, 2007.

Moore, Schuyler M. *The Biz: the Basic Business, Legal and Financial Aspects of the Film Industry*. 2nd edition. Silman-James Press, 2002.

Newton, Dale and Gaspard, John. *Digital Filmmaking 101: An Essential Guide to Producing Low-Budget Movies*. Michael Wiese Productions, 2001.

Schreibman, Myrl A. *The Indie Producer's Handbook: Creative Producing from A to Z*. Lone Eagle, 2001.

Additional Resources: Intellectual Property and Its Protection

TIP: Keyword search for ideas such as "public domain" and "fair use."

WEBLINK Center for the Study of the Public Domain at Duke University, Program in Intellectual Property:
www.law.duke.edu/ip
Center for Social Media, School of Communication, American University, Best Practices in Fair Use:
www.centerforsocialmedia.org/fairuse
Copyright Public Information Office:
www.copyright.gov/forms
The Copyright Office, Library of Congress:
www.copyright.gov
Creative Commons:
www.creativecommons.org
The Norman Lear Center at USC:
www.learcenter.org
Public Knowledge:
www.publicknowledge.org
Volunteer Lawyers for the Arts (VLA) (212) 319-ARTS:
www.vlany.org

Music Clearance Resources

WEBLINK ASCAP (American Society of Composers, Authors and Publishers):
www.ascap.com
BMI (Broadcast Music, Inc.):
www.bmi.com

Video Clearances

WEBLINK Motion Picture Licensing Corp.:
www.mplc.com

Cartoons Clearances

WEBLINK United Media:
www.unitedmedia.com

Print Clearances

WEBLINK Copyright Clearance Center:
www.copyright.com

Fair Use

WEBLINK Stanford University:
**www.fairuse.stanford.edu/Copyright_and_Fair_Use_Overview/
chapter 9/index.htm**

Television-Related Unions

WEBLINK The Screen Actors Guild (SAG):
www.sag.com
The Directors Guild of America (DGA):
www.dga.org
The Writers Guild of America (WGA):
www.wga.org or www.wgaeast.org

(Continued)

The National Association of Broadcast Engineer Technicians;
Communication Workers of America (NABET-CWA):
www.nabetcwa.org
The American Federation of Television and Radio Artists (AFTRA):
www.aftra.org
The American Federation of Musicians (AFM):
www.afm.org
The Producers Guild of America (PGA):
www.producersguild.org

CHAPTER 6. PITCHING AND SELLING THE PROJECT

Atchity, Kenneth and Wong, Chi-Li. *Writing Treatments That Sell: How to Create and Market Your Story Ideas to the Motion Picture and TV Industry*. 2nd edition. Holt Paperbacks, 2003.

Brody, Larry. *Television Writing from the Inside Out: Your Channel to Success*. Applause Books, 2003.

Koch, Jonathan, Kosberg, Robert, Norman, Tanya Meurer. *Pitching Hollywood: How to Sell Your TV and Movie Ideas*. Quill Driver Books, 2004.

Litwak, Mark. *Dealmaking in the Film and Television Industry: From Negotiations to Final Contract*. 2nd edition. Updated and revised. Silman-James Press, 2002.

Yoneda, Kathie Fong. *The Script-Selling Game: A Hollywood Insider's Look at Getting Your Script Sold and Produced*. Michael Wiese Productions, 2002.

CHAPTER 7. THE PLAN: PREPRODUCTION

Branston, Gill and Stafford, Roy. *The Media Student's Book*. 3rd edition. Routledge, 2003.

Campbell, Drew. *Technical Film and TV for Nontechnical People*. Allworth Press, 2002.

Cury, Ivan. *Directing & Producing for Television: A Format Approach*. 3rd edition. Focal Press, 2006.

Newton, Dale and Gaspard, John. *Digital Filmmaking 101: An Essential Guide to Producing Low-Budget Movies*. Michael Wiese Productions, 2001.

Rea, Peter and Irving, David K. *Producing and Directing the Short Film and Video*. 3rd edition. Focal Press, 2006.

Additional Resources: Preproduction

TIP: Keyword search for ideas such as "casting services" and "production software" and "payroll services."

Cast and Talent

WEBLINK Players Directory:
www.playersdirectory.com
The Screen Actors Guild:
www.sag.org
The American Federation of Television and Radio Artists (AFTRA):
www.aftra.org

Booking Crews

WEBLINK Crew Connection:
www.crewconnection.com
Crews Control:
www.crews-control.com
Crew Star, Inc.:
www.crewstar.com

Equipment Resources

WEBLINK www.sony.com
www.panasonic.com

CHAPTER 8. THE SHOOT: PRODUCTION

Branston, Gill and Stafford, Roy. *The Media Student's Book*. 3rd edition. Routledge, 2003.
Campbell, Drew. *Technical Film and TV for Nontechnical People*. Allworth Press, 2002.
Cury, Ivan. *Directing & Producing for Television: A Format Approach*. 3rd edition. Focal Press, 2006.
Malkiewicz, Kris and Mullen, Dave. *Cinematography*. 3rd edition. Fireside, 2005.
Newton, Dale and Gaspard, John. *Digital Filmmaking 101: An Essential Guide to Producing Low-Budget Movies.* Michael Wiese Productions, 2001.
Rea, Peter and Irving, David K. *Producing and Directing the Short Film and Video*. 3rd edition. Focal Press, 2006.
Schreibman, Myrl. A. *The Indie Producer's Handbook: Creative Producing from A to Z*. Lone Eagle, 2001.

CHAPTER 9. THE FINAL PRODUCT: POSTPRODUCTION

Bardosh, Karl. *The Complete Idiot's Guide to Digital Video*. Alpha, 2007.
Berger, John. *Ways of Seeing*. Penguin Books, 2003.
Button, Bryce. *Nonlinear Editing: Storytelling, Aesthetics, & Craft*. CMP Books, 2002.
Campbell, Drew. *Technical Film and TV for Nontechnical People*. Allworth Press, 2002.
Giannetti, Louis D. *Understanding Movies*. 11th edition. Prentice Hall, 2007.
Murch, Walter. *In the Blink of an Eye*. 2nd edition. Silman-James, 2001.
Rea, Peter and Irving, David K. *Producing and Directing the Short Film and Video*. 3rd edition. Focal Press, 2006.
Schreibman, Myrl A. *The Indie Producer's Handbook: Creative Producing from A to Z*. Lone Eagle, 2001.

Additional Resources: Postproduction

TIP: Keyword search for ideas such as "royalty-free stock footage," "stock music," and "nonlinear editing."

Stock Footage and Archival Footage

WEBLINK BBC Archives:
www.bbcmotiongallery.com
Getty Images:
www.gettyimages.com
Corbis Motion Brands:
www.corbismotion.com
DV Archive:
www.dvarchive.com
Historic Films:
www.historicfilms.com
IMAX:
www.imax.com
The National Archives:
www.archives.gov
Focal International:
www.focalint.org
Footage.net:
www.footage.net
Footage.info:
www.footage.info
Library of Congress:
www.loc.gov/rr/mopic/stock.html
NASA:
www.nasa.gov
Internet Archive:
www.archive.org
Fotosearch:
www.fotosearch.com
ABCNews VideoSource:
www.abcnewsvsource.com
National Geographic:
www.ngdigitalmotion.com
Independent Television News or ITN:
www.itnarchive.com
UCLA Film and Television Archive:
www.cinema.ucla.edu
WPA Film Library:
www.wpafilmlibrary.com

CHAPTER 10. IT'S A WRAP! NOW, THE NEXT STEPS

Badal, Sharon. *Swimming Upstream: A Lifesaving Guide to Short Film Distribution*. Focal Press, 2008.

Branston, Gill and Stafford, Roy. *The Media Student's Book*. 3rd edition. Routledge, 2003.

Fitzsimmons, April. *Breaking and Entering: Land Your First Job in Film Production.* Lone Eagle, 1997.

Honthaner, Eve Light. *Hollywood Drive: What it Takes to Break in, Hang in, and Make it in the Entertainment Industry.* Focal Press, 2005.

Karsh, Ellen and Fox, Arlen Sue. *The Only Grant-Writing Book You'll Ever Need: Top Grant Writers and Grant Givers Share Their Secrets.* Revised edition. Basic Books, 2006.

Landau, Camille and White, Tiare. *What They Don't Teach You at Film School: 161 Strategies to Making Your Own Movie No Matter What.* 3rd edition. Hyperion, 2000.

Lieberman, Al and Esgate, Pat. *The Entertainment Marketing Revolution: Bringing the Moguls, the Media, and the Magic to the World.* Financial Times Prentice Hall Books, 2002.

Rea, Peter and Irving, David K. *Producing and Directing the Short Film and Video.* 3rd edition. Focal Press, 2001.

Rowlands, Avril. *The Television PA's Handbook.* 2nd edition. Focal Press, 1993.

Warshawski, Morrie. *Shaking the Money Tree: How to Get Grants and Donations for Film and Video.* 2nd edition. Michael Wiese Productions, 2003.

Additional Resources: Next Steps

TIP: Keyword search for ideas such as "networking," "TV distribution," "grant," and "new media publications."

Organizations, Networking, Information, Seminars

WEBLINK Association of Independent Video and Filmmakers (AIVF):
www.aivf.org
Independent Film Project (IFP):
www.ifp.org
International Documentary Association (IDA):
www.documentary.org

Festivals

WEBLINK Festivals for television:
Film Festival Today:
www.filmfestivaltoday.com
Film Festivals.com:
www.filmfestivals.com
Without a Box (film and TV festivals site):
www.withoutabox.com

Publications and TV-Related Web Sites

WEBLINK FilmBuzz:
www.filmbuzz.co.uk
Filmmaker Magazine:
www.filmmakermagazine.com
Television Week:
www.tvweek.com
Cynopsis.com:
www.cynopsis.com
Markee:
www.markeemag.com
P3 Update Magazine: Preproduction,
Production, Postproduction:
www.p3update.com
HighDef Magazine:
www.highdef.com
Post:
www.postmagazine.com

Starting Your Own Business

WEBLINK Internal Revenue Service (IRS):
www.irs.gov.

Student Recommendations: Books and References

Note: The following books are recommended by students of producing and media as valuable sources of information. Their comments may or may not reflect the views of the author.

AMUSING OURSELVES TO DEATH: PUBLIC DISCOURSE IN THE AGE OF SHOW BUSINESS
Neil Postman (Penguin Books, 1986, 2005)

Postman addresses the real dangers of media misuse, and discusses how media shapes our lives with suggestions for ways we can shape the media in response.

> **STUDENT COMMENTS:** A great source of media evaluation and its culture, highlights the positive/negative effects the media can have on society.

ARISTOTLE'S POETICS FOR SCREENWRITERS: STORYTELLING SECRETS FROM THE GREATEST MIND IN WESTERN CIVILIZATION
Michael Tierno (Hyperion, 2002)

The author takes the classic work on storytelling, Aristotle's *Poetics*, and applies his thinking to modern-day writing and theory. Essentially "translating" Aristotle, the author examines elements of story such as plot structure, the fundamentals of screenwriting, plots and subplots, and dialogue. He uses examples from well-known films to show how Aristotle's ideas might apply to screenwriting today.

> **STUDENT COMMENTS:** It's very student-friendly, and is written in an easy way that makes Aristotle less overwhelming and extremely relevant.

THE ARTIST'S WAY (10TH ANNIVERSARY EDITION)
Julia Cameron (Jeremy P. Tarcher, 2002)

The author takes the reader on a journey into one's reservoirs of creativity, and explores the various blocks that often hinder the flow of creative juices. Through various exercises and thinking processes, the book gives the reader ways to find new confidence and productivity.

> **STUDENT COMMENTS:** Really interesting to read, and thought provoking. One of the best books for releasing the inner artist in each of us.

BASICS OF THE VIDEO PRODUCTION DIARY
Des Lyver, editor (Focal Press, 2001)

A good start for showrunners and would-be producers, with basic pointers for organization that are often overlooked. Helps improve management skills, paperwork, and maps out plans for producers in all stages of video production.

> **STUDENT COMMENTS:** An interesting resource. Shows how to create a "diary" or means of organizing and completing necessary paperwork, logically and professionally.

THE BIZ: THE BASIC BUSINESS, LEGAL AND FINANCIAL ASPECTS OF THE FILM INDUSTRY, 2ND EDITION
Schuyler M. Moore (Silman-James Press, 2003)

This text covers the extensive legal and financial elements involved in the film and television industries, and covers everything from raising financing, laws and contracts, dealing with unions, copyright issues, clearances, and sample forms and contracts.

> **STUDENT COMMENTS:** A little bit daunting but very helpful and comprehensive.

BOXED IN: THE CULTURE OF TV
Mark Crispin Miller (Northwestern University Press, 1988)

Through a collection of essays, the author uses wit and insight into television's effect on the life and culture of the American TV audience. He encourages critical awareness, for example, in watching TV commercials and the news, even game shows that diminish individuality and awareness and substitute with mediocrity.

> **STUDENT COMMENTS:** For students in media communications, it puts us on the spot and makes us take some responsibility for what we want to produce.

THIS BUSINESS OF TELEVISION
Howard J. Blumenthal and Oliver R. Goodenough (Watson-Guptill Pub, Inc., 1998)

A comprehensive, practical guide that examines how programming is financed, produced, and distributed. It describes ways that the FCC and federal laws can shape content.

> **STUDENT COMMENTS:** A good resource with tools for executives, writers, directors, and people already in the industry. A great desk bible, once you get the job!

CLEARANCE AND COPYRIGHT: EVERYTHING THE INDEPENDENT FILMMAKER NEEDS TO KNOW, 2ND REVISION
Michael C. Donaldson (Silman-James Press, 2003)

A clearly-written guide to legal issues that face producers and filmmakers, this text covers the range of rights and clearances elements in every stage of a project, from acquiring rights to an idea through to release and final distribution.

STUDENT COMMENTS: The language of this book makes it easier to understand a lot of the contracts and forms that are part of producing. It deals with things like rights of privacy and music clearances.

CONGLOMERATES AND THE MEDIA
Patricia Aufderheide and Erik Barnouw, Richard M. Cohen, Thomas Frank, David Leiberman, Mark Crispin Miller, Gene Roberts, and Thomas Schatz; introduction by Todd Gitlin (New Press, 1998)

Along with the rich history of radio and television, the authors discuss the decline of journalistic integrity and the impact of profit expectations on the news. Also covers merchandising and foreign rights, and resistance to conglomerate control of media. It explores the global reach of mass media.

STUDENT COMMENTS: Combines factual TV and radio history with attention to the current effects of media conglomerates on materials and culture.

CORPORATE MEDIA PRODUCTION
Ray DiZazzo (Focal Press, 2000)

The role of the Corporate Video Producer is examined with all aspects of a project, from the initial script through postproduction. It outlines roles of writer, producer, director, and client, and explores the dynamics and relationships between the key players.

STUDENT COMMENTS: Includes role descriptions and stages of production as well as the importance of positive professional relationships.

CREATIVE FILMMAKING FROM THE INSIDE OUT
Jed Dannenbaum, Carroll Hodge, and Doe Mayer (Fireside, 2003)

Three professors in the field of motion picture studies look at the creative process, outlining "the mysterious transformation of mere glimmers of thought into coherent stories, characters, images and sounds." The book breaks down the overall process of creative filmmaking into the Five "I"s: Introspection, Inquiry, Intuition, Interaction, and Impact.

STUDENT COMMENTS: Although it focuses on film, the information is easily transferable to TV, new media, or other genres of production. Written by filmmakers at USC, it addresses the work and commentary of each filmmaker.

CREATING UNFORGETTABLE CHARACTERS: A PRACTICAL GUIDE TO CHARACTER DEVELOPMENT IN FILMS, TV SERIES, ADVERTISEMENTS, NOVELS, AND SHORT STORIES
Linda Seger (Henry Holt and Company, Inc., 1990)

Focusing on the creation of strong, dimensional characters, the author offers a series of concepts that are designed to stimulate the creative process. It uses practical techniques and exercises, examines ways to avoid writer's block, and features interviews with writers for film and television, advertising and theatre.

STUDENT COMMENTS: We used this in our writing class, and it was really helpful. It makes imagining ideas easier to actually write down.

CREATIVITY IN TV AND CABLE MANAGING AND PRODUCING
William G. Covington Jr. (Rowman & Littlefield, 1999)

The author applies the concepts of goal-setting in business and cable management, and analyzes motivation and creativity among TV stations. It looks at a different side of the world of cable and networks.

> **STUDENT COMMENTS:** Some information on producing for television, although it is more business focused.

DIRECTING AND PRODUCING FOR TELEVISION, 3RD EDITION
Ivan Cury (Focal Press, 2006)

A comprehensive guide to producing, directing, and shooting television, especially in live TV format and studio production. It is based on the author's own experience in the industry and in university settings.

> **STUDENT COMMENTS:** The book covers a lot of ground, and though it's good for producers, it is more valuable for directors.

DOCUMENTARY FILMMAKERS SPEAK
Liz Stubbs (Allworth Press, 2002)

A book of interviews covering the history and evolution of cinema with a personal aspect; it gives the reader an opportunity really "hear" what filmmakers have to say.

> **STUDENT COMMENTS:** A collection that is inspirational and good for students to read—they can either relate to or understand the creative differences of filmmakers in the industry, all bound by the passion to make films.

DOCUMENTARY FOR THE SMALL SCREEN
Paul Kriwaczek (Focal Press, 2003)

This step-by-step approach to documentary filmmaking covers the organizational aspects and aesthetic styles and treatments to consider. It includes tips from leading documentary filmmakers in the industry.

> **STUDENT COMMENTS:** A great book for documentary makers. Provides interesting information on style choices from current doc makers, and it's written in a logical, straightforward way.

DOCUMENTARY STORYTELLING, 2ND EDITION: MAKING STRONGER AND MORE DRAMATIC NONFICTION FILMS
Sheila Curran Bernard (Focal Press, 2007)

As the author says, "Storytelling lies at the heart of most good documentaries," and "Our stories depend not on creative invention...but on creative arrangement." The book outlines the premise of execution of a story, and hones in on the process.

> **STUDENT COMMENTS**: The book offers tips for a manageable editing process, as well as an interesting perspective on the art of documentaries. It presents a variety of viewpoints that keep the reader enthused.

ENTERTAINMENT INDUSTRY ECONOMICS, 7TH EDITION
Harold L. Vogel (Cambridge University Press, 2007)

This book provides a fantastic overview of the various financial practices and strategies of several entertainment sectors including film, television, sports and digital technology.

> **STUDENT COMMENTS**: Vogel's most recent edition of this book provides a comprehensive foundation of the economic structures of several industries. This book was suggested by a professor at New York University and became extremely helpful when I began working in the industry.

THE ENTERTAINMENT MARKETING REVOLUTION: BRINGING THE MOGULS, THE MEDIA, AND THE MAGIC TO THE WORLD
Al Lieberman and Pat Esgate (Financial Times Prentice Hall, 2002)

Both authors are industry insiders, and Mr. Lieberman is a professor at New York University who created the Entertainment, Media, and Technology program at Stern. In the text, they cover the entire scope of marketing within the entertainment industry, and navigate the marketing processes for feature film, video, broadcast, cable, radio, music, print, games, sports, travel, theme parks, and more.

> **STUDENT COMMENTS**: Professor Lieberman enthusiastically shares his passion and amazing career with his students each semester. His book is just like his class!

FILM PRODUCTION MANAGEMENT, 3RD EDITION
Bastian Cleve (Focal Press, 2005)

This extensive text details the steps taken to bring a screenplay to the screen: organizing, staffing, budgeting, schedules, location, shooting, and postproduction. It includes sample forms, film festivals, marketing, training schools, and using the Internet. It is useful to the film student or film professional who may be looking for a career change within the industry.

> **STUDENT COMMENTS**: A thorough text with a lot of ideas from the film industry that can work for a producer in television.

HOLLYWOOD CREATIVE DIRECTORY (WWW.HCDONLINE.COM)

The directory offers the most comprehensive, up-to-date information available, listing the names, numbers, addresses, and current titles of entertainment professionals from the film, television, and music industries. HCD Online subscription includes additional film titles with contacts for writers, producers. and actors.

> **STUDENT COMMENTS**: The fastest way to find development executives for each channel or network. Also a good source for agents and other professionals.

I WAKE UP SCREENING: WHAT TO DO ONCE YOU'VE MADE THAT MOVIE
John Anderson and Laura Kim (Billboard Books, 2006)

This is a how-to guide for getting your film noticed in the overcrowded indie film arena. Packed with interviews with big industry names, this book offers a unique insight into what happens AFTER a film gets made and how to make all your hard work worth the effort.

> *STUDENT COMMENTS*: A quick and dirty, easy-read type of book—I felt like Anderson and Kim were talking to me. They lay it all out on the table and don't miss a nuance from dealing with publicists to knowing what materials to put on your EPK, from knowing the importance of getting a lawyer to recognizing when to give out a screener and when not to. I recommend it for a user-friendly guide.

THE INDEPENDENT FILM AND VIDEOMAKER'S GUIDE, 2ND EDITION
Michael Wiese (Michael Wiese Productions, 1998)

A guide for the beginning producer, the book examines the craft and the business of making films or video projects. It offers practical strategies for fundraising, scheduling, budgeting, marketing, and creative exercises for story development through the use of anecdotes and real-life examples.

> *STUDENT COMMENTS*: It isn't as relevant to TV, but it is helpful in relating what a producer does: finding resources, investors, etc. as well as developing or adapting a story.

THE INDIE PRODUCER'S HANDBOOK: CREATIVE PRODUCING FROM A TO Z
Myrl A. Schreibman (Lone Eagle Publishing Company, 2001)

The author is a professor at UCLA, and the text is a thorough, practical, and highly comprehensive guide for organizing and running a film, although much of the information is pertinent for the television producer as well.

> *STUDENT COMMENTS*: Good resource for the producer, not as relevant for television as it is for film.

THE INDEPENDENT VIDEO PRODUCER
Bob Jacobs (Focal Press, 1999)

The text details the legal and accounting process of forming an independent business, and includes information on the basic business, management, and communication skills necessary to an independent producer. It also acknowledges the current revolution in technology and the changing video markets.

> *STUDENT COMMENTS*: This is more about the business than the role of a producer, and focuses a lot on video, rather than TV. It is student-friendly and full of sample scripts, proposals, and forms.

INSIDE PRIME TIME
Todd Gitlin (University of California Press, 2000)

The author provides an insider's tour of the network executives' search for programming, and the processes they undertake to find and develop a hit show for broadcast. It appears on most recommended book lists in television studies departments, and is considered one of the more intelligent books written on the subject of the television business.

> **STUDENT COMMENTS:** This is a pretty realistic look at how daunting it can be to sell an idea for a show; it is well written and somehow still hopeful.

INTELLIGENCE REFRAMED: MULTIPLE INTELLIGENCES FOR THE 21ST CENTURY
Howard Gardner (Basic Books, 2000)

The author's groundbreaking theory on multiple intelligences—that intelligence is more than a single property of the human mind—has changed our basic viewpoints on education and overall human development. In this text, Gardner, a Harvard professor, explains the theories of multiple intelligences and their applications to our daily lives, as well as offers user-friendly guidelines for their use.

> **STUDENT COMMENTS:** A real eye-opener. It helped me understand myself better, as well as a lot of people around me like coworkers, friends, and family.

INTRODUCTION TO DOCUMENTARY
Bill Nichols (Indiana University Press, 2001)

Providing an overview of important topics and issues in documentary history and criticism, the text is designed for students in the media and outlines the many issues and concepts that are elements of documentary films and videos.

> **STUDENT COMMENTS:** The book provides a foundation in documentary filmmaking and gives examples of past documentaries. It explores boundaries (real and imaginary) of fiction and documentary film, and is quite thought provoking.

THE KID STAYS IN THE PICTURE
Robert Evans (Faber and Faber; New edition 2004)

The rise and fall of notorious producer and self-proclaimed bad boy Robert Evans. The title page says it all, "There are three sides to every story; yours, mine, and the truth."

> **STUDENT COMMENTS:** Love him or hate him, believe him or not, Robert Evans' autobiography *The Kid Stays in the Picture* is a must read for the aspiring producer. Written as though Evans were speaking, this autobiography is an unforgettable and fun read, chronicling his wild ride through Hollywood from the 1950s through the 1990s.

THE MEDIA STUDENT'S BOOK, 3RD EDITION
Gill Branston and Roy Stafford (Routledge, 2003)

This text combines practical elements of studying and producing ideas in various media, with lively debate and examination of cultural and ethical issues that face the media student. The authors analyze images, examine celebrity and marketing, and offer a range of resources, as well as a rare glimpse into television and media studies in the U.K..

> **STUDENT COMMENTS:** It has a distinctly British flavor, and is an excellent combination of theory, the practical, and anecdotes.

THE MOVIE BUSINESS: THE DEFINITIVE GUIDE TO THE LEGAL AND FINANCIAL SECRETS OF GETTING YOUR MOVIE MADE
Kelly Crabb (Simon & Schuster, 2005)

An accessible and informative read on the many aspects of entertainment law and its relation to producing a feature film.

> **STUDENT COMMENTS:** This book is a fantastic introduction and guide to entertainment law. Whatever area of entertainment you are interested in producing for, this book is an excellent resource for the aspiring (or established) producer.

MULTISKILLING FOR TELEVISION PRODUCTION
Peter Ward, Alan Bermingham, and Chris Wherry (Focal Press, 2000)

Written by trainers in television production who offer courses in "multiskilling," it is an introduction to the broad range of skills and technical knowledge necessary to succeed in the television industry.

> **STUDENT COMMENTS:** This book has an interesting perspective, and covers a wide range of topics. It is clearly laid out, and written in easily understood language.

THE PATH: CREATING YOUR MISSION STATEMENT FOR WORK AND FOR LIFE
Laurie Beth Jones (Hyperion, 1998)

The author gives the reader advice that is both practical and inspiring, bringing a fresh look at the process of defining and fulfilling one's mission—in work, family, and in life.

> **STUDENT COMMENTS:** It's not only easy to use, and full of humor, it actually works. It's the first time I've written a mission statement for myself that made sense. The process was fun to do.

PRACTICAL DV FILMMAKING, 2ND EDITION
Russell Evans (Focal Press, 2005)

Offering a variety of low-budget filmmaking principles, the text provides perspective on digital filmmaking through case studies and interviews. It assumes that the reader has little or no background knowledge, and combines technical knowledge with a stylistic approach to filmmaking while discussing all stages of a project's development.

> **STUDENT COMMENTS:** A great production resource, especially for beginners. In-depth discussion of production that thoroughly explores application of tools outlined in text.

PRIME TIME, PRIME MOVERS: FROM *I LOVE LUCY* TO *L.A. LAW*–AMERICA'S GREATEST TV SHOWS AND THE PEOPLE WHO CREATED THEM
David Marc and Robert J. Thompson (Syracuse University Press, 1995)

This inside look at the major creators of television is divided into sections on comedy, drama, soap operas, game shows, documentaries, and docudrama.

> **STUDENT COMMENTS:** Helpful, and just fun for people to read about shows they like. It's a good resource for retrieving info on specific shows or people involved in making them.

THE PRODUCER'S BUSINESS HANDBOOK, 2ND EDITION
John J. Lee, Jr. and Rob Holt (Focal Press, 2005)

A comprehensive examination of the complex business side of entertainment, focusing on legal and accounting necessities, the book also explores global production, licensing, and product exploitation.

> **STUDENT COMMENTS:** Very informative, and makes complicated information easier to understand. Takes a good look at important relationships in the global market and with other players in the film and television industries.

PRODUCING & DIRECTING THE SHORT FILM & VIDEO, 3RD EDITION
David K. Irving and Peter Rea (Focal Press, 2006)

This practical how-to book breaks down the entire process of making a short film or video, and details the role of the producer and the director throughout each stage of production.

> **STUDENT COMMENTS:** Very helpful, and well thought out. A step-by-step guide. Favors film and the director, but doesn't leave the producer or television out of the mix.

RICH MEDIA, POOR DEMOCRACY: COMMUNICATION POLITICS IN DUBIOUS TIMES
Robert W. McChesney (The New Press, 2000)

Winner of Harvard's Goldsmith Book Prize, this text openly questions the democratic process in our current commercial media sources, and states that the major beneficiaries of the industry are wealthy investors, advertisers, and a handful of enormous media, computer, and telecommunications corporations. McChesney examines the massive media mergers and acquisitions in the late 1990s, and aids the reader with ways to objectively critique and use the media for higher purposes.

> **STUDENT COMMENTS:** It definitely swings to the left, but it's incredibly revealing. This helped me understand just who controls the media, and what to look for as an educated television viewer.

STORY: SUBSTANCE, STRUCTURE, STYLE, AND THE PRINCIPLES OF SCREENWRITING
Robert McKee (Harper Entertainment, 1997)

Considered by many professionals as the ultimate book on writing for film and television, the author is renowned for his seminars and insightful teachings on screenwriting.

He writes that, "No one needs yet another recipe book on how to reheat Hollywood left-overs. We need a rediscovery of the underlying tenets of our art, the guiding principles that liberate talent." The text covers elements such as the story triangle, act climaxes, scene objective, character, and dialogue.

> **STUDENT COMMENTS:** Absolutely riveting. The best of all the classic books and texts on writing. It's required reading for all would-be screenwriters.

SWIMMING UPSTREAM: A LIFESAVING GUIDE TO SHORT FILM DISTRIBUTION
Sharon Badal (Focal Press, 2007)

For anyone interested in navigating the festival route for their short film or video, this book features interviews from dozens of festival experts. Men and women from Sundance, IFC, Netflix, Focus Features—to name just a few—offer their wisdom.

> **STUDENT COMMENTS:** I never really thought about getting involved in the world of festivals before, especially as a student, but this book took the fear away.

TECHNOPOLY: THE SURRENDER OF CULTURE TO TECHNOLOGY
Neil Postman (Vintage, 1993)

An in-depth examination of how technology affects our culture and what it means for the future. The esteemed author suggests ways to work with technical skills to enhance human functioning, rather than controlling it.

> **STUDENT COMMENTS:** Another great social evaluation from Postman. A valuable supplement to the creative decisions and audience targeting involved in media.

TELEVISION: CRITICAL METHODS AND APPLICATIONS, 3RD EDITION
Jeremy G. Butler (Lawrence Erlbaum, 2006)

This text is an analysis of videography, editing, acting, set design, lighting, and sound in terms of story telling, news and selling products to viewers. It includes critical and historical contexts, and discusses different approaches that have been applied to or are part of the evolution of TV styles in the past.

> **STUDENT COMMENTS:** Student-friendly is a plus. The supplemental web site augments the text with forms, sample papers, and video clips.

TELEVISION HISTORIES: SHAPING COLLECTIVE MEMORY IN THE MEDIA AGE
Gary R. Edgerton & Peter C. Rollins (eds.) (University Press of Kentucky, 2003)

The authors explore the tension between actual history and history as it is portrayed through the director's lens. It examines TV history, as well as the history of America and the way it is portrayed on television, by looking at individual styles and choices made in depicting social arenas of the past.

> **STUDENT COMMENTS:** An excellent resource. A combination of TV history, American history, and the changes and evolution of television.

TELEVISION PROGRAM MAKING
Colin Hart (Butterworth Heinemann, 1999)

This text provides a detailed guide to making a successful television program, and includes flowcharts, checklists, and examples from professionals in the business.

> *STUDENT COMMENTS:* Relevant and user friendly, especially for students, with hands-on charts and visual guides to the organizational process.

TUBE OF PLENTY: THE EVOLUTION OF AMERICAN TELEVISION, 2ND REVISED EDITION
Erik Barnouw (Oxford University Press, 1990)

An understanding of the future of television requires a look at its history. The author, who is one of the most respected scholars in his field, explores the development of television, as well as the current revolution in media and communications. He covers the explosion of cable and satellite television, premium channels such as HBO and Showtime, niche channels such as MTV, and their impact on the decline of the three major networks.

> *STUDENT COMMENTS:* This look at TV's history is easy to understand. The index and the chronology are student-friendly. An excellent read.

UNDERSTANDING MOVIES, 11TH EDITION
Louis D. Giannetti (Prentice Hall, Inc., 2007)

This classic text examines the forerunners of television, and takes the reader through the history of photography and filmmaking. The author looks at mise-en-scene, movement, editing, sound, documentary, drama, literature, avant garde, and theory. It is a valuable reference in understanding the overall evolution of media.

> *STUDENT COMMENTS:* Although it focuses only on film and photography, much of the information can be applied to all aesthetic production in general.

VIDEO PRODUCTION HANDBOOK, 3RD EDITION
Gerald Millerson (Focal Press, 2001)

This concise text focuses on video production on a budget, with explanations on camera controls, and other technical instructions. It gives tips for achieving specific looks and textures, using visual effects.

> *STUDENT COMMENTS:* A good source for technical details and style instructions.

INDEX

319